Learning Theories:
An Educational Perspective

Dale H. Schunk

University of North Carolina, Chapel Hill

Merrill, an imprint of
Macmillan Publishing Company
New York

Collier Macmillan Canada, Inc.
Toronto

Maxwell Macmillan International Publishing Group
New York   Oxford   Singapore   Sydney

Editor: Linda A. Sullivan
Production Editor: Sheryl Glicker Langner
Art Coordinator: Mark D. Garrett
Text Designer: Anne Daly
Cover Designer: Brian Deep

This book was set in Aster.

Macmillan Publishing Company
866 Third Avenue, New York, NY 10022

Collier Macmillan Canada, Inc.

Library of Congress Catalog Card Number: 90-60623
International Standard Book Number: 0-675-20644-8

Printing: 2   3   4   5   6   7   8   9   Year: 1   2   3   4

To Caryl and Laura

Preface

Recent years have witnessed many significant developments in the field of learning. An expanding research base, testing different theories, has changed our understanding of learning processes: Historical views of learning emphasized strengthening of associations between stimuli and responses; current accounts postulate that learning involves actively seeking and mentally processing information. Mounting evidence indicates that personal cognitions influence achievement behaviors and that outcomes of actions affect learners' thoughts. Although diverse perspectives on learning are presented in this book, the role of cognitions receives much emphasis.

Learning theorists and researchers increasingly are exploring learning in educational and other applied contexts. Much historical research has been conducted in laboratories using subhuman species as subjects or artificial tasks (word lists, nonsense syllables). Current researchers, however, are exploring how students acquire skills such as reading comprehension and mathematical problem solving. This shift in emphasis and context has sacrificed some of the experimental control possible in the laboratory, but it has generated important implications for teaching and invaluable knowledge of learning processes in contexts where learning normally occurs.

This book provides the student with an understanding of theories and research on learning and related processes and demonstrates their application in educational contexts. The text is intended for graduate students in schools of education or related disciplines, as well as for advanced undergraduates interested in education. It is assumed that most students using this text are pursuing or anticipate pursuing educationally relevant careers and that they possess minimal familiarity with psychological concepts and research methods.

Important historical theories are initially discussed, followed by accounts of current research. Differing views are presented, as well as criticism when warranted. A chapter is devoted to problem solving and learning in reading, writing, mathematics, and science. Although each of these subjects could be a separate chapter, I combined them because of space considerations and because many investigators view much domain-specific learning as a form of problem solving.

The chapters on motivation, self-regulation, and instructional processes address topics relevant to learning theories. These topics traditionally have shown little overlap with learning theories, but fortunately this situation is changing. Researchers are addressing such topics as how motivation can influence quantity and quality of learning, how instructional practices impact information processing, and how learning principles can be applied to develop self-regulated learners

The applications of learning principles focus on school-aged students, both because of personal preference and because most students are interested in working with children and teenagers. This is not to imply that learning principles are not relevant to younger and older learners. Much current research is exploring learning among preschoolers as well as throughout people's life span. We can expect exciting future developments.

I wish to acknowledge many individuals who helped make this book a reality. I owe a collective debt of gratitude to my professional colleagues, who have provided me with valuable insights into learning processes. Special thanks are due to Albert Bandura and Barry Zimmerman, whom I consider teachers, colleagues, and friends. My own research reported in this book has been supported by the National Science Foundation, Spencer Foundation, National Institute of Mental Health, University of North Carolina, and University of Houston. Through the years, I have been fortunate to work with many fine school administrators, teachers, and students who have taught me much about education. I also owe a special debt to many graduate students for their collaboration and assistance in various research projects.

With respect to the production of this book, my thanks to David Faherty, my editor at Merrill, for his support, patience, and editorial insights, as well as to the reviewers who critiqued the manuscript: Lou Carey, University of South Florida; Mary Gendernalik Cooper, University of North Carolina-Wilmington; Donald Cunningham, Indiana University-Bloomington; Clifton Harris, The University of Texas at Dallas; Sarah Huyvaert, Eastern Michigan University; CarolAnne Kardash, University of Missouri-Columbia; Mary Kelly, Teachers College, Columbia University; Gerald Kow-

PREFACE

itz, University of Oklahoma-Norman; David Lohman, University of Iowa-Iowa City; Rosemarie McCartin, University of Washington-Seattle; Robert Newhouse, Kansas State University; Glen Nicholson, University of Arizona-Tucson; and Jean Pierce, Northern Illinois University. At the University of North Carolina, Joan Hoffman and Amy Staples assisted with library research, Lorraine Sustana produced the tables and figures, and Jane Trexler did the word processing. I also benefited from the feedback given by many students who used this book in draft form.

Finally, I wish to thank my parents, Mil and Al Schunk, for their lifelong encouragement. I am deeply indebted to my wife, Caryl, for her patience, understanding, and support throughout this project. She drew on her years of school experience to contribute many of the ideas for the applications. While writing the manuscript, I was blessed with the birth of my daughter, Laura. I expect she will enrich my life with learning experiences for many years to come.

Contents

ix

CONTENTS

Chapter 1

The Study of Learning

Learning involves acquisition and modification of knowledge, skills, strategies, beliefs, and behaviors. As a fundamental process, learning takes many forms. On a rather simple level, children learn that 2 × 2 = 4 and that *d* is the fourth letter of the alphabet. More complex forms of learning involve solving long division problems and locating main ideas in text. In addition to cognitive and language skills, children learn motor skills (riding a bicycle, kicking a football) and social skills (interacting with peers, leading a group discussion).

This book focuses on human learning—how it occurs, which factors influence it, and how its principles apply in educational settings. The human capacity for learning is truly remarkable. Compared with the elementary behaviors animals learn, human learning is more rapid, extensive, and complex. The power and diversity of human learning are especially evident in schools.

Although everyone agrees that learning is important, there are different views on the causes, processes, and consequences of learning. These differences are examined in the chapters that follow. A central feature of this text is its emphasis on learning in educational contexts. We begin by defining learning and examining the types of situations to which learning principles apply.

LEARNING DEFINED

No definition of learning is uniformly accepted by theorists, researchers, and educational practitioners. Many definitions, however, employ common criteria to define learning. The following statement incorporates these criteria:

> *Learning* is an enduring change in behavior, or in the capacity to behave in a given fashion, which results from practice or other forms of experience. (Shuell, 1986)

One criterion for defining *learning* is *behavioral change,* or change in behavioral capacity. We use the label "learning" when a person becomes able to do or is capable of doing something different from what he could at an earlier point in time. Learning involves developing new behaviors or modifying existing ones. Student learning is assessed based on what students write, how they answer questions, what they verbalize, and so forth. The notion of a change in the capacity to behave in a new fashion is included in the definition because people may acquire knowledge without demonstrating it when learning occurs. Observational learning is an important type of learning (see the discussion of Modeling Processes in Chapter 4).

A second criterion used to define learning is that the behavioral change endures over time. This aspect of the definition excludes temporary behavioral changes brought about by such factors as drugs, alcohol, fatigue, and illness. At the same time, behavioral changes do not have to last for lengthy periods to be classified as learned; people forget things. It is debatable how long changes must endure to be classified as learned, but most theorists assume that momentary changes only lasting a few seconds are not examples of learning.

A third criterion for defining learning processes is that learning occurs through practice or other forms of experience (e.g., observing others). This criterion excludes behavioral changes that seem to be genetically determined, for example, such species-specific behaviors as birds building nests, tadpoles swimming, and moths flying toward light. Even with such behaviors, however, the distinction is not entirely clear cut. Species may be predisposed to act in given ways, but the actual development of the particular behaviors depends on a responsive environment. Monkeys' expressions of maternal behavior presumably are instinctive, but these behaviors are developed in females through their having had normal contact with their mothers (an environmental factor) (Harlow & Harlow, 1966).

The same considerations apply to such human maturational changes in behavior as crawling, walking, and talking. The maturational process predisposes the organism to different types of behaviors, but the actual behaviors expressed involve learning (Bandura, 1986). Language provides a good example. The human vocal apparatus matures so that it can produce sounds, but the actual sounds (words) produced are learned from interactions with others. Children raised by animals in the wilderness possess no human language and develop it slowly only with much tutoring (Lenneberg, 1967).

LEARNING THEORY AND RESEARCH

This section reviews the roles of theory and research in the study of learning. Some general functions of theory are discussed, along with important aspects of the research process, including ethics.

Functions of Theory

Theories are scientifically acceptable sets of principles offered to explain phenomena. They provide frameworks for interpreting environmental observations (Suppes, 1974) and serve as bridges between research and education. Without theories, research findings would simply be disorganized collections of data. For example, research shows that peer models do not always facilitate children's achievement and social behaviors compared with models dissimilar in age (Schunk, 1987). On its own, this conclusion does not help teachers decide when to employ peer models. However, linking this research finding with social cognitive learning theory can indicate when teachers should use peer models.

Theories reflect environmental phenomena and generate new research through the formation of *hypotheses,* or assumptions that can be empirically tested. Hypotheses can be cast as if-then statements: "If we do *X*, then *Y* should occur." The following hypothesis could be tested in a research study: "If we praise students when they work hard, then they should persist longer at the task than students who are not praised for hard work." Hypotheses supported by research data strengthen a theory. When hypotheses are not supported by data, the theory may have to be revised.

When we investigate an area in which there is little theory to guide us, we may formulate objectives or questions to be answered rather than hypotheses. Regardless of whether we are testing hypotheses or asking questions, we need to specify the research conditions as precisely as possible. Since research forms the basis for theory development and has valuable implications for teaching, we examine here the process of conducting research.

Conducting Research

In specifying the research conditions, we ask the following questions: Who will the subjects (participants) be? Where will the study be conducted? What measures will be collected? What procedures will be employed? We must define precisely the phenomenon we are studying. Using *operational definitions*, we specify the operations or procedures used to measure phenomena. Assume that we want to give students a pretest on some content, provide instruction, and follow with a posttest. Our operational definition of learning is the change in the number of correct test answers (posttest minus pretest). If we are interested in the rate of learning, we measure the time it takes students to master the material. In addition to defining learning, we need to specify other variables used in our study.

In experimental research, investigators systematically vary conditions (*independent variables*) and observe changes in outcomes (*dependent variables*). Assume that investigators exposed students to peer models or to adult models (independent variables) and then measured student learning (dependent variables). If using peer models resulted in greater learning, and if the researchers could rule out the influence of any extraneous factors, they could conclude the obvious: Exposure to peer models caused a greater gain in achievement than exposure to adult models.

Researchers are not always concerned with cause-effect relationships. *Correlational research* deals with relationships between variables, but it cannot specify cause-effect relationships. A researcher may hypothesize that student achievement is positively correlated with (related to) attitudes: Students who achieve at a higher level express more positive attitudes toward the subject matter. To test this relationship, researchers might give students an achievement test and an attitude survey, statistically correlating the scores to determine the nature and strength of the relationship. Correlational research, however, cannot determine whether higher achievement causes a positive attitude or vice versa. Either direction is possible, and the variables might well influence each other. Correlational research is especially valuable in clarifying the complexities of learning and in suggesting further direction for research.

Laboratory and Field Studies

Learning research studies are conducted in laboratories as well as in the field where participants work, live, play, go to school, and so forth. Much laboratory psychological research during the first half of the twentieth century used human subjects as well as infrahuman species such as monkeys, dogs, and rats. Today, much learning research is conducted in field settings, although laboratory research also remains popular.

Advantages and disadvantages exist in each type of research setting. The experimental laboratory offers a high degree of control over extraneous factors. Distractions are minimal or nonexistent: no ringing telephones, no one to interrupt the experiment, and no windows to look out of. The light, temperature, and sound can be controlled. All necessary equipment is readily available and can be left in place for the duration of the experiment.

Such control is not possible in the field. Schools are noisy and filled with activity. It often is difficult to find space to work. There inevitably are distractions: Students walk by, teachers interrupt, bells ring, announcements are made over the public address system, and fire drills are held. The space may be too bright or too dark, too hot or too cold. It also may be used for other purposes, so researchers may have to set up their equipment each time they work. These extraneous influences may affect the results of an experiment.

Field research has the advantage of being conducted where people typically learn. Its findings are highly generalizable: Researchers ought to be able to apply their results with some confidence to similar settings. In contrast, laboratory research findings are less generalizable: Laboratory researchers usually apply their findings to field settings with less confidence. Laboratory research has yielded many important findings on learning processes, and researchers often attempt to replicate laboratory findings in field settings.

Choosing the laboratory or the field depends on the purpose of the research, the availability of subjects, the cost, and the use of the results. By choosing the laboratory, researchers gain control but lose some generalizability. When using a field setting, researchers need to minimize potential extraneous influences so that they can be reasonably certain that their results are valid. Any research study has limitations. Researchers need to consider not only the results of their studies but also the potential limitations and the steps needed to address them.

Research with Human Subjects

It is the responsibility of investigators to protect the welfare of every person involved in research projects. Formal guidelines for the protection of human subjects have been promulgated by the U.S. Department of Health and Human Services and by the American Psychological Association (1982). Major considerations are summarized in this section.

Participation in projects must be voluntary. Researchers must obtain informed consent from all subjects unless the appropriate authorities specifically waive these rights or the participants are legally or physically incapable of giving consent. The latter subjects are considered to be "at risk." Children's legal rights, for example, are assigned to their parents or guardians. Researchers using children as subjects must obtain permission from the parents or guardians. They must also acknowledge that children have rights as research participants. Unless the children are not capable of giving assent as determined by the appropriate research review committee, their assent should be gained by explaining the project in language they can understand. Such protections also are applicable to other at-risk research populations, for example, subjects with physical disabilities (e.g., patients with brain damage) and prisoners.

Participants do not abdicate any rights by consenting to be research subjects. They have the right to withdraw from a research project at any time or refuse to participate without any loss of benefits to which they otherwise would be entitled. Subjects also have the right to receive appropriate professional care; to enjoy privacy and confidentiality in the use of personal information; and to be free from undue embarrassment, discomfort, anxiety, and harassment. Safeguarding information about participants that has been obtained in the course of an investigation is the obligation of the investigator.

Universities and other organizations conducting research have established committees to review all research proposals involving human subjects. These committees have representatives from the organizational units conducting research. In reviewing proposals, committees consider the factors shown in Table 1.1

Methodological requirements of some projects may require deception or involve stress to subjects. Prior to conducting such studies, the investigator must determine whether the use of such techniques is justified by the project's prospective scientific or practical benefit or whether alternative nondeceptive and nonstressful procedures would be adequate. Studies involving stress and deception are evaluated by human subjects committees in the same fashion as any other study. The central concerns are protecting the rights of subjects and determining the anticipated benefits and risks. When anxiety-provoking or deceptive procedures are employed, investigators must ensure that participants are provided with an adequate explanation (debriefing) as soon as possible (i.e., on completion of the project). If subjects require further services (e.g., counseling), investigators must be prepared to provide such services.

LEARNING THEORY ISSUES

Most theorists could accept in principle the definition of learning given at the beginning of this chapter. When we move beyond the definition, however, we find that theorists have different perspectives on several issues. The answers to the following issues are germane to each of the theories covered in this book.

How Does Learning Occur?

A basic issue concerns the process whereby learning occurs. In discussing this and the remaining issues, we distinguish between behavioral and cognitive theories of learning. *Behavioral theories* view learning as a change in

TABLE 1.1
Concerns for human subjects in research studies.

Concern	Explanation
Subjects' rights	Subjects' welfare considered carefully for each project
	Procedures presenting undue risks to subjects eliminated
	Appropriate safeguards and emergency measures provided
	Subjects' confidentiality preserved
	Subjects' mental and physical well-being protected
	Personal anguish, embarrassment, questions of conscience minimized
Reasonable risks	Risks reasonable in relation to anticipated benefits
	Human subjects not to be employed in poorly designed studies
Informed consent	Subjects informed of purpose and procedures including risks and benefits
	Risks explained in language subjects can understand
	Informed consent obtained from all subjects
	Only human subjects review committee can waive informed consent

the form or frequency of behavior as a consequence of environmental events. Behavioral theories contend that the learning process involves the formation of associations between stimuli and responses. The learner's environment is of tantamount importance. In Skinner's (1953) view, a response to a stimulus becomes more or less probable depending on the consequences of the response: Reinforcing consequences make responses more probable, whereas punishing consequences make them less likely.

Cognitive theories stress the acquisition of knowledge and cognitive structures. According to this view, learning is a mental activity that is inferred based on behavior. Cognitive theories focus on the mental processing of information. Knowledge acquisition involves rehearsing, coding, and storing information in memory; relating new information to information in memory; and retrieving information from memory when it is needed.

How learning occurs has important implications for education. Behavioral theories imply that teachers ought to arrange environmental conditions so that students can make the proper responses to stimuli. Cognitive theories emphasize making knowledge meaningful and helping learners organize and relate it to knowledge in memory. In short, how learning occurs

THE STUDY OF LEARNING

affects not only the structure and presentation of materials but also the types of student activities.

Which Factors Influence Learning?

Behavioral and cognitive theories acknowledge that learner (person) and environmental variables influence learning but differ in the relative emphasis given to these variables. For example, behavioral theories stress such environmental factors as the arrangement of stimuli and the consequences (reinforcements, punishments) of given behaviors. Learning requires that responses be performed. Behavioral theories assign less emphasis to learner variables than do cognitive theories. However, one learner variable—developmental status— is considered important because it can constrain learning. For instance, short people cannot dunk a basketball, and mental limitations hinder learning of complex skills. Learning is possible when the learner's biological equipment is adequate.

Cognitive theories acknowledge the role of environmental conditions as facilitators of learning. Teachers' explanations and demonstrations of concepts serve as environmental cues for students. Student practice of skills, along with corrective feedback, promotes learning. At the same time, cognitive theories contend that instructional features alone cannot fully account for students' learning (Pintrich, Cross, Kozma, & McKeachie, 1986). Key elements are how learners attend to, rehearse, transform, code, and store information. The way learners mentally process information determines the what and how of learning.

Cognitive theories emphasize the role of learners' thoughts, beliefs, attitudes, and values (Winne, 1985). For example, learners who doubt their abilities to learn may not properly attend to the task or may work halfheartedly on it, thus retarding learning (Schunk, 1989). Behavioral theories do not deny these mental activities exist, but rather contend that they do not explain learning.

What Is the Role of Memory?

Learning theories differ in how they view human memory. Traditional behavioral theories typically did not include memory as a research focus. Some behavioral theorists conceived of memory in terms of establishing neurological connections. Other theorists discussed the establishment of habits or responses with little attention to how these were stored by the individual for future use. Most behavioral theories viewed forgetting as a function of nonuse of a response over time.

Cognitive theories assign a more prominent role to memory. Information processing theories equate learning with encoding, that is, storing knowledge in memory in an organized, meaningful fashion. Information is stored in memory in verbal form; many theorists believe that information is also stored as images. Forgetting is the inability to retrieve information from memory because of interference, memory loss, or inadequate cues to access information.

How a theory views the role of memory has important implications for teaching. Behavioral theories typically posit that periodic, spaced reviews of behaviors maintain their readiness in learners' repertoires. Cognitive theories assign a prominent role to memory, stressing that teachers ensure that learners organize knowledge in memory for subsequent access and for relating it to other data previously acquired.

How Does Transfer Occur?

Transfer refers to knowledge being applied in new ways or situations (e.g., with different content). Transfer also concerns how prior learning affects new learning. Without transfer, all learning would be situationally specific.

Behavioral theories stress that transfer is a function of identical or similar features (stimuli) among situations. Behaviors generalize if situations have common elements. Cognitive theories postulate that transfer is a function of how information is coded in memory. Transfer occurs when learners understand how to apply knowledge in different contexts. The uses of knowledge must be stored in memory either with the knowledge itself or cross-referenced under different topics in memory that indicate types of situations to which the knowledge is applicable. Situations need not share common features. The key is the learners' belief that the knowledge may prove useful in a situation. Teachers should adapt instructional procedures to reflect their views of transfer.

Which Types of Learning Are Best Explained by the Theory?

Theories attempt to explain various types of learning but differ in their ability to do so (Bruner, 1985). Although professionals disagree, behavioral theories seem to explain best the simpler forms of learning that involve associations (e.g., memorizing multiplication facts and foreign language words). Because they emphasize mental structures, cognitive theories appear more appropriate for complex forms of learning (solving mathematical word problems, drawing inferences from text).

I am not suggesting that there are no commonalities among various types of learning. Learning to read is different from learning to play the violin in many ways, but both benefit from attention, effort, and persistence.

One challenge for future research is to specify the similarities and differences among different forms of learning.

LEARNING THEORY AND EARLY PHILOSOPHY

The remainder of this chapter addresses precursors of current learning theories, whose roots extend far into the past. The problems addressed by current researchers are not new but rather reflect a universal desire for people to understand themselves and others in their world.

From a philosophical perspective, learning can be discussed under the heading of *epistemology,* the study of the origin, nature, limits, and methods of knowledge. How can individuals know? How can they learn something new? Whence does knowledge arise? The complexity of how human beings learn is clearly illustrated in the following excerpt from Plato's (427?–347? B.C.) *Meno:*

> I know, Meno, what you mean. . . . You argue that a man cannot enquire either about that which he knows, or about that which he does not know; for if he knows, he has no need to enquire; and if not, he cannot; for he does not know the very subject about which he is to enquire. (1965, p. 16)

Two positions on the origin of knowledge and its relationship to the external environment are *rationalism* and *empiricism.* In varying degrees, these positions are recognizable in current learning theories.

Rationalism

Rationalism refers to the idea that knowledge derives from reason without aid of the senses. The distinction between mind and matter, which figures prominently in rationalist views of human knowledge, can be traced to Plato. Plato distinguished knowledge acquired via the senses from knowledge gained by reason. His view of knowledge can be summarized as follows: Material things in the world—houses, trees, automobiles, and so forth—are revealed to people via the senses. Humans acquire ideas, on the other hand, by reason or by thinking about what they already know. People have ideas about the world, and they learn ("discover") these ideas by reflecting upon them. Reason is the highest faculty, because through reason people learn abstract ideas. The true nature of houses, trees, and automobiles can be known only by reflecting upon the ideas of houses, trees, and automobiles.

Plato escaped from his dilemma concerning how humans learn by assuming that true knowledge, or the knowledge of ideas, is innate and is brought into awareness through reflection. To Plato, then, learning is recalling what exists in the mind. Information acquired via the senses—by observing, listening, and touching—constitutes raw materials, not ideas. The mind is innately structured to reason, providing meaning to disorganized incoming sensory information.

Centuries later, the rationalist doctrine was evident in the writings of René Descartes (1596–1650), a French philosopher and mathematician. Descartes employed doubt as a method of inquiry. By doubting, he arrived at conclusions that were absolute truths, that is, that were not subject to doubt. The fact that he could doubt led him to the belief that the mind (thought) exists as reflected in his famous dictum, "I think, therefore I am." Through deductive reasoning, or reasoning from general premises to specific instances, he proved the existence of God and concluded that ideas arrived at through reason must be true.

Like Plato, Descartes established a mind-matter dualism, although the latter's conception was different: The external world is mechanical, as are the actions of animals. People are distinguished in their ability to reason. The human soul, or the capacity for thought, influences the body's mechanical actions, but the body acts on the mind by bringing in sensory experiences. Although Descartes postulated dualism, he also hypothesized a type of mind-matter interactionism.

The rationalist perspective was further extended by Immanuel Kant (1724–1804), a German philosopher. Kant addressed mind-matter dualism in his 1781 book, *Critique of Pure Reason*. Kant noted that the external world is disordered yet is perceived as orderly because order is imposed by the mind. The mind takes in the external world through the senses and alters it according to subjective, innate laws. The world can never be known as it is, but rather as it is perceived. People's perceptions give the world its order. Although Kant reaffirmed the role of reason as a source of knowledge, he contended that reason operates within the realm of experience. Absolute knowledge untouched by the external world does not exist. Rather, knowledge is empirical in the sense that information is taken in from the world and is interpreted by the mind.

In summary, rationalism is the idea that knowledge arises through the mind. Although there is an external world from which humans acquire sensory information, ideas originate from the workings of the mind. Within this general framework, there are differences between philosophers. Descartes and Kant believed that reason acts upon information acquired from the world, whereas Plato felt that knowledge can be absolute in the sense that it is acquired by pure reason.

Empiricism

In contrast to rationalism, *empiricism* refers to the idea that experience is the only source of knowledge. This position originated with Aristotle (384–

THE STUDY OF LEARNING

322 B.C.), Plato's student and successor. Aristotle drew no sharp distinction between mind and matter. His philosophy of learning stated that the external world is the basis for human sense impressions, which in turn are interpreted as lawful (that is, consistent, unchanging) by the mind. The laws of nature cannot be discovered solely through sensory impressions; rather, they are discovered through reason by the mind, which takes in data from the environment. Unlike Plato, Aristotle believed that ideas do not exist independently of the external world, rather, the external world is the source of all knowledge.

Aristotle contributed to psychological theory with his principles of association as applied to memory. He believed that the recall of an object or idea triggers recall of other objects or ideas similar to (*similarity*), different from (*contrast*), or experienced close in time or space to (*contiguity*) the original object or idea. The more often objects or ideas were associated, the more likely recall of one would trigger recall of the other (*frequency*).

Another influential figure was the British philosopher John Locke (1632–1704). Locke contributed to the movement away from Plato's notion that ideas could be discovered through reason alone. Locke also developed a school of thought that was psychological in the sense of being empirical but that stopped short of being truly experimental (Heidbreder, 1933). Locke's views are summed up in his 1690 *Essay Concerning Human Understanding*.

Locke believed that there are no innate ideas, but rather that all knowledge derives from experience. There are two types of experience: sensory impressions of the external world and personal awareness. Ideas are derived from sensory experiences; nothing can be in the mind that does not originate in the senses. At birth, the infant's mind is a *tabula rasa* (blank tablet). Ideas are acquired from sensory impressions and personal reflection on these impressions. The mind is composed of ideas that have been combined in different ways. The mind can be understood only by breaking down ideas into simpler units. This *atomistic* notion of thought incorporates principles of association, because complex ideas are merely collections of simple ideas.

Locke made an important distinction between primary and secondary qualities of objects. *Primary qualities* are such characteristics as size, shape, weight, and number. They exist in the external world as part of the object or situation and are simply impressed onto the mind. In contrast, perception of *secondary qualities* (e.g., color, sound, taste) depends on the individual's sensory equipment and mind.

The issues raised by Locke were debated by such individuals as George Berkeley (1685–1753), David Hume (1711–1776), and John Stuart Mill (1806–1873). Berkeley believed that mind is the only reality. Only secondary qualities exist; there are no primary qualities. Berkeley is viewed as an empiricist, because he believed that ideas derive from experiences; however, he also felt that people impose qualities onto their sensory impressions. Hume agreed with Berkeley that people can never be certain about external reality, but Hume also believed that humans cannot be certain about their own ideas. He believed that individuals experience external reality only through their ideas, which is the only reality. At the same time, Hume accepted the empiricist notion that ideas derive from experience and become associated with one another. Mill was an empiricist and associationist, but he rejected the notion that simple ideas combine in orderly ways to form complex ideas. Mill felt that simple ideas generate complex ideas but that the latter need not be composed of the former. Simple ideas can produce a complex thought that might bear little obvious relationship to the ideas of which it is composed. Mill was essentially postulating the notion that the whole is greater than the sum of its parts, which is an integral assumption of Gestalt psychology (see the discussion of Historical Perspectives in Chapter 5).

In summary, empiricism postulates that experience is the only form of knowledge. Beginning with Aristotle, empiricists have contended that the external world serves as the basis for people's impressions. Most philosophers accept the notion that objects or ideas become associated to form complex stimuli or mental patterns. Locke, Berkeley, Hume, and Mill are among the better-known philosophers who espoused empiricist views.

LEARNING THEORY AND PSYCHOLOGY

Wundt's Psychological Laboratory

Who or what is responsible for the formal beginning of psychology as a science is much debated (Mueller, 1979). Most psychology texts note that the first psychological laboratory was begun in 1879 by Wilhelm Wundt (1832–1920) in Leipzig, Germany, although William James started a psychological laboratory at Harvard 4 years earlier. Wundt generally is given the credit largely because it was his clear intention to establish psychology as a new science. His laboratory acquired an international reputation with an impressive list of visitors, and Wundt started a journal to report psychological research.

The establishment of a laboratory marked the transition from the formal theorizing characteristic of philosophers to the emphasis on experimentation. This transition was guided in part by Wundt's 1873 book, *Principles of Physiological Psychology*. Psychology, according to Wundt, is the study of the mind. The psychological method should be patterned after the physiological method: The process being studied should be investigated in terms of controlled stimuli and measured responses by means of experimentation and introspection. (The latter are discussed in the section on Titchener later in this chapter.)

Wundt's laboratory attracted a "new breed" of scientist who accepted the challenge to establish psychology as a science. The researchers blended experimentation with introspection and investigated diverse problems in sensation and perception, reaction times, verbal associations, attention, feelings, and emotions. Although Wundt's laboratory was not credited with any one great discovery, it established psychology as a discipline and experimentation as its method of acquiring knowledge.

Ebbinghaus's Verbal Learning

Hermann Ebbinghaus (1850–1909) was a German psychologist who, although not connected with Wundt's laboratory, helped establish psychology and the experimental method. Ebbinghaus addressed higher mental processes by studying memory. He accepted the principle of association and believed that learning and the subsequent recall of learned material depend on the frequency of exposure to the material. A proper test of this hypothesis required material with which subjects were unfamiliar. Ebbinghaus invented *nonsense syllables*, three-letter (consonant–vowel–consonant) combinations (e.g., *cew, tij*).

Ebbinghaus was an avid researcher who used himself as the subject. In a typical experiment, Ebbinghaus would devise a list of nonsense syllables, look at each syllable briefly, pause, and then look at the next syllable. In this fashion, he would determine how many trials it took to learn the entire list. He found that he made fewer errors with repeated study of the list, that he needed more trials to learn more syllables, that he forgot rapidly at first but then more gradually, and that he required fewer trials to relearn than to learn. Many times he studied a list of syllables some time after original learning and calculated a *savings score*, the time or trials necessary for relearning as a percentage of the time or trials required for original learning. He also memorized some meaningful passages and found that meaningfulness made learning easier. Ebbinghaus (1885/1964) compiled the results of his studies in the book *Memory*.

Major shortcomings of Ebbinghaus's research are that he employed only one subject (himself) and that he was not an unbiased observer. Nonetheless, his results have been experimentally validated by numerous researchers in subsequent years. He was a pioneer in bringing higher mental processes into the experimental laboratory, which helped establish psychology as a science.

Titchener's Structuralism

Edward B. Titchener (1867–1927) was a student of Wundt's in Leipzig. Although Titchener was a British citizen, in 1892 he became the director of the psychological laboratory at Cornell University. Titchener imported Wundt's methods and helped establish the experimental method in the United States.

The psychology of Titchener had no particular name, although it eventually became known as *structuralism*. Structuralism represented a blend of associationism and the experimental method. Structuralists were interested in studying the makeup or structure of mental processes, and they believed that human consciousness is a legitimate area of scientific investigation. They postulated that the mind is composed of associations of ideas and that to study the complexities of the mind one must break down these associations into entities or single ideas (Titchener, 1909).

The experimental method used by Wundt, Titchener, and other structuralists was *introspection*, actually a type of self-analysis. Titchener noted that all scientists rely on observation of phenomena and that introspection is a form of observation. Subjects in introspection experiments verbally reported their immediate experiences following exposure to objects or events. If subjects were shown a table, they would report their perceptions of shape, size, color, texture, and so forth. They were not to "label," that is, to report their knowledge about the object or the meanings of their perceptions. If, for example, they said "table" while viewing a table, they were committing an error by attending to the stimulus rather than to their conscious processes. Labeling interfered with the study of the pure organization of consciousness.

As a method, introspection was held in high regard by many of the new psychologists. It was peculiar to the new science of psychology and helped legitimize psychology by demarcating it from other sciences. Introspection was a method that required special training in proper use. A trained introspectionist could determine when subjects were examining their own conscious processes rather than their interpretations of phenomena.

Introspection often was problematic and unreliable. When shown a table, people would immediately think of the word *table*, the uses of a table, and other related knowledge. Forcing people to ignore meanings and labels became recognized as an unnatural exercise that inaccurately reflected the mind's structure. (As seen in later chapters, much evidence exists indicating that information is stored in memory in verbal form.) By ignoring meanings, introspectionists were disregarding a central aspect of the mind. Watson and other behaviorists (Chapter 2) decried the use of introspection and used its problems to rally support for an objective psychology that studied only observable behavior (Heidbreder, 1933).

Structuralists studied associations of ideas, but they had little to say about how these associations are acquired. Also at issue was whether introspection was an appropriate method to study such higher mental processes as thinking and judging, which are removed from immediate sensations and perceptions. While Titchener was at Cornell, developments elsewhere challenged the validity of structuralism. Among these developments was the work of the functionalists.

James's Functionalism

Functionalism is the view that mental processes and behaviors of living organisms help them adapt to their environments (Heidbreder, 1933). This school of thought flourished at the University of Chicago largely through the work of John Dewey (1867–1949) and James R. Angell (1869–1949). Before discussing the contributions of Dewey and Angell, the psychology of William James (1842–1910), which was influential in functionalist thinking, is examined.

James's (1890) principal work was the two-volume series, *The Principles of Psychology;* he also published an abridged version designed for classroom use (1892). James was an empiricist who believed that experience is the starting point for examining thought, but he was not an associationist. He thought that simple ideas are not passive copies of environmental inputs; rather, they are the product of abstract thought and study.

James (1890) postulated that consciousness, a continuous process rather than a collection of discrete bits of information, has five characteristics:

1. Every thought tends to be part of a personal consciousness.
2. Within each personal consciousness thought is always changing.
3. Within each personal consciousness thought is sensibly continuous.
4. It always appears to deal with objects independent of itself.
5. It is interested in some parts of these objects to the exclusion of others, and welcomes or rejects—*chooses* from among them, in a word—all the while. (Vol. I, p. 225)

The "stream of thought" changes as experiences change. "Consciousness, from our natal day, is of a teeming multiplicity of objects and relations, and what we call simple sensations are results of discriminative attention, pushed often to a very high degree" (Vol. I, p. 224). James thus described the purpose of consciousness as assisting organisms to adapt to their environments.

Functionalists incorporated James's ideas into their doctrine. Dewey's (1896) article, *The Reflex Arc Concept in Psychology*, marks the beginning of the movement. Dewey argued that psychological processes could not be broken into discrete parts, rather that consciousness should be viewed in wholistic fashion. "Stimulus" and "response" describe the roles played by objects or events, but these roles could not be divorced from the overall reality. Dewey cited an example from James (1890) about a baby who sees a candle burning, reaches out to grasp it, and experiences burned fingers. From a stimulus-response perspective, sight of the candle is a stimulus and reaching is a response, getting burned (pain) is a stimulus for the response of withdrawing the hand. Dewey argued that this sequence is better viewed as one large coordinated act in which seeing and reaching influence each other.

Functionalists were strongly influenced by Darwin's writings on evolution and survival. They believed that mental processes could not be dissociated from the environments in which they occur. Functionalism studied the utility of mental processes in helping organisms adapt to their environments and survive (Angell, 1907). The following factors were found to be functional: bodily structures (because they allow organisms to survive); consciousness (because it has survived); and such cognitive processes as thinking, feeling, and judging. Functionalists were interested in how mental processes operate, what they accomplish, and how they vary with environmental conditions. They also saw the mind and body not as existing separately but as interacting with each other.

Functionalists opposed introspection as a method, not because it studied consciousness but rather *how* it studied consciousness. Introspection attempted to reduce consciousness to discrete elements, which functionalists believed was not possible. The latter contended that studying a phenomenon in isolation does not reveal how it contributes to an organism's survival.

Dewey (1900) argued for the relevance of psychology to education, believing that the results of psychological experiments should be applicable to everyday life. Although this goal was laudable, it also was problematic in that it attempted to do too much. Its research agenda was too broad to offer a clear focus. Thus, functionalism was replaced by behaviorism as the dominant force in American psychology. The latter is the subject of Chapter 2.

SUMMARY

The study of human learning focuses on how individuals acquire and modify their knowledge, skills, strategies, beliefs, and behaviors. Most researchers agree that learning is an enduring change in behavior, or the capacity to behave in a given fashion, which results from practice or other experiences. This definition excludes temporary changes in behavior due to illness, fatigue, or drugs, as well as maturational and instinctive behaviors, although many of the latter require responsive environments to manifest themselves.

Theories provide frameworks for making sense of environmental observations, serving as bridges between research and educational practices and as tools to organize and translate research findings into recommendations for educational practice. In research, the effects of one or more independent variables on one or more dependent variables are often examined. Types of research include laboratory and field experiments, and the methodology must be based on the purpose of the research. Each research type has advantages and disadvantages.

In conducting research, investigators are responsible for the welfare of research subjects and the protection of their rights. Potential risks to subjects must be avoided unless the risks are outweighed by potential benefits, as determined by the appropriate human subjects review committee. Research requires obtaining informed consent from subjects for their participation, that is, informing them of the project's purpose, procedures, and potential risks. Subject participation always is voluntary and may be withheld or withdrawn at any time without penalty or reduction in services normally provided.

Theories of learning differ on a number of criteria. Some of the more important concern how learning occurs, which factors influence learning, what the role of memory is, how transfer occurs, and which types of learning are best explained by the theory.

As a scientific discipline, learning traces its philosophical roots to epistemology, the study of knowledge. Two opposing schools of thought are rationalism and empiricism. Rationalism contends that knowledge derives from reason without aid of the senses, whereas empiricism teaches that experience is the only source of knowledge. The roots of rationalism can be traced to Plato and also are reflected in the writings of Descartes and Kant. Plato's student Aristotle espoused empiricism, a doctrine evident in the works of Locke, Berkeley, Hume, and Mill.

The beginning of psychology as a science often is ascribed to Wundt, because he established a psychological laboratory in Leipzig, Germany. The laboratory included an active group of researchers who investigated learning and perceptual phenomena. Although not affiliated with Wundt's laboratory, Ebbinghaus conducted verbal learning research using himself as a subject. Structuralism, an early American school of thought, studied the structure of mental events. Under Titchener, structuralists employed introspection to study human consciousness. Problems with structuralism included its narrow research focus and its use of introspection, a scientific method of questionable legitimacy. Another school of thought, functionalism, maintained that the mental processes and behaviors of living organisms help them adapt environmentally. Functionalism drew from the writings of William James and flourished at the University of Chicago through the work of Dewey and Angell. Functionalism's research agenda was found to be too broad to offer a clear focus.

Chapter 2

Historical Foundations

Psychology was an infant science at the beginning of the twentieth century, but exciting developments were occurring in America and abroad. Two prominent schools of thought were structuralism and functionalism. Under the strong guidance of Titchener, structuralism maintained its unique research focus despite the problems of the introspection method. Structuralists did not incorporate Darwin's work on adaptation and evolution into their thinking as did functionalists. Although structuralism had a research agenda, it was out of touch with important developments in science. If an overly restrictive research agenda was structuralism's problem, functionalism suffered from an overly broad agenda. Angell (1907) proposed that research address behavioral adaptation and the functions of various mental processes; Dewey (1900) encouraged research that applied to the real world (e.g., schools). Functionalism lacked a clear focus, because its leading proponents advocated too many research directions.

Against this background, behaviorism began its rise to become the leading psychological discipline. Its most strident proponent was John B. Watson. Watson (1924) contended that if psychology was to become an objective, experimental science, it must deal with observable, scientific subject matter. For psychologists, that which was observable was behavior.

This chapter presents some important historical views of learning. Much of the research conducted by proponents of these perspectives was done in experimental laboratories with subhuman species. Although most of this work was never applied to educational contexts, understanding the historical theories gives a better perspective on current theories. The theories of Thorndike, Pavlov, Watson, Guthrie, and Hull occupy a prominent position in the history of learning. The work of these psychologists is the subject of the remainder of this chapter.

THORNDIKE'S CONNECTIONISM

The learning theory of Edward L. Thorndike (1874–1949) was dominant in the United States during the first half of the twentieth century. Thorndike began his study of learning with a series of laboratory experiments on animals (Thorndike, 1911). Unlike many psychologists of his day, he was highly interested in education, especially in the areas of learning, transfer, individual differences, and intelligence. He applied an experimental approach to the study of educational processes by measuring the achievement outcomes of students in school. Under Thorndike's influence, the quantitative approach to educational research grew. Thorndike's impact on education is reflected in the Thorndike Award, which is the highest honor awarded by the Division of Educational Psychology of the American Psychological Association and which is given for distinguished contributions to educational psychology.

Thorndike's major work was the three-volume series, *Educational Psychology* (1913a, 1913b, 1914). Thorndike's views on learning did not remain constant throughout his lifetime. He modified his theory because his own research and that of other investigators did not support some of his early ideas. Although a comprehensive treatment of Thorndike's theory is beyond the scope of this book, some of his more important ideas (and their subsequent revisions) are discussed in the following sections.

Trial-and-Error Learning

Thorndike (1913b) postulated that the most fundamental type of learning involves the forming of associations (connections) between sensory experiences (perceptions of stimuli or events) and neural impulses (responses) that manifest themselves behaviorally. The *stimulus-response* (S-R) theory of learning thus emphasizes the associations between stimuli and responses.

From his early animal experiments, Thorndike felt that learning often occurs by *trial and error,* or by selecting and connecting. Organisms (humans and animals) find themselves in problem situations in which they attempt to reach a goal (e.g., obtain food, reach a particular location). From among the various responses of which they are capable of performing, they select one, perform it, and experience the consequences (outcomes). The more often they make a response to a stimulus, the more firmly that response becomes connected to that stimulus. In a typical experimental situation, a cat was placed in a cage. By pushing a stick or pulling a chain, the cat could open an escape hatch. After an initial series of random responses, the cat would make the response that opened the hatch, and it would escape. The cat then would be placed back into the cage. Over time, the cat would reach the goal (escape) more quickly and would make fewer errors prior to making the correct response. A typical plot of results is shown in Figure 2.1.

Thorndike believed that learning occurs gradually; successful responses become established and unsuccessful ones are abandoned. In this *incremental* view of learning, connections are "stamped in" or "stamped out" through their being performed or not being performed repeatedly in a situation. Animals do not "catch on" or "have insight" into a solution; rather, they form connections automatically in mechanistic fashion. Thorndike realized that human learning is much more complex and postulated that humans also engage in other forms of learning—connection (forming) of ideas, analysis, and reasoning (Thorndike, 1913b). At the same time, the similarity between animal and human learning seen in the research findings led Thorndike to explain complex learning using elementary learning principles. He proposed that an educated adult possesses millions of connections between stimuli and responses. By avoiding mentalistic explanations of learning, Thorndike set the stage for the subsequent dominance of behaviorism in psychological theory and research.

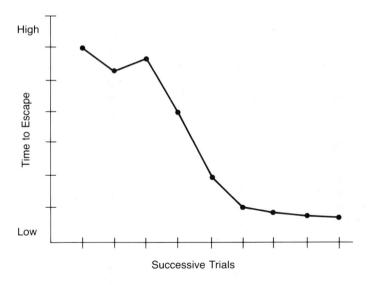

FIGURE 2.1
Incremental performance improvement over trials exemplifying Thorndike's trial-and-error learning.

Laws of Exercise and Effect

Thorndike's basic ideas about learning were embodied in the Law of Exercise and the Law of Effect. The *Law of Exercise* postulates learning (unlearning or forgetting) through repetition (nonrepetition) and includes the Law of Use and the Law of Disuse. The *Law of Use* states, "When a modifiable connection is made between a situation and a response, that connection's strength is, other things being equal, increased" (Thorndike, 1913b, p. 2). Thorndike viewed the strength of the connection in terms of the probability of the connection being made in that situation in the future. The *Law of Disuse* states, "When a modifiable connection is *not* made between a situation and response during a length of time, that connection's strength is decreased" (p. 4). The longer the time interval before a response is made to a situation, the greater the decline in the connection's strength (more forgetting).

The *Law of Effect* is as follows (Thorndike, 1913b):

> When a modifiable connection between a situation and a response is made and is accompanied or followed by a satisfying state of affairs, that connection's strength is increased: When made and accompanied or followed by an annoying state of affairs, its strength is decreased. (p.4)

With regard to satisfiers and annoyers, Thorndike (1913b) said,

> By a satisfying state of affairs is meant one which the animal does nothing to avoid, often doing things which maintain or renew it. By an annoying state of affairs is meant one which the animal does nothing to preserve, often doing things which put an end to it. (p.2)

The Law of Effect emphasizes the *consequences* of behavior as contributing to learning. In today's terminology, the Law of Effect might be restated as follows: Responses resulting in rewarding consequences are learned, and responses producing punishing consequences are not learned. Thorndike's Law of Effect represents a highly functional account of learning, proposing that responses leading to desirable outcomes allow organisms to adapt better to their environments. In a sense, Thorndike was well ahead of his time, because the idea that behavioral consequences influence what people learn and do is accepted today. In an experimental demonstration of the Law of Effect (Thorndike, 1927), subjects were shown 50 strips of paper one at a time. The strips ranged from 3 to 27 centimeters in length. Alongside each test strip was a strip that subjects knew to be 10 centimeters long. Subjects initially estimated the length of each strip without being given feedback. Following this pretest, the 50 strips were presented again one at a time. Following each estimate, subjects were told "right" or "wrong" by the experimenter. After the 50 strips were repeatedly presented over several days, they were again presented to the subjects, once more without feedback about their length judgments. Following training, subjects' length estimates more closely approximated the actual length of the strips than their previous estimates had. Thorndike concluded that these results, which were strikingly similar to experiments in which animals are rewarded with food or freedom, support the idea that satisfying connections between stimuli and responses are strengthened and unsatisfying ones are weakened.

Other Principles

Thorndike's theory included several other important features, two of which were the Law of Readiness and Associative Shifting. The *Law of Readiness* describes circumstances that are and are not conducive to connections being formed:

> When any conduction unit is in readiness to conduct, for it to do so is satisfying. When any conduction unit is not in readiness to conduct, for it to conduct is annoying. When any conduction unit is in readiness to conduct, for it *not* to do so is annoying. (Thorndike, 1913b, p. 2)

Thorndike felt that readiness ultimately could be explained in terms of the sensitivity of one's neurological mechanisms to conduct impulses. In terms of behavior, the Law of Readiness states that when an organism is prepared to act, to do so is satisfying and not to do so is annoying. Thus, if an organism is hungry, responses that lead it to food are in a state of readiness; whereas other responses not leading it to food are not in a state of readiness. If an organism is fatigued, it is annoyed if forced to exercise. Applying this idea to human learning: When students are ready to learn a particular behavior, they are satisfied when engaging in activities to foster this learning. Learning under these conditions is more profitable than it is when students are not ready to learn the particular behavior.

The term *associative shifting* has the following meaning: Responses made to a particular stimulus eventually can be made to an entirely different stimulus if, on repeated trials, there are small changes in the nature of the stimulus. These small changes involve adding some elements and removing others (Thorndike, 1913b). Associative shifting could be applied to memorizing a poem. Initially, the student studies the poem printed on a sheet of paper. The student then studies the poem printed on a different sheet on which some of the words are missing. On successive sheets, more words are left out. Finally, the student can recite the poem from memory with no cues.

Revisions

Thorndike subsequently revised the Laws of Exercise and Effect based on empirical evidence that failed to support them (Thorndike, 1932). Thorndike discarded the Law of Exercise because he found that mere repetition of a situation does not necessarily alter responses. In a prototypic experiment (Thorndike, 1932), subjects with eyes closed drew a series of lines they thought were 2 inches, 4 inches, 6 inches, and 8 inches long, hundreds of times over several days. During this time they were never given feedback regarding the accuracy of the lengths. Each of these subject-drawn lines was carefully measured. If the Law of Exercise was correct, then for any given length the response occurring most frequently during the first hundred or so drawings ought to become more frequent thereafter. Thorndike found no support for this idea. Rather than the status quo being maintained, the mean lengths changed over time, although the variability in lengths diminished. In short, he found that mere repetition of a situation does not enhance the future likelihood of its occurrence.

Thorndike's initial statement of the Law of Effect postulated that the effects of satisfiers and annoyers were opposite but comparable. Subsequent research showed that the effects are not parallel. Thorndike (1932) concluded that, whereas rewarding consequences tend to strengthen connections, punishing consequences do not necessarily weaken connections. Connections are weakened indirectly by strengthening alternative connections. A series of experiments conducted by Thorndike showed this lack of parallelism. In one study, subjects were presented with uncommon English words (e.g., *edacious, eidolon, ern*). Each word was followed by five common English words, one of which was a correct synonym. On each trial, subjects chose a synonym and underlined it, after which the experimenter rewarded (or punished) them by saying "right" or "wrong." Saying "right" strengthened the connections, but saying "wrong" did not diminish the probability of that response occurring to that stimulus word. Punishment did not weaken connections sufficiently to overcome the strength they had gained by just occurring. Thorndike (1932) concluded, "The wrong connections wane in relative frequency, not because they weaken intrinsically, but because they are supplanted by the right connections" (p. 288).

Punishing (annoying) consequences suppress responses, but the responses do not disappear. Punishment is an ineffective means of altering behavior, because it does not replace the unwanted response with a more productive one. A teacher, for example, may reprimand students who are talking rather than working. The punishment only temporarily stops the talking. The students are likely to talk with one another in the future at inappropriate times.

Students sometimes learn skills incorrectly. Brown and Burton (1978) have shown that students often learn "buggy algorithms," or incorrect rules for solving mathematical problems. A common buggy algorithm is to subtract the smaller number from the larger number in each column without regard for direction (e.g., $4371 - 2748 = 2437$). When students are told that this method is wrong and are given corrective feedback and practice solving problems, they learn the correct method. However, although they no longer perform the incorrect steps, they may not forget them. The difference is that they realize that their past solutions are incorrect.

Educational Principles

Thorndike was a professor of education at Columbia University. He wrote several books that addressed such topics as educational aims, learning processes, teaching methods, curricular sequences, and measuring techniques for educational products (Thorndike, 1906, 1912; Thorndike & Gates, 1929). Thorndike's contributions to education could easily fill a volume. This section only summarizes his research and writings on some educational topics.

Principles of Teaching. Thorndike believed that a central outcome of schooling is the formation of habits. For teachers to help students form good habits, the teachers must apply the Law of Effect. Thorndike (1912) summarized principles of teaching habit formation:

1. Form habits. Do not expect them to create themselves.
2. Beware of forming a habit which must be broken later.
3. Do not form two or more habits when one will do as well.
4. Other things being equal, have a habit formed in the way in which it is to be used. (pp. 173–174)

The latter principle cautions against teaching content removed from its application. As Thorndike exemplified, "Since the forms of adjectives in German or Latin are always to be used with nouns, they should be learned with nouns" (p. 174). Today we would say that students need to understand how to apply the knowledge and skills they acquire and that these uses can be taught in conjunction with the content.

Sequence of Curricula. Thorndike addressed where and how particular content should be included in the educational curricula. A fact or skill should be introduced (Thorndike & Gates, 1929) as follows:

1. At the time or just before the time when it can be used in some serviceable way
2. At the time when the learner is conscious of the need for it as a means of satisfying some useful purpose
3. When it is most suited in difficulty to the ability of the learner
4. When it will harmonize most fully with the level and type of emotions, tastes, instinctive and volitional dispositions most active at the time

APPLICATION 2.1: Sequence of Curricula

Thorndike's views on the sequence of curricula closely parallel the current emphasis on integrated learning. His ideas suggested that as teachers plan units of study they should not segregate related subject matter. For example, an elementary teacher planning a unit in the fall might focus on pumpkins. The students could study the significance of pumpkins to the colonists (history) and where pumpkins are grown (geography). They also could measure and chart the various sizes of pumpkins (mathematics), carve the pumpkins (art), plant pumpkin seeds and study their growth (science), and read and write stories about pumpkins (language arts). This approach provides a meaningful experience for children and "real life" learning of various skills.

5. When it is most fully facilitated by immediately preceding learnings and when it will most fully facilitate learnings which are to follow shortly (pp. 209–210)

Thorndike and Gates noted that strict application of these principles goes against the grain of much content placement in schools. Content typically is segregated by subject (e.g., history, geography, science). A better arrangement is to focus on knowledge and skills and then show how they cut across a variety of subjects. For instance, the concept of tragedy should be taught to high school students not only in English class but in history and current events classes as well.

Transfer.   In Thorndike's theory, the term *transfer* refers to the extent to which a strengthening (weakening) of one bond produces a similar change in another connection. Thorndike (1913b) contended that transfer occurs only when two connections are in part identical, that is, when situations have *identical elements* and call for similar responses. In a series of studies, Thorndike and Woodworth (1901) found that practice or training in a skill in a specific context does not produce gains in subjects' ability to execute that skill generally. For example, training on estimating the area of rectangles does not improve subjects' ability to estimate the areas of triangles, circles, and irregular figures. For skills to be applied by students, the skills must be taught in conjunction with different types of educational content.

Mental Discipline.   Mental discipline, the belief that learning certain subjects (e.g., the classics, mathematics) enhances mental functioning better than other subjects, was popular in Thorndike's day. Thorndike (1924) tested this idea with 8,500 students in grades 9 to 11. Students were given intelligence tests one year apart, and their courses of study during that year were compared to determine whether certain courses produced greater intellec-

APPLICATION 2.2: Transfer

Thorndike suggested that drilling students on a specific skill does not help them master it nor does it teach them how to apply the skill in different contexts. For example, when teachers instruct secondary students how to use map scales, they must teach them to calculate miles from inches at the same time. Students become more proficient if they actually apply the skill on various maps and create maps of their own surroundings than if they are just given numerous problems to solve.

tual gains. The results yielded no support for the mental discipline notion that some subjects were more valuable to human intelligence than others. Thorndike concluded as follows:

> If our inquiry had been carried out by a psychologist from Mars, who knew nothing of theories of mental discipline, and simply tried to answer the question, "What are the amounts of influence of sex, race, age, amount of ability, and studies taken, upon the gain made during the year in power to think, or intellect, or whatever our stock intelligence tests measure," he might even dismiss "studies taken" with the comment, "The differences are so small and the unreliabilities are relatively so large that this factor seems unimportant." The one causal factor which he would be sure was at work would be the intellect already existent. Those who have the most to begin with gain the most during the year. Whatever studies they take will seem to produce large gains in intellect. (p. 95)

In Thorndike's research, the students who had greater ability to begin with made the best progress regardless of which subject they studied. The intellectual value of studies resided not in how much they improved students' ability to think but rather in how they affected students' interests and goals. Thorndike's research was influential among educators and led to the redesign of curricula away from the mental discipline idea.

PAVLOV'S CLASSICAL CONDITIONING

Basic Processes

Ivan Pavlov (1849–1936), a Russian physiologist, won the Nobel Prize in 1904 for his work on digestion (Frolov, 1937). His contributions to psychology came from his classic experiments with dogs (Cuny, 1965). Pavlov studied the animals' reflexive actions produced by neurological activity in response to environmental stimulation. Pavlov's (1927, 1928) legacy to learning theory was his work on *classical conditioning*. While Pavlov was the director of the physiological laboratory at the Institute of Experimental Medicine in Petrograd, he noticed that dogs often would salivate at the sight of the attendant bringing them food or even at the sound of the attendant's footsteps. Pavlov realized that the attendant was not a natural environmental stimulus for producing salivation, but that the attendant acquired this power by being associated with food. Pavlov defined salivation in response to food as an *unconditioned reflex* and salivation in response to someone or something associated with food as a *conditioned reflex*.

Classical conditioning involves presenting an *unconditioned stimulus* (UCS), which elicits an *unconditioned response* (UCR). In his experiments, Pavlov placed a hungry dog in an apparatus. The dog would salivate (UCR) when presented with meat powder (UCS). Thus, conditioning involves repeatedly presenting an initially neutral stimulus for a brief period before presenting the UCS. Pavlov used a ticking metronome as the neutral stimulus in many experiments. In the early trials, the ticking of the metronome produced no salivation. Eventually, the dog would salivate in response to the ticking metronome prior to the presentation of the food powder. The metronome had become a *conditioned stimulus* (CS) that elicited a *conditioned response* (CR) similar to the original UCR. This process is summarized in Table 2.1. Repeated presentations of the CS alone cause the CR to diminish in intensity and disappear, a phenomenon known as *extinction*.

Pavlov (1932b) believed that conditioning and extinction involve excitatory and inhibitory processes. This neurological explanation was speculative and not addressed by Pavlov's research. It is presented here to place his theory in its proper historical context. Pavlov (1928) described the conditioning process as follows:

> If a new, formerly indifferent stimulus, entering into the cerebrum, meets in the nervous system at the moment, a focus of strong excitation, this newly arriving stimulation begins to concentrate, and to open a road, as it were, to this focus, and through it onward to the corresponding organ, becoming in this way a stimulator of that organ. In the opposite case, i.e., if no such focus of excitation exists, the new stimulation is dispersed without any marked effect in the mass of the cerebrum. (p. 124)

Pavlov hypothesized that presentation of a CS neurally activates a portion of the cortex, which then associates with the portion activated by the UCS. Neural centers excited by external stimulation thus become associated with one another. *Inhibition*, a type of excitation, works antagonistically to other excitations and diminishes the intensity of or extinguishes the CR. External inhibition arises when an outside agent interferes with the CS (e.g., a subject is distracted by a noise at the moment the CS is presented). Internal inhibition decreases excitation due to nonpairing of the CS with the UCS. Such inhibition causes the CR to extinguish.

TABLE 2.1
Classical conditioning procedure.

Phase	Stimulus	Response
1	UCS (food powder)	UCR (salivation)
2	CS (metronome), then UCS (food powder)	UCR (salivation)
3	CS (metronome)	CR (salivation)

Other Phenomena

Occasionally after a time lapse in which the CS is not presented, the CR may be elicited by presentation of the CS. This sudden recurrence, termed *spontaneous recovery*, suggests that the CR was not extinguished but only inhibited. The lapse of time allowed the inhibition to dissipate; however, a CR that recovers will not endure unless the CS is presented again. Pairings of the CS with the UCS restore the CR to full strength.

In Pavlov's research, the excitation associated with conditioning also helps to explain generalization and discrimination. *Generalization* means that the CR occurs to test stimuli similar to the CS (Figure 2.2). Once an animal is conditioned to salivate in response to a metronome ticking at 70 beats per minute, it also may salivate in response to a metronome ticking faster or slower, as well as to ticking clocks or timers. Generalization presumably occurs because excitation spreads throughout the cortex, a process known as *irradiation*. The neural activity associated with the original CS spreads to other areas activated by ticking sounds. The more dissimilar the test stimulus is to the CS, the less generalization occurs. *Discrimination*, the complementary process to generalization, means that the organism learns to respond to the CS but not to other, similar stimuli. To train discrimination, an experimenter might pair the CS *with* the UCS and also present other, similar stimuli *without* the UCS. If the CS is a metronome ticking at 70 beats per minute, it is presented with the UCS, whereas other cadences (e.g., 50, 60, 80, 90 beats per minute) are presented but not paired with the UCS. Pavlov believed that discrimination results when the spread of activation is limited, that is, when excitation is concentrated in a small area.

Pavlov (1927) found that once a stimulus becomes conditioned, it can function as a UCS and further conditioning is possible. This process is known as *higher-order conditioning*. If a dog has been conditioned to salivate at the sound of a metronome ticking at 70 beats per minute, the ticking metronome can function as a UCS. A new neutral stimulus (such as a buzzer) can be sounded for a few seconds, followed by the ticking metronome. If,

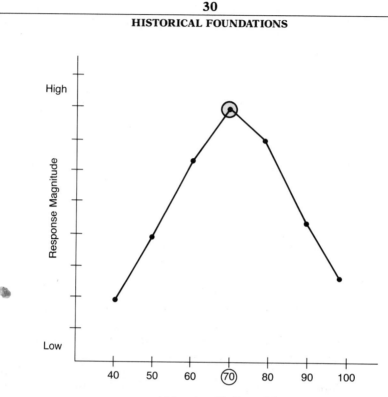

FIGURE 2.2
Generalization curve showing decreased magnitude of conditioned response as a function of increased dissimilarity with the conditioned stimulus.

after several trials, the dog begins to salivate at the sound of the buzzer, the buzzer has become a CS of the second order. Conditioning of the third order is possible, as the CS of the second order can serve as the UCS and a new neutral stimulus paired with it. Pavlov (1927) reported that conditioning beyond the third order is difficult and often unsuccessful. He believed that higher-order conditioning occurs when excitation associated with the original CS has spread to the region of the brain associated with the new neutral stimulus. The spread of activation lessens as the distance from the original UCS increases. Inhibition connected with failing to present the original UCS may weaken the spread of activation.

Higher-order conditioning is complex, and its mechanism is not well understood (Rescorla, 1972). The concept is theoretically interesting, because it might help to explain why some social phenomena, such as failure on a test, can cause conditioned emotional reactions (e.g., anxiety) among students. For example, failure—an initially neutral event—often is associated with reproof from parents and teachers. The disapproval by others could serve as a UCS and elicit anxiety.

Conditioned stimuli capable of producing conditioned responses in organisms are called *primary signals*. This *first signal system* is shared by animals and humans. Pavlov recognized that because people have the additional capacity for speech, human language (the *second signal system*) greatly expands the potential for conditioning. Words referring to events or objects become conditioned stimuli, because words are labels attached to events and objects. An experimenter might condition a hungry dog to salivate to the spoken word *meat* by repeatedly pairing the word *meat* with meat powder. Thus a particular sound pattern is being conditioned; the dog might also salivate to phonetically similar words such as *beat*. In contrast, saying "meat" to a hungry individual might produce salivation, but it is the *meaning* of the word that produces the response, not the sound pattern.

Informational Variables

Pavlov believed that conditioning is an automatic process that occurs with repeated CS-UCS pairings and that repeated nonpairings extinguish the CR. In humans, conditioning can occur rapidly, sometimes with only a single CS-UCS pairing. Repeated nonpairings of the CS and UCS may not extinguish the CR. However, Pavlov's description of the conditioning process does not adequately address these findings. Conditioning depends not so much on CS-UCS pairings as on the extent to which the CS conveys information to the individual about the likelihood of the UCS occurring (Rescorla, 1972, 1976). Assume there are two stimuli: One is always followed by a UCS, the other sometimes is followed by it. Conditioning occurs to the first stimulus, because it reliably predicts the onset of the UCS (Egger & Miller, 1963). No actual CS-UCS pairings are necessary; simply telling people about their relationship can produce conditioning (Brewer, 1974). In similar fashion, repeated CS-UCS nonpairings are not necessary for extinction; telling people the contingency is no longer in effect reduces or extinguishes the CR.

People form expectations concerning the probability of the UCS occurring (Rescorla, 1987). For a stimulus to become a CS, it must convey information to the individual about the time, place, quantity, and quality of the UCS. Even when a stimulus is predictive, it may not become conditioned if another stimulus is a better predictor. Rather than conditioning being automatic, it appears to be mediated by cognitive processes (Fuhrer & Baer, 1965). If people do not realize there is a CS–UCS link, conditioning does not occur. Even when there is no CS-UCS link, conditioning occurs if people *believe* there is a link.

Biological Constraints

Pavlov (1927) believed that conditioning is general in the sense that any perceived stimulus can be conditioned to any reflex that can be made. Pavlov (1928) also noted, "It follows that any natural phenomenon chosen at will may be converted into a conditioned stimulus" (p. 86). Biological constraints limit the generality of these statements. Within any species, responses can be conditioned to some stimuli but not to others. How well conditioning occurs, or if at all, depends on how compatible the stimulus and response are with species-specific reactions (Bolles, 1972). As Garcia and Garcia y Robertson (1985) noted,

> Behavior is manifested at the juncture between the organism and its niche, and learning is an adjustive process that eases the misfits at that juncture. All organisms inherently possess the basic behavioral patterns that enable them to survive in their niches, but learning provides the fine tuning necessary for successful adaptation. (p. 197)

An experiment by Garcia and Koelling (1966) with rats demonstrates this phenomenon. Some rats drank water that was accompanied by bright lights and noise (aversive stimulus—bright, noisy water). Rats either were shocked immediately or treated so that they became nauseous some time later. Other groups of rats were either shocked or became nauseous after drinking regular (saccharin) water. Bright, noisy water plus shock led to a conditioned aversion to the water, but bright, noisy water plus nausea did not. Regular (saccharin) water plus nausea led to an aversion to the water, but regular water plus shock did not. It appears that the shock (an external event) was easily associated with the bright lights and noise (also external cues) but not to an internal event like nausea. The latter became a conditioned response to an internal stimulus—taste. Among the problems with this study is that the interval between drinking the water and nausea was about an hour, much too long to satisfy a classical conditioning model. Nonetheless, the results suggest that rats have developed an evolutionary mechanism to guard against taste aversions, which is further evidence for the complexity of classical conditioning.

Conditioned Emotional Reactions

Pavlov (1932a, 1934) became interested in applying classical conditioning research findings to abnormal behavior. His views on how neuroses and other pathological states might develop via conditioning were speculative and unsubstantiated, although classical conditioning principles have been applied by others to dysfunctional behavior. A notable example is *systematic desensitization*, which is often used with individuals who possess debilitating fears (Wolpe, 1958). Desensitization comprises three phases. In the first

APPLICATION 2.3: Emotional Conditioning

Principles of classical conditioning are relevant to some dysfunctional behaviors. Children entering kindergarten or first grade may possess fears related to the new experiences. At the beginning of the school year, primary teachers might develop procedures to desensitize some of the children's initial fears. Teachers could plan preschool visitation sessions giving students the opportunity to meet their teacher and other students and to see their classroom and the seat with their name on it. On the first few days of school, the teacher might plan fun but relatively calm activities involving students getting to know their teacher, classmates, room, and school building. Students could tour the building, return to their room, and draw pictures. They might talk about what they saw. Students can be taken to offices to meet the principal, assistant principal, nurse, and counselor. They also could play name games in which they introduce themselves and then try to recall names of classmates.

These activities represent an informal desensitization procedure. For some children, cues associated with the school serve as stimuli eliciting anxiety. The fun activities elicit pleasurable feelings, which are incompatible with anxiety. Pairing fun activities with cues associated with school may cause the latter to become less anxiety producing.

phase, therapist and client jointly develop an anxiety hierarchy of situations graded from least to most anxiety producing for the client. For a test-anxious student, low-anxiety situations might be hearing a test announcement in class and deciding when to study for a test. Situations of moderate anxiety might be studying the night before the test and walking into class on the day of the test. High-anxiety situations could include receiving a copy of the test in class and not knowing the answer to a test question. The number of situations included on the hierarchy is decided by client and therapist.

In the second phase, the client is taught to relax by imagining pleasant scenes and cuing relaxation (e.g., saying "relax" to oneself). In the third phase, the client, while relaxed, imagines the lowest scene on the hierarchy. This may be repeated several times, after which the client imagines the next scene. Treatment proceeds up the hierarchy until the client can imagine the most anxiety-producing scene without feeling anxious. If the client reports anxiety while imagining a scene, the client drops back down the hierarchy to a scene that does not produce anxiety. Total treatment may require several sessions.

Desensitization involves a type of counterconditioning. The relaxing scenes that one imagines (UCS) produce relaxation (UCR). Anxiety-produc-

ing cues (CS) are paired with the relaxing scenes. Relaxation is incompatible with anxiety. By initially pairing a weak anxiety cue with relaxation
and by slowly working up the hierarchy, all of the anxiety-producing cues
eventually elicit relaxation (CR). As a therapeutic procedure, desensitization is quite effective. One advantage is that desensitization can be accomplished in a therapist's or counselor's office. It does not require therapist
and client to perform the activities on the hierarchy. A disadvantage is that
the client must be able to imagine scenes. People differ in their ability to
form mental images (see the discussion of Mental Imagery in Chapter 6).
Desensitization also requires the skill of a professional therapist or counselor and should not be attempted by anyone unskilled in its application.

WATSON'S BEHAVIORISM

Pavlov's research had a strong impact on John B. Watson (1878–1958), generally considered to be the founder of modern behaviorism (Heidbreder,
1933). Watson rejected as unscientific schools of thought and research methods that dealt with the mind. He believed that for psychology to become a
science, it had to structure itself along the lines of the physical sciences,
which examine phenomena that can be observed and measured, and that
the proper material for psychologists to study is behavior. Watson (1914)
argued that if consciousness can only be studied through introspection, it
should not be studied at all because introspection is too unreliable:

> Psychology, as the behaviorist views it, is a purely objective, experimental
> branch of natural science which needs introspection as little as do the
> sciences of chemistry and physics. It is granted that the behavior of
> animals can be investigated without appeal to consciousness. . . . The
> position is taken here that the behavior of man and the behavior of
> animals must be considered on the same plane; as being equally essential
> to a general understanding of behavior. It can dispense with conscious-
> ness in a psychological sense. (p. 27)

Functionalism was similarly rejected because it dealt with consciousness. Thorndike's satisfiers and annoyers were subjective mental concepts
that were unobservable and unmeasurable; thus, they had no place in psychology (Watson, 1919). Even thinking—a hallmark of human consciousness—was considered to be nothing more than talking to oneself (Watson,
1924; Watson & MacDougall, 1929).

Basic Processes

Watson (1916) felt that Pavlov's conditioning model was appropriate to use
in building a science of human behavior. Watson was impressed with Pavlov's precise measurement of observable behaviors. Watson did not believe

that the model was limited to reflexive actions, but rather that it could be extended to account for diverse forms of learning and personality characteristics.

Watson (1926a) believed that newborns are capable of displaying three emotions: love, fear, and rage. Through Pavlovian conditioning, these emotions become attached to various stimuli to produce the complexities of an adult's emotional life. Fear in infants, for example, can arise from loud noises and loss of maternal support. Through pairing with unconditioned stimuli, objects and places become conditioned stimuli. Children who become separated from their parents and get lost in the woods might develop a conditioned fear of the woods. Higher-order conditioning can produce additional conditioned reactions. The power of conditioning is captured in Watson's (1926b) famous pronouncement:

> Give me a dozen healthy infants, well-formed, and my own specified world to bring them up in and I'll guarantee to take any one at random and train him to become any type of specialist I might select—a doctor, lawyer, artist, merchant-chief and, yes, even into beggar-man and thief, regardless of his talents, penchants, tendencies, abilities, vocations and race of his ancestors. (p.10)

Little Albert Experiment

Conditioning was purportedly demonstrated in the well-known Little Albert experiment (Watson & Rayner, 1920). Albert was an 11-month-old infant who initially showed no fear of a white rat. During conditioning, a hammer was struck against a steel bar behind Albert as he reached out for the rat. "The infant jumped violently and fell forward, burying his face in the mattress" (p.4). This sequence was immediately repeated. One week later when the rat was presented, Albert began to reach out but then withdrew his hand. The previous week's conditioning had had some effect. During the second session, the rat and loud noise were paired several times, after which the rat was presented alone. Albert's reaction was as follows:

> The instant the rat was shown the baby began to cry. Almost instantly he turned sharply to the left, fell over on left side, raised himself on all fours and began to crawl away so rapidly that he was caught with difficulty before reaching the edge of the table. (p.5)

Subsequent tests over the next few days showed that Albert reacted emotionally to the rat's presence. There also was evidence of generalization of fear to a rabbit, dog, and fur coat. Albert was retested a month later with the rat, and he showed a mild emotional reaction, which was greatly diminished from its original intensity.

The Little Albert study is widely cited as showing how conditioning can produce emotional reactions, but the influence of conditioning is not as powerful as this study indicates (Harris, 1979). Classical conditioning is a complex phenomenon; one cannot condition any response to any stimulus. Species have evolved mechanisms predisposing them to some forms of conditioning and not to others. Among humans, conditioning occurs only when people are aware of the contingency, and information that the contingency is no longer in effect can produce extinction. Efforts to replicate Watson and Rayner's study did not uniformly meet with success. Valentine (1930a), for example, found no evidence of conditioning when he used objects as the CS instead of animals.

Watson's research had little relevance for education because it was mostly confined to the laboratory. Nevertheless, he is an important figure in the history of psychology because he helped establish it as a science. He spoke and wrote with conviction, and his adamant stance on behaviorism helped it become the predominant influence in American psychology from around 1920 until the early 1960s. In the years since Watson, behavioristic research has made significant contributions to the study of human learning.

GUTHRIE'S CONTIGUOUS CONDITIONING

Edwin R. Guthrie (1886–1959) was a psychologist whose views on learning placed him clearly within the S-R tradition. Guthrie did not formulate a theory of learning. Rather, he postulated only a few principles that reflected the idea of associationism. Guthrie (1952) too believed that a science of human behavior must be based on observable phenomena:

> The ability to learn, that is, to respond differently to a situation because of past response to the situation, is what distinguishes those living creatures which common sense endows with minds. This is the practical descriptive use of the term "mind." Another use, the theological or mythological notion of mind as a substance, as a mysterious hidden cause of action, we may dismiss at once. Our interest is scientific, and we are dealing only with observable features of the world about us. (p.3)

Guthrie's focus on observables rules out such constructs as Thorndike's satisfiers and annoyers and Pavlov's spread of activation. His views require no special assumptions concerning the makeup of the nervous system, as is the case with Pavlov's and Thorndike's theories (Mueller & Schoenfeld, 1954).

Guthrie emphasized the applicability of his ideas to everyday living. He discussed many practical applications concerning how habits are formed and altered. At the same time, Guthrie (1952) did not believe that the outcomes or usefulness of behaviors should be the primary focus of psychology. "We must know *how learning occurs* as well as *what it accomplishes*" (p. 292). He rejected the Law of Effect and reinforcement as key processes influencing learning. He felt that although the outcomes of learning are important for practical reasons, the job of psychologists is to describe observable behavior, not what it accomplishes (Guthrie, 1940).

Acts and Movements

The basic principle in Guthrie's system reflected the notion of *contiguity:*

> A combination of stimuli which has accompanied a movement will on its recurrence tend to be followed by that movement. (Guthrie, 1952, p. 23)

And alternatively,

> Stimulus patterns which are active at the time of a response tend, on being repeated, to elicit that response. (Guthrie, 1938, p. 37)

Movements, of primary importance in Guthrie's system, refer to discrete behaviors that result from muscle contractions. Guthrie distinguished movements from *acts,* or classes of movements that produced some outcome or result. Playing the piano is an act comprising many movements. A particular act may be accompanied by a variety of movements; the act does not specify the movements. In basketball, sinking a basket (an act) can be accomplished with a variety of movements.

The contiguity principle, roughly translated, says that if one performs a certain behavior in a situation, one will tend to repeat that behavior the next time the situation occurs. "What is being noticed becomes a signal for what is being done" (Guthrie, 1959, p. 186). At any given moment, the organism is confronted with many stimuli, and associations cannot be made to all of them. Rather, only a small number of stimuli are selected, and associations are formed between them and responses. The contiguity principle also applies to memory, which refers to verbal cues associated with stimulus conditions or events at the time of learning (Guthrie, 1952). *Forgetting* involves new learning and is due to interference in which an alternative response is made to an old stimulus.

Associative Strength

The process by which learning occurs involves pairing of stimulus and response. Guthrie (1942) addressed a second important principle, associative strength:

> A stimulus pattern gains its full associative strength on the occasion of its first pairing with a response. (p. 30)

Guthrie rejected the notion of associationism through frequency, as embodied in Thorndike's original Law of Exercise (Guthrie, 1930). However, Guthrie was not suggesting that people learn complex behaviors by performing them once. Rather, he believed that what becomes associated after the first trial is one or more movements; and repetition of a situation is important to add movements, to combine movements into acts, and to establish the act under different environmental conditions. "It appears that practice is necessary to the extent that the response must be elicitable from a variety of situations" (Guthrie, 1942, p. 32).

The Guthrie and Horton (1946) experiment with cats was interpreted as supporting this *all-or-none* notion of learning. Guthrie and Horton used a puzzle box similar to Thorndike's. Touching a post in the center triggered the mechanism that sprung open the door, allowing the cat to escape. When cats initially were placed in the box, they explored it and made a series of random movements. Eventually they made a response that released the mechanism and allowed for escape. Some cats hit the post with a paw; others brushed against it; others backed into it. The last response made by the cat in the box was successful in that it opened the door. The last response is the one predicted by Guthrie's contiguity principle. The investigators found that the cats repeated their successful response when put back into the box. Guthrie and Horton argued that the last movement (e.g., hitting the pole) became associated with the puzzle box, because it allowed the animal to escape. Therefore no new response became associated with the box.

Guthrie's position does not imply that once students successfully solve a long division problem or balance a chemical equation they have mastered the requisite skills. Practice linked the various movements involved in the acts of solving problems and balancing equations. The acts themselves have many variations (types of problems and equations), and they should transfer, that is, students should be able to solve problems and balance equations in different contexts. Guthrie accepted Thorndike's notion of identical elements. Little transfer is expected in different situations. Behaviors need to be practiced in the exact situations in which they will be called for. Students need to practice solving problems and balancing equations at the board, at their desks, in small groups, and at home.

Rewards and Punishments

Guthrie believed that reward is not necessary for learning to occur. The key mechanism is contiguity (close pairing in time) between stimulus and response. It does not matter whether the response results in a satisfying state of affairs. A simple pairing without any consequences could lead to learning.

> The future response to a situation can be best predicted in terms of what an animal has done in that situation in the past. Stimuli acting during a response tend on later occasions to evoke that response. (Guthrie, 1952, p. 127)

Guthrie disputed Thorndike's Law of Effect on conceptual grounds. Satisfiers and annoyers refer to the effects of actions. Because they occur after the organism acts, they cannot influence the learning of associations:

> We may go on to inquire how any stimulus becomes an annoyer in the first place, a question which Thorndike did not consider. He defined an annoyer as a state of affairs which the animal avoids or changes. But this ability to avoid is just what it is necessary to explain. Hammering the thumb or bumping one's head on a beam is not an annoyer according to this definition unless we assume that the learning has already occurred, for the victim cannot avoid it after it has happened. If he avoids it at all it must be in time, and this implies that the learning which we hoped to explain has already taken place. (Guthrie, 1952, pp. 128–129)

In short, satisfiers and annoyers (rewards and punishments) cannot influence previous connections but only subsequent ones. Reward could help prevent *unlearning* because it removes the organism from the situation and thwarts new responses from being associated with stimulus cues. In the Guthrie and Horton (1946) experiment, the reward (escape from the box) took the organism out of the learning context and precluded the animal from acquiring new associations to the box. Similarly, punishment can lead to unlearning only if it causes the organism to learn something else. Punishment may also lead to responding differently to cues in the future.

Contiguity is a central feature of school learning. Flashcards help students learn arithmetic facts. Students learn to associate a *stimulus* (e.g., 4 × 4) with a *response* (16). Foreign language drills also use the principle of contiguity. Foreign language words are associated with their English equivalents. In German, students study *das Buch* along with its English translation, "the book."

As noted above, rewards can prevent unlearning. Consider a student who answers "16" in response to the flashcard "4 × 4 =" and receives teacher praise ("Good"). In Guthrie's view, the next time the student is presented with the same flashcard, the student is apt to reply with 16 rather than with another number. Receiving praise temporarily removes the student from the learning context and prevents new associations from being formed to the flashcard.

Habit Formation and Change

Guthrie (1952) felt that habits are nothing more than behaviors established to a wide variety of cues:

> The chief difficulty in the way of avoiding a bad habit is that the responsible cues are often hard to find, and that in many bad habit systems they are extremely numerous. Each rehearsal is responsible for a possible

APPLICATION 2.4: Breaking Habits

Guthrie's contiguity principle offers practical suggestions for how to break habits. One application of the *threshold* method involves the time young children spend on academic activities. Young children have short attention spans, so the length of time they can sustain work on one activity is limited. Most activities are scheduled to last no longer than 30 to 40 minutes. However, at the start of the school year, attention spans quickly wane and behavior problems often result. To apply Guthrie's theory, a teacher might, at the start of the year, limit activities from 15 to 20 minutes. Over the next few weeks the teacher could gradually increase the time students spend working on a single activity.

The threshold method is also applied to teaching printing and handwriting. When children first learn to form letters, their movements are awkward and they lack fine motor coordination. The distances between lines on a page are purposely wide so children can fit the letters into the space. If papers with narrow lines are initially introduced, students' letters would spill over the borders and students might become frustrated. Once students can form letters within the larger borders, they can use paper with smaller borders to help them refine their skills.

The *fatigue* method can be applied when disciplining disruptive students who build paper airplanes and sail them across the room. The teacher could remove the students from the classroom, give them a large stack of paper, and tell them to start making paper airplanes. After the students have made several airplanes, the activity should lose its attraction. Thus paper will have become a cue for not building airplanes.

The *incompatible response* method can be used with students who talk and misbehave while in the media center. Reading is incompatible with talking. The media center teacher could ask the students to find interesting books and read them while in the center. Assuming that the students find the books enjoyable, the media center will, over time, become a cue for selecting and reading books rather than for talking with other students.

---

addition of one or more new cues which tend to set off the undesired action. (p. 116)

Teachers who want students to behave well in school need to link the school rules with as many cues as possible. A rule, such as "Treat others with respect" needs to be linked with the classroom, halls, cafeteria, gymnasium, auditorium, and playground. By associating all of these contexts with this rule, students' respectful behaviors toward others become habitual. If students believe they only have to practice respect in the classroom, respecting others will not become a habit.

The key to changing behavior is to "find the cues that initiate the action and to practice another response to these cues" (Guthrie, 1952, p. 115). Guthrie (1952) identified three methods for altering habits—the threshold, fatigue, and incompatible response methods (Table 2.2). Although these methods appear distinct on the surface, they all present cues for an habitual action but arrange for it not to be performed. In the *threshold* method, the cue for the undesired response is initially introduced at such a low level or weak strength that it does not elicit the response; it is below the "threshold" level of the response. Gradually the stimulus is introduced at greater levels until it finally is presented at full strength. Were the stimulus to be introduced at its greatest level initially, the response would be the behavior that is to be changed (the habit). Some children react to the taste of spinach by spitting it out and refusing to eat it. To alter this habit, parents should introduce spinach in small bites or mixed with a food that the child enjoys. Over time, the amount of spinach the child eats can be increased.

In the *fatigue* method, the cue for engaging in the behavior is transformed into a cue for avoiding it. This is the opposite of the threshold method in that the stimulus is introduced at full strength and the individual per-

TABLE 2.2
Guthrie's methods for breaking habits.

Method	Explanation	Example
Threshold	Introduce weak stimulus. Increase stimulus, but keep it below threshold value that will produce unwanted response.	Introduce academic content in short blocks of time for young children. Gradually increase session length, but not to where students become frustrated or bored.
Fatigue	Force subject to make unwanted response repeatedly in presence of stimulus.	Give child who makes paper airplanes in class stack of paper and have child make each sheet into a plane.
Incompatible response	In presence of stimulus, have subject make response incompatible with unwanted response.	Pair cues associated with media center with reading rather than talking.

forms the undesired response until exhausted. The stimulus becomes a cue for not performing the response. To alter a child's behavior of repeatedly throwing toys, parents should make the child continue to throw toys until it is no longer fun.

The third method (*incompatible response*) requires that the cue for the undesired behavior be paired with a response incompatible with the undesired response. Responses are incompatible when they cannot be performed simultaneously. The response to be paired with the cue must be more attractive to the individual than the undesired response. The stimulus becomes a cue for performing the alternate response. To stop snacking while watching TV, one needs to keep the hands busy—sewing, painting, working crossword puzzles. Over time, watching TV becomes a cue for engaging in the other activity rather than snacking.

Guthrie believed that punishment is an ineffective means of altering habits. Punishment following a response cannot affect the stimulus-response association. Punishment given while a behavior is being performed may disrupt the habit but will not change it. Punishment does not establish an alternate response to the stimulus. The threat of punishment even can prove to be exciting and can encourage the habit rather than discourage it. Regarding children's misbehaviors, Guthrie (1952) noted, "Drawing on the walls, saying 'I won't,' spilling food, uttering forbidden words, all take on the fascination that big-game hunting has for the adult" (p. 117). In short, punishment may temporarily suppress a response but does not eliminate it from one's behavioral repertoire.

HULL'S SYSTEMATIC BEHAVIOR THEORY

Clark L. Hull (1884–1952) formulated an elaborate learning theory that he continually tested and modified. A basic assumption of the theory is that behavior is lawful and can be described precisely. Like the views of Thorndike, Pavlov, Watson, and Guthrie, Hull's theory concerns the study of observable behavior and deals with how associations are formed between stimuli and responses.

In describing S-R relationships, Hull employed *intervening variables*, or theoretical constructs that mediate the relationship between a stimulus and response. Intervening variables are nonobservable and are inferred from antecedent conditions and present contextual variables. Prominent intervening variables in Hull's system are habit strength, drive, inhibition, and incentive motivation.

Hull employed a rigorous approach to theorizing. His theory is logical-deductive and consists of a series of postulates from which theorems are derived. The theorems and corollaries are testable and serve as the basis for experimentation. The theory also is quantitative, because postulates are expressed in mathematical terms (Hull, 1935; Hull, et al., 1940). The most comprehensive account of Hull's theory is found in his *Principles of Behavior* (1943). He wrote a short book describing major changes to his theory (Hull, 1951) and finished a second major volume shortly before his death (Hull, 1952). Kenneth W. Spence (1907–1967) collaborated extensively with Hull and was primarily responsible for several modifications to the theory. Following Hull's death, Spence (1960) continued to revise the theory based on findings from his own research.

Comprehensive treatment of Hull's theory is beyond the scope of this book. The ensuing sections are largely nonmathematical; mathematical formulas are stated without being derived. Interested readers should consult Hull (1943) for derivations. Other extensive treatments of Hull's theory are found in Koch (1954), Logan (1959), and Spence (1960).

Hull's system is no longer a viable theory of learning. Hull attempted to quantify the learning process, which made the theory easy to test empirically. The complexities of behavior, however, yielded many research findings that conflicted with predictions. These failures did not detract from Hull's position in the field of learning. Rather, the theory helped establish the experimental method in studying learning and generated a tremendous amount of research on many important learning variables. Several individuals who collaborated with Hull or who worked within his theoretical framework subsequently established their own research reputations, including Neal Miller, Kenneth Spence, O. Hobart Mowrer, Frank Logan, Abram Amsel, and Robert Sears. Readers interested in a Neo-Hullian perspective on learning should consult Logan (1976). Dollard and Miller (1950) presented a Neo-Hullian view of psychotherapy and behavior change.

Learning and Reinforcement

Hull (1937) was strongly influenced by the work of Darwin. Like Darwin, Hull viewed behavior in an adaptive sense. A state of *primary need* exists whenever the conditions necessary for survival are lacking or deviate markedly from an optimal level (Hull, 1943). Primary needs are often fulfilled by innate mechanisms. When a piece of food lodges in their throat, people automatically begin coughing. This response usually expels the food and allows normal breathing. Often there is a hierarchy of responses such that if the first is not effective, the second occurs. If dirt lodges in the eye, the eye automatically begins watering to expel the object. If the amount of dirt is large, one begins to rub the eye.

Learning is part of the process of adaptation to the environment to ensure survival. Learned mechanisms are required when innate ones fail to satisfy needs. Once a response is learned, no new learning occurs as long as the previously learned one is effective. Learning occurs only when a need exists and innate mechanisms or previously learned responses do not satisfy the need.

Hull (1943) viewed learning as the process of establishing receptor-effector (neurological) reactions in response to need situations:

> It is evident, however, that such an arrangement of ready-made (inherited) receptor-effector tendencies, even when those evoked by each state of need are distinctly varied, will hardly be optimally effective for the survival of organisms living in a complex, highly variable, and consequently unpredictable environment. For the optimal probability of survival of such organisms, inherited behavior tendencies must be supplemented by learning. . . . Just as the inherited equipment of reaction tendencies consists of receptor-effector connections, so the process of learning consists in the strengthening of certain of these connections as contrasted with others, or in the setting up of quite new connections. (pp. 68–69)

Like Thorndike and Pavlov, Hull spoke of learning in terms of neurological connections. In behavioral terms, Hull's theory says that responses are learned to satisfy needs when innate mechanisms fail to do so. These learned responses are adaptive because they satisfy needs.

Basic Learning Model

Hull's system comprises three types of variables. *Independent variables* are contextual aspects (stimuli) impinging on the organism. *Dependent variables* are responses made by the organism, such as type, amount, and duration of a particular response. *Intervening variables* are processes occurring within the organism. These variables are not directly observable but can be operationally defined. Three important intervening variables are drive, habit strength, and inhibition.

Drive. A need state exists whenever the actual or potential survival of the individual or species is threatened. A need produces a drive to reduce the need. Drive (D) is a motivational construct; it energizes the organism and propels it into action. Obtaining reinforcement to satisfy a need is known as *drive reduction*. Hull recognized that much behavior is not immediately oriented toward obtaining primary reinforcement. Stimulus situations could acquire reinforcing power (*secondary reinforcement*) by being paired with primary reinforcement. People work to earn money, which in turn is used to buy food, clothing, and so on. Hull (1943) also noted that once a situation acquires secondary reinforcing properties, it can reinforce other situations through pairing.

Habit Strength. Responding to a situation that results in reinforcement creates a habit. *Habit strength* $(_sH_R)$, the strength of the association between a stimulus and response, increases with the number of reinforced S-R pairings.

The probability that a learned response will be made to a situation is known as *reaction potential* ($_sE_R$). Reaction potential is a multiplicative function of drive and habit strength:

$$_sE_R = D \times {}_sH_R$$

If either drive or habit strength is at or near zero, there is no action no matter how high the other variable. Repeated responses not followed by reinforcement produce *extinction* of the habit, or a decrease in its strength to a value too low to produce the response in the presence of the stimulus.

Inhibition.   Drive and habit strength lead organisms to make responses; inhibition causes them *not* to make responses. *Inhibition* is an intervening variable that comprises *reactive inhibition* and *conditioned inhibition*. Responding requires work, and work produces fatigue. This fatigue, or reactive inhibition (I_R), disrupts responding. When no responses occur over time, fatigue dissipates, and *spontaneous recovery* occurs. When the organism is fatigued, *not responding* is reinforced. The learned response of not responding (*conditioned inhibition*) ($_sI_R$) becomes conditioned. Inhibition is subtracted from the reaction potential to give the *effective reaction potential* ($_s\bar{E}_R$):

$$_s\bar{E}_R = D \times {}_sH_R - (I_R + {}_sI_R)$$

Other Important Constructs

Oscillation.   Hull (1943) postulated that the full force of the effective reaction potential is rarely manifested. Rather, it is subject to moment-to-moment fluctuations around a mean value lower than the effective reaction potential. This process is known as *oscillation*. Oscillation explains why a learned behavior may be demonstrated on some occasions and not on others, even when external conditions and (presumably) intervening variables are comparable.

Generalization.   A response may occur not only to the original stimulus but to other, similar stimuli. The more the original and generalization situations are qualitatively alike, the greater the generalization effect. Less generalization is expected as stimuli become more dissimilar.

Fractional Antedating Goal Reactions.   A chain of events typically leads up to the response that obtains reinforcement. If a hungry rat runs through a maze, the rat will obtain food. Along the way, the rat responds to stimuli associated with the maze; the rat runs straight, turns left, runs straight, turns right, and so forth. Each of these responses becomes conditioned to the appropriate stimuli. When the animal finally reaches the goal, neurological traces of the intermediate stimuli and responses remain. The reinforcement becomes conditioned to the consummatory response and to the traces of the intermediate responses. When the rat subsequently runs the maze, the intermediate stimuli elicit parts (fractions) of the goal response prior to the rat reaching the goal. These *fractional antedating goal reactions* (r_Gs) maintain goal-directed behavior (Hull, 1952). One important function of r_Gs is to create secondary reinforcers, because responses to stimuli leading to the goal are reinforcing. The closer (in space or time) the fractional antedating goal reactions are to the primary reinforcement, the more strongly they become conditioned. This is the essence of the *goal-gradient hypothesis:*

> The goal reaction gets conditioned most strongly to the stimuli preceding it, and the other reactions of the behavior sequence get conditioned to their stimuli progressively weaker as they are more remote (in time or space) from the goal reaction. (Hull, 1932, p. 26)

Presumably the goal-gradient hypothesis accounts for the experimental finding that errors in a chain of behavior are more readily eliminated the closer they occur to the terminal response. During training, it helps to establish clear cues along the route (e.g., mark alternate routes in different colors), so that fewer errors occur in conditioning.

Habit-Family Hierarchy. Many situations offer multiple ways of reaching the goal. For any given situation, the possible ways of reaching a goal constitute a family and can be ordered in a hierarchy according to likelihood. Less likely alternatives to the goal are chosen only when more likely ones are thwarted. An animal in a maze would take a detour only if the preferred (shortest, most direct) route is blocked. Hierarchies presumably become established as a function of r_Gs, with those more remote from the goal becoming less strongly conditioned to it.

Incentive Motivation

Hull's theory specifies that reinforcement increases habit strength and effective reaction potential. Hull (1943) postulated that a large reward leads to better learning (i.e., greater habit strength) than a small reward:

> Therefore, given a normal hunger drive, the organism will execute the correct one of several acts originally evoked by the situation more promptly, more vigorously, more certainly, and more persistently when a large amount of food is stimulating its receptors than when they are stimulated by a small amount. (p. 132)

Hull believed that the amount and timing of reinforcement influence the maximum acquired amount of habit strength. Stronger habits are developed when large rewards are delivered immediately after goal attainment. As reward size decreases and the delay between response and reward increases, the upper limit of habit strength is lowered.

These ideas, however, are not substantiated by research. Tolman's research on latent learning did show that rats learn to run mazes without being rewarded (see the discussion of Historical Perspectives in Chapter 4). Other research demonstrated that shifts in performance (e.g., speed of maze running) occur subsequent to learning as a function of changes in reward size (Crespi, 1942). The latter finding could not be attributed to altered habit strength, which was hypothesized to increase gradually with repeated reinforcements. Hull (1951, 1952) eventually modified his position to include an *incentive motivation factor* (K):

$$_s\bar{E}_R = D \times {_sH_R} \times K - I$$

where I equals inhibition.

The incentive motivation construct was explored by Spence (1960), who argued that reward does not affect habit strength but rather performance of the response and that incentive motivation is a performance variable, not a learning variable. Spence postulated that the incentive motivation factor (K) combines in additive fashion with drive to produce a complex movitational variable:

$$_s\bar{E}_R = (D + K) \times {_sH_R} - I$$

The idea that reward influences the frequency and amount of behavior but is not necessary for learning to occur has been subsequently substantiated (Chapter 4).

Discrimination Learning

Discrimination learning requires the organism to respond differently depending on the stimulus presented. In laboratory studies with animals, a pigeon may learn to discriminate a green disk from a red disk by pecking at the green one and not pecking at the red one. Discrimination learning is important with humans; it allows differentiation of concepts with similar meanings (e.g., chair, stool). It also is important in distinguishing symbols (the letters *b* and *d*).

Spence (1936) postulated that discrimination learning involves conditioning. Reinforced responding toward the positive stimulus builds "excitatory tendencies"; nonreinforced responses weaken these tendencies by increasing inhibition. Once responses become conditioned or weakened, they can generalize to other similar stimuli (Spence, 1937). Spence's view is a *continuity* position, because it postulates that changes in the tendencies

APPLICATION 2.5: Discrimination Learning

Teachers might apply the spirit of Spence's discrimination learning principles in the following ways. Many young children learning to read are confused about their left and right and on which side of the word or page they should begin. Teachers working with small reading groups might place brightly colored objects, such as rubber bands or plastic bracelets, around the children's left wrists to help them remember which side is left. When children begin reading their word lists, flashcards, or sentences on a page, teachers could reward students by placing another object around their wrists if they read correctly from left to right or do other tasks correctly. At the end of the period, children can exchange their rubber bands or bracelets for free time.

Intermediate students learning to solve long division problems often have difficulty discriminating among the appropriate applications of division, multiplication, and subtraction. Teachers could help students color code the various computations as students complete them. Students could be given differently colored pencils or markers to use for each mathematical operation (e.g., red markers for multiplication, blue for subtraction). This learning technique increases students' awareness of the various steps in completing problems.

for organisms to respond (or not to respond) occur gradually with repeated reinforcement (or nonreinforcement). Discrimination becomes errorless once the excitatory potential to respond to the positive stimulus sufficiently outweighs any residual potential to respond to the negative stimulus. Learning requires several trials in which organisms initially respond randomly but gradually respond more correctly with fewer errors.

The continuity theory of discrimination learning has been disputed by cognitive theorists, who believe that individuals form hypotheses about correct patterns of responding and act based on their beliefs more than on their reinforcement history. There also is evidence that discrimination learning can occur without any errors, which calls into question the gradual buildup of excitatory tendencies (see the discussion of Basic Processes in Chapter 3). Nonetheless, Spence's research has remained influential for many years and constitutes an exemplary research program on an important topic.

SUMMARY

The systematic development of learning theories began at the start of the twentieth century. Structuralism and functionalism were active schools of

SUMMARY

thought, but they suffered from problems that limited their widespread applicability to psychology. As theorists attempted to define psychology as a science, they sought to establish a focus of study and an appropriate methodology. Led by Watson and others, a behaviorist movement gained prominence that focused its research on observable behavior.

The learning theories of Thorndike, Pavlov, Watson, Guthrie, and Hull are of historical importance. Although there are theoretical differences among them, each theory views learning as a process of forming associations between stimuli and responses. Thorndike believed that responses to stimuli are strengthened when followed by satisfying consequences. Pavlov experimentally demonstrated how stimuli could be conditioned to elicit responses by being paired with unconditioned stimuli. Watson believed that Pavlov's model could be extended to cover diverse forms of learning and personality development. Guthrie hypothesized that a contiguous relationship between stimulus and response establishes their pairing. Hull postulated that behavior is a complex function of drive, habit strength, inhibition, and other variables and that learning occurs with reinforced responding.

Although these theories are no longer viable in their original forms, many of their principles are evident in current learning theories. These historical theories, along with the research they generated, have helped establish psychology as a science and learning as an area of study.

Chapter 3

Operant Conditioning

Operant conditioning is a behavioristic theory formulated by B.F. (Burrhus Frederic) Skinner. Beginning in the 1930s, Skinner published a series of papers reporting results of laboratory studies with animals, in which he identified the various components of operant conditioning. Much of this early work is summarized in Skinner's (1938) influential book, *The Behavior of Organisms*.

Skinner has been a prolific writer and has applied his ideas to the solution of human problems. Early in his career he became interested in education and developed teaching machines and programmed instruction. Skinner's (1968) book *The Technology of Teaching* addressed such topics as instruction, motivation, discipline, and creativity. In 1948, after a difficult period in his life, he published *Walden Two*, which described how behavioral principles can be applied to create a utopian society. Skinner (1971) addressed the problems of modern life and advocated applying a behavioral technology to the design of cultures in *Beyond Freedom and Dignity*. Other investigators have applied operant conditioning principles to such diverse contexts as school learning and discipline, child development, social behaviors, mental illness, medical problems, substance abuse, and vocational training (Karoly & Harris, 1986).

Skinner was born in Pennsylvania in 1904. His upbringing was uneventful except for his younger brother dying suddenly during adolescence. Skinner received his undergraduate degree from Hamilton College. His aspiration was to be a writer, but that career never materialized (Skinner, 1970):

> I built a small study in the attic and set to work. The results were disastrous. I frittered away my time. I read aimlessly, built model ships, played the piano, listened to the newly-invented radio, contributed to the humorous column of a local paper but wrote almost nothing else, and thought about seeing a psychiatrist. (p. 6)

He became interested in psychology and read Pavlov's (1927) *Conditioned Reflexes* and Watson's (1924) *Behaviorism*. Eventually he began graduate study in psychology at Harvard. After completing his doctoral dissertation on conditioned reflexes in 1931, he stayed at Harvard as a postdoctoral fellow for five years. His first faculty position was at the University of Minnesota. He became chairman of the psychology department at Indiana University in 1945. In 1947 he gave the William James lectures at Harvard and was asked to become a faculty member. He moved to Harvard in 1948, where he remains today. Despite his admission, "I had failed as a writer because I had had nothing important to say" (Skinner, 1970, p. 7), he has most effectively channeled his literary aspiration into scientific writing.

CONCEPTUAL FRAMEWORK

Scientific Assumptions

Thorndike and Pavlov viewed behavior as a manifestation of neurological functioning. Both theories traced the ultimate locus and explanation of learning to the nervous system. Skinner (1938) did not deny that neurological functioning is relevant to behavior, but he believed a psychology of behavior can be understood in its own terms without reference to neurological events. Behavior needs to be concerned with the whole organism, not with its individual parts.

Hull postulated that needs give rise to drives, the latter of which are the energizing sources of behavior. Skinner (1953) dismissed such internal drives and other intervening variables as causes of behavior. Skinner believed that the search for intervening variables downgrades the importance of variables in the immediate environment and the organism's environmental history, which are available for scientific analysis:

> When we say that a man eats *because* he is hungry, smokes a great deal *because* he has the tobacco habit, fights *because* of the instinct of pugnacity, behaves brilliantly *because* of his intelligence, or plays the piano well *because* of his musical ability, we seem to be referring to causes. But on analysis these phrases prove to be merely redundant descriptions. A single set of facts is described by the two statements: "He eats" and "He is hungry." . . . Such terms as "hunger," "habit," and "intelligence"

convert what are essentially the properties of a process or relation into what appear to be things. Thus we are unprepared for the properties eventually to be discovered in the behavior itself and continue to look for something which may not exist. (p. 31)

Skinner raised similar objections to modern cognitive views of learning that emphasize how people mentally process information. *Private events*, or responses made "within the organism's own skin," are accessible only to the organism. They can be studied through people's verbal reports (Skinner, 1953). Skinner and other behavior theorists do not deny the existence of attitudes, beliefs, opinions, desires, and other forms of self-knowledge. Rather, Skinner (1974) qualified the role of these inner realities in a science of human behavior:

A behavioristic analysis does not question the practical usefulness of reports of the inner world that is felt and introspectively observed. They are clues (1) to past behavior and the conditions affecting it, (2) to current behavior and the conditions affecting it, and (3) to conditions related to future behavior. Nevertheless, the private world within the skin is not clearly observed or known. (p. 31)

Skinner (1987) contended that people do not experience consciousness or emotions but rather their own bodies, and that internal reactions are responses to internal stimuli:

Cognitive psychologists like to say that "the mind is what the brain does," but surely the rest of the body plays a part. The mind is what the *body* does. It is what the *person* does. In other words, it is behavior, and that is what behaviorists have been saying for more than half a century. (p. 784)

Furthermore, internal events often are problematic. The reason for certain behaviors may not be known. Translating private events into language is difficult, because language does not completely capture the dimensions of an internal experience (e.g., pain). Much of what is called *knowing* involves using language (verbal behavior). Thoughts are types of behavior that are brought about by other stimuli (environmental or private) and that give rise to responses (overt or covert). To the extent that private events are expressed as overt behaviors, behaviorists can determine their role in a functional analysis.

Functional Analysis of Behavior

Skinner (1953) referred to his means of examining behavior as *functional analysis:*

The external variables of which behavior is a function provide for what may be called a causal or functional analysis. We undertake to predict and control the behavior of the individual organism. This is our "dependent variable"—the effect for which we are to find the cause. Our "independent variables"—the causes of behavior—are the external conditions of which behavior is a function. Relations between the two— the "cause-and-effect relationships" in behavior—are the laws of a science. A synthesis of these laws expressed in quantitative terms yields a comprehensive picture of the organism as a behaving system. (p. 35)

Learning is "the reassortment of responses in a complex situation"; *conditioning* refers to "the strengthening of behavior which results from reinforcement" (Skinner, 1953, p. 65). There are two types of conditioning: Type S and Type R. *Type S* is Pavlovian conditioning, characterized by the pairing of the reinforcing stimulus with another stimulus. The *S* calls attention to the importance of the stimulus in eliciting a response from the organism. The behavior paired with the eliciting stimulus is known as *respondent behavior.*

Although Type S conditioning explains such behaviors as conditioned emotional reactions, most human behaviors are *emitted* in the presence of stimuli rather than elicited by stimuli. The consequences of the behavior (posterior event or stimulus) control the response, not the antecedent stimulus. This type of behavior, which Skinner termed *Type R* to emphasize the response aspect, is *operant* in the sense that it operates to produce an effect. Type R conditioning and extinction are explained as follows (Skinner, 1938):

> If the occurrence of an operant is followed by presentation of a reinforcing stimulus, the strength is increased. . . . If the occurrence of an operant already strengthened through conditioning is not followed by the reinforcing stimulus, the strength is decreased. (p. 21)

Unlike respondents, which prior to conditioning have a zero probability of producing a conditioned response, the probability of occurrence of operants is never zero, because the response must be made for reinforcement to be provided. Reinforcement changes the likelihood of occurrence of the response. Operants act upon their environment and become more likely to occur because of reinforcement.

BASIC PROCESSES

Reinforcement

Reinforcement is the mechanism responsible for response strengthening— increasing the rate of responding or making responses more likely to occur, that is, it is any stimulus or event that leads to response strengthening: "The only defining characteristic of a reinforcing stimulus is that it reinforces" (Skinner, 1953, p. 72). A reinforcer cannot be determined in advance or independently of its effects:

> The only way to tell whether or not a given event is reinforcing to a given organism under given conditions is to make a direct test. We observe the frequency of a selected response, then make an event contingent upon it and observe any change in frequency. If there is a change, we classify the event as reinforcing to the organism under the existing conditions. (Skinner, 1953, pp. 72–73)

Reinforcers apply to individual organisms at given times under given conditions. What is reinforcing to a particular student at one moment may not be an hour later. What is reinforcing to a particular student during reading may not be during math. Despite this specificity, stimuli or events that reinforce behavior can, to some extent, be predicted:

> We achieve a certain success in guessing at reinforcing powers only because we have in a sense made a crude survey; we have gauged the reinforcing effect of a stimulus upon ourselves and assume the same effect upon others. We are successful only when we resemble the organism under study and when we have correctly surveyed our own behavior. (Skinner, 1953, p. 73)

Students typically find reinforcing such events as teacher praise, free time, privileges, and high grades. Nonetheless, Skinner cautioned that researchers cannot know whether an event is reinforcing until they present the event contingent on a response and see whether behavior changes.

Three-Term Contingency. People sometimes behave in the absence of any stimulus antecedent. For example, a child may kick a rock down a street or tap a pencil on a desk. Most human behavior, however, bears a functional relationship with aspects of the environment. The basic operant model of conditioning is the following three-term contingency:

$$S^D \rightarrow R \rightarrow S^R$$

A *discriminative stimulus* (S^D) sets the occasion for a *response* (R) to be emitted, which is followed by a *reinforcing stimulus* (S^R, or reinforcement). The reinforcing stimulus is any stimulus (event, consequence) that increases the probability the response will be emitted in the future when the discriminative stimulus is present.

Positive and Negative Reinforcement. There are two types of reinforcement. *Positive reinforcement* involves presenting stimuli, or adding something to a situation, for example, presenting food, water, praise, a high grade. A *positive reinforcer* is a stimulus that, when presented following a response, increases the future likelihood of the response occurring in that situation. *Negative reinforcement* involves removing stimuli, or taking something away from a situation, for example, removing a loud noise, a bright light, criticism, a low grade. A *negative reinforcer* is a stimulus that, when

APPLICATION 3.1: Positive and Negative Reinforcement

Teachers can use positive and negative reinforcement as motivators to increase students' mastery of skills and time on the task. For instance, in teaching concepts included in a science unit, a teacher asks students to complete questions at the end of the chapter following the teacher's explanation of a particular topic. The teacher also sets up activity centers around the room that involve hands-on experiments related to the lesson. Students circulate and complete the experiments contingent on their successfully answering the chapter questions (positive reinforcement). This contingency reflects the Premack principle (discussed below) of providing the opportunity to engage in a more-valued activity (experiments) as a reinforcer for engaging in a less-valued one (completing chapter questions). Students who complete 80% of the questions correctly and who participate in a minimum of two experiments do not have to complete homework. This negative reinforcement assumes that students perceive homework as a negative reinforcer.

removed by a response, also increases the future likelihood of the response occurring in that situation. Positive and negative reinforcement have the same effect—they increase the future probability of the response. These two processes are portrayed in Table 3.1.

Assume that a teacher is holding a question and answer session with the class. The teacher asks a question (S^D); calls on a student volunteer, who gives the correct answer (R); and praises the student (S^R). If student volunteering increases or remains at a high level, praise is operating as a positive reinforcement. Now assume that the teacher asks a question (S^D); calls on a student volunteer, who gives the correct answer (R); and removes a question from that night's homework (S^R). If student volunteering increases or remains at a high level, the removal of homework questions is operating as a negative reinforcement.

Extinction

Extinction involves the decline of response strength due to nonreinforcement. Rats who run mazes for food at the end may cease running if food is no longer presented. Students who raise their hands in class but never get called on may stop raising their hands. When people write many unanswered letters to the same individual, they may eventually quit writing.

How rapidly extinction occurs depends on the reinforcement history (Skinner, 1953). Extinction occurs quickly if few preceding responses have been reinforced. Responding is much more durable with a lengthier history

TABLE 3.1
Reinforcement and punishment processes.

	S^D ⟶ Discriminative Stimulus	R ⟶ Response	S^R Reinforcing (Punishing) Stimulus
Positive reinforcement (Present positive reinforcer)	T gives ⟶ independent study time*	L ⟶ studies*	T praises L for good work
Negative reinforcement (Remove negative reinforcer)	T gives ⟶ independent study time	L studies ⟶	T says L does not have to do homework
Punishment (Present negative reinforcer)	T gives ⟶ independent study time	L wastes ⟶ time	T gives homework
Punishment (Remove positive reinforcer)	T gives ⟶ independent study time	L wastes ⟶ time	T says L will miss free time

T refers to teacher and L to learner.

of reinforcement. Extinction is not to be confused with *forgetting*, which is a true loss of conditioning with the passage of time in which the occasions for the behavior have not been present.

Primary and Secondary Reinforcers

Such stimuli as food, water, and shelter are called *primary reinforcers;* they are necessary for survival. Much human behavior that is maintained over lengthy periods is indirectly associated with primary reinforcement; people work long hours to receive paychecks, which they exchange for money to buy food and pay the rent and utilities. *Conditioned (secondary) reinforcers* are intervening events that become associated with primary reinforcers. A conditioned reinforcer that becomes paired with more than one primary reinforcer is a *generalized reinforcer.*

Much social behavior can be explained by generalized reinforcers. Attention is a generalized reinforcer. Children sometimes behave in ways to "get attention" from adults. Attention is reinforcing because it is paired with primary reinforcers from adults (e.g., food, water, protection). Much the same can be said about behaviors that draw approval from others. In the nonsocial realm, money is a generalized reinforcer because it can be exchanged for numerous primary reinforcers. In education, generalized reinforcers are teachers' praise, high grades, honor roll, and diplomas. These reinforcers often are paired with other generalized reinforcers, such as approval (from parents and friends) and money (diploma from prestigious school leading to high-paying job).

Premack Principle

Premack (1962, 1971) described a means for ordering reinforcers that allows prediction of which stimuli and events should function as reinforcers. According to Premack, the opportunity to engage in a more-valued activity reinforces engaging in a less-valued activity. Premack defined *value* in terms of the amount of responding or time spent on the activity in the absence of explicit reinforcers. The Premack principle says that if a contingency is arranged such that the value of the contingent event is higher than the value of the instrumental event, an increase will be expected in the probability of occurrence of the instrumental event (the reward assumption). If the value of the contingent event is lower than that of the instrumental event, the likelihood of occurrence of the instrumental event ought to decrease (the punishment assumption).

Suppose a child is periodically given free time and the choice of working on an art project, going to the media center, reading a book in the classroom, or working at the computer. Over the course of 10 free-time sessions, this child goes to the media center 6 times, works at the computer 3 times, works on an art project 1 time, and never reads a book in the classroom. For this child, the opportunity to go to the media center is valued the most and should be an effective reinforcer for reading a book in the classroom. Considerable empirical evidence supports Premack's ideas, especially with respect to the reward assumption (Dunham, 1977).

The Premack principle offers guidance about how to predict the outcome of an operant contingency: Observe what people do when they have a choice, and order those behaviors in terms of likelihood. The order is not permanent, since the value of reinforcers can change. Any reinforcer, when applied often, can result in *satiation* and lead to decreased responding. Teachers who employ the Premack principle need to conduct periodic checks of students' preferences by observing and asking what they like to do.

Punishment

Unlike reinforcement, *punishment* decreases the future likelihood of a response being made in the presence of a stimulus. There are two types of punishment: withdrawing a positive reinforcer or presenting a negative reinforcer contingent on a response. Punishment is exemplified in Table 3.1. Assume that during a question and answer session a student repeatedly pokes another student when the teacher is not watching (teacher not watching = S^D; misbehavior = R). The teacher spots the misbehavior and says to the student, "Stop bothering him" (S^R). If the student's poking ceases, the teacher's criticism has functioned as a punishment, that is, the teacher presented a negative reinforcer. Instead of criticizing the student, assume that the teacher says, "You'll have to stay inside during recess today." If the student's poking ceases, the loss of recess has functioned as a punishment, that is, the teacher removed a positive reinforcer.

Punishment *suppresses* a response but does not eliminate it; when the threat of punishment is removed, the punished response may return. In a classic experiment by Estes (1944), rats were trained to press a lever to get food reinforcement. Extinction was then implemented: Lever pressing no longer produced food. Some rats received shock as they pressed the lever during early extinction trials. Although the shocked rats initially made fewer responses than the nonshocked rats, once punishment (i.e., the shocking) was discontinued, the shocked rats responded at a higher rate than the others.

The effects of punishment are complex. Punishment often brings about responses that are incompatible with the punished behavior and that are strong enough to suppress it (Skinner, 1953). Spanking a child for misbehaving may produce guilt and fear, which can suppress misbehavior. If the child misbehaves in the future, the conditioned guilt and fear reaction may reappear and lead the child quickly to stop misbehaving. Punishment also conditions responses that help the organism escape or avoid punishment. Students whose teacher criticizes incorrect answers soon learn to avoid punishment by not volunteering answers. Punishment can condition maladaptive behaviors, because punishment does not teach how to behave more productively. Punishment can further hinder learning by creating a conflict such that the individual vacillates between responding one way or another. If the teacher sometimes criticizes students for incorrect answers and sometimes does not, students never know when criticism is forthcoming. Such variable behavior can have lasting effects. The emotional byproducts of punishment—fear, anger, and crying—all interfere with learning.

Alternatives to Punishment. Skinner has discussed various alternatives to punishment. One can determine which aspects of the environment are producing the negative behavior. Often a simple change in the environment eliminates the behavior being punished. Teachers follow this strategy when they change the seat of a disruptive student who is misbehaving with a neighbor. Teachers can also allow the individual to continue the unwanted behavior until he or she becomes *satiated,* which is similar to Guthrie's fatigue method (see the discussion of Guthrie's Contiguous Conditioning in Chapter 2). One can also extinguish an unwanted behavior by ignoring it. Extinction can be effective with minor behaviors, but when behaviors become disruptive, teachers need to act in other ways.

Another alternative is to condition *incompatible behavior* with positive reinforcement. Teacher praise for productive work habits helps condition those habits. The primary advantage of this alternative over punishment is that it shows the student how to behave more adaptively. Rather than punishing the child for misbehaving, positive reinforcement teaches the child how to behave acceptably. Although this technique is more time consuming than punishment, it is much more effective in the long run.

Schedules of Reinforcement

Much research has addressed how different reinforcement schedules influence responding (Ferster & Skinner, 1957; Skinner, 1938; Zeiler, 1977). One distinction is between continuous and intermittent schedules. *Continuous reinforcement* is reinforcement for every response and is especially desirable while skills are being acquired: Students receive feedback after each response concerning the accuracy of their work. In this fashion, incorrect responses are not inadvertently acquired.

Most behaviors in and out of school are not continuously reinforced. People are not reinforced every time they go to a movie, call a friend, or read a book. *Intermittent reinforcement* (some but not all responses are reinforced) is common in classrooms, because it is impossible for teachers to reinforce each student for every response. Students are not called on every time they raise their hands, they do not receive feedback after working each problem, and they are not continuously told they are behaving appropriately.

Intermittent schedules are defined in terms of time or number of responses. *Interval schedules,* or time schedules, call for the first response after a specific time period to receive reinforcement. In a *fixed interval (FI) schedule,* the time interval is constant from one reinforcement occasion to the next. An FI5 schedule means that reinforcement is delivered for the first response made after 5 minutes. Students who receive 30 minutes of free time every Friday (contingent on good behavior during the week) are operating under a fixed interval schedule. In a *variable interval (VI) schedule,* reinforcement is contingent on the first response after a given time period, but the interval varies from occasion to occasion around some average value. A VI5 schedule means that on the average the first response after 5 minutes is reinforced, but the time interval varies from trial to trial (e.g., 2, 3, 7, or 8 minutes). Students who receive 30 minutes of free time (contingent on good behavior) on the average of once per week, but not necessarily on the same day each week, are operating under a variable interval schedule.

Ratio schedules depend directly on the number of responses or rate of responding. In a *fixed ratio (FR) schedule*, every *n*th response is reinforced, where *n* is constant from trial to trial. An FR10 schedule means that every 10th response receives reinforcement. In a *variable ratio (VR) schedule*, every *n*th response is reinforced, but the value varies from trial to trial around an average number *n*. A teacher may give free time after every fifth workbook assignment is completed (FR5) or periodically following a completed assignment but on the average for every fifth one (VR5).

Reinforcement schedules produce characteristic patterns of responding, as shown in Figure 3.1. In general, ratio schedules produce higher rates than interval schedules, provided that the ratio is not too high. A limiting factor in ratio schedules is fatigue due to rapid responding. Fixed interval schedules produce a scalloped pattern. Responding drops off immediately after reinforcement but picks up toward the end of the interval between reinforcements. The variable interval schedule produces a steady rate of responding, which usually is preferable to ratio schedules over lengthy periods. Unannounced quizzes operate on VI schedules and typically keep students studying regularly.

Intermittent schedules are more resistant to extinction than continuous schedules: When reinforcement is discontinued, responding continues for a longer time if reinforcement has been given intermittently rather than continuously. In studies by Humphreys (1939a, 1939b), college students displayed significantly higher rates of responding during extinction when they had been reinforced previously only 50% of the time, compared with students who had received continuous (100%) reinforcement. The durability of intermittent schedules can be seen in such diverse life events as playing slot machines, casting fishing lines into water, and making trips to bargain stores.

Generalization and Discrimination

Generalization.   Once a certain response has been conditioned to occur in the presence of a given stimulus, the response also may occur in the presence of other stimuli. The spread of the effect of the reinforcement contingency to other stimuli is called *generalization* (Skinner, 1953). As an experimental demonstration of laboratory generalization, a pigeon is trained to peck at

OPERANT CONDITIONING

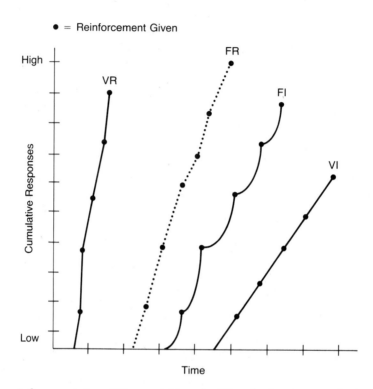

● = Reinforcement Given

Note: ● = *reinforcement given; VR = variable ratio; FR = fixed ratio; FI = fixed interval; VI = variable interval.*

FIGURE 3.1
Patterns of responding under different reinforcement schedules.

a bright red disk on an intermittent food reinforcement schedule. If the disk color is changed to orange or yellow, the pigeon also may peck, though perhaps without the same frequency or intensity. The color of the disk is an important stimulus property but not the only one—size and shape of the disk are also involved.

Recall that Thorndike postulated that transfer of responses occurs when the old and new situations share common elements. Generalization of a response to a situation in which it has never been reinforced seems troublesome for the operant position. Skinner explained this by noting that people execute many behaviors that typically lead to the final (reinforced) response. These component behaviors are often part of the chains of behavior of different tasks and therefore are reinforced in different contexts. When in a new situation, people are likely to execute the component behaviors, which produce an accurate response or rapid acquisition of the correct response. As with other aspects of the operant analysis, which features of a situation individuals respond to (and what type of generalization occurs) cannot be known in advance. Rather, minor changes are made to stimulus features to determine whether the response generalizes to those changes.

Students with good academic habits come to class, attend to and participate in the activities, take notes, do the required reading, and keep up with the assignments. These behaviors produce high scores on exams and assignments, as well as high course grades. When such students begin a new class, it is not necessary that the content be similar to other classes in which they have been enrolled. Rather, the component behaviors have received repeated reinforcement and, by virtue of the reinforcement history, are likely to occur in the new setting. The new class will have elements in common with prior courses (classroom, instructor, tables and chairs, books), but the prior reinforcement history produces generalization.

This is not to suggest that generalization occurs automatically. O'Leary and Drabman (1971) noted, "Generalization is not . . . a magical procedure or an explanation of a phenomenon but a description of a behavioral change which must be programmed like any other behavioral change" (p. 393). One problem with many behavior modification programs is that behaviors are changed while the reinforcement contingencies are in effect, but the new behaviors do not generalize outside the training context. O'Leary and Drabman (1971) offered the following suggestions for facilitating generalization:

Parental involvement	Involve parents in behavioral change programs
High expectations	Convey to students they are capable of performing well
Self-evaluation	Teach students to evaluate their behaviors
Contingencies	Withdraw artificial contingencies (tokens) and replace with natural ones (privileges)

APPLICATION 3.2: Generalization

Generalization can advance skill development across subject areas. Finding main ideas is relevant in language arts, social studies, mathematics (word problems), and so forth. For instance, during a language arts class, an instructor teaches students a strategy for finding main ideas. Once students master this strategy reasonably well, the teacher explains how to modify its use for other academic subjects. By teaching the strategy well in one domain and cuing students to its use in other domains, teachers save much time and effort, because they do not have to reteach the strategy in each subject area.

Participation	Allow students to participate in specifying behaviors to be reinforced and reinforcement contingencies
Academics	Provide a good academic program because many students with behavior problems have academic deficiencies
Benefits	Show students how behavioral changes will benefit them by linking changes to activities of interest
Reinforcement	Reinforce students in different settings to reduce discrimination between reinforced and nonreinforced situations
Consistency	Prepare teachers in regular classes to continue to shape behaviors of students in special classes when they are mainstreamed into the regular program

Discrimination. Discrimination is the complementary process to generalization. *Discrimination* involves responding differently (intensity, rate) depending on the stimulus or features of a situation (Rilling, 1977). Although teachers want students to generalize what they learn to other situations, they also want them to respond discriminately. In solving mathematical word problems, teachers want students to adopt a general problem-solving approach (e.g., determine the given and the needed information, draw a picture, generate useful formulas) and to discriminate word problem types (e.g., area, time-rate-distance, interest rate). Being able to identify the type of problem enhances students' chances for success.

Recall from Chapter 2 Spence's idea that in order to train subjects to discriminate, researchers should reinforce some responses and not others so that the subjects' response to the nonreinforced features is extinguished. (see Hull's Systematic Behavior Theory in Chapter 2). Terrace (1963) showed how to train animals to make errorless discriminations; that is, the animal never responds to the nonreinforced stimulus. Using pigeons, Terrace initially introduced the nonreinforced stimulus (pecking key) for short durations and at low intensities. Over trials, the duration and intensity of the key were increased. Birds not trained in errorless discrimination showed gradual learning of the discrimination; they occasionally responded to the nonreinforced stimulus in "emotional" fashion (fright, turning away).

Errors generally are thought to be disruptive and to produce learning of incorrect responses. Educators try to keep student errors to a minimum. Whether all errors need to be eliminated is debatable. There is evidence that students who learn to deal with errors in an adaptive manner subsequently persist longer on difficult tasks than do students who have experienced errorless learning (see the discussion of attribution change programs in the section on Attribution Theory in Chapter 8).

BEHAVIORAL CHANGE

Successive Approximations (Shaping)

When operants exist in one's behavioral repertoire, reinforcement (punishment) given contingent on their occurrence increases (decreases) their future likelihood of occurrence. Much of the time students are in school, however, operants in their behavior do not exist in the final, polished form. If teachers waited to deliver reinforcement until learners emitted the proper responses, many learners would never receive reinforcement because they never would acquire the responses. Even learners who had acquired some aspects of a complex skill would not be reinforced, because they would not perform the behavior in its final form.

The operant conditioning method of behavioral change is *shaping*, which involves *differential reinforcement* of *successive approximations* to the desired form or rate of behavior (Morse & Kelleher, 1977). In some instances, behavior is shaped by naturally occurring environmental contingencies. Consider a student attempting to shoot a basket from a particular point on the court. The student's first shot falls short of the basket. The student shoots harder the second time, and the ball hits the backboard. The student does not shoot quite as hard the third time, and the ball hits the right rim and bounces off. On the fourth attempt, the student shoots as hard as the third attempt but aims left. The ball hits the left rim and bounces off. Then the student shoots just as hard but aims slightly to the right, and the ball goes into the basket.

Formal application of the shaping process uses the following sequence:

1. Identify what the student can do now (entry behavior)
2. Identify the desired (terminal) behavior
3. Identify potential reinforcers in the student's environment
4. Break the terminal behavior (step 2) into small substeps to be mastered sequentially
5. Move the student from the entry behavior to the terminal behavior by successively reinforcing each approximation to the terminal behavior

Consider a hyperactive student who can work on a task for only about 2 minutes before becoming distracted. The goal is to shape the student's behavior so she can work uninterrupted for 30 minutes. It is unrealistic to wait until the student has worked for 30 minutes to deliver reinforcement. Instead, the teacher must first identify what the student can do now, that is, work for 2 minutes. If the student works productively for 2 minutes, a reinforcer is delivered; if not, no reinforcement is given. After several 2-minute intervals in which the student receives reinforcement, the criterion for reinforcement is raised to 3 minutes. Assuming that the student works uninterrupted for several 3-minute periods, the criterion is raised to 4 minutes. This process continues to the goal of 30 minutes as long as the student reliably performs at the criterion level. If the student encounters difficulty at any point, the criterion for reinforcement is decreased to a level at which the student can perform successfully.

Teaching skills can be shaped in the same fashion. To teach a student the 6-table ($6 \times 1 = 6$; $6 \times 2 = 12$; etc.), the instructor must assess the student's initial performance level. Assume that the student only knows $6 \times 1 = 6$ and $6 \times 2 = 12$. To earn reinforcement, the student must correctly recite these two plus $6 \times 3 = 18$. After the student can do this reliably, the criterion for reinforcement is raised to include $6 \times 4 = 24$. This process is continued until the student accurately recites the entire table.

Chaining

Most human behavior comprises more than just one three-term contingency. Such skills as reading comprehension and balancing chemical equations involve a unified sequence of responses. A response alters the environment, and this altered condition serves as the stimulus for the next response. *Chaining* is the process of producing or altering some of the variables that serve as stimuli for future responses (Skinner, 1953).

Consider a student balancing chemical equations. The first element of the first problem serves as the S^D, to which the student makes the appropriate response (R). This completed operation—the S^R—is also the S^D for the next response necessary to balance the equation. This progression continues until the equation is balanced, which serves as the S^D to move to the next equation. Operations within each equation constitute a chain, and the entire problem set constitutes a chain.

A chain consists of a series of operants, each of which sets the occasion for further responses. Some chains acquire a functional unity; the chain is an integrated sequence such that successful implementation defines a skill. When skills are well honed, execution of the chain occurs automatically. Riding a bicycle consists of several discrete acts, yet an accomplished rider executes these with little or no conscious effort. Chains also become automatic with cognitive skills (e.g., reading, solving problems).

Complex chains have been constructed in experiments for purposes of clarifying the nature of their operation (Gollub, 1977; Keller & Schoenfeld, 1950). Skinner (1978) said that chaining is the process whereby complex responses are developed:

> Long chains of responses can be built up by conditioning reinforcers. In a typical classroom demonstration a rat executes a series of perhaps ten different responses, each of which is reinforced by the opportunity to execute the next, until a final, usually unconditioned, reinforcer appears.

The first step seems to be taken "for the sake of the last," which lies in the fairly distant future. Something of the same sort occurs, when, for example, a person builds a shelter. The last step brings protection from the weather, but it can be taken only after earlier stages have been completed. As the shelter is constructed, each step is reinforced by the opportunity to take another step. (p. 21)

Behavior Modification

Behavior modification (behavior therapy) refers to the systematic application of learning principles to facilitate adaptive behaviors (Ullmann & Krasner, 1965). The conceptual basis for behavior modification is derived from work by Skinner and his colleagues examining the relationship between environmental changes (stimuli, reinforcement contingencies) and changes in people's behaviors. Behavior modification has been employed with adults and children in such diverse contexts as classrooms, counseling settings, prisons, and mental hospitals. Behavior modification has been used to treat phobias, dysfunctional language, disruptive behaviors, negative social interactions, poor childrearing, and low self-control (Ayllon & Azrin, 1968; Becker, 1971; Keller & Ribes-Inesta, 1974; Ulrich, Stachnik, & Mabry, 1966). Lovaas (1977) used behavior modification to teach language to autistic children.

Regardless of subjects, context, or therapeutic goal, the basic techniques include reinforcement of desired behaviors and extinction of undesired ones. Although rarely employed, punishment more often involves removing a positive reinforcer than presenting a negative reinforcer. Researchers also have blended behavior modification with cognitive elements. In *cognitive behavior modification*, learners' thoughts (when verbalized) function as discriminative and reinforcing stimuli. Cognitive behavior modification techniques often are applied with handicapped learners (Hallahan, Kneedler, & Lloyd, 1983) and are incorporated into self-regulation programs (Chapter 9). Meichenbaum's self-instructional training is an example of cognitive behavior modification (see Modeling Processes in Chapter 4).

In deciding on a program of change, behavior modifiers (therapists) typically focus on the following three issues (Ullmann & Krasner, 1965):

1. Which of the subject's behaviors are maladaptive, and which should be increased (decreased)
2. What environmental contingencies currently support the subject's behaviors (either to maintain undesirable behaviors or to reduce the likelihood of performing more adaptive responses)
3. What environmental features can be manipulated to alter the subject's behavior

APPLICATION 3.3: Behavioral Change

Behavioral change for disruptive students is difficult, because these students rarely display appropriate responses to be positively reinforced. A teacher might use shaping to address a specific annoying behavior. For instance, assume that Erik pushes and shoves other students when the class gets in line to go somewhere in the building. When the class is going only a short distance, the teacher could inform Erik that if he stays in line without pushing and shoving, he will be the line leader on the way back to the classroom, and that if he pushes or shoves, he immediately will be removed from the line. If Erik is able to stay in the line appropriately, he is allowed to lead the line on the return walk. This procedure can be repeated until Erik can handle short distances. The teacher then can allow him to walk with the class for progressively longer distances until he can walk with other class members for any distance.

The first step in establishing a program is to define the problem objectively in behavioral terms. "Keith is out of his seat too often" refers to overt behavior that can be measured: One can keep a record of how often and for how long Keith is out of his seat. General expressions referring to unobservables ("Keith has a bad attitude") do not allow for objective problem definition.

The next step is to determine the contingencies maintaining undesirable behavior. Perhaps Keith is getting teacher attention only when he gets out of his seat and not when he is seated. A simple environmental alteration is to have the teacher attend to Keith while he is seated and engaged in academic work and to ignore him when he gets out of his seat. If the amount or number of times Keith gets out of his seat decreases, teacher attention is a positive reinforcer.

A behavior modification program might employ such generalized reinforcers as points or tokens that students can exchange for tangible rewards, free time, or privileges. Generalized reinforcers can be exchanged for different backup reinforcers, so at least one backup reinforcer is effective for each student at all times. A behavioral criterion must be established in order to earn reinforcement. The five-step shaping procedure (discussed previously) can be employed. The criterion is initially defined as the level of entry behavior and progresses in small increments toward the terminal behavior. A point or token is given to the student each time the criterion is satisfied. Additionally, to extinguish undesirable behavior in Keith's case, the teacher should try not to give him too much attention if he gets out of his seat, but rather should inform him privately that he does not satisfy the criterion and therefore does not earn a point or token.

Punishment should be used infrequently, but it may be needed when behavior becomes so disruptive that it cannot be ignored (students who are fighting or bringing drugs or weapons to school). On a lesser level, a common punishment technique is *time out* (from reinforcement). During time out, the student is removed from the classroom social context and is confined to a corner or separate room. There the student may continue to engage in academic work, but without the possibility of peer social interaction or the opportunity to receive points, free time, or teacher approval. Other punishments remove such positive reinforcers as free time, recess, and privileges.

Critics have argued that behavior modification in schools is too often used to shape quiet and docile behaviors (Winett & Winkler, 1972). Although a reasonable amount of quiet is needed to ensure that learning occurs, some teachers seek a quiet classroom at all times, even when some noise (e.g., social interactions) would facilitate learning. The use of behavior modification should not be confused with the techniques. It can be used to produce a quiet classroom or to promote social initiations by withdrawn children (Strain, Kerr, & Ragland, 1981). Like the techniques themselves, the goals of behavior modification need to be thought out by those implementing the procedures.

Misbehavior of Organisms

Skinner (1956) assumed that any response the organism is capable of making can be conditioned with operant methods. For any given species, however, responses cannot be classically conditioned to any stimulus (Chapter 2). Evidence from different sources indicates that such selectivity also is the case with operant behaviors. We consider evidence relating to instinctual drift, autoshaping, and superstitious behavior.

Instinctual Drift.   Breland and Breland (1961) were animal trainers who had applied operant conditioning to train 6,000 animals representing 38 species. Despite these successes, the Brelands encountered several problems. Once they tried to condition a raccoon to pick up a coin and put it in a metal box. The raccoon easily learned to pick up the coin, but would not drop it into the box. The raccoon would rub the coin against the inside of the container, then pull it back out and clutch it firmly. When handling two coins, the animal would frequently rub them together and dip them into the container. The rubbing became worse over time despite nonreinforcement. Another time the Brelands tried to condition pigs to pick up large wooden dollars and put them in a piggy bank. The pigs easily learned the behavior and engaged in it repeatedly. Over weeks, however, the pigs began to drop the coins, root them, pick them up, root them, pick them up and toss them into the air, and so forth. These behaviors became progressively worse as time went on.

Breland and Breland (1961) labeled such "misbehaviors" as *instinctual drift:* The direction of the drift is toward instinctive behaviors naturally associated with obtaining food by the species:

> After 14 years of continuous conditioning and observation of thousands of animals, it is our reluctant conclusion that the behavior of any species cannot be adequately understood, predicted, or controlled without knowledge of its instinctive patterns, evolutionary history, and ecological niche. (p. 684)

The Brelands' results suggest that operant conditioning depends not only on the particular elements of the three-term contingency but also on the elements' natural relationship for members of the species. When the behavior to be conditioned is associated with an instinctive pattern, over time the animal's behaviors may drift to the instinctive pattern even when reinforcement contingencies are in effect. Instinctual drift modifies Skinner's contention about the generality of operant conditioning principles.

Autoshaping.   *Autoshaping,* or the organism's efforts to shape its own behaviors to obtain reinforcement, also seems to reflect instinctive behavior. In a classic demonstration of autoshaping (Brown & Jenkins, 1968), pigeons were exposed to a plastic disk that during each trial was illuminated for a few seconds, after which food reinforcement was delivered automatically regardless of whether the pigeon pecked at the disk. Even though the pigeons were not shaped to peck at the disk and food was not contingent on pecking, all pigeons eventually pecked at the disk while it was illuminated. In a variation of this procedure, Williams and Williams (1969) arranged the contingency such that pecking the disk prevented food reinforcement from being delivered. Although pecking was nonadaptive, there nonetheless was a high rate of responding under these negative conditions.

To account for autoshaping, Brown and Jenkins suggested that pecking is a response hungry pigeons make because it facilitates obtaining food under natural conditions. When the disk is illuminated, the bird notices it and pecks. Rather than pecking being reinforced by the food, pecking occurs naturally and the object of pecking—the disk—is not linked with food. The lighted object prompts instinctive behavior that has a high likelihood of occurring under the circumstances. In short, the pecking likely reflects instinctive behavior rather than learning.

Superstitious Behaviors.   A third line of evidence comes from experiments on *superstitious behaviors,* or those conditioned accidentally and not instrumental in producing a response. Consider a conditioning experiment in which a pigeon is given a small amount of food every 30 seconds regardless of what it is doing (noncontingent reinforcement). When the food tray is presented the first time, the pigeon is doing something—bobbing its head, turning, pecking. The behavior it was engaged in at that moment should be strengthened. If the pigeon is performing the same behavior the next time the food tray is presented, that behavior will be strengthened further. If the pigeon is performing a different behavior, that behavior should be strengthened. Over trials, the pigeon develops a superstitious behavior ritual prior to food reinforcement. The pigeon might peck at a disk, turn around, hop, turn around the other way, hop again, and so forth.

Superstitious behaviors are not confined to animals. People engage in superstitious behaviors because they believe such behaviors bring good luck. Some students always use a particular pen or pencil to take a test. Athletes often engage in ritualistic behaviors on the day of a game—eat the same meal, arrive at the stadium at the same time, and wear certain clothing. Skinner (1953) explained superstitious behavior by stating that the pigeon's behavior prior to reinforcement serves as an operant and that any behavior can become conditioned in this superstitious fashion as follows:

> Nor need there be any permanent connection between a response and its reinforcement. We made the receipt of food contingent upon the response of our pigeon by arranging a mechanical and electrical connection. Outside the laboratory various physical systems are responsible for contingencies between behavior and its consequences. But these need not, and usually do not, affect the organism in any other way. So far as the organism is concerned, the only important property of the contingency is temporal. The reinforcer simply follows the response. How this is brought about does not matter. (pp. 84–85)

Staddon and Simmelhag (1971) examined pigeons' superstitious behaviors closely and found that the birds displayed two types of behaviors during the interval between food reinforcements. Interim activities occurred right after food delivery. These behaviors were random and varied between pigeons. Terminal responses occurred close to the time food was to be delivered and involved pecking at or near the food location. The terminal responses were food related, because pigeons peck while eating or anticipating eating. Rather than strengthening operant behaviors, the noncontingent reinforcement prompted the pigeons to display food-related behaviors. Staddon and Simmelhag noted that Skinner did not distinguish the two types of activities, so it is unclear what behavior was being conditioned in Skinner's (1953) study. Staddon and Simmelhag's explanation does not seem to account for human superstitious behaviors, but the point is that Skinner's explanation appears to be incomplete.

Taken together, the findings in this section do not disprove the principles of operant conditioning, but they highlight the complexity of behavior. Animals display species-specific behaviors that appear to be conditioned but actually are instinctive given the context. The instinctual drift, auto-shaping, and superstitious behavior phenomena limit the generality of operant conditioning (especially the role of reinforcement) in producing behavioral change.

VERBAL BEHAVIOR

Acquisition

Skinner (1957) extended the operant conditioning model to language with the publication of *Verbal Behavior.* He defined *verbal behavior* as follows: "Behavior shaped and maintained by mediated consequences . . . behavior reinforced through the mediation of other persons" (Skinner, 1957, p. 2). Verbal behavior can be conditioned and shaped by the same stimuli and reinforcement contingencies that condition and shape nonverbal behavior. Skinner acknowledged the unique biological endowment of human beings— the vocal apparatus, the predisposition to vocalize, and the susceptibility to reinforcement contingencies. Other than this endowment, there is nothing special about language; no new principles are needed to explain its acquisition or use.

Verbal Responses

Skinner classified verbal behaviors in terms of their controlling variables. One type is the *mand*, which Skinner (1957) defined as "a verbal operant in which the response is reinforced by a characteristic consequence and is therefore under the functional control of relevant conditions of deprivation or aversive stimulation" (pp. 35–36). Skinner chose the term *mand* because it is found in such words as *command* and *demand.* "Listen!" "Stop!" "More bread," and "Pass the salt" produce their unique consequences (the verbalized acts) when heard by another person. The utterance of mands is controlled by deprivation or aversive states; one asks for the salt when one needs (is deprived of) salt. Mands are not under the control of particular environmental stimuli; they specify their consequences regardless of the prevailing environmental circumstances. Mands do not have to be cast as commands. They can be polite requests: "Do you have the time?" "May I borrow your notes?" Regardless of form, fulfillment of the mand by a listener is reinforcing and increases the likelihood the mand will be uttered in the future when a similar aversive state arises.

Skinner (1957) described another type of verbal behavior, the *tact*, which reflects the notion that the behavior makes "contact" with the environment:

> A tact may be defined as a verbal operant in which a response of a given form is evoked (or at least strengthened) by a particular object or event or property of an object or event. We account for the strength by showing that in the presence of the object or event a response of that form is characteristically reinforced in a given verbal community. (pp. 81–82)

Unlike mands, tacts are under the control of prevailing environmental conditions; tacts name or describe discriminative stimuli. Because the same tact is often associated with many different reinforcements, it can become generalized and can be uttered in the presence of various people in different circumstances. When young children point to and name different objects, their utterances are often reinforced by adults with smiles, hugs, and verbal acknowledgments (e.g., "Yes, that's a top"). Whereas a mand informs the listener about the speaker's internal state, a tact tells the listener something about circumstances regardless of the speaker's internal state.

A third type of verbal behavior is the *echoic.* One form of echoic behavior is simple imitation. A father says to his infant, "Dada"; the infant responds, "Dada"; the father smiles and hugs the infant. A second type of echoic behavior is based on the following types of associations: "Say the first word you think of after I say a word. You cannot repeat the same word." Examples of echoics are "eggs" to "ham" and "butter" to "bread." Echoics help one learn words, as when one hears a new word, repeats it several times, and looks it up in a dictionary.

Textual behavior is controlled by texts. Verbal operants become established under the control of visual stimuli (tactual in Braille). Textual behavior is reinforced by teachers and parents when children read well. It also is reinforced when it helps establish other verbal responses. For example, reading books or looking up words in dictionaries establishes new word meanings, and individuals subsequently use these new words in their speech and writing. Students who study vocabulary words in preparation for the SAT or GRE are reinforced if some of the words they learned appear on the test.

Autoclitic behavior is "behavior which is based upon or depends upon other verbal behavior" (Skinner, 1957, p. 315). Some autoclitics inform listeners of the types of verbal operants they accompany; for example, "I see that . . . " and "I recall that . . . " Autoclitics can preface mands ("I ask you to pass the salt") and tacts ("I tell you that it's raining"). Other types of autoclitics convey strength of verbal response: "I suppose," "I guess," "I imagine." Autoclitics also describe the relation between a response and another response of speaker or listener ("I agree," "I admit"); convey the emotional or motivational state of the speaker ("I hate to tell you this . . . ," "I know you'll be glad to hear . . . "); and express negative verbal behavior

("I doubt that . . . ," "I don't remember . . . "). Adverbs and adjectives are autoclitics, as are expressions modifying or indicating the order or position of what follows (e.g., "for example," "so to speak," "just between you and me").

Verbal Behavior presents a theoretical analysis of how human language can be acquired and maintained. Unfortunately, it contains only informal data to support Skinner's arguments, and the theory has received little empirical testing. Behaviorists generally have been interested in issues other than verbal behavior, and psycholinguists typically have tested cognitive theories of language acquisition and use (Segal, 1977). Much controversy exists over Skinner's reinforcement analysis of language. The issue is not whether individuals acquire any language via reinforcement; reinforcement undoubtedly plays a role. Rather, the issue is whether reinforcement is the mechanism primarily responsible for language acquisition.

Chomsky's Critique

Skinner's (1957) *Verbal Behavior* received a critical review from the linguist Noam Chomsky (1959), who argued that a conditioning model is inappropriate for explaining language acquisition and comprehension:

> Careful study of this book (and of the research on which it draws) reveals . . . that the insights that have been achieved in the laboratories of the reinforcement theorist, though quite genuine, can be applied to complex human behavior only in the most gross and superficial way, and that speculative attempts to discuss linguistic behavior in these terms alone omit from consideration factors of fundamental importance that are, no doubt, amenable to scientific study. (p. 28)

Chomsky raised issues that he believed an operant analysis could not adequately address. One issue concerned the nature of the stimulus to which one responds with verbal behavior. Chomsky contended that the stimulus must be specified or else it loses its objectivity and meaning as a scientific concept. Skinner (1957) gave the following example of stimulus control:

> The student who is learning to "spot" the composer of unfamiliar music or to name the artist or school of an unfamiliar picture is subjected to the same contingencies of differential reinforcement. Responses such as *Mozart* or *Dutch* are brought under the control of extremely subtle properties of stimuli when they are reinforced with "right" or punished with "wrong" by the community. (p. 108)

Chomsky (1959) disputed this point as follows:

> Suppose instead of saying *Dutch* we had said *Clashes with the wall-paper, I thought you liked abstract work, Never saw it before, Tilted, Hanging too*

low, Beautiful, Hideous, Remember our camping trip last summer?, or whatever else might come into our minds when looking at a picture (in Skinnerian translation, whatever other responses exist in sufficient strength). Skinner could only say that each of these responses is under the control of some other stimulus property of the physical object. (p. 31)

Another issue Chomsky raised concerned the process whereby language is acquired. Chomsky (1959) contended that an operant analysis deals only with surface features of language. As such, it cannot explain how people acquire the grammar of a language or its underlying, abstract set of rules. The following sentences have different surface structures but identical "deep" structures and meanings: "The snake bit the boy." "The boy was bitten by the snake." At best, reinforcement can account for a small part of language acquisition:

A child may pick up a large part of his vocabulary and "feel" for sentence structure from television, from reading, from listening to adults, etc. Even a very young child who has not yet acquired a minimal repertoire from which to form new utterances may imitate a word quite well on an early try, with no attempt on the part of his parents to teach it to him. It is also perfectly obvious that, at a later stage, a child will be able to construct and understand utterances which are quite new, and are, at the same time, acceptable sentences in his language. Every time an adult reads a newspaper, he undoubtedly comes upon countless new sentences which are not at all similar, in a simple, physical sense, to any that he has heard before, and which he will recognize as sentences and understand; he will also be able to detect slight distortions or misprints. (Chomsky, 1959, p. 42)

Other issues raised by Chomsky are not summarized here, but they point to the same conclusion. Language cannot be addressed adequately without considering the mental life of the individual. Most researchers who study language acquisition and comprehension adopt a cognitive perspective, not Skinner's position. Although MacCorquodale (1970) attempted to address Chomsky's criticisms, the general consensus within the scientific community is that Chomsky's points are especially persuasive.

INSTRUCTION

Skinner (1954, 1961, 1968, 1984) has written extensively on how his ideas can be applied to education. Skinner discussed the problems facing the American educational system. For one, there is too much aversive control. Although students rarely receive corporal punishment, they often work on assignments not because they want to learn or enjoy school but rather to avoid such negative outcomes as teacher criticism, loss of privileges, and being sent to the principal. For another, reinforcement is given infrequently and often not at the proper times. Teachers attend to each student for only a few minutes each day. While students are engaged in seatwork, several minutes elapse between when the students finish an exercise and when they receive teacher feedback. Consequently, students perform operations incorrectly, and the teacher must spend additional time giving corrective feedback. Third, the scope and sequence of curricula are not sufficient to ensure that all students acquire skills. Students do not learn at the same pace. To cover much material, teachers usually move to the next lesson before all students have mastered the previous one.

These types of problems cannot be solved by paying teachers more money, lengthening the school day and year, or raising teacher certification requirements. Rather, better use of instructional time is needed. It is unrealistic to expect students to move through the curriculum at the same rate. Schooling would become twice as efficient by individualizing instruction.

"Teaching is simply the arrangement of contingencies of reinforcement" (Skinner, 1968, p. 5). No new principles are required in applying operant conditioning to education. Instruction is more effective when (1) teachers present the material in small steps, (2) learners actively respond rather than passively listen, (3) teachers give feedback immediately contingent on learners' responses, and (4) learners move through the material at their own pace.

The basic process of instruction involves *shaping*. The goal of instruction (terminal behavior) is defined, and the students' entry behaviors are identified. A series of substeps (behaviors) is formulated leading from the entry behavior to the terminal behavior. Each substep represents a small modification of the preceding one. Students are moved through the sequence using various approaches including demonstrations, small group work, and individual seatwork. Students actively respond to the material and receive immediate feedback concerning their accuracy.

This instructional approach involves specifying learners' present knowledge and desired objectives in terms of what learners *do*. Terminal behaviors often are specified as *behavioral objectives*, to be discussed shortly. Individual differences are taken into account by beginning instruction at learners' present performance levels and allowing them to progress at their own rates. Given the prevailing teaching methods in our educational system, these goals seem impractical: Teachers would likely have to begin instruction at different points and cover material at different rates for individual students. *Programmed instruction* circumvents these problems; learners begin at the point in the material corresponding to their performance level and progress at their own rates.

Behavioral Objectives

Objectives are clear statements of the intended student outcomes of instruction. Specifying objectives is a necessary first step in teaching and learning. Objectives can range from general to specific. General or vague objectives such as "improve student awareness" can be fulfilled by almost any kind of instruction. At the opposite extreme, overly specific objectives can document every minute change in student behavior. Besides being time consuming, formulating such specific objectives can cloud the most important learning outcomes. Optimal objectives fall somewhere between these extremes.

A *behavioral objective* describes the following: "What the student will be doing when demonstrating his achievement and how you will know he is doing it" (Mager, 1962, p. 53). The four parts of a good objective are (1) the specific group of students, (2) the actual behaviors students are to perform as a consequence of instructional activities, (3) the conditions or contexts in which the students are to perform the behaviors, and (4) the criteria for assessing student behaviors to determine whether objectives have been accomplished. The following is a sample objective:

> Given *8 addition problems with fractions of unlike denominators,* (3)
>
> the *fourth-grade math student* (1)
>
> *will write* the correct sums (2)
>
> for *at least 7* of them. (4)

Behavioral objectives can help determine the important learning outcomes, those that aid in lesson planning and testing to assess student learn-

---

APPLICATION 3.4: Behavioral Objectives

As teachers prepare lessons and complete lesson plans, it is important that they decide on specific behavioral objectives and plan activities to assist students in mastering these objectives. Instead of an art teacher planning a lesson with the objective, "Have students complete a pen and ink drawing of the front of the building," the teacher should decide on the major objective for the students to master. Is it to use pen and ink or to draw the front of the school building? The objective is better stated as follows: "Have the students draw the major lines of the front of the building in correct perspective" (materials/medium: drawing paper, pens, ink). When teachers specifically address learning outcomes, students are aware of expectations and teachers have clearer standards against which to evaluate student progress.

ing. Formulating objectives also helps teachers decide what content is attainable by students. Given unit teaching objectives and a fixed amount of time to cover them, teachers can decide which objectives are more important and focus on them. Although objectives for lower-level learning outcomes (factual knowledge) are generally easier to specify, good behavioral objectives can be written to assess higher-order outcomes (synthesis, evaluation) as well.

Research reveals some benefits of objectives on student achievement. Students provided with behavioral objectives show better verbatim recall of verbal information compared with students not provided with such information (Faw & Waller, 1976; Hamilton, 1985). Providing objectives may cue students to process the information at the appropriate level; when students are given objectives requiring recall, they engage in activities (rehearsal) that facilitate that type of recall. Research also shows that providing students with objectives does not enhance their learning of material unrelated to the objectives (Duchastel & Brown, 1974). Perhaps students concentrate on learning material relevant to the objectives and disregard other material.

The effect of objectives on learning depends on students' prior experience with them and on their perceived importance of information. Training in using objectives or familiarity with criterion-based instruction leads to better learning compared with the absence of such training or familiarity. When students can determine what material is important to learn, providing them with objectives does not facilitate learning. Objectives are more important for information students judge unimportant.

The type of text structure may moderate the effect of objectives on learning. Target information made salient by being in a prominent semantic position is recalled well even when objectives are not provided (Muth, Glynn, Britton, & Graves, 1988). Duchastel (1979) cited the example of text entitled, "Fast Breeder Reactors," covering future electrical needs, rational utilization of fossil fuels, nuclear reactors, nuclear breeding, and doubling time. "Nuclear reactors" is high in the content structure of the text because it precedes more detailed nuclear fission content. A passage entitled "Future Energy Sources" covered emerging alternative energy sources, solar energy, nuclear reactors, geothermal resources, and laser fusion. Although "nuclear reactors" is in the same (third) position, it is one of many alternatives, so its semantic highlighting is diminished. According to Duchastel's study, providing students with objectives helps to enhance recall when target information is low in the content structure; however, Muth et al. (1988) found benefits of objectives on recall regardless of whether content was high or low in text. These authors suggest that rehearsal prompted by objectives produces better memory storage.

Programmed Instruction

Programmed instruction (PI) refers to instructional materials developed in accordance with behavioral principles of learning (O'Day, Kulhavy, Anderson, & Malczynski, 1971). An historical influence was work in the 1920s by Sidney Pressey, who designed machines to use in intelligence testing. Students were presented with multiple-choice questions, and they pressed a button corresponding to their choice. If students responded correctly, the machine presented the next choice; if they responded incorrectly, the error was recorded and they continued to respond to the item.

Pressey's ideas were revived by Skinner in the 1950s and modified to incorporate instruction (Skinner, 1958). Skinner's *teaching machines* presented students with material in small steps (*frames*). Each frame required students to make an overt response. Material was carefully sequenced and broken into small units to minimize student error rates. The material also minimized errors by prompting students for correct answers. Students received immediate feedback on the accuracy of each response. Assuming their answer was correct, they moved to the next frame. When they answered incorrectly, supplementary material was provided in the next frame.

The material used in teaching machines is a form of PI. PI, however, does not require the use of a machine; many programs are in book form. A book by Holland and Skinner (1961) is a program teaching behavioral principles. Today, many computer software programs are forms of PI incorporating principles of behavioral instruction.

APPLICATION 3.5: Programmed Instruction

Instructional programming involves designing instruction to move students systematically in small steps through material. This notion is especially useful with slow learners. For example, a high school biology instructor is teaching students to identify the major bones in the human body. The average and accelerated students are able to handle all of the body bones at the same time, but the slower learners are having great difficulty mastering such identification. The teacher decides to modify the method of instruction for the slow learners by dividing the unit into a series of short lessons. Each lesson addresses the bones associated with a major body part (i.e., head, chest, arm, leg) and provides students with much practice and feedback to learn the names of bones. At the end of each lesson, students are drilled on the lesson's content as well as on the bone names learned during previous lessons.

There are several PI principles (O'Day et al., 1971). First, behavioral objectives specify what students should perform on completion of the instruction. Second, the unit is subdivided into sequenced frames, each of which presents a small bit of information and a test item to which learners respond. Although a large body of material may be included in the program, the frame-to-frame increments are small. Third, learners work at their own pace. Fourth, learners respond to questions as they work through the program. Responses can include supplying words in blanks, providing numerical answers, and choosing which of several statements best describes the idea being presented. Fifth, feedback is given contingent on the learner's response. If the learner is correct, the next item is given. If the learner answers incorrectly, additional remedial information is presented and the idea is tested in slightly different form.

Because PI reflects the shaping process, performance increments are small and learners almost always respond correctly. *Linear* and *branching programs* are distinguished according to how they treat learner errors.

Linear Programs.   Students proceed through linear programs in the same sequence. Regardless of whether students respond correctly or incorrectly to a frame, they move to the next frame where they receive feedback on the accuracy of their answer. Linear programs are based on the notion that answering incorrectly increases the likelihood of future incorrect responding. Programs minimize the probability of errors by covering the same material in more than one frame and by prompting student responses. Some frames from a linear program are shown in Figure 3.2.

Branching Programs.   Students move through branching programs depending on how they answer the questions. Each frame in a branching program asks a question and follows it with two or more alternative answers. The student's next frame depends on the answer. In a book, each alternative may list a page to turn to; a software program will automatically present a new frame after the student responds. Branching programs take into account individual differences in learning ability: Students who learn the material quickly skip frames and bypass much of the repetition of linear programs, whereas slower learners receive additional instruction. A disadvantage is that working through a branching program in book form can be very confusing. Should students lose their place, it may be time consuming to find it. Sample frames from a computer branching program are portrayed in Figure 3.3.

Research shows that linear and branching programs promote student learning equally well, and that PI—whatever its form—is as effective as conventional classroom teaching (Bangert, Kulik, & Kulik, 1983; Lange, 1972; Silberman, Melaragno, Coulson, & Estavan, 1961). Whether PI is used instead of traditional instruction depends in part on how well existing

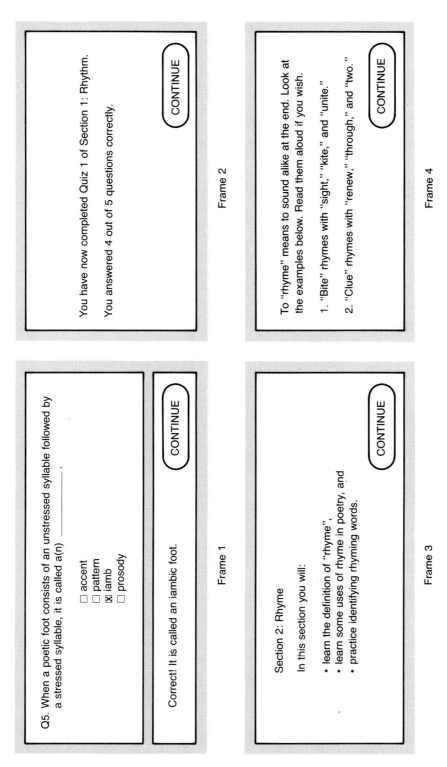

Q5. When a poetic foot consists of an unstressed syllable followed by a stressed syllable, it is called a(n) _____.

☐ accent
☐ pattern
☒ iamb
☐ prosody

Correct! It is called an iambic foot.

(CONTINUE)

Frame 1

You have now completed Quiz 1 of Section 1: Rhythm.

You answered 4 out of 5 questions correctly.

(CONTINUE)

Frame 2

Section 2: Rhyme

In this section you will:

• learn the definition of "rhyme",
• learn some uses of rhyme in poetry, and
• practice identifying rhyming words.

(CONTINUE)

Frame 3

To "rhyme" means to sound alike at the end. Look at the examples below. Read them aloud if you wish.

1. "Bite" rhymes with "sight," "kite," and "unite."
2. "Clue" rhymes with "renew," "through," and "two."

(CONTINUE)

Frame 4

FIGURE 3.2
Frames from a linear program.

81

programs cover the required scope and sequence of instruction. PI seems especially useful with students who demonstrate skill deficiencies; working through programs provides them with needed remedial instruction and practice. PI programs also are useful for students desiring additional study of a topic, since they work through the programs on their own.

Contingency Contracts

A *contingency contract* is an agreement between teacher and student specifying what work a student must accomplish to earn a particular reinforcer (Homme, Csanyi, Gonzales, & Rechs, 1970). A contract can be agreed upon orally, although it usually is written. Teachers can devise the contract and ask if the student agrees with it, but it is customary for teacher and student to jointly formulate it. An advantage of joint participation is that students may feel greater commitment to the terms of the contract. Goal-setting research shows that when people participate in goal selection, they often are more committed to attaining goals than when they are excluded from the selection process (Locke, Shaw, Saari, & Latham, 1981).

Contracts specify goals in terms of particular behaviors to be demonstrated by the student and their outcomes, "If you do *X*, then you will receive *Y*." Contracts need to describe behaviors specifically: "I will complete pages 1–30 in my math book with at least 90% accuracy." "I will stay in my seat during reading period." Such contract conditions as "I will work on my math" or "I will behave appropriately" are unacceptable because they are not specific. Time periods are best kept short, especially with young chil-

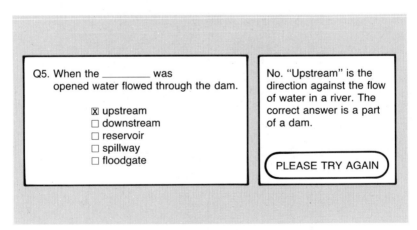

Frame 1

FIGURE 3.3
Frames from a branching program.

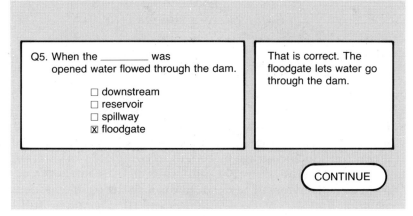

Frame 2

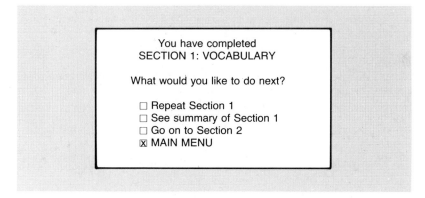

Frame 3

```
                    MAIN MENU

    □ Section 1: VOCABULARY
    □ Section 2: CAUSES OF FLOODING
    □ Section 3: CONSEQUENCES OF FLOODING
    □ Section 4: FLOOD CONTROL
    □ Section 5: SIMULATION
    □ Section 6: CONSEQUENCES OF CONTROL
    □ QUIT
```

Frame 4

FIGURE 3.3
Continued

APPLICATION 3.6: Contingency Contracting

A contingency contract represents a systematic application of reinforcement principles to change behavior. A major advantage of the contract is that students see the relationship between behavior and its consequences.

Assume that a teacher has tried unsuccessfully to apply several motivational techniques to encourage a student to complete work in language arts. The teacher and student might jointly develop a contract to address the inappropriate behaviors. They should discuss the problem, identify the desired behavior, and list the consequences and time frame for fulfilling the terms of the contract. A sample contract might be as follows:

Contract for the Week of January 9–13

I will complete my language arts seatwork with 80% accuracy in the time allotted during class.

If I complete my seatwork, I will be allowed to participate in a learning center activity.

If I do not complete my seatwork, I will miss recess and complete my work at that time.

Monday: _____ completed _____ not completed
Tuesday: _____ completed _____ not completed
Wednesday: _____ completed _____ not completed
Thursday: _____ completed _____ not completed
Friday: _____ completed _____ not completed

Bonus: If I complete my work 3 out of 5 days, I will be able to work in the computer center for 30 minutes on Friday afternoon.

_____ _____

Student signature/Date   Teacher signature/Date

dren. However, they can cover more than one time period, such as behaviors to be demonstrated during successive 30-minute periods or the work to be accomplished during each social studies period for one week. Contracts can include academic and nonacademic behaviors.

Drawing up contracts with students is time consuming. Contracts seem especially helpful as a means of assisting students to work on assignments more productively. A lengthy, long-term assignment can be subdivided into a series of short-term goals with due dates. This type of plan assists students in keeping up with the work and turning in material in a timely fashion.

Contracts are based on sound principles. Research shows that goals that are specific, temporally close at hand, and difficult but attainable maximize performance. Goals enhance performance when people commit themselves to attempt them (Locke et al., 1981). To the extent that contracts reinforce student progress in learning or in accomplishing more on-task behavior, they are likely to raise student achievement. Most students, however, do not require contracts to behave appropriately or accomplish work.

Keller Plan

The Keller Plan, or Personalized System of Instruction (PSI), reflects many operant conditioning principles (Keller, 1966, 1968). The central features are student self-pacing, mastery learning, and extensive self-study of the course material (Keller, 1977). The course is divided into units, and students must pass each unit exam with a minimum score (e.g., 80%) before they can progress to the next unit. There often are fewer whole-class meetings compared with conventionally taught courses. Students study the course materials on their own or in small groups, and they often consult with teaching assistants. Students decide how fast or slowly they want to complete the material. Grades are based on the number of units completed, with a certain percentage of the grade based on a final exam. The Keller Plan has been used most extensively in college undergraduate courses and has been applied to diverse content—psychology, engineering, biology, and others. Keller and Sherman (1974) describe appropriate Keller Plan procedures.

Evaluations of the effectiveness of Keller Plan courses in fostering learning have been positive (Robin, 1976; Ryan, 1974). Kulik, Kulik, and Cohen (1979) reviewed 75 studies comparing Keller Plan courses with courses taught in conventional fashion. Outcome measures included instructors' course grades, course ratings, course completions, and student study time. PSI generally led to higher student achievement, less variability in achievement, and higher student ratings; no differences were obtained for course withdrawal or student study time.

The latter findings are interesting because students who do not adequately pace themselves will fall behind and may drop the course; Robin (1976) found higher withdrawal rates in PSI courses than in conventionally taught courses. Robin also noted that study time was higher in PSI courses; however, when the number of hours students spent in lectures was added to the time for conventional courses, there was no difference in study time. Kulik et al. (1979) found differential effectiveness across subject areas: PSI was particularly effective in mathematics, engineering, and psychology courses. Differences in the outcomes of PSI and conventional courses were smaller when some PSI features (e.g., unit tests) were incorporated into conventional courses.

BEHAVIORAL CONTROL

Freedom and Control

Skinner moved beyond the domains of psychology and education to address how principles of operant conditioning can apply to daily life. Skinner's (1948/1976) youthful dream of becoming a literary writer was realized in 1948 with the publication of *Walden Two*, the story of a successful utopian community employing principles of behavior modification. As Skinner noted in the preface of a republished (1976) version, "The 'behavioral engineering' I had so frequently mentioned in the book was, at the time, little more than science fiction" (p. vi). The book details how people can lead happy and productive lives through the systematic application of operant conditioning principles. The key is to teach people how to regulate their lives within societal boundaries (Skinner, 1948/1976):

> We already had worked out a code of conduct—subject, of course, to experimental modification. The code would keep things running smoothly if everybody lived up to it. Our job was to see that everybody did. Now, you can't get people to follow a useful code by making them into so many jacks-in-the-box. You can't foresee all future circumstances, and you can't specify adequate future conduct. You don't know what will be required. Instead you have to set up certain behavioral processes which will lead the individual to design his own "good" conduct when the time comes. We call that sort of thing "self-control." But don't be misled, the control always rests in the last analysis in the hands of society. (p. 96)

Walden Two is a fictional account of how behavioral conditioning might solve the problems of living. In everyday life, behaviors are controlled by environmental stimuli and reinforcement contingencies. People act on the basis of their conditioning histories and of the prevailing environmental stimuli, not because of inner wills or desires. Environmental control is sometimes obvious, as when one pulls one's car off the road when a police car is behind with siren on and lights flashing. Much of the time, however, environmental control is more subtle. People may seem to be acting freely, but inconspicuous reinforcement contingencies are actually affecting their behavior. As Skinner (1971) said in *Beyond Freedom and Dignity*,

> Autonomous man is a device used to explain what we cannot explain in any other way. He has been constructed from our ignorance, and as our understanding increases, the very stuff of which he is composed vanishes. Science does not dehumanize man, it de-homunculizes him, and it must do so if it is to prevent the abolition of the human species. To man *qua* man we readily say good riddance. Only by dispossessing him can we turn to the real causes of human behavior. Only then can we turn from the inferred to the observed, from the miraculous to the natural, from the inaccessible to the manipulable. (pp. 200–201)

Skinner's ideas appear to contradict many Western societal beliefs. People are taught from childhood that they are free and responsible for their actions, that they pay the consequences for those actions, and that they set and pursue goals. Yet to Skinner, freedom is mostly an illusion. Freedom does not allow people to do what they please, rather it gives them choices among alternative actions. The issue is not whether people's choices are determined (because they are), but rather *how* they are determined, specifically, by whom and to what end? Skinner's (1966) free society is one that is free of aversive controls and that allows choices between desirable (reinforcing) activities:

> If we are not to rely solely upon accident for the innovations which give rise to cultural evolution, we must accept the fact that some kind of control of human behavior is inevitable. We cannot use good sense in human affairs unless someone engages in the design and construction of environmental conditions which affect the behavior of men. Environmental changes have always been the condition for the improvement of cultural patterns, and we can hardly use the more effective methods of science without making changes on a grander scale. We are all controlled by the world in which we live, and part of that world has been and will be constructed by men. The question is this: Are we to be controlled by accident, by tyrants, or by ourselves in effective cultural design? (p. 15)

Cultural Redesign

Skinner argued that cultural redesign is needed to incorporate behavioral technology, which could solve such serious problems as population growth, inadequate food supplies, and contaminated air and water. As part of the cultural redesign, societies need to re-establish the strengthening effects of reinforcers (Skinner, 1986). People have become "pleasure seekers" and are reinforced for pushing buttons on appliances, hiring people to do work for them, and working repetitively on tasks. The specialization of labor and greater wealth have led to a divorce between people's actions and the reinforcing effects or, as Karl Marx noted, the "alienation of the worker from the product of his work."

For example, in times past people chopped wood to build homes and to burn for cooking and heating. People canned vegetables for eating, and they knitted and sewed clothes for wearing. The effects of wood chopping, canning, knitting, sewing, and many other activities were reinforcing. Today people buy their firewood, food, and clothes. Those who chop wood, can vegetables, and make clothes are reinforced with money and work-related benefits rather than the effects of their efforts.

Another way that modern societies separate workers' behaviors from their immediate (reinforcing) consequences is through specialization. Workers perform only one act; for example, they assemble small parts or monitor assembly operations. Individuals spend much time doing the same thing over and over. On an assembly line, each worker engages in only one small aspect of the task, rather than producing the entire product.

Skinner advised examining the strength of the links between reinforcers and their immediate effects and redesigning cultures as needed to produce stronger links. In education, for example, students study material to earn good grades. The reinforcer for learning is the grade, which might lead to college or a job, not the immediate usefulness of the learning. Learning should provide immediate rewards, such as their application to improve everyday life. Teachers can make school learning more immediately reinforcing by taking it out of the classroom and showing students how to apply what they have learned to their lives.

SUMMARY

Operant conditioning is based on the assumption that features of the environment (stimuli, situations, events) set the occasion for responding. Reinforcement strengthens responses and increases their likelihood of occurrence when the stimuli are present. It is not necessary to refer to underlying physiological or mental mechanisms to explain behavior. The proper subject matter for psychological study is overt behavior.

The basic operant conditioning model is a three-term contingency involving a discriminative stimulus, response, and reinforcing stimulus. The consequences of behaviors are defined by their effects. Reinforcing consequences increase behavior; punishing consequences decrease behavior. Other important concepts are extinction, generalization, discrimination, primary and secondary reinforcers, and reinforcement schedules.

Shaping is the process used to alter behavior. Shaping involves differential reinforcement of successive approximations of the desired behavior. Complex behaviors are formed by chaining together successive three-term contingencies. Behavior modification programs have been commonly applied in diverse contexts to promote more adaptive behaviors.

The generality of the operant model has been challenged by animal experiments on instinctual drift, autoshaping, and superstitious behavior. The natural relationship a response bears to the effect it produces can outweigh the effect of reinforcement contingencies. Skinner's application of the operant model to language acquisition and use has been criticized by Chomsky and psycholinguists who view language as governed by underlying mental structures.

Behavioral principles have been applied to many aspects of teaching and learning. Foremost is their use in behavioral objectives, programmed instruction, contingency contracting, and the Keller Plan. Research evi-

SUMMARY

dence generally shows positive effects of these applications on student learning.

Skinner extended his views to problems of modern life. He contended that freedom in the traditional sense is an illusion. People are not free to do as they please; there are many constraints on their actions. To solve pressing problems requires application of a behavioral technology. Societies should eliminate methods of aversive control and reinstitute means of directly reinforcing individuals for their actions.

Chapter 4

Social Cognitive Theory

Social cognitive learning theory highlights the idea that much human learning occurs in a social environment. By observing others, people acquire knowledge, rules, skills, strategies, beliefs, and attitudes. Individuals also learn the functional value and appropriateness of modeled behaviors by observing their consequences, and they act in accordance with their beliefs concerning the expected outcomes of actions.

This chapter focuses on Albert Bandura's (1986) social cognitive theory. Bandura was born in Alberta, Canada, in 1925. He received his doctorate in clinical psychology from the University of Iowa in 1952 and accepted a faculty appointment at Stanford University, where he continues to teach. While at Iowa, Bandura was influenced by Miller and Dollard's (1941) book *Social Learning and Imitation*, which is discussed later in this chapter. After arriving at Stanford, Bandura began a research program exploring the influences on social behavior. He believed contemporary learning theories offered incomplete explanations of the acquisition and performance of prosocial and deviant behaviors:

> During the past half century, learning-theory approaches to personality development, deviant behavior, and psychotherapy have been favored by the majority of research-oriented psychologists. Generally speaking, however, these conceptualizations have not been highly effective in accounting for the processes whereby social behavior is acquired and modified. Indeed, most prior applications of learning theory to issues concerning prosocial and deviant behavior . . . have suffered from the fact that they

have relied heavily on a limited range of principles established on the basis of, and mainly supported by, studies of animal learning or human learning in one-person situations. (Bandura & Walters, 1963, p. 1)

Bandura formulated a comprehensive theory of observational learning that he has gradually expanded to encompass acquisition and performance of diverse skills, strategies, and behaviors. Bandura and others have tested predictions of his theory with cognitive, motor, social, and self-regulatory skills.

Bandura has been a prolific writer. Beginning with *Social Learning and Personality Development,* written in 1963 with Richard Walters, he also has authored *Principles of Behavior Modification* (1969), *Aggression: A Social Learning Analysis* (1973), and *Social Learning Theory* (1977b). In a recent book, *Social Foundations of Thought and Action: A Social Cognitive Theory* (1986), Bandura expanded his theory to address ways people seek control over important events of their lives through self-direction of their thoughts and actions. Individuals set goals for themselves; judge anticipated outcomes of their actions; evaluate progress toward goal attainment; and regulate their thoughts, emotions, and actions.

Many points addressed by Bandura bear some similarity to ideas discussed in other theories that include social learning processes. Especially relevant are Tolman's purposive behaviorism, Rotter's social learning theory, and theories of imitation.

HISTORICAL PERSPECTIVES

Tolman's Purposive Behaviorism

Edward C. Tolman (1886–1959) was born in West Newton, Massachusetts. He received his bachelor's degree from the Massachusetts Institute of Technology in 1911 and his Ph.D. in psychology from Harvard University in 1915. Following a teaching assignment at Northwestern University, he joined the faculty at the University of California at Berkeley. Tolman's learning theory is described in depth in his major work *Purposive Behavior in Animals and Men* (1932). Many of his articles were compiled into a book (Tolman, 1951). Shortly before his death, Tolman (1959) published a comprehensive statement of his position. One of the best summaries of Tolman's theory is found in MacCorquodale and Meehl (1954). On a personal level, Tolman was a pacifist and expressed his distaste of war in a short book *Drives Toward War* (1942), which, despite its title, is primarily about learning and motivation.

Molar Behavior. Like most psychologists of his time, Tolman was trained in behaviorism. From a methodological perspective, Tolman's experiments resembled those of conditioning theorists because they dealt with responses to stimuli under varying environmental conditions. At the same time, he was greatly influenced by the work of the Gestalt psychologists (see the discussion of Historical Perspectives in Chapter 5), especially Kohler's problem-solving experiments. He disagreed with behaviorists on their molecular definition of behavior as a series of stimulus-response connections and on their analysis of discrete actions. He contended that conditioning theories do not adequately explain the learning process, because learning is more than the mere strengthening of responses in the presence of stimuli. Tolman recommended a focus on *molar behavior*, a large sequence of behavior that is goal-directed. Behavior is more than the sum of its parts; it is a phenomenon to be studied in its own right:

> It will be contended by us . . . that "behavior-acts," though no doubt in complete one-to-one correspondence with the underlying molecular facts of physics and physiology, have, as "molar" wholes, certain emergent properties of their own. And it is these, the molar properties of behavior-acts, which are of prime interest to us as psychologists. (Tolman, 1932, p.7)

According to Tolman (1932), some examples of molar behaviors are the following:

> A rat running a maze; a cat getting out of a puzzle box . . . a psychologist reciting a list of nonsense syllables; my friend and I telling one another our thoughts and feelings—*these are behaviors* (qua *molar*). (p. 8)

Goal-Directed Behavior.   Tolman's theory is often referred to as *purposive behaviorism*. The primary characteristic of behavior is that it is goal-directed: "Behavior . . . always seems to have the character of getting-to or getting-from a specific goal-object, or goal-situation" (Tolman, 1932, p. 10).

> The rat's behavior of "running the maze" has as its first and perhaps most important identifying feature the fact that it is a getting to food. Similarly, the behavior of Thorndike's kitten in opening the puzzle box would have as its first identifying feature the fact that it is a getting away from the confinement of the box, or, if you will, a getting to the freedom outside. Or, again, the behavior of the psychologist reciting nonsense syllables in the laboratory has as its first descriptive feature the fact that it is a getting to (shall we say) "an offer from another university." Or, finally, the gossiping remarks of my friend and myself have as their first identifying feature a set of gettings to such and such mutual readinesses for further behaviors. (p. 10)

Environmental stimuli (e.g., objects, paths) are means to goal attainment. They cannot be studied in isolation; rather, the entire behavioral sequences must be studied to understand why people engage in particular actions. High school students whose goal is to attend a leading university study hard in their classes. By focusing only on the studying, researchers would miss the purpose of the behavior. The students do not study because they have been reinforced for studying in the past. Rather, studying is a means to intermediate goals (learning, high grades), which, in turn, enhance the likelihood of acceptance to the university.

Because behavior is purposive, it is also cognitive. "And such purposes and such cognitions are just as evident . . . if this behavior be that of a rat as if it be that of a human being" (Tolman, 1932, p. 12). Tolman's suggestion that rats and other lower animals pursue goals and act based on cognitions was not well received by behavioral researchers. Tolman qualified his use of the terms *purpose* and *cognition* by noting they are defined objectively. The behavior of people and animals is goal-oriented, that is, organisms are acting "as if" they were pursuing a goal and "as if" they had chosen a means for goal attainment. Although Tolman was aligned with behavioral psychologists because he studied overt behavior, he went beyond simple stimulus-response associations to discuss underlying cognitive mechanisms.

Expectancy Learning. Tolman (1949) identified six kinds of learning; for present purposes, the most important is *field expectancy*. An expectancy is "an immanent cognitive determinant aroused by actually presented stimuli" (Tolman, 1932, p. 444). Expectancies involve relationships between stimuli (S1–S2) or between a stimulus, response, and stimulus (S1–R–S2). Relations between stimuli concern what stimulus was apt to follow what other stimulus; for example, the sound of thunder follows lightning. More important are the three-term relations in which people develop the belief that a certain response to a given stimulus produces a certain result. If one's goal is to get to a roof (S2), the sight of the ladder (S1) could lead one to think, "If I place this ladder against the house [R], I can get to the roof." This is similar to Skinner's three-term contingency, except that Tolman conceived of this type of relation as reflecting a cognitive expectancy.

Expectancies are acquired from one's experiences with environmental events. Simple contiguity of stimuli and responses form expectancies. Expectancies are important because they help people attain goals. Tolman postulated that people form *cognitive maps*, or internal plans comprising expectancies of which actions are needed to attain their goals. Individuals follow *signs* to a goal; they learn *meanings* rather than discrete responses. When in problem-solving situations, people use their cognitive maps to determine the best course of action to take to attain their goals.

Tolman tested his ideas in an ingenious series of experiments (Tolman, Ritchie, & Kalish, 1946a, 1946b). In one study, rats were trained to run an apparatus, shown in Figure 4.1 (Maze 1). Subsequently, the apparatus was replaced with one in which the original pathway was blocked. The conditioning theory prediction was that the animals would choose a pathway close to the original one, as shown in Figure 4.1 (Maze 2a). Surprisingly, the results were that the most frequently chosen path was aimed in the direction where food was originally found, as illustrated in Maze 2b. These results support the idea that the animals formed a cognitive map of the location of the food and responded based on that map rather than on prior responses to stimuli.

Latent Learning. Additional evidence to support cognitive map learning was obtained in experiments on latent learning. *Latent learning* occurs in the absence of a goal or reinforcement, thus contradicting the operant conditioning principle that learning involves behavior change through reinforced practice.

Tolman and Honzik (1930) allowed two groups of rats to wander through a maze for 10 trials. One group always was fed in the maze, whereas the other group was never fed. Rats fed in the maze quickly reduced their time and number of errors in running the maze, but time and errors for the other group remained high. Starting on the eleventh trial, some rats from the nonreinforced group were given food for running the maze. Both their time and number of errors quickly dropped to the levels of the group that always had been fed; the running times and error rates for those rats that continued to be nonreinforced did not change. Rats in the nonreinforced group had learned features of the maze by wandering through it without reinforcement. When food was introduced, the latent learning quickly displayed itself.

Tolman's research demonstrated that learning can occur even when the behavior is not displayed at the time it is learned. This distinction between learning and the performance of learned behaviors is central to Bandura's social cognitive theory. Further, Tolman showed that reinforcement does not strengthen S-R connections or shape behaviors, but rather serves as a motivational inducement. In short, reinforcement affects performance rather than learning.

Rotter's Social Learning Theory

The social learning theory of Julian Rotter represents an integration of learning and personality theories (Phares, 1976). The theory is social in nature because "it stresses the fact that the major or basic modes of behaving are learned in social situations and are inextricably fused with needs requiring for their satisfaction the mediation of other persons" (Rotter, 1954, p. 84). Although originally a social learning theory of personality, Rotter's theory has been applied to other domains—learning (including education), social psychology, measurement, psychopathology, and behavioral change (Rotter, Chance, & Phares, 1972).

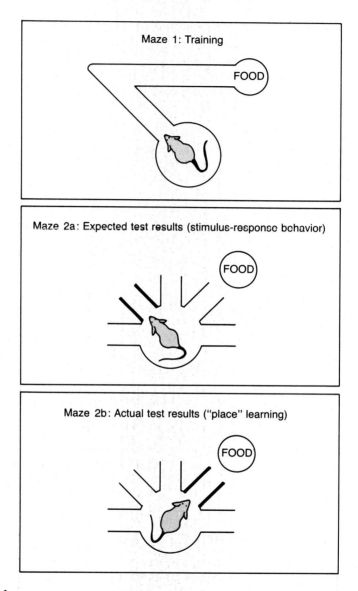

FIGURE 4.1
Experimental arrangement to study expectancy learning (*Source:* Adapted from Tolman, Ritchie, & Kalish, 1946a).

The theory comprises four basic constructs: behavior potential (BP), expectancy (E), reinforcement value (RV), and the psychological situation (Rotter, 1982). The potential for a particular behavior to occur in a given situation in relation to a certain reinforcement is a function of the expectancy of occurrence of that reinforcement following the behavior and of the value of that reinforcement in that situation. This relationship is symbolized as follows:

$$BP = E \& RV$$

Behavior potential refers to the probability that an individual will act in a certain fashion relative to alternative behaviors. In any given situation, an individual may engage in different actions. Behavior potential orders these possibilities in terms of likelihood. In Rotter's view, behavior includes observable actions as well as such covert acts as thinking and planning, which are often manifested behaviorally.

Expectancy is the individual's belief concerning the likelihood a particular reinforcement will occur as a consequence of a specific behavior. One may believe various outcomes are possible consequences of an action, but each outcome has a probability of occurrence. Expectancy is subjective and may bear little relation to reality. Students may believe if they study hard they will make an A on an English test, even though they never have made an A on an English test when they studied hard. Rotter et al. (1972) noted that reinforcements may be internal (reinforcing to the individual) or external (reinforcing to the group or culture to which the person belongs).

Reinforcement value refers to how much the individual values a particular outcome relative to other potential outcomes. Expectancy and reinforcement value are independent of each other. Of several potential outcomes of a behavior, the most likely outcome may be more or less desired by the individual relative to other potential outcomes.

The *psychological situation* implies that the context of behavior is important. The way in which the individual views the situation can affect both reinforcement value and expectancy. In unpleasant situations, for example, one might view all potential outcomes as negative. Thus, the least negative one might be the most desirable.

As a result of experiences with others, people form expectancies about the likely outcomes of behaviors, and they act in accordance with their expectancies and the value they place on the potential outcomes (Rotter et al., 1972). Assuming that one believes a given reinforcement (outcome) will occur following a behavior and that one values that outcome, the theory predicts one will engage in that behavior. People will attempt difficult tasks if they expect reinforcement and if they value that reinforcement. A student may volunteer to do a difficult project if the student expects teacher praise and peer approval to be forthcoming and values those reinforcements.

SOCIAL COGNITIVE THEORY

Although Rotter's theory assumes that behavior is situationally specific, it does not imply that there is no generality across situations. Expectancies for reinforcement can generalize to similar situations. "Expectancies in each situation are determined not only by specific experiences in that situation, but also, to some varying extent, by experiences in other situations which the individual perceives as similar" (Rotter, 1982, p. 304). The notion of generalized expectancies is captured by the motivational construct *locus of control*. (See also the discussion of Attribution Theory in Chapter 8.)

Rotter's theory says that individuals consider the likely consequences of their actions in a given situation and act based on their beliefs. In contrast to Skinner's contention that individuals act in accordance with prior reinforcement, Rotter postulates that people do what they believe will lead to valued reinforcements. When subjective belief contradicts prior experience—when previously reinforced but not believing they will be again—people are more likely to act on the basis of belief than experience.

Imitation

Throughout history, imitation has been viewed as an important means of transmitting behaviors (Rosenthal & Zimmerman, 1978). The ancient Greeks used the term *mimesis* to refer to learning through observation of the actions of others and of abstract models exemplifying literary and moral styles. More recent views concerning imitation are summarized as follows:

View	Assumptions
Instinct	Observed actions elicit an instinctive drive to copy those actions.
Developmental	Children imitate actions that fit with existing cognitive schemes.
Conditioned	Through shaping, behaviors are imitated and reinforced. Imitation becomes a generalized response class.
Instrumental behavior	Imitation becomes a secondary drive through repeated reinforcement of responses matching those of models. Imitation results in drive reduction.

Imitation Is an Instinct. Scientific attention was increasingly directed toward imitation at the beginning of the twentieth century. The dominant view was that people possess a natural instinct to imitate the actions of others (Tarde, 1903). James (1890) also treated imitation as an instinct:

> There is the more direct propensity to speak and walk and behave like others, usually without any conscious intention of so doing. And there is

the imitative tendency which shows itself in large masses of men, and produces panics, and orgies, and frenzies of violence, and which only the rarest individuals can actively withstand. This sort of imitativeness is possessed by man in common with other gregarious animals, and is an instinct in the fullest sense of the term, being a blind impulse to act as soon as a certain perception occurs. (Vol. 2, p. 408)

James believed that imitation is largely responsible for children's socialization, but he did not explain the process by which imitation occurs. McDougall (1926) restricted his definition of imitation to the instinctive overt copying by one person of the actions of another: Observed actions elicit an instinct or drive to copy those actions.

The instinct notion was rejected by behaviorists because it assumed the existence of a drive—and possibly a mental image—intervening between a stimulus (action of another person) and response (copying of that action). Watson (1924) stated,

There are then for us no instincts—we no longer need the term in psychology. Everything we have been in the habit of calling an "instinct" today is a result largely of training—belongs to man's *learned behavior.* (p. 74)

Imitation Is Limited by Development. A different view of imitation was offered by Piaget (1962), who believed that human development involves the acquisition of *schemes.* A scheme is a type of cognitive structure or capacity that underlies and makes possible organized thought and action (Flavell, 1985). Thoughts and actions are not synonymous with schemes; they are overt manifestations of schemes. Schemes available to individuals determine how they react to events. Schemes reflect prior experiences and comprise the totality of one's knowledge at any given time.

Schemes presumably are developed by maturation and experiences slightly more advanced than one's existing cognitive structures. Imitation is restricted to activities corresponding to existing schemes. Children may imitate actions they understand, but they should not imitate actions incongruent with their cognitive structures. Development, therefore, must precede imitation. This view severely limits the potential of imitation to create and modify cognitive structures.

Research does not support the developmental position (Rosenthal & Zimmerman, 1978). In an early study, Valentine (1930b) found that infants could imitate actions within their capabilities but which they previously had not performed. There were numerous instances of purposeless imitation that followed the infant's attention to a visual display and served no biological purpose. Infants showed a strong tendency to imitate unusual actions commanding attention. The imitation was not always immediate, and actions often had to be repeated before infants would imitate them. The individual performing the original actions also was important: Infants were most likely to imitate their mothers.

Imitation Is Conditioned. Researchers in the behavioristic tradition have construed imitation in associationist terms. Humphrey (1921) wrote that imitation is a type of circular reaction in which each response serves as a stimulus for the next response. A baby may start crying (response) because of a pain (stimulus). The baby hears its own crying (auditory stimulus), which then serves as a stimulus for subsequent crying. Through conditioning, small reflex units form progressively more complex response chains.

Reinforcement theorists view imitation in the same fashion as other behaviors. According to Skinner (1953), imitation is a generalized response class. In the three-term contingency ($S^D \rightarrow R \rightarrow S^R$), a modeled act serves as the S^D (discriminative stimulus). Imitation occurs when an observer performs the same response (R) and receives reinforcement, or reinforcing stimulus (S^R). This contingency becomes established early in life. For example, a parent makes a sound ("Dada"), the child imitates, and the parent delivers reinforcement (smile, hug). Once an imitative response class is established, it can be maintained on an intermittent reinforcement schedule. The child imitates the behaviors of models (its parents) as long as the models remain discriminative stimuli for reinforcement.

One limitation of this view is that the imitated response must exist in the imitator's behavioral repertoire; one can imitate only those responses one can perform. In fact, much research shows that diverse types of behaviors can be acquired through observation (Rosenthal & Zimmerman, 1978). Another limitation concerns the necessity of reinforcement for imitated behaviors. Observers learn from models in the absence of reinforcement to models or observers (Bandura, 1986). Tolman showed that reinforcement primarily affects learners' performance of responses that have been learned.

Imitation Is Instrumental Behavior. An elaborate theory of imitation, or *matched-dependent behavior,* was proposed by Miller and Dollard (1941), who rejected the associationist notion in favor of a Hullian view of drive reduction. Imitation is instrumental learned behavior because it leads to reinforcement. Matched-dependent behavior is matched to (i.e., is the same as) that of the model and is dependent on or elicited by the model's action. Miller and Dollard (1941) described matched-dependent behavior in the following example of two children playing in their bedroom adjacent to the kitchen.

> The kitchen opened upon a back stairway. It was six o'clock in the evening, the hour when father usually returned home, bearing candy for the two children. While playing in the bedroom, Jim heard a footfall on the stairs; it was the familiar sound of father's return. The younger child,

however, had not identified this critical cue. Jim ran to the kitchen to be on hand when father came in the back door. Bobby happened on this occasion to be running in the direction of the kitchen and behind Jim. On many other occasions, probably many hundreds, he had not happened to run when Jim did. He had, for instance, remained sitting, continued playing with his toys, run to the window instead of the door, and the like; but on this occasion, he was running behind his brother. Upon reaching the kitchen, Jim got his candy and Bobby his. (p. 94)

In this scenario, the behavior (running) of the imitator (Bobby) is elicited by and identical to that of the model (Jim). Miller and Dollard believed that initially the imitator responds to behavioral cues in trial-and-error fashion, but eventually the imitator performs the correct response and is reinforced. Responses performed by imitators exist in their behavioral repertoires. Repeated reinforcement of imitated behavior establishes imitation as a secondary (learned) drive.

Miller and Dollard's conception of imitation as learned instrumental behavior was an important advance in its scientific study, but the view contains problems: New responses are not created through imitation; imitation represents performance of learned behaviors. This view also could not account for delayed imitation (i.e., when imitators perform the matching responses some time after the actions are performed by the model) or for imitated behaviors that are not reinforced (Bandura & Walters, 1963). This narrow conception of imitation restricts its usefulness to imitative responses corresponding closely to those portrayed by models.

CONCEPTUAL FRAMEWORK

Social cognitive theory makes several assumptions about learning and the performance of behaviors. These assumptions address the reciprocal interactions among persons, behaviors, and environments; enactive and vicarious learning (i.e., the ways learning occurs); and the distinction between learning and performance.

Reciprocal Interactions

Bandura (1978, 1982a) discussed human behavior within a framework of *triadic reciprocality*, or reciprocal interactions among behaviors, environmental variables, and personal factors such as cognitions (Figure 4.2):

In the social cognitive view people are neither driven by inner forces nor automatically shaped and controlled by external stimuli. Rather, human functioning is explained in terms of a model of triadic reciprocality in which behavior, cognitive and other personal factors, and environmental

SOCIAL COGNITIVE THEORY

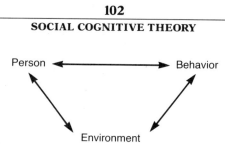

FIGURE 4.2

Triadic reciprocity model of causality (*Source:* From Albert Bandura, SOCIAL FOUNDATIONS OF THOUGHT & ACTION, © 1986, p. 24. Adapted by permission of Prentice Hall, Inc., Englewood Cliffs, N.J.).

events all operate as interacting determinants of each other. (Bandura, 1986, p. 18)

Triadic reciprocality can be exemplified with an important construct in Bandura's (1982b) theory: *perceived self-efficacy,* or beliefs concerning one's capabilities to organize and implement actions necessary to attain designated performance levels. With respect to the interaction of self-efficacy (personal factor) and behavior, research shows that self-efficacy beliefs influence such achievement behaviors as choice of tasks, persistence, effort expenditure, and skill acquisition (Schunk, 1989). In turn, students' actual behaviors modify self-efficacy. As students work on tasks they note their progress toward their learning goals (e.g., completing workbook pages, finishing sections of a term paper). Such progress indicators convey to students that they are capable of performing well and enhance their self-efficacy for continued learning.

The interaction between self-efficacy and environmental factors has been shown in learning disabilities research. Many learning disabled students hold a low sense of self-efficacy for performing well (Licht & Kistner, 1986). Individuals in students' social environments may react to students based on attributes typically associated with the learning disabled rather than on the actual abilities of the individual students. Teachers often judge learning disabled students less capable than nondisabled students and hold lower academic expectations for them, even in content areas where learning disabled students are performing adequately (Bryan & Bryan, 1983). In turn, teacher feedback can impact self-efficacy. When a teacher tells a student, "I know you can do this," the student is likely to feel more confident about succeeding.

Students' behaviors and classroom environments influence one another in many ways. Consider a typical instructional sequence in which the teacher presents information and asks students to direct their attention to the chalkboard. Environmental influence on behavior occurs when students look at the chalkboard without much conscious deliberation. Students' behaviors often alter the instructional environment. If the teacher asks questions and students give the wrong answers, the teacher may reteach some points rather than continue the lesson.

Enactive and Vicarious Learning

In social cognitive theory, "Learning is largely an information-processing activity in which information about the structure of behavior and about environmental events is transformed into symbolic representations that serve as guides for action" (Bandura, 1986, p. 51). Learning occurs either *enactively* by actually performing or *vicariously* by observing models perform (watching TV, reading, and so forth). Enactive learning involves learning from the consequences of one's actions: Behaviors that result in successful consequences are retained; those that lead to failures are discarded.

Operant conditioning theory also says that people learn by doing, but social cognitive and conditioning theories have different explanations. Skinner (1953) noted that cognitions may accompany behavioral change but they do not influence it. Social cognitive theory contends that behavioral consequences, rather than strengthening behaviors as postulated in operant theory, serve as sources of information and motivation. Consequences inform people of the likely outcomes of the behavior. If the outcome is failure, they know that they are doing something wrong and they take steps to produce success the next time. While learning, people selectively process information; they engage in such activities as attending to instruction and rehearsing information, which they believe will promote learning. From a motivational perspective, people strive to learn behaviors they value and believe will have desirable consequences.

Much human learning occurs vicariously, that is, in the absence of overt performance by the learner. Common sources of vicarious learning are observing or listening to others (live, on TV or radio, videotapes, slides, filmstrips) and reading. Vicarious sources accelerate learning over what would be possible if people had to perform every behavior for learning to occur. Vicarious sources also save people from personally experiencing negative consequences. They learn that poisonous snakes are dangerous by reading books rather than by experiencing the unpleasant consequences of their bites.

Complex skills typically involve enactive and vicarious learning. Aspiring golfers, for example, do not simply watch professionals; rather, they engage in much practice and receive corrective feedback from qualified instructors. In school, students observe teachers explain and demonstrate skills. Through observation, students often learn some components of a complex skill and not others. Student practice gives teachers the opportunity to provide corrective feedback to help students perfect their skills. As with enactive learning, response consequences from vicarious sources inform and motivate observers. Observers are more apt to learn modeled behaviors leading to successes than those resulting in failures. When people believe that modeled behaviors are useful, they attend carefully to models and mentally rehearse the behaviors.

Learning and Performance

A third assumption made by social cognitive theory involves the distinction between learning and performance of previously learned behaviors. By observing models, people acquire knowledge they may not demonstrate at the time of learning (Rosenthal & Zimmerman, 1978). Although some school activities (review sessions) involve performance of previously learned skills, much time is spent learning. Students acquire *declarative knowledge* in the form of facts, scripts (e.g., events of a story), and organized passages (words in a song or poem). Students also acquire *procedural knowledge* (concepts, rules, algorithms) as well as *conditional knowledge* (knowing when to employ forms of declarative and procedural knowledge and why it is important to do so) (Paris, Cross, & Lipson, 1984; Paris, Lipson, & Wixson, 1983). Any of these forms of knowledge can be acquired but not demonstrated when learning occurs. For example, students might learn that skimming is a useful procedure for acquiring the gist of text but may not employ that knowledge until they are at home reading a newspaper.

The model portrayed in Figure 4.2 does not imply that the directions of influence are always the same. At any given time, one factor may predominate: When environmental influences are weak, personal factors predominate. For instance, students allowed to write a report on a book of their choosing will select one they enjoy. However, a person caught in a burning house is apt to behave in accordance with the situation; here environmental factors predominate over personal factors.

Much of the time the three factors interact. As a teacher presents a lesson to the class, students think about what the teacher is saying (environment influences cognitions). Students who do not understand a point raise their hands to ask a question (cognitions influence behavior). The teacher reviews the point (behavior influences environment). Eventually the teacher gives students work to accomplish (environment influences cognitions, which influence behavior). As students work on the task, they believe they are performing it well (behavior influences cognitions). They decide they like the task, ask the teacher if they can continue to work on it, and are allowed to do so (cognitions influence behavior, which influences environment).

MODELING PROCESSES

Functions of Modeling

Modeling is a general term that refers to behavioral, cognitive, and affective changes deriving from observing one or more models (Berger, 1977; Rosenthal & Bandura, 1978; Zimmerman, 1977). A distinction is usually drawn between *live models*, who appear in person, and *symbolic models*, who are presented via oral or written instructions or in pictures, TV, films, or other audiovisual displays (Bandura & Walters, 1963). Models may be nonhuman (e.g., televised talking animals and cartoon characters). Bandura postulated that modeling serves the following three functions:

Function	Underlying Process
Inhibition and disinhibition	Modeled behaviors create expectations in observers that similar consequences will occur should they model the actions.
Response facilitation	Social prompts create motivational inducements for observers to model the actions ("going along with the crowd").
Observational learning	Subprocesses include attention, retention, production, and motivation.

Inhibition and Disinhibition. Observing a model can strengthen or weaken inhibitions over behaviors previously learned. Observing models perform threatening or prohibited activities without experiencing negative consequences can lead observers to perform the behaviors. Observing models punished for performing certain actions may inhibit observers' responding. Inhibitory and disinhibitory effects occur because of information conveyed to observers that similar consequences are likely should they perform the modeled behaviors.

Classroom misbehavior is inhibited or disinhibited by the teacher's actions. Unpunished student misbehavior can have a disinhibiting effect: Students who observe modeled misbehavior not followed by punishing consequences might start misbehaving themselves. Conversely, misbehavior in other students is often inhibited when the teacher disciplines one student for misbehaving. Observers are likely to believe they, too, will be disciplined if they continue to misbehave and are spotted by the teacher.

Response Facilitation. There are many behaviors people learn but typically do not perform because of insufficient motivational inducements rather than prohibitions. Response facilitation refers to modeled actions that serve as social prompts for observers to behave accordingly. Consider a teacher who has set up an attractive display in a corner of the classroom. When the first students enter in the morning, they spot the display and immediately go to look at it. When other students enter the room, they see a group in the corner, so they, too, move to the corner to see what everyone is looking at. Several students together serve as a social prompt for others to join them, even though the latter students do not know why the others are gathered in the corner.

Response facilitation effects are similar to inhibitory and disinhibitory effects in that behaviors reflect actions people have learned. Unlike inhibitory and disinhibitory effects, response facilitation effects are neutral in the sense the behaviors are socially acceptable and not accompanied by potential restraints (Bandura, 1986).

Observational Learning. Observational learning through modeling occurs when observers display new patterns of behavior that prior to modeling had a zero probability of occurrence even with motivational inducements in effect (Bandura, 1969). A key mechanism in observational learning is the information conveyed by models. Models inform observers of ways to produce new behaviors (Rosenthal & Zimmerman, 1978). Observational learning is hypothesized to comprise the following four subprocesses:

Subprocess	Activities
Attention	Student attention is directed by physically accentuating relevant task features, subdividing complex activities into parts, using competent models, and demonstrating usefulness of modeled behaviors.
Retention	Retention is increased by rehearsing information to be learned, coding in visual and symbolic form, and relating new material to information previously stored in memory.
Production	Behaviors produced are compared to one's conceptual (mental) representation. Feedback helps to correct deficiencies.
Motivation	Consequences of modeled behaviors inform observers of functional value and appropriateness. Consequences motivate by creating outcome expectations and raising self-efficacy.

Observer *attention* to relevant environmental events, the first subprocess, is necessary for them to be meaningfully perceived. At any given time, there are countless activities to which one can attend. As discussed later in this chapter, factors associated with model and observer influence one's attention to models. Distinctive activities also command attention. An activity can "grab one's attention" because of its size, shape, color, sound, or unusual location. Teachers apply this principle when they add such distinctive features to their modeled demonstrations as bright colors and oversized cutouts. Modeled activities differ in their perceived *functional value;* those judged by observers as important and likely to lead to rewarding outcomes command greater attention. An important reason why students attend to teachers is that teachers' activities are viewed as highly functional. Students are expected to learn the modeled behaviors; they will have to perform them or be tested on them. Coupled with functional value is the students' belief that the teacher is highly competent. Perceived model competence is inferred from the results of the modeled actions (success, failure) and symbols signifying competence (title, position).

The second subprocess is *retention*. Retention activities include coding and transforming modeled information for storage in memory, as well as cognitively rehearsing information. Observational learning relies upon two means for cognitively storing informing: imaginal and verbal (Bandura, 1977b). A modeled display leads observers to store the acquired information as an image, in verbal form, or both. Imaginal coding is especially important for activities not easily described in words; for example, motor skills performed so rapidly that individual movements merge into a larger sequence (e.g., golf swing). Much cognitive skill learning relies upon verbal coding, such as statements of rules or procedures.

Chapters 5 to 7 present a detailed analysis of the information processing view of learning, which involves encoding incoming information in meaningful fashion and integrating it with information already in memory. Rehearsal (mentally reviewing information) serves a key function in this view of learning. Bandura and Jeffery (1973) presented adults with complex modeled movement configurations. Some subjects coded these movements at the time of presentation by assigning numerical or verbal designators to them. Other subjects were not given coding instructions but were told to subdivide the movements to remember them. In addition, subjects either were or were not allowed to rehearse the codes or movements following presentation. Both coding and rehearsal enhanced retention of modeled events; subjects who coded and rehearsed showed the best recall. Rehearsal without coding and coding without rehearsal were less effective.

Production, the third observational learning subprocess, involves translating visual and symbolic conceptions of modeled events into overt behaviors. Problems in producing modeled behaviors arise because information is inadequately coded or because learners experience difficulty translating coded information into overt behavior. Rarely are complex behaviors learned solely through observation. Learners often code information improperly, act based on the faulty knowledge, or find it difficult to translate knowledge in memory into overt action.

Most complex skills are learned through a combination of modeling, guided practice, and corrective feedback. Learners usually acquire at least a rough approximation of a complex skill by observing modeled demonstrations (Bandura, 1977b). By actually practicing skills, learners refine their skills, especially when teachers provide corrective feedback and reteach troublesome aspects.

Motivation, the fourth subprocess, is induced by direct, vicarious, and self-produced experiences. Individuals do not demonstrate all the knowledge, skills, and behaviors they acquire through observation. People perform actions they believe will result in rewarding outcomes and avoid acting in ways they believe will result in negative outcomes (Schunk, 1987). They form expectations about anticipated outcomes of actions based on consequences experienced by them and models. In addition, individuals act based on their beliefs and values. They perform activities they value and avoid those they find dissatisfying, regardless of the consequences to themselves or others. People forego money, prestige, and power when the activities they must engage in to receive these rewards are devalued (e.g., questionable business practices).

Cognitive Skill Learning

Observational learning expands the range and rate of learning over what could occur through a shaping process, where each response must be performed and reinforced. Modeled portrayals of cognitive skills are standard features in classrooms. In a typical instructional sequence, a teacher explains and demonstrates the skill to be acquired, after which the students receive guided practice while the teacher checks for student understanding. The skill is retaught if students experience difficulty. When the teacher is satisfied students have a basic understanding, they engage in independent practice while the teacher periodically monitors their work.

APPLICATION 4.1: Teacher Modeling

Teachers serve as models since they help students acquire skills. Modeled demonstrations typically are incorporated into lessons designed to teach students such diverse skills as solving mathematics problems, diagramming sentences, installing batteries in cars, and joining together pieces of wood.

Modeled demonstrations are used to teach elementary children how to head their papers properly. The teacher might draw on a transparency or section of a chalkboard a sketch of the paper students are using. The teacher then can review the heading procedure step by step, explaining and demonstrating how to complete it.

In a home economics class, students can learn how to insert a sleeve into a garment through modeled demonstrations. Teachers might begin by describing the process, after which they use visual aids to portray the procedure. Teachers could conclude the lesson by demonstrating the process at a sewing machine.

MODELING PROCESSES

Cognitive Modeling. *Cognitive modeling* incorporates modeled explanation and demonstration with verbalization of the model's thoughts and reasons for performing given actions (Meichenbaum, 1977). In teaching division skills, a teacher might verbalize the following in response to the problem 276 ÷ 4:

> First I have to decide what number to divide 4 into. I take 276, start on the left and move toward the right until I have a number the same as or larger than 4. Is 2 larger than 4? No. Is 27 larger than 4? Yes. So my first division will be 4 into 27. Now I need to multiply 4 by a number that will give an answer the same as or slightly smaller than 27. How about 5? 5 × 4 = 20. No, too small. Let's try 6. 6 × 4 = 24. Maybe. Let's try 7. 7 × 4 = 28. No, too large. So 6 is correct.

Cognitive modeling can include other types of statements. Errors are built into the modeled demonstration to show students how to recognize and cope with them. Self-reinforcing statements (e.g., "I'm doing well") also are useful, especially with students who encounter difficulties learning and doubt their capabilities to perform well.

Explanation together with modeling is more effective in teaching skills than explanation alone (Rosenthal & Zimmerman, 1978). Schunk (1981) compared the effects of cognitive modeling with those of didactic instruction on children's self-efficacy and long division skills. Children deficient in division skills participated in a long division training program. Cognitive modeling subjects observed an adult model explain and demonstrate division operations while applying them to sample problems. Didactic subjects received the same instructional material that explained and demonstrated the operations, but children studied the material independently. Cognitive modeling enhanced children's division skill learning and self-efficacy for successfully solving division problems better than didactic instruction.

Self-Instructional Training. Meichenbaum and Goodman (1971) incorporated cognitive modeling into a self-instructional training procedure. Their subjects were impulsive second graders in a special education class. The following 5-step procedure was used:

1. *Cognitive modeling:* Adult tells children what to do while adult performs the task.
2. *Overt guidance:* Children perform under direction of adult instruction.
3. *Overt self-guidance:* Children perform while instructing themselves aloud.
4. *Faded overt self-guidance:* Children whisper instructions while performing task.
5. *Covert self-instruction:* Children perform task while guided by inner silent speech.

Various tasks were used to help children control their behaviors with self-instructions. One objective of the training was to slow down children's rate of performing tasks. The following sample statements were employed by the adult model for a line-drawing task in Meichenbaum and Goodman's (1971) study:

> Okay, what is it I have to do? You want me to copy the picture with the different lines. I have to go slow and be careful. Okay, draw the line down, down, good; then to the right, that's it; now down some more and to the left. Good, I'm doing fine so far. Remember go slow. Now back up again. No, I was supposed to go down. That's okay, just erase the line carefully. . . . Good. Even if I make an error I can go on slowly and carefully. Okay, I have to go down now. Finished. I did it. (p. 117)

In this example, the model made a mistake and showed how to cope with it. This is an important aspect for impulsive students and those with other behavioral deficits, because they often become frustrated and quit easily following errors. Meichenbaum and Goodman found that cognitive modeling slowed down children's response times, but that the addition of the self-instructional training led to a significant decrease in errors.

Cognitive modeling has been used in training programs with a variety of tasks and types of students (Fish & Pervan, 1985) and is especially useful in teaching students to work on tasks in strategic fashion. In teaching reading comprehension, the beginning of the preceding instructions can be modified as follows: "What is it I have to do? I have to find the topic sentence of the paragraph. The topic sentence is what the paragraph is about. I start by looking for a sentence that sums up the details or tells what the paragraph is about" (McNeil, 1987, p. 96). Statements for coping with difficulties (e.g., "I haven't found it yet, but that's all right") can be built into the modeled demonstration.

Rule Learning

Observational learning is an effective means of acquiring rules governing language use and concept attainment (Zimmerman & Rosenthal, 1974). In contrast to Skinner's ideas about language acquisition, social cognitive theory assumes that very little language is acquired through shaping or mimicry of verbalizations by others. Social cognitive research has not explored the "deep" cognitive structures that are of concern to psycholinguists, but rather it has investigated whether rule-governed language use is facilitated through exposure to models.

The general procedure involved in language rule learning is to expose the observer to one or more models using a grammatical construction reflecting the rule. Over time, the rule is held constant while nonrelevant task aspects (e.g., words used by the model) are varied. Subsequent modeling of the construction by the observer reflects rule learning rather than simple imitation of words or sound patterns.

In an early study, Bandura and Harris (1966) showed young children common nouns, and the children constructed a sentence with each noun. Several treatments were implemented. Some children were exposed to models who demonstrated the desired construction (e.g., passive verbs) and who took turns with them in making up sentences. Reinforcement (stars exchangeable for gifts) was given to some children for making up passive constructions, as well as to the models for children assigned to a modeling condition. In another condition (problem-solving set), children were advised to determine what aspect of the construction earned them a star. This study also investigated the effects of these treatments on a second type of grammatical construction—prepositional phrases.

The use of passive constructions remained generally low after training; modeling combined with reinforcement and set produced the greatest number. With prepositional phrases, reinforcement combined with set (with or without modeling) yielded significant increases following training. The children did not simply mimic the model's responses; they acquired the grammatical rule and generated their own sentences, some of which were quite novel. This study showed that social influences can modify grammatical constructions of young children.

A number of research studies have demonstrated that exposure to models is effective in teaching children abstract nonlinguistic rules (Rosenthal & Zimmerman, 1978). Rosenthal, Moore, Dorfman, and Nelson (1971) studied the acquisition and transfer of a simple coordination rule. Children observed a model demonstrate the rule: Construct a three marble triangle in the same color as the disk stimulus (e.g., construct two blue triangles if two blue disks are presented). For some subjects, the model also verbalized while responding. Prior to modeling, children showed no evidence of the modeled response. Modeling produced increases in the appropriate response; the addition of verbalized descriptive statements by the model facilitated children's transfer of the rule to disks of mixed colors. These results highlight the efficacy of using modeled demonstrations to teach concepts (see the discussion of concept learning in the section on Procedural Knowledge in Chapter 6).

Motor Skill Learning

According to social cognitive theory, motor learning involves constructing a mental model that provides the conceptual representation of the skill for

APPLICATION 4.2: Motor Skill Learning

Principles of observational learning are relevant to the learning of motor skills. To teach students to dribble a basketball, physical education teachers begin with various skill exercises from standing stationary and bouncing the ball to actually moving and bouncing the ball with each step. As teachers introduce each skill leading to the final sequence, they should demonstrate slowly and precisely what the students are to model. The students should practice the particular skill following the modeled demonstration. If students have difficulty on a particular step, teachers need to repeat the modeled demonstration before the students continue practicing.

response production and that serves as the standard for correcting responses subsequent to feedback (Carroll & Bandura, 1982). The conceptual representation is formed by transforming observed sequences of behaviors into visual and symbolic codes to be cognitively rehearsed. Individuals often have a mental model of a skill before they attempt to perform it. For example, individuals construct a mental model of such activities as the serve, volley, and backhand by watching tennis players. These models are rudimentary in that they require feedback and correction to be perfected, but they allow learners to perform some approximation of the skill at the outset of training. In the case of novel or complex behaviors, learners may have no prior mental model and need to observe modeled demonstrations before attempting the behaviors.

A problem in motor skill learning is that learners cannot observe many aspects of their performances because they lie outside of their field of vision. Whether people are swinging a golf club, kicking a football, throwing a baseball, high jumping, or pole vaulting, they cannot observe many aspects of these sequences. When one cannot see what one is doing, one must rely on kinesthetic feedback and compare it with one's conceptual representation. The absence of visual feedback makes learning difficult.

Carroll and Bandura (1982) exposed subjects to models performing a motor skill, after which subjects were asked to reproduce the motor pattern. Some subjects were given concurrent visual feedback of their performances by running a video camera and allowing subjects to observe their ongoing performances on a monitor. Other subjects were not given visual feedback. Visual feedback, given before subjects formed a mental model of the motor behavior, had no effect on performance. Once subjects had an adequate model in mind, visual feedback enhanced their accurate reproduction of the modeled behaviors. Visual feedback eliminated discrepancies between the subjects' conceptual model and actions once the former was in place.

INFLUENCES ON LEARNING AND PERFORMANCE

Engaging in a task or observing models does not guarantee that learning will occur or that learned behaviors will be performed later. Several factors influence enactive and vicarious learning and performance of learned behaviors. These factors affect what individuals attend to, how they process information, whether they perceive learning as useful, and how they gauge their capabilities for learning and performance. Influential factors include the following:

Characteristic	Effects on Modeling
Developmental status	Improvements with development include longer attention and increased capacity to process information, to use strategies, to compare performances with memorial representations and to adopt intrinsic motivators.
Model prestige and competence	Observers pay greater attention to competent, high-status models. Consequences of modeled behaviors convey information about functional value. Observers attempt to learn actions they believe they will need to perform.
Vicarious consequences	Consequences to models convey information about behavioral appropriateness and likely outcomes of actions. Valued consequences motivate observers. Similarity in attributes or competence signals appropriateness and heightens motivation.
Outcome expectations	Observers are more likely to perform modeled actions they believe are appropriate and will result in rewarding outcomes.
Goal setting	Observers are likely to attend to models who demonstrate behaviors that help observers attain goals.
Self-efficacy	Observers attend to models when they believe they are capable of learning or performing the modeled behavior. Observation of similar models affects self-efficacy ("If they can do it, I can too").

Developmental Status of Learners

Students' abilities to learn from models depend on developmental factors (Bandura, 1986). Young children have difficulty attending to modeled events for long periods and distinguishing relevant from irrelevant cues. Such information processing functions as rehearsing, organizing, and elaborating (Chapters 5 and 6) improve with development. As they grow, children acquire a more extensive knowledge base to help them comprehend new information, and they become more capable of using memory strategies. Young children may encode modeled events in terms of physical properties, whereas older children often represent information visually or symbolically.

With respect to the production process, information acquired through observation cannot be performed if children lack the requisite physical capabilities. Production also requires translating into action information stored in memory, comparing performance with memorial representation, and correcting performance as necessary. The ability to self-regulate one's actions for longer periods increases with development. Motivational inducements for action also vary depending on development. Young children are motivated by the immediate consequences of their actions. As children mature, they are more likely to perform modeled actions they find personally satisfying.

Prestige and Competence of Models

Modeled behaviors vary in usefulness. Behaviors that successfully deal with the environment command greater attention than those that deal less effectively. People attend to a model in part because they believe they might face the same situation themselves and they want to learn the necessary actions to succeed. Students attend to a teacher because the teacher prompts them to do so but also because they believe they will have to demonstrate the same skills and behaviors. When models compete for attention, people are more likely to attend to the models displaying those behaviors they believe they will have to perform.

Model competence is inferred from the outcomes of modeled actions (success, failure) but also from symbols that denote competence. An important attribute is prestige. Models who have gained distinction are more apt to be attended to than those of lower prestige. In most instances, high-status models have ascended to their positions because they are competent and typically perform well. Their actions have greater functional value for observers, who are apt to believe that rewards will be forthcoming if they act accordingly.

Parents and teachers are high-status models for most children. The scope of adult influence on children's modeling can be quite general. Although teachers are important models in the development of children's intellectual skills, their influence typically spreads to such other areas as social behaviors, educational attainments, and even dress and mannerisms (Rosenthal & Bandura, 1978). The effects of model prestige often generalize

APPLICATION 4.3: Model Prestige and Competence

People attend to models partly because they believe they will have to face the same situations themselves. Effective use of model prestige and competence can help motivate secondary students to attend to lessons related to such topics as drugs, alcohol, suicide, and sex education.

If the use of alcohol has become a problem in a high school, school personnel might develop a program on alcohol education and abuse (prevention, treatment) to include outside speakers. Influential speakers would be recent high school and college graduates prominent in the community who have successfully overcome problems with alcohol or who work with persons who have. The relative similarity in age of the models to the students, coupled with the personal experiences of the models, should make the models appear highly competent. Such individuals are likely to have a greater impact on the students than literature or lessons taught by teachers and counselors.

to areas in which models have no particular competence, as when children adopt the food preferences of prominent athletes appearing in commercials. Although modeling becomes more prevalent with development, even young children are highly susceptible to adult influence (Hartup & Lougee, 1975).

Vicarious Consequences to Models

As noted earlier, the *functional value* of behavior—whether it results in success or failure, reward or punishment—influences observer modeling. Vicarious consequences to models can affect observers' learning and performance of modeled actions. Observers who view models rewarded for their actions are more likely to attend to the models and rehearse and code their actions for retention. Vicarious rewards motivate observers to perform the same actions themselves. In short, vicarious consequences have an informational and a motivational function (Bandura, 1986).

Informational Function. The consequences experienced by models convey information to observers about the types of actions likely to be effective. Vicarious consequences exert their effects on observers through their judgments of probable outcomes contingent on similar actions. Observing competent models perform successful actions conveys information to observers about the sequence of actions people should use to succeed. By observing modeled behaviors and their consequences, people form beliefs concerning which behaviors will be rewarded and which punished.

In a classic demonstration of the role of vicarious consequences on behavior, Bandura, Ross, and Ross (1963) exposed children to live aggressive models, filmed aggression, or aggression portrayed by cartoon characters. The models, who pommeled a Bobo doll by hitting, throwing, kicking, and sitting on it, were neither rewarded nor punished. Children subsequently were allowed to play with a Bobo doll. Compared with control subjects not exposed to aggression, children who viewed aggressive models displayed significantly higher levels of aggression. The type of aggressive model (live, filmed, cartoon) made no difference in the aggression level.

Similarity to models is hypothesized to be an important source of information for gauging behavioral appropriateness and forming beliefs (Schunk, 1987). The more alike observers are to models, the greater is the probability that similar actions by observers are socially appropriate and will produce comparable results. Model attributes often are predictive of the functional value of behaviors. Most social situations are structured so that behavioral appropriateness depends on such factors as age, sex, or status. Similarity ought to be especially influential when observers have little information about functional value. For example, modeled behaviors on tasks with which observers are unfamiliar or those that are not immediately followed by consequences may be highly susceptible to influence by similarity in model attributes (Akamatsu & Thelen, 1974).

As noted earlier, social cognitive theory postulates that reinforcement informs and motivates rather than strengthens responses. Seeing others reinforced for an action conveys to observers it is socially desirable. People are apt to believe they will be rewarded if they act in the same fashion, which can motivate them to behave accordingly.

Some psychological theories postulate that children are more likely to attend to and learn from models of their own sex. More recently, investigators have suggested that the sex of model affects *performance* rather than *learning* of behaviors (Perry & Bussey, 1979; Spence, 1984). Children learn behaviors from models of both sexes and categorize behaviors as appropriate for both sexes or as more appropriate for members of one sex. To the extent that children perform behaviors appropriate for members of either sex or for members of their sex, they may do so because they believe those behaviors have greater functional value than sex-inappropriate behaviors; that is, they believe the former behaviors are more likely to be rewarded (Schunk, 1987). Model sex, therefore, seems important as a conveyor of information about task appropriateness (Zimmerman & Koussa, 1975). When children are uncertain about the sex-appropriateness of a modeled behavior, they may model same-sex peers, because they have been rewarded for doing so in the past.

Model-observer similarity in age is important when children perceive the actions of same-age peers to be more appropriate for themselves than the actions of younger or older models (Schunk, 1987). Whether children are more likely to emulate peers or adults depends on their perceptions of which actions have greater functional value. There is no evidence to suggest that children learn any better or worse from peers or adults. There is some evidence, however, that peers and adults use different teaching strategies: Child teachers often use nonverbal demonstrations and link instruction to specific items; adults typically employ more verbal instruction and relate information to be learned to other material (Ellis & Rogoff, 1982). Peer instruction may be quite beneficial with learning disabled students and other students who do not process verbal material particularly well.

The highest degree of model-observer similarity is attained when one is one's own model. Behavioral change that occurs from observing one's own behaviors is called *self-modeling* (Dowrick, 1983). Self-modeling has been used to develop social, vocational, motor, and cognitive skills and is commonly used in teacher training programs. In a typical procedure, one is videotaped while performing skills and subsequently views the tape. Observing a self-model tape is a form of review and is especially informative for skills one cannot watch while performing (e.g., gymnastic routines).

Performances that contain errors are problematic (Hosford, 1981). Commentary from a knowledgeable individual while one is viewing one's tape helps to prevent the performer from becoming discouraged; the expert can explain how to execute the skills better the next time. Errorless performances are portrayed by videotaping a skillful performance or by editing errors out of the tape. Viewing one's skillful performance conveys that one is capable of learning and can continue to make progress with further work, which raises self-efficacy.

Motivational Function.   Vicarious consequences serve a motivational function. Observers who see models rewarded become motivated to act accordingly. Perceived similarity enhances motivational effects. Observing similar others perform a behavior can lead observers to try it. These motivational effects depend in part on self-efficacy (Bandura, 1982b). Observing similar others succeed raises observers' self-efficacy and motivates them to perform the task; they are apt to believe that if others can succeed, they can as well. Such motivational effects are common in classrooms. Students who observe other students performing a task well may become motivated to try their best, because they believe that if others can do it, they can too.

Reinforcing consequences to models influence observers' behaviors (Rosenthal & Zimmerman, 1978). Of particular educational importance is the observation of effort that leads to success (Schunk, 1989). In tasks involving such underlying abilities as reading and mathematics, observers may become more motivated from watching similar others succeed than those superior in competence. People often believe they are incapable of attaining an expert's performance level.

This is not to suggest that vicarious success will sustain behavior over long periods. Actual performance successes eventually become necessary. Motivation is enhanced when students observe teachers giving praise and high grades to others for hard work and good performances; motivation is sustained when students believe their own efforts are leading to better performances.

Outcome Expectations of Learners

Outcome expectations, or beliefs concerning the anticipated outcomes of actions, influence learning and performance. The outcome expectation construct is similar to the expectancies discussed by Tolman and Rotter. People form beliefs about what will be the consequences of given actions. Individuals select courses of action they believe will be successful, and they attend to models they believe will teach them valued skills. Outcome expectations sustain behaviors over long periods when people believe their actions will eventually produce desired outcomes.

Outcome expectations can refer to external events (e.g., "If I study hard, I should make a good grade on this exam") and to personal standards and attitudes ("If I work hard on this term paper, I'll feel good about myself"). An important type of outcome expectation relates to progress in skill learning ("If I work hard, I'll become a better reader"). Students who believe they are making little or no progress in learning may become demoralized and lackadaisical. In many instances, progress occurs slowly and students notice little day-to-day change. Reading comprehension is a good example. Students improve their skills in reading longer and more difficult passages, in finding main ideas, in drawing inferences, and in reading for details, but progress is slow. Teachers need to inform students explicitly of their progress when it may not be immediately apparent.

Goal Setting and Learners

Much human behavior is sustained over long periods in the absence of immediate external incentives. An important cognitive mechanism operates through goal setting and self-evaluation of one's progress. *Goal setting* involves establishing a standard or objective to serve as the aim of one's actions. A goal reflects one's purpose and refers to quantity, quality, or rate of performance (Locke et al., 1981). People can set their own goals, or goals can be established by others (i.e., parents, teachers, supervisors). An important source of goal information is modeled standards, as when students strive to perform a task as well as or better than their teacher or peers.

Goals enhance learning and performance through people's self-evaluative reactions (Bandura, 1986). Initially, people must commit themselves

APPLICATION 4.4: Goal Setting in Lesson Design

Goal properties are easily incorporated into lesson designs. For example, elementary teachers might introduce a new spelling unit to their classes by stating the following goal:

> Of our 20 words this week, I know that all of you will be able to learn to spell the first 15. We are going to work very diligently in class on these words, and I expect you to do the same at home. With our work at school and at home, I know that all of you will be able to spell these words correctly by Friday. The last 5 words are more difficult. These will be our bonus words.

This goal is specific, but for young children it is distant and might be viewed as too difficult. To help students achieve the overall goal, teachers might set short-term goals each day: "Today we are going to work on these 5 words. By the end of class time I know that all of you will be able to spell these 5 words." Children should view the daily goals as easier to attain than the weekly goal. To further ensure goal attainment, teachers should make sure that the 15 words selected for mastery by Friday challenge the students but are not overly difficult.

to attaining a goal. As they work on the task, they compare their current performances with goals. Perceived negative discrepancies create dissatisfaction, which leads to additional effort. People are more likely to attend to models when they believe the modeled behaviors will help attain their goals. Goals do not automatically enhance learning and motivation. Rather, certain goal properties such as the following serve as incentives:

Goal Property	Effects on Behavior
Specificity	Goals with specific standards of performance increase motivation and raise self-efficacy because goal progress is easy to gauge.
Proximity	Proximal goals increase motivation and efficacy; especially important for young children, who may not subdivide a long-term goal into short-term goals.
Difficulty	Challenging but attainable goals raise motivation and efficacy better than easy or hard goals.

Goal Specificity. Goals that incorporate specific standards of performance are more likely to enhance learning and activate self-evaluative reactions than are such general goals as, "Do your best" (Locke et al., 1981). Specific goals boost task performance through greater specification of the amount of effort required for success and the self-satisfaction anticipated when accomplished. Specific goals also promote self-efficacy because progress toward an explicit goal is easy to gauge.

Much research attests to the effectiveness of specific goals in raising task performance (Locke et al., 1981). Specific goals are especially effective with children (Bandura & Schunk, 1981). Elementary school activities tend to be structured as a series of specific goals, which keeps motivation and learning high.

Goal Proximity.   Goals are distinguished by how far they project into the future. Proximal goals are closer at hand, are achieved more quickly, and result in greater motivation directed toward attainment than more temporally distant goals. Proximal goals are especially influential with children, who have short time frames of reference and are not fully capable of representing distant outcomes in thought. Proximal goals fit well with normal lesson planning, as elementary teachers plan activities around blocks of time. Goals are often proximal and specific, as when teachers ask children to finish five workbook pages in the next half hour.

Goal Difficulty.   Goal difficulty refers to the level of task proficiency required as assessed against a standard. The amount of effort people expend to attain a goal depends on the proficiency level required. Individuals expend greater effort to attain a difficult goal than an easy goal.

Difficulty level and performance do not bear an unlimited positive relationship to each other. Positive effects due to goal difficulty depend on students having sufficient ability to reach the goal. Difficult goals do not enhance performance in the absence of prerequisite skills. Also people's beliefs in their abilities are important. When people believe they do not possess the ability to reach a goal, they hold low expectations for success, do not commit themselves to reaching the goal, and work halfheartedly at the task. Students often believe they cannot accomplish a task. Teachers need to encourage students to work on the task and to give them feedback concerning their progress.

Gaa (1973, 1979) showed that goal-setting conferences enhance students' learning and self-evaluations. First and second graders were assigned to one of three conditions: conferences with goal setting, conferences without goal setting, or no conferences (Gaa, 1973). All children received the same in-class reading instruction. Children in the goal-conference condition met with the researcher once a week for 4 weeks. They received a list of reading skills and selected those they would attempt to accomplish the following week. They also received feedback on their previous week's goal accomplishments. Children who participated in conferences without goals met with the experimenter for the same amount of time but received only general information about material covered previously and what would be covered the following week. Children who participated in goal-setting conferences attained the highest level of reading achievement. At the end of training, they showed the smallest discrepancy between goals set and mastered. Thus, proximal goal setting was shown to promote accurate perceptions of capabilities.

Self-Efficacy of Learners

Perceived self-efficacy refers to judgments of one's capability to organize and implement actions necessary to attain designated performances (Bandura, 1977a, 1977b). As previously noted, self-efficacy is a belief about whether one is capable of accomplishing an act; it is not simply a matter of knowing what to do. In gauging efficacy, individuals assess their skills and abilities to translate those skills into actions. Efficacy is not synonymous with outcome expectations. Students may believe that a positive outcome will result from their actions but doubt that they have the capability to produce those actions. For example, students may believe that if they correctly answer their teacher's questions, they will receive praise (positive outcome expectation), and they might desire the teacher's praise. But they may not volunteer answers if they doubt their capabilities to answer the questions (low self-efficacy). In school, however, outcome expectations and self-efficacy usually are related. Students who perform well are confident of their learning capabilities and expect (and usually receive) positive outcomes for their efforts.

Efficacy is a domain-specific construct; it is meaningful to speak of efficacy for drawing inferences from text, balancing chemical equations, solving fraction problems, and so on. Efficacy is distinguished from the global construct of self-concept, which refers to one's collective self-perceptions formed through experiences with and interpretations of the environment and which is heavily influenced by reinforcements and evaluations by significant others (Wylie, 1979).

Efficacy depends in part on student abilities. In general, high-ability students feel more efficacious about learning compared with low-ability students; however, efficacy is not another name for ability. Collins (1982) identified high-, average-, and low-ability students in mathematics. Within each level, she found students of high and low efficacy. Students were given problems to solve and could rework those they missed. Ability was related to skillful performance, but students with high self-efficacy solved more problems correctly and chose to rework more problems they missed (regardless of ability level) than those with low self-efficacy.

Self-efficacy is hypothesized to have diverse effects in achievement settings (Schunk, 1989). Efficacy can influence choice of activities. Students with low efficacy for learning may avoid tasks; those who judge themselves efficacious should participate more eagerly. Efficacy also can affect effort expenditure, persistence, and learning. When facing difficulties, students who feel efficacious about learning generally expend greater effort and persist longer than students who doubt their capabilities. In turn, these behaviors promote learning.

People acquire information about their efficacy in a given domain from their performances, observations of models (vicarious experiences), forms of social persuasion, and physiological indexes (e.g., heart rate, sweating). Performances offer the most valid information for assessing efficacy. In general, successes raise efficacy and failures lower it, although an occasional failure (success) after many successes (failures) should not have much effect.

In classrooms, students acquire much information about their capabilities through knowledge of how others perform. Similarity to others is an important cue for gauging one's efficacy (Brown & Inouye, 1978; Rosenthal & Bandura, 1978). Observing similar others succeed raises observers' efficacy and motivates them to try the task because they believe that if others succeed, they can as well. At the same time, a vicarious increase in efficacy can be negated by subsequent personal failures. Students who observe peers fail may believe they lack the competencies to succeed, which can dissuade them from attempting the task.

Students often receive persuasive information from teachers that they possess the capability to perform well (e.g., "You can do this"). Although positive feedback enhances efficacy, this increase will be short-lived if students subsequently perform poorly. Students also acquire some efficacy information from their physiological reactivity; for instance, students can interpret emotional symptoms (sweating, trembling) as meaning they are not capable of learning. When students notice they are reacting more calmly to academic demands, they may experience heightened efficacy for mastering the task.

Information acquired from these sources does not influence efficacy automatically but is cognitively appraised (Bandura, 1982b). Efficacy appraisal is an inferential process in which persons weigh and combine the contributions of personal and situational factors. In forming efficacy assessments, students consider such factors as ability, effort expended, task difficulty, teacher assistance, number and pattern of successes and failures (Bandura, 1981).

Self-efficacy is especially germane to school learning. Individuals usually do not judge their efficacy for accomplishing habitual routines or tasks requiring well-established skills. People are more apt to assess their capabilities when they are learning or when they believe altered personal or situational conditions may thwart performance. Although some school time is spent on review, much of the time students are learning new tasks or applying new skills.

Even when students are appraising efficacy primarily from their own performances, their appraisals are not mere reflections of those performances. Educational practices can moderate the effects of successes and failures on efficacy judgments (Schunk, 1989). At the outset of a learning activity, students differ in how efficacious they feel about acquiring the skills or strategies being taught. Students should develop a higher sense of efficacy for learning as they work at a task and experience success. Some educational practices validate this sense of efficacy by clearly conveying to students they are acquiring knowledge and skills, which sustains motivation and enhances learning. Other practices offer less clear information about skill acquisition or convey that students are not particularly skillful, which retards motivation and leads students to wonder whether they are capable of learning (Chapter 8).

Peer Models. Observing a similar peer performing a task well can instate a sense of efficacy in other students for learning, which is validated when they work at the task and experience success. An important variable is number of models. Compared with a single model, multiple models increase the probability observers will perceive themselves as similar to at least one of the models (Thelen, Fry, Fehrenbach, & Frautschi, 1979). Students who might easily discount the successes of a single model may be especially swayed by observing several peers accomplishing a task.

Another way to raise efficacy is to use *coping models,* who initially demonstrate the typical fears and deficiencies of observers but gradually improve their performance and gain confidence in their capabilities. Coping models illustrate how determined effort and positive self-thoughts overcome difficulties. In contrast, *mastery models* demonstrate faultless performance and high confidence from the outset (Thelen et al., 1979). Coping models enhance perceived similarity and efficacy for learning among students likely to view their initial difficulties and gradual progress as more similar to their typical performances than the rapid learning of mastery models.

Schunk and Hanson (1985) showed elementary school children, who had encountered difficulties learning subtraction with regrouping, videotapes portraying a peer mastery model, a peer coping model, a teacher model, or no model. In the peer-model conditions, an adult teacher repeatedly provided instruction, after which the peer solved problems. The peer mastery model easily grasped operations and verbalized positive achievement beliefs reflecting high self-efficacy and ability, low task difficulty, and positive attitudes. The peer coping model initially made errors and verbalized negative achievement beliefs but gradually performed better and verbalized coping statements (e.g., "I need to pay attention to what I'm doing"). Eventually, the coping model's problem-solving behaviors and verbalizations matched those of the mastery model. Teacher-model subjects observed videotapes portraying only the teacher providing instruction; no-model subjects did not view videotapes. All children judged self-efficacy for learning to subtract and participated in an instructional program.

APPLICATION 4.5: Building Efficacy with Peer Models

Observing similar peers performing a task increases students' self-efficacy for learning. This idea is applied when a teacher selects certain students to complete mathematics problems at the chalkboard. By demonstrating success, the peer models help raise observers' self-efficacy for performing well. If ability levels in a class vary considerably, the teacher might pick peer models at different levels of ability. Students in the class are likely to perceive themselves as similar in competence to at least one of the models.

Peers who readily master skills may help teach skills to observing students but may not have much impact on the efficacy of those experiencing learning difficulties. For the latter, low achievers who have mastered skills may be excellent models.

Teachers also can instruct peer models while other students observe. Teachers can convey coping strategies by stressing concentration and hard work to the models. Teachers monitoring seatwork can provide learners with social comparative information (e.g., "See how well Kevin is doing? I'm sure that you can do just as well"). Teachers need to ensure that learners view the comparative performance as one they can attain; judicious selection of referent students is necessary.

Peers also can enhance students' efficacy during small-group work. Successful groups are those in which each member has some responsibility and members share rewards based on their collective performance. Using such groups reduces negative ability-related social comparisons by low achievers. Teachers need to carefully select tasks, because unsuccessful groups do not raise efficacy.

Self-efficacy and skill were enhanced more by observing a peer model than by observing a teacher model or no model; the teacher-model condition promoted these outcomes better than no model. No differences were obtained between the mastery and coping conditions. It is possible that children focused more on what the models had in common (task success) than on their differences. Although subjects' prior successes in subtraction were limited to problems without regrouping, they had these experiences to draw on and may have concluded that if the model could learn, they could as well.

Schunk, Hanson, and Cox (1987) employed a similar methodology to investigate the effects of single coping and mastery models and multiple coping and mastery models. These authors used a task (fractions) on which children had experienced few prior successes. Viewing a single coping model or multiple coping or mastery models enhanced self-efficacy and skill better than viewing a single mastery model. For these low achievers, the coping models were more effective, although observing several peers learn rapidly yielded comparable effects.

Peer models have been used to promote prosocial behaviors in students. Strain et al. (1981) discussed how peers are trained to initiate social play with withdrawn children by using verbal signals (e.g., "Let's play blocks") and motor responses (handing child a toy). Such peer initiations typically increase target children's subsequent social initiations. Training peer initiators is time consuming but well worth the effort, since methods of remedying social withdrawal (prompting, reinforcement) require nearly continuous teacher involvement.

Clinical Applications. Bandura and his colleagues investigated how well self-efficacy predicts behavioral changes in clinical settings. In one study (Bandura, Adams, & Beyer, 1977), adult snake phobics received a *participant modeling* treatment in which a therapist initially modeled a series of progressively more threatening encounters with a snake. After subjects jointly performed the various activities with the therapist, they were allowed to perform them on their own to help enhance their efficacy. Compared with subjects who only observed the therapist model the activities and with those who received no training, participant modeling subjects demonstrated the greatest increases in self-efficacy and approach behaviors toward the snake. Regardless of treatment, self-efficacy for performing tasks was found to be highly related to subjects' actual behaviors. In a related study, Bandura and Adams (1977) found participant modeling superior to systematic desensitization. These results support Bandura's (1982b) contention that performance-based treatments combining modeling with practice offer the best basis for gauging efficacy and produce greater behavioral change.

Self-efficacy has generated much research. There is evidence that self-efficacy predicts such diverse outcomes as smoking cessation, pain tolerance, athletic performance, career choices, assertiveness, coping with feared events, recovery from heart attack, and sales performances (Bandura, 1986). These studies have employed diverse settings, subjects, measures, treatments, tasks, and time spans. The generality of the self-efficacy construct undoubtedly will be extended in future research.

SUMMARY

Social cognitive theory highlights the idea that people learn from their social environments. Theories of imitation, along with those of Tolman and Rotter, offer valuable insights on social learning processes.

Bandura discussed human functioning as a series of reciprocal interactions between personal factors, behaviors, and environmental events. Within this framework, learning is construed as an information processing

SOCIAL COGNITIVE THEORY

activity in which knowledge is cognitively represented as symbolic representations serving as guides for action. Learning occurs enactively through actual performances and vicariously by observing models, listening to instructions, reading, or through audiovisual means (TV, videotapes, films).

The consequences of behavior are especially important. Behaviors that result in successful consequences are retained; those that lead to failures are discarded. Modeling greatly expands the range and rate of learning. Various modeling effects are distinguished: inhibition and disinhibition, response facilitation, and observational learning. Observational learning through modeling expands the learning rate, as well as the amount of knowledge acquired. Subprocesses of observational learning are attention, retention, production, and motivation.

In the social cognitive view, performing a behavior or observing a model does not guarantee learning or later performing the behaviors. Factors affecting learning and performance are developmental status of learners, prestige and competence of models, vicarious consequences to models, outcome expectations, goal setting, and perceived self-efficacy.

Bandura's theory has been tested in a variety of contexts and applied to cognitive, social, motor, and self-regulatory skills. Much learning of complex skills occurs through a combination of enactive and vicarious learning. Observers acquire a rough approximation of the skill by observing models. Subsequent practice of the skill allows teachers to provide corrective feedback to learners. With additional practice, learners refine skills and retain them for future use.

Chapter 5

Information Processing

Information processing theories focus on how people attend to environmental events, encode information to be learned and relate it to knowledge in memory, store new knowledge in memory and retrieve it as needed. As a scientific discipline, information processing has been influenced by advances in communications and computer technology.

Information processing is not the name of a single theory; it is a generic name applied to theoretical perspectives dealing with the sequence and execution of cognitive events. Information processing approaches have been applied to the study of learning, memory, problem solving, visual and auditory perception, cognitive development, and artificial intelligence.

Early information processing research was conducted in experimental laboratories and focused on such phenomena as eye movements, recognition and recall times, attention to stimuli, and interference in perception and memory. More recently, researchers have addressed cognitive processes involved in such school learning domains as reading, writing, and mathematics. Before current conceptions of human cognition are discussed, two theoretical traditions of historical importance are reviewed: Gestalt psychology and verbal learning.

HISTORICAL PERSPECTIVES

Gestalt Psychology

Background. The Gestalt movement began in Germany with a small group of psychologists in the early twentieth century. In 1912, Max Wertheimer wrote an article on apparent motion. The article was significant among German psychologists yet had no influence on the Gestalt movement in the United States, which didn't occur until years later. The subsequent publication in English of Kurt Koffka's *The Growth of the Mind* (1924) and Wolfgang Kohler's *The Mentality of Apes* (1925) helped the Gestalt movement spread to America. These three men eventually settled in the United States, where they applied their ideas to a wide range of psychological phenomena.

Early Gestalt psychology involved the perceptual phenomenon of apparent motion. In a typical demonstration, two lines close together are exposed successively for a fraction of a second with a short time interval between each exposure. An observer sees not two lines but rather a single line moving from the line exposed first toward the line exposed second. The timing of the demonstration is critical. If the time interval between exposure of the two lines is too long, the observer sees the first line and then the second but no motion. If the interval is too short, the observer sees two lines side by side but no motion.

This apparent motion is known as the *phi phenomenon* and demonstrates that subjective experiences cannot be explained by referring to the objective elements involved. Observers perceive movement though there is none. Phenomenological experience (apparent motion) differs from sensory experience (exposure of lines). The attempt to explain this and related phenomena led Wertheimer to challenge psychological explanations of perception as the sum of one's sensory experiences, because these explanations did not take into account the unique wholeness or meaningfulness of perception.

Meaningfulness of Perception. As an example of this meaningfulness, imagine a young woman named Betty who is 5 feet tall. When we view Betty at a distance, our retinal image is much smaller than when we view Betty close up. Yet Betty is 5 feet tall no matter how far away she is. Although the perception (retinal image) varies, the meaning of the image remains constant.

There is no English word that corresponds to the German word *Gestalt*. Roughly translated it means "form, shape, or configuration" (Kohler, 1947/1959). The essence of the Gestalt view is that objects or events are viewed as organized wholes. The basic organization involves a *figure* (what one focuses on) against a *ground* (the background). The configuration is meaningful, not the individual parts (Koffka, 1922). A tree is not a random collection of leaves, branches, roots, and trunk; it is a meaningful configuration of these elements. When viewing a tree, people typically do not focus on individual elements but rather the organized whole. The human brain transforms objective reality into mental events organized as meaningful wholes. This capacity to view things as wholes is an inborn quality, although perception is modified by experience and training (Leeper, 1935). As Kohler (1947/1959) explained,

> There is, in the first place, what is now generally called the *organization* of sensory experience. The term refers to the fact that the sensory fields have in a way their own social psychology. Such fields appear neither as uniformly coherent continua nor as patterns of mutually indifferent elements. What we actually perceive are, first of all, specific entities such as things, figures, etc., and also groups of which these entities are members. This demonstrates the operation of processes in which the content of certain areas is unified, and at the same time relatively segregated from its environment. (p.71)

As previously mentioned, Gestalt theory originally applied to perception, but when its European proponents emigrated to the United States, they confronted the American emphasis on learning theory. Applying Gestalt ideas to learning was not difficult. In the Gestalt view, learning is a cognitive phenomenon involving perceptions of things, people, or events in a different way (Koffka, 1922, 1926). One reorganizes experiences into a different perception. Much human learning is *insightful,* which means that the transformation from ignorance to knowledge occurs rapidly. When confronted with a problem, individuals figure out what is known and what needs to be determined. They then think about possible solutions. Insight occurs when people suddenly "see" how to solve the problem.

Gestalt theorists disagreed with many assumptions of the early schools of psychology. One objection to behaviorism was that it discards consciousness. Another disagreement concerned the principle of associationism, that complex phenomena could be broken into elementary parts. In an associationist view, the whole is the sum of the parts. The Gestaltists disputed this, because they believed the whole to be meaningful and devoid of meaning when reduced to individual components. Gestalt theorists postulated the whole to be greater than the sum of its parts. In similar fashion, Gestaltists objected to the method of introspection, not because it attempted to study consciousness but because it attempted to modify perceptions to correspond to objective reality. Introspectionists tried to divorce meaning from perception, and Gestaltists believed that perception is meaningful.

Principles of Organization. Gestalt psychologists felt that people use various principles to organize their perceptions. Some of the most important principles involve figure-ground relationship, proximity, similarity, common direction, simplicity, and closure (Koffka, 1922; Kohler, 1926, 1947/1959).

The principle of the *figure-ground relationship* postulates that any perceptual field may be subdivided into a figure against a background. Such salient features as size, shape, color, and pitch distinguish a figure from its background. When figure and ground are ambiguous, perceivers may alternatively organize the sensory experience one way and then another. Figure 5.1(a) portrays an ambiguous example of the figure-ground relationship.

The principle of *proximity* states that elements in a perceptual field are viewed as belonging together according to their closeness to one another in space or time. Individuals are apt to view the lines in Figure 5.1(b) as three groups of three lines each, although other ways of perceiving this configuration are possible. This principle of proximity also is involved in individuals' perception of speech. Humans hear (organize) speech as a series of words or phrases separated with pauses. When people are unfamiliar with speech sounds (foreign languages), they have difficulty discerning pauses.

The principle of *similarity* means that elements in a perceptual field similar in such respects as size or color are viewed as belonging together. Viewing Figure 5.1(c), people tend to see a group of three short lines, followed by a group of three tall lines, and so on. Proximity can outweigh similarity; when dissimilar stimuli are closer together than similar ones (Figure 5.1[d]), the perceptual field tends to be organized into four groups of two lines each.

The principle of *common direction* implies that elements of a field appearing to constitute a pattern or flow in the same direction are perceived as a figure. The lines in Figure 5.1(e) are likely to be perceived as forming a distinct pattern. The principle of common direction also applies to an alphabetic or numeric series in which one or more rules define the order of items. The next letter in the series *abdeghjk*—is *m*, as determined by the rule: Beginning with the letter *a* and moving through the alphabet sequentially, list two letters and omit one.

The principle of *simplicity* states that people organize their perceptual fields in simple, regular features and tend to form good Gestalts comprising symmetry and regularity. This idea is captured by the German word *Pragnanz*, which roughly translated means "terseness or precision." Individuals are likely to see the visual patterns in Figure 5.1(f) as one geometrical pattern overlapping another rather than as several irregularly shaped geometric patterns.

The principle of *closure* means that people fill in incomplete patterns or experiences. Despite the missing lines in the pattern shown in Figure 5.1(g), people tend to complete the pattern and see a meaningful picture.

Productive Thinking. An important educational application of Gestalt theory was to productive thinking, or problem solving (Duncker, 1945; Lu-

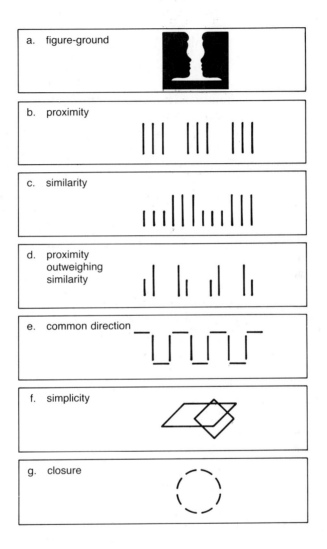

FIGURE 5.1
Examples of Gestalt principles.

chins, 1942; Wertheimer, 1945). Rote memorization is an inefficient and rarely used mode of learning in real life. People learn most things through *understanding*, that is, comprehending the meaning of some event or grasping the principle underlying task performance. Some organization exists in most facets of life, and one can use built-in organization to facilitate learning.

Research by Katona (1940) demonstrated the utility of rule learning compared with memorization. In one study, subjects were asked to learn

---

APPLICATION 5.1: Role of Understanding in Learning

Teachers want students to understand concepts rather than simply memo-rize how to complete tasks. Gestalt psychologists believed that an empha-sis on drill and practice, memorization, and reinforcement results in trivial learning and that understanding is achieved by grasping rules and principles underlying concepts and skills.

Teachers often use hands-on experiences to help students understand the structure and principles involved in learning. In biology, students might memorize what a cross-section of a bean stem looks like under a microscope, but they may have difficulty conceptualizing the structures in the living organism. Mock-ups assist student learning. A large, hands-on model of a bean stem that can be taken apart to illustrate the internal structures should enhance student understanding of the stem's composi-tion and how the parts function.

---

number sequences (e.g., 816449362516941). Some subjects learned the se-quences by rote, whereas others were given clues to aid learning (e.g., "Think of squared numbers"). Subjects who determined the rule for gen-erating the sequences retained them better than subjects who memorized by rote.

Rules lead to better learning and retention than memorization, be-cause they give a simpler description of the phenomenon; thus, there is less information to learn. In addition, rules help organize material. To recall information, one recalls the rule and then fills in the details. In contrast, memorization entails recalling more pieces of information.

Some well-known work on problem solving was done by Kohler (1926) with apes on the island of Tenerife during World War I. In one experiment, Kohler put a banana just out of reach of an ape in a cage; the ape could fetch the banana by using a long stick or by putting two sticks together. Kohler concluded that problem solving is *insightful:* Animals would survey the situation, suddenly "see" the means for attaining the goal, and test out the solution. The apes' first problem-solving attempts failed as they tried different ineffective strategies (e.g., throwing a stick at the banana). Even-tually they saw the stick as an extension of their arms and used it accordingly.

A barrier to problem solving is *functional fixedness*, or the inability to perceive different uses for objects or new configurations of elements in a situation (Duncker, 1945). In a study by Luchins (1942), subjects were given problems requiring obtaining a given amount of water using three jars of different sizes. Subjects from 9 years of age to adulthood easily learned the formula that always produced the correct amount. Intermixed in the problem set were some problems that could be solved using a simpler formula. Subjects generally continued to apply the original formula blindly. Cuing subjects that there might be an easier solution led some to discover the simpler method, although many continued to use the original formula. Thus it was shown that when students lack understanding of a phenomenon, they blindly apply a known algorithm and seem unaware that easier methods exist.

As a formal view of learning, Gestalt psychology was thought-provoking but generated little research and did not develop into a major theory. The rise of behaviorism in America led to Gestalt psychology being branded as nonobjective. Behaviorists argued that psychology involves the study of behavior, not the mind. Gestalt theory is important because it challenged the basic assumptions of early psychological theories and offered a different way of understanding behavior. Interestingly, Gestalt ideas concerning organization and meaningfulness have reemerged in current cognitive views of learning.

Verbal Learning

S-R Associations. The impetus for research on verbal learning derived from the work of Ebbinghaus (Chapter 1), who construed learning as gradual strengthening of associations between verbal stimuli (words, nonsense syllables). With repeated pairings, the response *dij* became more strongly connected with the stimulus *wek*. Other responses also could become connected with *wek* if subjects were learning a list of paired nonsense syllables, but these associations became weaker over trials.

Ebbinghaus's work showed that various factors affect the ease or speed with which one typically learns a list of items. Three important factors are meaningfulness of items, degree of similarity between them, and length of time separating study trials (Klatzky, 1980). Words (meaningful items) are learned more readily than nonsense syllables. With respect to similarity, the more alike items are to one another, the harder it is to learn them. Similarity in meaning or sound can cause confusion. A subject asked to learn several synonyms (*gigantic, huge, mammoth,* and *enormous,* among others) may fail to recall some of these but instead may recall words similar in meaning but not on the list (*large, behemoth*). With nonsense syllables, confusion occurs when the same letters are used in different positions (*xqv, khq, vhx, vkq*). The length of time separating study trials can vary from quite short (massed practice) to longer (distributed practice). When interference effects are likely (discussed below), distributed practice yields better learning (Underwood, 1961).

Learning Tasks. Verbal learning research uses three types of experimental tasks: serial learning, paired-associate learning, and free-recall learning. In *serial learning*, the subject's task is to recall the verbal stimuli in the order presented. Serial learning is involved in such school tasks as memorizing a poem or ordered procedures. Results of many serial learning studies yielded a *serial position curve* (Figure 5.2). Words at the beginning and end of the list are readily learned, whereas middle items require more trials for learning. The serial position effect may arise due to differences in distinctiveness of the various positions. People must remember not only the items themselves but also their positions in the list. The ends of a list appear to be more distinctive and are therefore "better" stimuli than the middle positions of a list.

In *paired-associate learning*, one stimulus is provided for one response item (e.g. *cat–tree, boat–roof, bench–dog*). The subject's task is to respond with the correct response upon presentation of the stimulus. There are three aspects of paired-associate learning: discrimination among the stimuli, learning the responses, and learning which responses accompany which stimuli. Debate has centered on the process by which paired-associate learning occurs and the role of cognitive mediation. Researchers originally as-

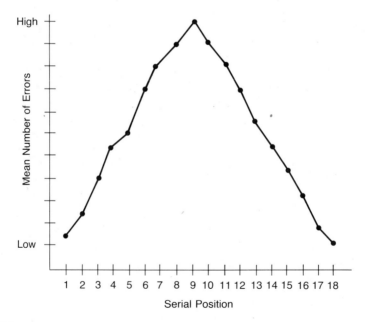

FIGURE 5.2
Serial position curve showing errors in recall as a function of item position.

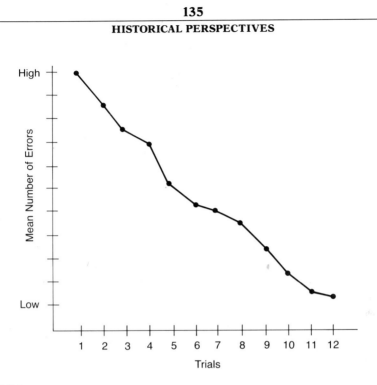

FIGURE 5.3
Learning curve showing errors as a function of study trials.

sumed learning is incremental and each S-R association is gradually strengthened. This view is supported by the typical learning curve (Figure 5.3). The number of errors subjects make is high at the beginning, but errors decrease with repeated exposures of the subjects to the list.

Work by Estes (1970) and others suggested a different perspective. Although subjects' learning of a list improves with repetition, learning of any given item has an all-or-none character: The learner either knows the correct association or does not know it. Over trials, the number of learned associations increases. A second issue involves *cognitive mediation*. Rather than simply memorizing responses, subjects often impose their organization to make material meaningful. Subjects may form cognitive mediators to link stimulus words with their responses. For the pair *cat–tree,* one might picture a cat running up a tree or think of the sentence, "The cat ran up the tree." When presented with the word *cat,* one recalls the image or sentence and responds with *tree.* Research shows that verbal learning processes are more complex than originally believed (Klatzky, 1980).

In *free-recall learning,* subjects are presented with a list of items and recall them in any order. Free recall lends itself well to subject-imposed organization to facilitate memory. It is not unusual during recall for subjects to group words presented far apart on the original list (Bower, 1970). Groupings often are based on similar meaning or membership in the same category (e.g., rocks, fruits, vegetables).

In a classic demonstration of the phenomenon of *categorial clustering*, subjects were presented with a list of 60 nouns, 15 each drawn from the following categories: animals, names, professions, and vegetables (Bousfield, 1953). Words were presented in scrambled order; however, subjects tended to recall members of the same category together. The tendency to cluster increases with the number of repetitions of the list (Bousfield & Cohen, 1953) and with longer presentation times for items (Cofer, Bruce, & Reicher, 1966). Clustering has been interpreted in associationist terms (Wood & Underwood, 1967); that is, words recalled together tend to be associated under normal conditions, either to one another directly (e.g., pear–apple) or to a third word (fruit). A cognitive explanation is that subjects learn both the words presented and the categories of which they are members (Cooper & Monk, 1976). The category names serve as mediational cues: When subjects are asked to recall, they retrieve category names and then their members. Clustering provides insight into the structure of human memory and supports the Gestalt notion that individuals organize their experiences.

Interference Theory. One of the contributions of the verbal learning tradition was the *interference theory of forgetting*. According to this theory, once associations are learned, they are never completely forgotten. Forgetting results from competing associations that lower the probability of the correct association being recalled; that is, other material becomes associated with the original stimulus (Postman, 1961; Underwood, 1957). The problem

---

APPLICATION 5.2: Interference

Proactive and retroactive interference occur often in teaching and learning. Teachers may not be able to completely eliminate interference, but they can minimize its effects by recognizing areas in the curricula that easily lend themselves to interference. For example, students learn to subtract without regrouping and then to subtract with regrouping. Teachers often find that when they give students review problems not requiring regrouping, some students erroneously regroup. To minimize interference, teachers should give students the underlying rules and principles, having them practice applying the skills in different contexts. Teachers also need to point out similarities and differences between the two types of problems and to teach students how to decide whether regrouping is necessary. Frequent review of old material also helps minimize interference.

lies in retrieving information from memory, rather than in memory itself (Crouse, 1971).

Two types of interference were experimentally identified (Table 5.1). *Retroactive interference* occurs when new verbal associations make it difficult for one to remember prior associations, whereas *proactive interference* refers to older associations that make newer learning more difficult.

To experimentally demonstrate retroactive interference, an experimenter might ask two groups of subjects to learn word list A. Group 1 then learns word list B, while group 2 engages in a competing activity to prevent rehearsal of list A. Both groups then attempt to recall list A. Retroactive interference occurs if the recall of group 2 is better than that of group 1. For proactive interference, group 1 learns list A while group 2 does nothing. Both groups then learn list B and attempt to recall list B. Proactive interference occurs if the recall of group 2 surpasses that of group 1.

Retroactive and proactive interference occur often in school. Retroactive interference is seen among students who learn words with regular spellings, then learn words that are exceptions to spelling rules. If, after some time, they are tested on the original words, they might alter the spellings to that of the exceptions. Proactive interference is evident among students taught first to multiply and then to divide fractions. When subsequently tested on division, they may simply multiply without first inverting the second fraction.

Interference theory represented an important step in specifying memory processes. As discussed in Chapter 2, early theories of learning postulated that learned connections leave a memory "trace" that weakens and decays with nonuse. Skinner did not postulate an internal memory trace

TABLE 5.1
Interference and forgetting.

	Retroactive Interference		Proactive Interference	
	Word list		**Word list**	
Task	**Group 1**	**Group 2**	**Group 1**	**Group 2**
Learn	A	A	A	—
Learn	B	—	B	B
Test	A	A	B	B

Note: Each group learns the task to some criterion of mastery. The — indicates a period of time in which the group is engaged in another task that prevents rehearsal but does not interfere with the original learning. Interference is demonstrated if Group 2 outperforms Group 1 on the test.

but suggested that forgetting results from lack of opportunity for a response to be emitted in the presence of a stimulus due to the stimulus being absent for some time. Both of these views have shortcomings. The memory trace notion is vague and difficult to verify experimentally. The nonuse position holds at times, but there are exceptions. It is not unusual for people to recall information after many years of nonuse (names of their third-grade teachers). Interference theory surmounted these problems by postulating how information in memory becomes confused with other information. It also specified a research model for investigating these processes.

Interference is not the only theory of forgetting. Postman and Stark (1969) suggested that suppression, rather than interference, could account for these types of forgetting results. Subjects participating in learning experiments hold in active memory material they believe will have to be recalled later. Subjects who learned list A and then were given list B were apt to suppress their responses to the words on list A. Such suppressions would last while subjects were learning list B and for a while thereafter. In support of this point, the typical retroactive interference paradigm produces little forgetting when subjects are given a recognition test on the original word list A rather than asked to recall the words (Klatzky, 1980).

Tulving (1974) postulated that forgetting represents inaccessibility of information due to improper retrieval cues. Information in memory does not decay nor is it confused or lost. Rather, the memory trace is intact but cannot be accessed. Memory of information depends on the trace being intact and on having adequate retrieval cues. People often cannot remember an old home phone number. They have not forgotten it; rather, the memory is submerged because their new environment is different from that of years ago and the cues associated with their old home phone number—where they lived, with whom they lived, where they worked or went to school—are absent. The principle of cue-dependent forgetting also is compatible with the common finding that subjects perform better on recognition than on recall tests. In the cue-dependent view, in recognition tests, subjects should perform better because more retrieval cues are provided; whereas in recall tests, subjects supply their own cues.

Current interference research suggests that interference occurs (e.g., people confuse elements) when the same cognitive schema or plan is used on multiple occasions (Thorndyke & Hayes-Roth, 1979; Underwood, 1983). Schemata are discussed later in this chapter and in Chapter 6 in the section on Propositions in LTM. Interference theory continues to provide a viable framework for investigating forgetting.

Verbal learning research identified the course of acquisition of verbal material and mechanisms that produce forgetting. The idea that learning of verbal material could be explained by associations was too simplistic.

This became apparent when researchers moved beyond simple list learning to more meaningful forms such as learning from text. From an educational perspective, one might question the relevance of learning lists of nonsense syllables or words paired in arbitrary fashion. In school, verbal learning occurs within meaningful contexts, for example, word pairs (e.g., state capitals, English translations of foreign words); ordered phrases and sentences (poems, songs); and meanings for vocabulary words. With the advent of information processing views of learning and memory, many of the ideas propounded by verbal learning theorists were discarded or substantially modified. Recent work by information processing researchers has addressed learning and memory of context-dependent verbal material.

INFORMATION PROCESSING SYSTEM

Assumptions

Information processing theorists challenge the idea that all learning involves the formation of associations between stimuli and responses. Although these theorists do not dismiss associationism, they focus less on external conditions and more on *internal processes,* or mental activities intervening between stimuli and responses. Learners are viewed as active seekers and processors of information. They select and attend to environmental aspects, transform and rehearse information, relate new information to previously acquired knowledge, and organize knowledge to make it meaningful.

Information processing researchers differ in their views about how learners engage in cognitive processes, but they have certain commonly held assumptions (Klatzky, 1980). One assumption is that information processing occurs in stages that intervene between receiving a stimulus and producing a response. A corollary is that the form of information, or how it is represented mentally, differs depending on the stage. The stages are *qualitatively* different from one another.

Another commonly held assumption is that human information processing is analogous to computer processing, at least metaphorically. The human system functions similar to a computer: It receives information, stores it in memory, and retrieves it as necessary. Researchers differ in how far they extend this analogy. For some, the computer analogue is nothing more than a metaphor. Other researchers employ computers to simulate activities of the human system. The field of *artificial intelligence* is concerned with programming computers to engage in such human activities as thinking, using language, and solving problems (see the section on Computer Learning in Chapter 10).

Information processing researchers also generally assume that information processing impacts all cognitive activities: perceiving, rehearsing, thinking, solving problems, remembering, forgetting, and imaging. Information processing extends beyond the domain of human learning as traditionally delineated. This chapter is concerned primarily with those information processes most germane to learning: sensory reception, encoding, and memory.

Two-Store (Dual-Memory) Model

A human information processing model is shown in Figure 5.4. This model incorporates stages of processing and closely corresponds to the model proposed by Atkinson and Shiffrin (1968, 1971).

Information processing begins when a stimulus item (e.g., visual, auditory) impinges on one or more senses (e.g., hearing, sight, touch). The *sensory register* receives the input and holds it briefly in sensory form. It is here that *pattern recognition* (or *perception*) occurs, which is the process of assigning meaning to a stimulus. This does not involve naming, because information stays in the sensory register for only a fraction of a second. Rather, pattern recognition involves equating a stimulus with known information.

The sensory register transfers information to *short-term memory* (STM). STM is a *working memory* (WM) and corresponds roughly to awareness, or what one is conscious of at a given moment. STM is limited in capacity. Miller (1956) proposed that STM holds only 7 plus or minus 2 units of

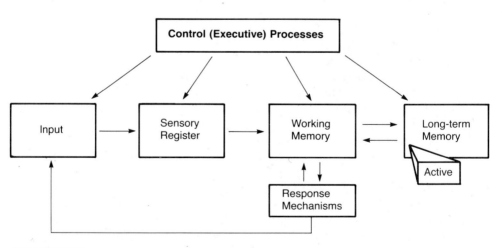

FIGURE 5.4
Information processing memory model.

information. A *unit* is a meaningful item: a letter, word, number, or common expression (e.g., "bread and butter"). STM also is limited in duration; for units to be retained in STM they must be rehearsed. Without rehearsal, information is lost after a few seconds.

While information is in STM, related knowledge in *long-term memory* (LTM), or permanent memory, is *activated* and placed in STM to be integrated with the new information. To name all the state capitals beginning with the letter *A*, students recall the names of states—perhaps by region of the country—and scan their capital names. If students do not know the capital of Maryland, once they learn "Annapolis," they can store it with "Maryland" in LTM.

There is debate over whether information ever is lost from LTM. Some researchers contend that information can be permanently lost. Other say that recall failures are due to not having good retrieval cues, rather than to forgetting. If an individual cannot recall her third-grade teacher's name (e.g., Mapleton), she might be able to recall it if someone hinted, "Think of trees." Regardless of theoretical perspective, researchers agree that information in LTM stays in the memory a long time.

Control (executive) processes regulate the flow of information throughout the information processing system. Rehearsal is an important control process that occurs in WM. For verbal material, rehearsal takes the form of repeating the information aloud or subvocally. Other control processes include coding (putting information into a meaningful context), imaging (visually representing information), implementing decision rules, organizing information, monitoring one's level of understanding, and using retrieval strategies.

The two-store model can account for many research results. One of the most consistent research findings is that when people are given a list of items to learn, they tend to recall best the initial items (*primacy effect*) and the last items (*recency effect*), as portrayed in Figure 5.2. According to the two-store model, initial items receive the most rehearsal and are transferred to LTM, whereas last items are still in WM at the time of recall. Middle items are recalled the poorest because they are no longer in WM at the time of recall (having been pushed out by subsequent items), they receive fewer rehearsals than initial items, and they are not properly stored in LTM.

One problem is that this model does not fully specify how information moves from one store to the other. The control processes notion is plausible but vague. For instance, what mechanism decides that information has been rehearsed long enough and transfers it into LTM, and how is information in LTM selected to be activated? Another concern is that this model seems best suited to handle verbal material. It is not clear how nonverbal representation occurs with material not readily verbalizable, such as a modern art painting or a well-established skill.

The model also is vague about what really is learned. Consider subjects learning word lists. With nonsense syllables, subjects have to learn the words themselves. When subjects already know the words, they must learn the positions in which the words appear; for example, the word *cat* appeared in the fourth position followed by *tree*. Subjects have to take into account their purpose in learning and modify learning strategies accordingly. What is the mechanism whereby these processes occur?

Whether all components of the system are used at all times is also an issue. For example, STM is useful when people are acquiring knowledge and need to relate incoming information to knowledge in LTM. But there are many things individuals do automatically: get dressed, walk, ride a bicycle, respond to simple requests, e.g., "Can you tell me what time it is?" For many adults, reading (decoding) and simple computations are automatic processes that place little demand on their cognitive processes. Such automatic processing may not require the operation of STM. A question, then, is how does automatic processing develop and what mechanism governs it?

These and other concerns (e.g., role of motivation in learning) do not disprove the two-store model; rather they are issues researchers need to address to show that the model represents a viable account of human learning. Although most information processing researchers accept in principle some variation of this memory model, there is an alternative conception of the information processing system—levels of processing.

Levels of Processing Model

Levels of processing conceptualizes memory according to the type rather than the location of processing that information receives (Craik, 1979; Craik & Lockhart, 1972; Craik & Tulving, 1975; Lockhart, Craik, & Jacoby, 1976). This view does not incorporate such stages or structural components as STM or LTM. Rather, there are different ways or levels of processing information: physical (surface), acoustic (phonological, sound), and semantic (meaning). These three levels are dimensional, with semantic processing being the "deepest" level. For example, suppose one is reading and the next word is *wren*. This word can be processed on a surface level (e.g., whether it is capitalized), a phonological level (rhymes with *den*), or a semantic level (small bird). Each level represents a more elaborate type of processing than the preceding level; processing the meaning of *wren* expands upon the information of the item more than acoustic processing, which expands more than surface-level processing.

These three levels seem conceptually similar to the sensory register and short- and long-term stores of the two-store model. Both views contend that processing becomes more elaborate with succeeding stages or levels. The levels of processing model, however, does not assume that the three types of processing constitute stages. In levels of processing, one does not have to move to the next process to engage in more elaborate processing; depth of processing can vary within a level. *Wren* can receive low-level semantic processing (small bird) or more extensive semantic processing (a wren's similarity to and difference from other birds, its features, etc.).

Another difference between the two information processing models concerns the *order* of processing. The two-store model assumes that information is processed in order by the sensory register, STM, and LTM. Levels of processing does not make a sequential assumption. To process at the meaning level, it is not necessary to process information at the surface and sound levels beyond that required for information to be received (Lockhart et al., 1976).

The two models also have different views of how type of processing affects memory. In levels of processing, the "deeper" the level at which an item is processed, the better the memory, because the more ingrained the memory trace. Once an item is processed at a particular point within a level, additional processing at that point should not improve memory because the memory trace will not be any deeper. In contrast, the two-store model contends that memory can be improved with additional processing of the same type. The more a list of items is rehearsed, the better it will be recalled.

There is some evidence to support levels of processing. Craik and Tulving (1975) presented subjects with words. As each word was presented, subjects were given a question to answer. The questions were designed to facilitate processing at a particular level. For surface processing subjects were asked, "Is the word in capital letters?" For phonological processing they were asked, "Does the word rhyme with *train?*" For semantic processing, "Would the word fit in the sentence, 'He met a _____ in the street'?" The time that subjects spent processing at the various levels was controlled. Subjects recalled items best when they were processed at a semantic level, next best at a phonological level, and worst at a surface level.

Levels of processing implies that greater student understanding occurs when material is processed at deeper levels. Glover, Plake, Roberts, Zimmer, and Palmere (1981) found that having students paraphrase ideas while they read essays significantly enhances recall compared with activities that do not draw on previous knowledge (e.g., identifying key words in the essays). Simple instructions to read slowly and carefully do not assist students during subsequent recall.

Despite the findings noted above, the levels of processing theory has problems. One might question whether semantic processing always is deeper than the other levels. The sounds of some words (*kaput*) are at least as distinctive as their meanings ("ruined"). In fact, recall depends not only on level of processing but also on type of recall task. Morris, Bransford, and Franks (1977) found that, given a standard recall task, semantic coding produces better results than rhyming coding; however, given a recall task emphasizing rhyming, asking rhyming questions during coding produces better recall than semantic questions. Moscovitch and Craik (1976) proposed that deeper processing during learning results in a higher potential memory performance, but whether that potential is realized depends on whether conditions at retrieval match those during learning.

Another problem with the levels of processing theory is the belief that additional processing at the same level can produce better recall. Nelson (1977) gave subjects one or two repetitions of each stimulus (word) processed at the same level. Two repetitions produced better recall, contrary to the levels of processing hypothesis. Additional research is necessary to determine whether Nelson's finding applies generally or whether the effect of number of repetitions on recall varies with aspects of the task (Jacoby, Bartz, & Evans, 1978).

A final criticism concerns the nature of a level. Investigators have argued that an objective measure of level does not exist, so it is unknown how processing at different levels affects learning and memory (Baddeley, 1978; Nelson, 1977). Time is a poor criterion of level, because some surface processing (e.g., "Does the word have the following letter pattern: consonant–vowel–consonant–consonant–vowel–consonant?") can take longer than semantic processing ("Is it a type of bird?"). Neither is processing time within a given level indicative of deeper processing (Baddeley, 1978). This criticism does not imply that levels of processing should be discarded, but it does limit its usefulness to explain human memory.

Future research might determine whether the levels approach can be combined with the two-store model to produce a refined memory model. For example, information in WM might be related to knowledge in LTM superficially or more elaborately. Also, the two separate memory stores might be found to include levels of processing within each store. Semantic coding in LTM may be seen to result in a more extensive network of information and in a more meaningful way to remember information, than surface or phonological coding.

ATTENTION AND SENSORY RECEPTION

From an information processing perspective, human learning requires attention, perception, encoding, storage, and retrieval. This section discusses the processes of attention and perception. Encoding processes are described in the next section—Memory Stores; storage and retrieval are addressed in Chapter 6.

Attention

The word *attention* is heard often in educational settings: Students do not pay attention to instructions or directions; they have a short attention span or an attention deficit disorder. These expressions describe students who do not attend to the teacher or the instructional material. Even high-achieving students do not always attend to instructionally relevant stimuli. At any point in time, individuals' senses are bombarded with sights, sounds, smells, tastes, and sensations; they cannot or need not attend to them all. People's attentional capabilities are limited; they can only attend to a few stimuli at a given moment. *Attention* is thus construed as the process of selecting some of many potential inputs.

Alternatively, *attention* can refer to a limited human resource expended to accomplish one's goals and to mobilize and maintain various cognitive processes (Grabe, 1986). Attention is not a bottleneck in the information processing system through which only so much information can pass. Rather it describes a general limitation on the entire human information processing system.

Theories of Attention. Research has explored how people select inputs for attending. Much work has been done using *dichotic listening* tasks in which subjects wear headphones and receive different messages in each ear. Subjects are asked to "shadow" one message (report what they hear). Most subjects can do this quite well. Cherry (1953) was concerned with what happened to the unattended message. He found that the subjects knew when it was present, whether it was a human voice or a noise, and when it changed from a male to a female voice. They typically did not know what the message was, what words were spoken, which language was being spoken, or whether words were repeated.

Broadbent (1958) proposed a model of attention known as *filter theory.* In this view, incoming information from the environment is held briefly in a sensory system. Based on their physical characteristics, pieces of information are selected for further processing by the perceptual system. Information not acted on by the perceptual system is filtered out, that is, not processed beyond the sensory system. Attention is selective because it lets only some messages through for further processing. In dichotic listening studies, filter theory proposes that subjects select a channel based on instructions given to them. They know only some details about the other message because the physical examination of information occurs prior to filtering.

Subsequent work by Treisman (1960, 1964) identified problems with Broadbent's filter model. Treisman found that during dichotic listening experiments subjects routinely shift their attention between ears depending on the location of the message they are shadowing. If subjects are shadowing the message coming into their left ear, and if the message suddenly shifts to the right ear, they continue to shadow the original message and not the new message coming into the left ear. Selective attention depends not only on the physical location of the stimulus but also on its meaning. Treisman proposed that attention, rather than blocking out messages, simply turns them down to make them less salient than those being attended to. Information inputs initially were subjected to different tests for physical characteristics and content. Following this preliminary analysis, one input was selected for attention.

Treisman's model is problematic in that much analysis must precede attending to an input, which is puzzling because presumably the original analysis involves some attention. To circumvent this problem, Norman (1976) proposed that all inputs are attended to in sufficient fashion to activate a portion of LTM. At that point, one input is selected for further attention based on the degree of activation, which depends on the context. An input is more likely to be attended to if it fits into the context established by prior inputs. While people read, for example, many outside stimuli impinge on their sensory system, yet they attend to the printed symbols.

For Norman, then, stimuli activate portions of LTM, but attention involves more complete activation. Neisser (1967) suggested that *preattentive processes* are involved in head and eye movements (e.g., refocusing attention) and in guided movements (walking, driving). Preattentive processes are automatic—people implement them without conscious mediation. In contrast, attentional processes are deliberate and require conscious activity. Recent research (Chapter 7) shows that much cognitive skill processing becomes automatic. Distinguishing preattentive from attentional processes fits well with the automaticity notion.

Attention and Learning. Attention is a necessary prerequisite of learning. In learning to distinguish letters, a child learns the distinctive features: To distinguish *b* from *d*, students must attend to the position of the vertical line on the left or right side of the circle, not to the mere presence of a circle. To learn from the teacher, students must attend to the teacher's voice and ignore other sounds. To develop reading comprehension skills, students must attend to the printed words and ignore such irrelevancies as page size and color.

As skills become routinized, information processing requires less conscious attention. In learning to work multiplication problems, students must carefully attend to each step in the process and check their compu-

---

APPLICATION 5.3:
Focusing and Maintaining Student Attention

Various practices help keep classrooms from becoming too predictable and repetitive, which decreases attention. Teachers can vary their presentations, materials used, student activities, and such personal qualities as dress and mannerisms. Lesson formats for young children especially should be kept short. Teachers can keep a high level of activity through student involvement and by moving about to check on student progress.

Teachers might include the following activities in a language arts lesson. As students begin each section of a teacher-directed exercise, they can point to the location on their papers or in their book. The way sections are introduced can be varied: Students can read together in small groups, individual students can read and be called on to explain, or the teacher can introduce the section. The way students' answers are checked also can be varied: Students can use hand signals or respond in unison, or individual students can answer and explain their answers. As students independently complete the exercise, the teacher should move about the room checking progress and assisting those having difficulty learning or maintaining task focus.

---

tations. Once students learn multiplication tables and the algorithm, working problems becomes automatic. Such automatic processing is triggered by the input of information.

Differences in the ability to control attention are associated with student age, hyperactivity, intelligence, and learning disabilities (Grabe, 1986). Attentional deficits notably are associated with learning problems. Hyperactive students, for example, are characterized by excessive motor activity, distractibility, and low academic achievement. They have difficulty focusing and sustaining attention on academic material. They may be unable to effectively block out irrelevant stimuli, which overloads their processing systems. The primary task may be lost among competing stimuli. Sustaining attention over time requires that students work in a strategic manner and monitor their level of understanding.

Teachers can spot attentive students by noting their eye focus, their ability to begin working on cue (after directions are completed), and physical signs (e.g., handwriting) indicating they are engaged in work (Good & Brophy, 1984). Physical signs alone may not be sufficient; strict teachers can keep students sitting quietly even though students may not be engaged in class work.

Teachers can assist student attention in the design of classroom activities. Eye-catching displays or actions at the start of lessons draw student attention. Teachers who move around the classroom—especially when students are engaged in seatwork—help sustain student attention on the task. Other suggestions for focusing and maintaining student attention are the following:

Signals	Signal to students at the start of lessons or when they are to change activities.
Movement	Move while presenting material to the whole class. Move around the room while students are engaged in seatwork.
Variety	Use different materials and teaching aids. Use gestures. Do not speak in a monotone.
Interest	Introduce lessons with stimulating material. Appeal to students' interests at other times during the lesson.
Questions	Ask students to explain a point in their own words. Stress that they are responsible for their own learning.

Attention and Reading. A consistent research finding is that students are more likely to recall important text elements than less important ones (R. Anderson, 1982; Grabe, 1986). Good and poor readers locate important material and attend to it for longer periods (Ramsel & Grabe, 1983; Reynolds & Anderson, 1982). What distinguishes these readers is not attention control but rather subsequent processing and comprehension. Perhaps poor readers, being more preoccupied with basic reading tasks (e.g., decoding), become distracted from important material and do not process it adequately for retention and retrieval. Research has not established what good and poor readers do while attending to important material, though it may be that good readers relate the information to what they know, make it meaningful, and rehearse it, all of which improve comprehension (Resnick, 1981).

Research suggests that the importance of text material affects subsequent recall through differential attention (R. Anderson, 1982). Text elements apparently are processed to some minimal level so importance can be assessed. Based on this evaluation, the text element either is dismissed in favor of the next element (unimportant information) or receives additional attention (important information). Comprehension suffers when students do not pay adequate attention. Assuming attention is sufficient, the actual types of processing students engage in must differ to account for subsequent comprehension differences. Better readers may engage in much automatic processing initially and attend to information deemed important, whereas poorer readers might engage in automatic processing less often.

Perception

Perception, or *pattern recognition*, refers to the meaning attached to environmental inputs received through the senses. For an input to be perceived, it must be held in a sensory register and compared with knowledge in LTM.

Sensory Registers. Environmental inputs are received through the senses: vision, hearing, touch, smell, and taste. Each sense has its own register in which information is briefly held in the same form in which it is received; that is, visual information is held in visual form, auditory information in auditory form, and so on. Information stays in the sensory register for only a fraction of a second. Some sensory input is transferred to WM for further processing. Other input is erased and replaced by new input. The sensory organs are the only components of the information processing system that operate in parallel fashion, because several senses can be engaged simultaneously and independently of one another. The two sensory memories that have been most extensively explored are the *icon* (vision) and the *echo* (hearing) (Neisser, 1967).

In a typical experiment to investigate iconic memory, subjects are presented with rows of letters briefly (e.g., 50 milliseconds) and report as many as they remember. Subjects commonly report only 4 to 5 letters from an array. Early work provides insight into iconic storage (Sperling, 1960). Sperling presented subjects with rows of letters, after which they were cued to report letters from a particular row. Sperling estimated that, after exposure to the array, subjects actually could recall about 9 letters. Sensory memory could hold more information than was previously believed, but while subjects were recalling letters, the traces of other letters quickly faded. Sperling also found that recall varied inversely with length of time between the end of a presentation of the array and the beginning of recall: The longer the interval, the poorer the recall, which supports the trace decay idea. Trace decay refers to the loss of a stimulus from a sensory register.

Whether the icon is actually a memory store or a persisting image is debated. Sakitt argues that the icon is located in the rods of the eye's retina (Sakitt, 1976; Sakitt & Long, 1979). The active role of the icon in perception is diminished (but not eliminated) if the icon is a physical structure. Many researchers do not agree with Sakitt's position, and further research is necessary.

There is evidence for an auditory structure (echo) similar in function to the icon. Experiments by Darwin, Turvey, and Crowder (1972) and by Moray, Bates, and Barnett (1965) yielded results comparable to Sperling's (1960). Subjects heard three or four sets of recordings simultaneously and then were asked to report one. Findings showed that the echo is capable of holding more information than can be recalled. Similar to iconic information, traces of echoic information rapidly decay following removal of stimuli. The echoic decay does not seem to be quite as rapid as the iconic, but periods beyond 2 seconds between cessation of stimulus presentation and onset of recall produce poorer recall.

LTM Comparisons. Perception depends on objective characteristics and prior experiences. Environmental inputs have tangible physical properties.

Assuming normal color vision, everyone who looks at an orange golf ball will recognize it as an orange object, but only those familiar with golf will recognize it as a golf ball. The variety of information people have acquired accounts for the different meanings they assign to objects.

Perception also is affected by people's expectations. They perceive the expected and fail to perceive the unexpected. Most individuals have had the experience of hearing their name spoken, only to realize that another name was being called. For instance, while waiting to meet a friend at a public place or to pick up an order in a restaurant, people hear their name because they expect to hear it. Also, people may not perceive things whose appearance has changed or which occur out of context. For example, people may not recognize co-workers they meet by chance on the beach, because they do not expect to see them away from the work place.

Many of the concepts embodied in Gestalt theory are relevant to our perceptions; however, Gestalt principles are quite general and do not address the actual mechanisms of perception. To say that individuals perceive similar items as belonging together does not explain how they perceive items as similar in the first place. Gestalt principles are illuminating but not explanatory.

An early theory of perception was *template matching*. In this view, people store templates, or miniature copies of stimuli, in LTM. When they encounter a stimulus, they compare it with existing templates and identify the stimulus if a match is found. This view is appealing but problematic. People would have to carry around millions of templates in their heads to be able to recognize all their actions. Such a large stock would exceed the human brain's capability. Template theory also has difficulty accounting for stimulus variations. Chairs, for example, come in all sizes, shapes, colors, and designs; hundreds or thousands of templates would be needed just to perceive a chair.

The problems concerning templates can be solved by assuming that templates can have some variation. *Prototypes* are abstract forms that include the basic ingredients of stimuli (Klatzky, 1980). Prototypes are stored in LTM and are compared with encountered stimuli that are subsequently identified based on the prototype they match or resemble in form, smell, sound, and so on. Some research supports the existence of prototypes (Franks & Bransford, 1971; Posner & Keele, 1968).

A major advantage of prototypes over templates is that one carries around only one prototype for each stimulus instead of countless variations; thus, identification of a stimulus should be easier because it is not necessary to compare it with several templates. One concern with prototypes deals with the amount of acceptable variability of the stimuli, i.e., how closely a stimulus must match a prototype to be identified as an instance of that prototype.

A variation of the prototype model involves *feature analysis* (Klatzky, 1980). In this view, one learns the critical features of stimuli and stores them in LTM as images or verbal codes. When a stimulus enters the sensory register, its features are compared with memorial representations. If enough of the features match, the stimulus is identified. For a chair, the critical features may be legs, seat, and a back. Many other features (e.g., color, size) are irrelevant. Any exceptions to the basic features need to be learned (e.g., football-game chairs, which rest on bleachers and have no legs). Unlike the prototype analysis, information stored in memory is not an abstract representation of a chair but rather of its critical features. One advantage of feature analysis is that there is not one prototype for each stimulus, which partially addresses the concern about the amount of acceptable variability. There is some empirical support for feature analysis, and future research is likely to clarify this process (Klatzky, 1980).

Regardless of how LTM comparisons are made, research shows that pattern recognition proceeds in two fashions: bottom-up and top-down processing. (Anderson, 1980; Bobrow & Norman, 1975; Lindsay & Norman, 1977; Resnick, 1985). *Bottom-up processing* analyzes features and builds a meaningful representation to identify stimuli. Beginning readers typically use bottom-up processing when they encounter letters and new words and attempt to sound them out. People also use bottom-up processing when experiencing unfamiliar stimuli (e.g., someone else's handwriting).

Perception would proceed very slowly if the memory always analyzed features in detail. In top-down processing, individuals develop expectations regarding perception based on the context. Once they become familiar with situations, they anticipate events and perceive in accordance with those. Skilled readers build a mental representation of the context while reading and expect certain words and phrases in the text (Resnick, 1985). The earlier example of people erroneously hearing their name called (because they expect to hear it) and not recognizing co-workers (because they did not expect to see them) are instances of top-down processing. Effective top-down processing depends on extensive prior knowledge.

MEMORY STORES

Short-Term Memory

Once a stimulus is attended to and perceived, the input is transferred to short-term memory (STM), or working memory (WM). STM (WM) is our immediate consciousness. Incoming information is stored for a short time and is worked on by being rehearsed or related to information activated in LTM. As students read a text, WM holds for a few seconds the last few words or sentences they read. Students might try to remember a particular point by repeating it several times (rehearsal) or by asking how it relates to a topic discussed earlier in the book (relate to information in LTM). As another example, assume that a student is multiplying 45 by 7. WM holds these numbers (45 and 7), along with the product of 5 and 7 (35), the number carried (3), and the answer (315). The information in WM ($5 \times 7 = $?) is compared with activated knowledge in LTM ($5 \times 7 = 35$). Also activated in LTM is the multiplication algorithm, and these procedures direct the student's actions.

Research has provided a reasonably detailed picture of the operation of WM. WM is severely limited in *duration:* If not acted upon quickly, information in WM decays. In a classic study (Peterson & Peterson, 1959), subjects were presented with a nonsense syllable (e.g., *khv*), after which they performed an arithmetic task before attempting to recall the syllable. The purpose of the arithmetic task was to prevent subjects from rehearsing the syllable, but because the numbers did not have to be stored, they did not interfere with storage of the syllable in WM. The longer subjects spent on the distracting activity, the poorer was their recall of the nonsense syllable. These findings imply a fragile WM; information is quickly lost if not learned well. If, for example, people are given a phone number to call but then are distracted before being able to dial it or write it down, they cannot recall it.

WM is also limited in *capacity:* It can hold only a small amount of information. Miller (1956) suggested that the capacity of WM is 7 items plus or minus 2 items, where items are such meaningful units as words, letters, numbers, and common expressions. One can increase the amount of information by *chunking,* or combining information in a meaningful fashion. The phone number 555-1952 consists of 7 items, but it can easily be chunked to 2 as follows: "Triple 5 plus the year Eisenhower was elected President."

Sternberg's (1969) research on *memory scanning* provides insight into how information is retrieved from WM. Subjects were presented rapidly with a small number of digits not exceeding the capacity of WM. They then were given a test digit and were asked whether it was in the original set of digits. Because the learning was easy, subjects rarely made errors, so the reaction time was tested. As the original set increased from two to six items, the time to respond increased about 40 milliseconds per additional item. Sternberg concluded that people retrieve information from active memory by successively scanning items.

Control (executive) processes, as previously mentioned, direct the processing of information in WM, as well as the movement of knowledge into and out of WM. Control processes include rehearsal, predicting, checking, and monitoring. Control processes are goal directed; they select information relevant to people's plans and intentions from the various sensory receptors. Information deemed important is rehearsed. *Rehearsal,* or repeating information to oneself (aloud or subvocally), can maintain information in WM indefinitely. Not surprisingly, rehearsal improves recall (Rundus, 1971; Rundus & Atkinson, 1970).

Environmental or self-generated cues activate a portion of LTM, which then is more accessible to WM. The working (active) memory holds a representation of events occurring recently, such as a description of the context and the content. There is debate whether active memory constitutes a separate memory store or merely an activated portion of LTM (Calfee, 1981).

Long-Term Memory

Research in recent years has shown that knowledge representation in LTM depends on frequency and contiguity (Calfee, 1981). The more often an idea is encountered, the stronger its representation in memory. Further, two experiences that occur closely in time are apt to be linked in memory, so that when one is remembered the other also is activated. Thus information in LTM is represented in *associative structures*.

Information processing models often use computers for analogies, but there are some important differences, as highlighted by associative structures. Human memory is *content addressable:* Information on the same topic is stored together, so that knowing what is being looked for will likely lead to recalling the information (Calfee, 1981). In contrast, computers are *location addressable:* Computers have to be told where information is stored. The nearness of one program or data set on a disk to others on the same disk is purely arbitrary. Another difference is that information is stored precisely in computers. Human memory is less precise but often more colorful or informative. The name Daryl Crancake stored in a computer's memory stays there in the same form. The same name stored in human memory may stay there in the same form or become distorted. For instance, Daryl might become Darrell, Darel, or Derol, and Crancake might change to Cupcake, Cranberry, or Crabapple.

A useful analogy for the human mind is a library. Information in a library is content addressable in that books on similar content are stored under similar call numbers. Information in the mind (as in the library) is also *cross-referenced* (Calfee, 1981). Knowledge that cuts across different content areas can be accessed through either area. For example, a person may have a memory slot devoted to his twenty-first birthday. The memory includes what he did, who he was with, and what gifts he received. These topics can be cross-referenced as follows: the jazz tapes he received as gifts are cross-referenced in the memory slot dealing with music. The fact that his next-door neighbor attended is filed in the memory slot devoted to the neighbor and neighborhood.

Knowledge stored in LTM varies in its richness. Each person has vivid memories of pleasant and unpleasant experiences. These memories can be exact in their details covering who, what, where, and when. Other types of knowledge stored in memories are mundane and impersonal: word meanings, arithmetic operations, and excerpts from famous documents.

To account for the differences in memory, Tulving (1972, 1983) proposed a distinction between episodic and semantic memory. *Episodic memory* includes information associated with particular times and places that is personal and autobiographical. The fact that the word *cat* occurs in position three on a learned word list is an example of episodic information, as is information about what a person did on his twenty-first birthday and which night this week Joe called. *Semantic memory* involves general information and concepts available in the environment and not tied to a particular context. Examples include the words to the "Star Spangled Banner" and the chemical formula for water (H_2O). The knowledge, skills, and concepts learned in school are semantic memories. The two types of memories often are combined, as when a child tells a parent, "Today I learned [episodic memory] that Columbus discovered America in 1492 [semantic memory]."

Another important issue concerns the form or structure in which knowledge is stored in LTM. Paivio (1971) proposed that knowledge is stored in verbal and visual form, each of which is functionally independent though interconnected. Concrete objects—dog, tree, book—tend to be stored as images, whereas abstract concepts—love, truth, honesty—and linguistic structures are stored in verbal codes. It is possible for knowledge to be stored both visually and verbally: One can have a pictorial representation of one's house and also can describe it verbally. Paivio postulated that for any piece of knowledge, an individual has a preferred storage mode activated more readily than the other. Dual-coded knowledge may be remembered better, which confirms the general teaching principle of explaining (verbal) and demonstrating (visual) new material.

Paivio's work is discussed further in the section on Mental Imagery in Chapter 6. Paivio's views have been criticized on the grounds that a visual memory exceeds the brain's capacity and requires some brain mechanism to read and translate the pictures (Pylyshyn, 1973). Some theorists contend that knowledge is stored only in verbal codes (J. Anderson, 1976, 1980; Collins & Quillian, 1969; Newell & Simon, 1972; Norman & Rumelhart, 1975; Quillian, 1969). Verbal models do not deny that knowledge can be represented pictorially but postulate that the ultimate code is verbal and that pictures in memory are reconstructed from verbal codes. Some characteristics and distinctions of memory systems are as follows:

Type of Memory	Characteristics
Short-term	Limited capacity (about seven items), short duration (in absence of rehearsal), and immediate consciousness

MEMORY STORES

Long-term	Theoretically unlimited capacity, permanent storage, and information activated when cued
Episodic	Information in long-term memory associated with particular events, times, and places
Semantic	Information in long-term memory involving general knowledge and concepts; not tied to specific contexts
Verbal	Propositions (units of information) and procedures coded verbally
Visual	Information in pictures, images, and scenes

The associative structures of LTM are *propositional networks,* or interconnected sets comprising nodes or bits of information (Anderson, 1990; Calfee, 1981). A proposition is the smallest unit of information that can be judged true or false. The statement "My 80-year-old uncle lit his awful cigar," consists of the following propositions:

- I have an uncle.
- He is 80 years old.
- He lit a cigar.
- The cigar is awful.

Various types of propositional knowledge are represented in LTM. *Declarative knowledge* refers to facts, subjective beliefs, scripts (e.g., events of a story), and organized passages (e.g., Declaration of Independence). *Procedural knowledge* consists of concepts, rules, and algorithms. *Conditional knowledge* is knowing when to employ forms of declarative and procedural knowledge and why it is beneficial to do so (R. Gagné, 1985; Paris et al., 1983).

Response Mechanisms. Learning can occur in the absence of overt behavior because learning involves the formation or modification of propositional networks; however, overt performance typically is required from students to ensure they have acquired skills. Research on skilled actions shows that people typically execute behaviors according to a sequence of planned segments (Bilodeau, 1966; Fitts & Posner, 1967). Individuals select a performance routine they expect will produce the desired outcome, periodically monitor their performances, make corrections as necessary, and alter their performances following corrective feedback. Since individuals' performances often need to vary to fit contextual demands, they find it helpful to practice adapting skills in different contextual situations. Although these points derive from work on motor skills, they also seem applicable to cognitive skills.

Transfer refers to the links between propositions in memory and depends on information being cross-referenced or the uses of information being stored with it. Students understand that skills and concepts are applicable in different domains if that knowledge is stored in the respective networks. Teaching students how information is applicable in different contexts ensures that appropriate transfer occurs.

INFLUENCES ON ENCODING

Encoding is the process of putting new (incoming) information into the information processing system and preparing it for storage in LTM. Encoding usually is accomplished by making new information meaningful and integrating it with known information in LTM. It should be noted that information does not have to be meaningful to be learned; one unfamiliar with geometry could memorize the Pythagorean theorem without knowing its meaning. Meaningfulness does, however, improve learning and retention.

Simply attending to and perceiving stimuli does not ensure that information processing will continue. Many things teachers say in class go unlearned—even though students attend to the teacher and the words are meaningful—because students do not continue to process the information. Important factors that influence encoding are organization, elaboration, and schema structures.

Organization

Gestalt theory and research showed that well-organized material is easier to learn and recall (Katona, 1940). Miller (1956) argued that learning is enhanced by classifying and grouping bits of information into organized chunks. Memory research demonstrates that even when items to be learned are not organized, subjects often impose organization on the material, which facilitates recall (Klatzky, 1980). Organized material improves memory because items are linked to one another systematically. Recall of one item prompts recall of items linked to it.

One way to organize material is to use a hierarchy into which pieces of information are integrated. A sample hierarchy for animals is shown in Figure 5.5. The animal kingdom as a whole is on top, and underneath are the major categories (e.g., mammals, birds, reptiles). Individual species are found on the next level, followed by breeds.

Other ways of organizing information include the use of mnemonic devices (see the discussion in section on Information Processing Theory in Chapter 9) and mental imagery (see Chapter 6). *Mnemonic devices* enable learners to enrich or elaborate material; for example, by forming the first letters of words to be learned into an acronym, familiar phrase, or sentence. Some mnemonic techniques employ imagery; in remembering two words, one might imagine them interacting with each other. The educational im-

INFLUENCES ON ENCODING

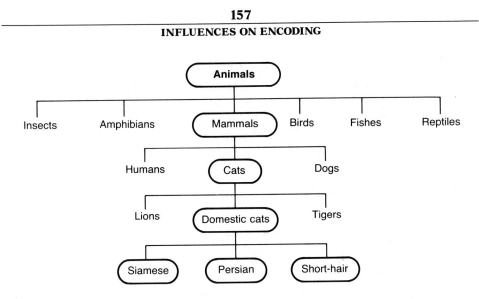

FIGURE 5.5
Memory network with hierarchical organization.

plications are to use audiovisuals in instruction and teach students to use imagery and mnemonic devices.

Elaboration

Elaboration is the process of expanding upon new information by adding to it or linking it to what one knows. Elaborations assist encoding and retrieval because they link the to-be-remembered information with other knowledge. Newly learned information is easier to access in this expanded memory network. Even when the new information is forgotten, people often can recall the elaborations (Anderson, 1990).

Rehearsing information keeps it in WM but does not elaborate it. People can distinguish *maintenance rehearsal* (repeating information over and over) from *elaborative rehearsal* (relating the information to something already known). Students learning American history can simply repeat the idea that D-day was June 6, 1944, or they can elaborate it by relating it to something they know (e.g., the same year that Roosevelt was elected President for the fourth time).

Mnemonic devices elaborate information in different ways. Once such device is to form the first letters into a meaningful sentence. For example, to remember the order of the planets one might learn the sentence, "My very educated mother just served us nine pizzas," in which the first letters correspond to those of the planets (Mercury, Venus, Earth, Mars, Jupiter, Saturn, Uranus, Neptune, Pluto). During recall, students first recall the sentence and then reconstruct the order based on the first letters.

Students may be able to devise elaborations, but there is no need for them to labor endlessly when teachers can provide effective elaborations. To assist storage in memory and retrieval, elaborations must make sense. Elaborations that are too unusual may not be remembered. Precise and sensible elaborations facilitate memory and recall (Bransford et al., 1982; Stein, Littlefield, Bransford, & Persampieri, 1984).

Schemata

A *schema* is a structure that organizes large amounts of information into a meaningful system. Larger units are needed to organize propositions representing bits of information into a coherent whole (Anderson, 1990). A schema is a stereotype specifying a standard pattern or sequence of steps associated with a particular concept, skill, or event (Rumelhart & Ortony, 1977). Schemata are types of plans we learn and use during our environmental interactions.

In an early study, Bartlett (1932) found that schemata aid the comprehension of information. A subject read a story about an unfamiliar culture, after which the subject attempted to reproduce the story for a second subject. The second subject reproduced the story for a third subject, and so on. By the time the story reached the tenth subject, its unfamiliar context had been changed to one subjects were familiar with (e.g., a fishing trip). Bartlett found that as stories were repeated they changed in predictable ways. Unfamiliar information was dropped, a few details were retained, and the stories became more like the subjects' experiences. Incoming information was altered to fit subjects' preexisting schemata.

Any well-ordered sequence can be represented as a schema. One type of schema is "going to a restaurant." The steps consist of such activities as being seated at a table, looking over a menu, ordering food, being served by a waiter or waitress, not cleaning up the dishes, receiving a bill, leaving a tip, and paying the bill. Schemata are important because they indicate what to expect in a situation. People recognize a problem when reality and the schema do not match. Most people have had the experience of being in a restaurant where one of the expected steps does not occur, e.g., the waiter or waitress brings them a menu but never returns to take their order.

Common educational schemata involve laboratory procedures, studying, and comprehending stories. When given material to read, students activate the type of schema they believe is required. If students are to read a passage and answer questions about main ideas, they may periodically stop and quiz themselves on what they believe are the main points (Resnick, 1985).

Schemata assist encoding because they elaborate new material into a meaningful structure. Using a schema highlights important information.

APPLICATION 5.4: Schema Structures

Teachers can increase learning by helping students develop schemata. A schema is especially helpful when learning can occur by applying an ordered sequence of steps. Instructors might teach the following schema to young children to assist their reading of unfamiliar words: (1) Read the word in the sentence to see what might make sense. (2) Look at the beginning and ending letters of the word; it is easier to read the beginning or ending than the whole word. (3) Think of words that would make sense in the sentence and that would have the same beginning and ending. (4) Sound out all the letters in the word. (5) If these steps do not help identify the word, look the word up in a dictionary. (With slight modifications, this schema for figuring out new words can be used by students of any age.)

When learning material, students attempt to fit information into the schema's spaces. Less important or optional schema elements may or may not be learned. In reading works of literature, students who have formed the schema for a tragedy can easily fit the characters and actions of the story into the schema. They expect to find such elements as the struggle of good against evil, human frailties, and a dramatic ending. When these events occur, they are not surprising but rather are fit into the conceptual framework students have activated for the story.

Schemata may facilitate recall independently of their encoding effects. Anderson and Pichert (1978) presented college students with a story about two boys skipping school. Subjects were advised to read it from the perspective of either a burglar or a homebuyer; the story had elements relevant to both. Subjects recalled the story and later recalled it a second time. For the second recall, half of the subjects were advised to use their original perspective and the other half the other perspective. On the second recall, subjects recalled more information relevant to the second perspective but not to the first perspective and less information unimportant to the second perspective that was important to the first perspective. Kardash, Royer, and Greene (1988) also found that schemata exerted their primary benefits at the time of recall rather than at encoding. Collectively, these results suggest that at retrieval, people recall a schema and attempt to fit elements into it. This reconstruction may not be accurate but will include most schema elements.

SUMMARY

Information processing theories focus on attention, perception, encoding, storage, and retrieval of knowledge. These theories explain learning in terms of internal events, specifically, the movement and transformation of information through the processing system. Gestalt psychology and research on verbal learning were important precursors of information processing. Gestalt psychologists believed that perception is subjective and that learning involves perceiving things and events in a different way. They also saw perception as influenced by such laws as proximity, similarity, and common direction. Gestalt psychologists objected to the molecular focus of behaviorists on discrete behaviors; rather, they felt that learning depends on perceiving meaningful wholes and patterns. Learning often occurs suddenly through insight, and people learn best when some degree of organization is present.

Verbal learning research identified the course of acquisition of verbal material, along with ways that interference causes forgetting. Learning tasks are serial learning, paired-associate learning, and free-recall learning. Free-recall studies showed that organization improves recall and that people impose their own organization when none is present.

In information processing theories, information enters through the sensory registers. Although there is a register for each system, most research has been conducted on the icon (visual) and echo (auditory) registers. At any one time, only a limited amount of information can be attended to. It is unknown whether attention acts as a filter or a general limitation on capacity of the human system. Inputs attended to are perceived by being compared with information in LTM.

Information in STM is rehearsed and encoded for storage in LTM. Encoding is facilitated through organization, elaboration, and preexisting schema structures. LTM is organized by content, and information is cross-referenced with related content. Control processes monitor and direct the flow of information through the system.

Learning is facilitated by making new information more meaningful to learners and relating it to what students know. Meaningfulness integrates information into the appropriate LTM schema. Transfer of learning is facilitated when students are shown how knowledge is useful in different contexts, which creates links between LTM networks.

Chapter 6

Knowledge Acquisition and Representation

The preceding chapter presented a simple characterization of the long-term memory (LTM) and its structure. Knowledge is represented in LTM as locations or nodes in networks, and the networks are connected or associated with one another. This chapter expands on this view by considering (1) the integration of knowledge into networks, (2) the linking of networks, and (3) the retrieval of knowledge from memory.

When discussing networks, we deal primarily with *declarative knowledge* (knowing facts, beliefs, things, and events). In this chapter, we also discuss *procedural knowledge* (knowing how to perform cognitive activities), *conditional knowledge* (knowing when to employ forms of declarative and procedural knowledge and why it is important to do so), and *metacognitive activities* (those that monitor and direct one's cognitive processing). It is assumed that knowledge is stored in LTM in verbal codes, but we also address the role of *imagery*. A point to keep in mind is that the human information processing system is complex; researchers have only tapped the surface and new research findings are continually updating our views on LTM. We can expect exciting new developments in the coming years, which will have important implications for teaching and learning.

PROPOSITIONS IN LTM

Nature of Propositions

Propositions form *networks*, which are composed of individual *nodes* or *locations*. Nodes can be thought of as individual words, although their exact

161

nature is unknown but very probably abstract. For example, students taking a history class very likely have a "history class" network comprising such nodes as "book," "teacher," "location," "name of student who sits on their left," and so forth.

Individual nodes are important because they are combined to express meaning. The basic units of knowledge and meaning in LTM are *propositions* (Kosslyn, 1984; Norman & Rumelhart, 1975). Each of the following is a proposition:

- The Declaration of Independence was signed in 1776.
- 2 + 2 = 4.
- Aunt Frieda hates turnips.
- I'm good in math.
- The main characters are introduced early in a story.

As with nodes, the exact nature of propositions is not well understood. In a loose sense, a proposition can be thought of as a sentence. According to J. Anderson (1976, 1990), however, propositions are not actually sentences but rather the meanings of those sentences. Research supports the point that we store information in memory as propositions rather than as complete sentences. Kintsch (1974) gave subjects sentences to read that were of the same length but varied in the number of propositions they contained. The more propositions contained in a sentence, the longer it took subjects to comprehend it. This implies that, although students can generate the sentence, "The Declaration of Independence was signed in 1776," what they likely have stored in memory is a proposition containing only the essential information (Declaration of Independence—signed—1776). There are exceptions (memorizing a poem), but in general it seems that people store meanings rather than precise wordings.

A *proposition* may be defined as the smallest unit of information that can be judged true or false. Each of the sample propositions above can be judged true or false. Note, however, that people may disagree on their judgments. I may judge the statement, "I'm good in math," as true and have it stored in memory, but my teacher may judge it as false and have the opposite stored in his memory.

Propositional Networks

Propositions are formed according to a set of rules. Researchers disagree on which rules constitute the set, but there is general agreement that rules combine nodes into propositions and, in turn, propositions into higher-order structures or *networks*, which are sets of interrelated propositions.

Anderson's ACT* model (J. Anderson, 1976) is an example of a network model of LTM with a propositional structure. A proposition is formed by combining two nodes with a *subject-predicate* link or association; one node constitutes the subject and another node the predicate. Examples are (implied information): "Fred (is) rich" and "Shopping (takes) time." A second type of association is the *relation-argument* link, the relation being a verb (in meaning) and the argument the recipient of the relation or what is affected by the relation. Examples are "eat cake" and "solve puzzles." Relation-arguments can serve as subjects or predicates to form complex propositions. Examples are "Fred eat(s) cake" and "solv(ing) puzzles (takes) time."

Propositions are interrelated when they share a common element. Common elements allow people to solve problems, cope with environmental demands, draw analogies, and so on. If there were no common elements, all knowledge would be stored separately and information processing would occur slowly. One would simply not "recognize" that knowledge relevant to one domain is also relevant to other domains.

An example of a propositional network is shown in Figure 6.1. The common element is *"cat,"* because it is part of the propositions, "The cat walked across the front lawn" and "The cat caught a mouse." One can imagine that the former proposition is linked with other propositions relating to one's house, whereas the latter is linked with propositions about mice.

Propositions are organized in hierarchical structures. Collins and Quillian (1969) showed that people store information at the highest level of generality. For example, the LTM network for "animal" would have stored at the highest level such facts as "moves" and "eats." Under this category would come such species as "birds" and "fish." Stored under "birds" are "has wings," "can fly," and "has feathers." The fact that birds eat and move is not stored at the level of bird because that information already has been stored at the higher level of animal. Collins and Quillian found that retrieval

Propositions:

"The cat walked across the front lawn."
"The cat caught a mouse."

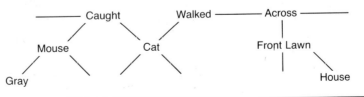

FIGURE 6.1
Sample propositional network.

times increased the farther apart concepts were stored in memory. The hierarchical organization idea has been modified somewhat by recent research showing that familiar information may be stored both with its concept and at the highest level of generality (Anderson, 1990). If you have a bird feeder and you often watch birds eating, you might have "eats" stored with both "birds" and "animal." This finding does not detract from the central idea that propositions are organized and interconnected.

Acquisition of Declarative Knowledge

Declarative knowledge is knowing *that* something is the case (Paris et al., 1983) and includes facts, beliefs, opinions, generalizations, theories, hypotheses, and attitudes. In short, it is knowledge of oneself, others, and world events, and it is measured by recall or by verifying information.

Declarative knowledge is acquired when a new proposition is stored in LTM, usually with related propositions in a network (J. Anderson, 1976, 1990). The basic process operates as follows. First, new information is presented to the learner, as when the teacher makes a statement or the learner reads a sentence in a book. Next, the new information is translated into one or more propositions in the learner's short-term memory (STM) or working memory (WM). At the same time, related propositions in LTM are cued. The new propositions are associated with the related propositions in WM; in the process, learners might generate additional propositions. Finally, all the new propositions—those presented and those generated by the learner—are stored together in LTM (Hayes-Roth & Thorndyke, 1979).

This process is illustrated in Figure 6.2. Assume that a teacher is presenting a unit on the U.S. Constitution and says to the class, "The Vice President of the United States serves as President of the Senate but does not vote unless there is a tie." This statement may cue other propositional knowledge stored in students' memories relating to the Vice President (e.g., elected with the President, becomes President when the President dies or leaves office, can be impeached for crimes of treason) and the Senate (e.g., 100 members, two elected from each state, 6-year terms). Putting these various propositions together, the students should infer that the Vice President would vote in the Senate if 50 senators voted for a bill and 50 voted against it.

A problem occurs when there are no preexisting propositions with which new information can be linked. Students who have never heard of the U.S. Constitution and do not know what a constitution is will draw a blank when they hear the word for the first time. Conceptually meaningless information can be stored in LTM, but better learning takes place when new information is related to something students know. Showing students a

Statement:

"The Vice President of the United States serves as President of the Senate but does not vote unless there is a tie."

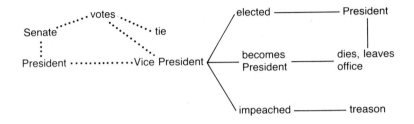

Note: Dotted lines represent new knowledge; solid lines indicate knowledge in long-term memory.

FIGURE 6.2
Acquisition of declarative knowledge.

facsimile of the U.S. Constitution or relating it to something they have studied (e.g., Declaration of Independence) gives them a referent to link with the new information.

Even when students have studied related material, they may not automatically link it with new information. Teachers usually need to make the links explicit. In the example above, teachers could remind students of the composition of the U.S. Senate and the other roles of the Vice President when discussing the function of the Vice President in the Senate. Propositions sharing a common element are stored in LTM as described only if they are active in WM simultaneously. This point helps to explain why students might fail to see how new material relates to old material, even though the link is clear to the teacher. Teaching that establishes propositional networks in students' minds incorporates review, organization of material, and reminders to students of things they know but are not thinking of at the moment.

Spreading Activation. A concept important for linking new information to knowledge in LTM is *spreading activation* (Anderson, 1983, 1984; Collins & Loftus, 1975). The basic underlying principles are as follows (Anderson, 1984):

1. Human knowledge can be represented as a network of nodes, where nodes correspond to concepts, and links to associations among these concepts.

KNOWLEDGE ACQUISITION AND REPRESENTATION

2. The nodes in this network can be in various states that correspond to their levels of activation. More active nodes are processed "better."
3. Activation can spread along these network paths by a mechanism whereby nodes can cause their neighboring nodes to become active. (p. 61)

Anderson (1990) cites the example of an individual presented with the word *dog*. This word is associatively linked with such other concepts in LTM as "bone," "cat," and "meat." In turn, each of these concepts is linked to other concepts. The activation of "dog" in LTM will spread beyond "dog" to linked concepts, with the spread lessening with concepts farther away from "dog."

Experimental support for the existence of spreading activation was obtained by Meyer and Schvaneveldt (1971). These investigators used a reaction time task in which subjects were presented with two strings of letters and responded whether both were words. Words associatively linked (*bread* and *butter*) were recognized faster that words not linked (*nurse* and *butter*).

Spreading activation results in a larger portion of LTM being activated than knowledge immediately associated with the content of one's WM. Activated information stays in LTM unless it is deliberately accessed, but this information is more readily accessible for use in WM. Spreading activation also facilitates transfer. Transfer depends on propositional networks in LTM being activated by the same cue, so students recognize that knowledge is applicable in the different domains.

Schemata.   Propositional networks represent small pieces of knowledge. As discussed in Chapter 5, however, much knowledge is organized into larger networks, or *schemata*. Schemata represent the structure of objects, persons, and events (Anderson, 1990). Structure is represented with a series of "slots," each of which corresponds to an attribute. In the schema or slot for "houses," some attributes (and their values) might be as follows: material (wood, brick), contains (rooms), function (human dwelling). Schemata are hierarchical; they are joined to superordinate ideas (building) and subordinate ones (roof).

Strong support for the underlying nature of schemata was obtained by Brewer and Treyens (1981). Subjects were asked to wait in an office for a brief period, after which they were brought into a room. They were asked to write down everything they could recall about the office. Their recall reflected the strong influence of a schema for "office." Subjects correctly recalled the office having a desk and a chair (typical attributes) but not a skull (nontypical attribute). Although the office contained no books, many subjects incorrectly recalled books (typical attribute).

Schemata are important during teaching and for transfer. Once students learn a schema, teachers can activate this knowledge when they teach any content to which the schema is applicable. Suppose an instructor teaches a general schema for describing geographical formations (e.g., mountain, volcano, glacier, river). The schema might contain the following attributes: height, material, and activity. Once students learn the schema, they can employ it to categorize new formations they study. In so doing, they would create new schemata for the various formations.

Retrieval Strategies

What happens when a student is asked such a question as, "What does the Vice President of the United States do in the Senate?" The question enters the student's WM and is broken into propositions, which activate associated networks in LTM. Through spreading activation, related propositions are activated and examined to determine if they answer the question. If they do, that information is translated into a sentence and verbalized to the questioner or into motor patterns to be written. If the activated propositions do not answer the query, activation spreads until the answer is located. When insufficient time is available for spread of activation to locate the answer, students may make an educated guess (J. Anderson, 1976).

Much cognitive processing occurs automatically. People are often unaware of all the steps taken to answer a question. However, when people must judge several activated propositions to determine whether the propositions properly answer the question, they are more aware of the process.

Because knowledge is encoded in propositional form, retrieval proceeds even though the information to be retrieved does not exist in exact form in memory. If a teacher asks whether the Vice President would vote on a bill when the initial vote was 51 for and 49 against, students could retrieve the proposition that the Vice President votes only when there is a tie. Thus, by implication, the Vice President would not vote. Such processing takes longer than when a question requires information that is coded in memory in the same form, but students should respond correctly assuming they activate the relevant propositions in LTM.

Encoding Specificity. Retrieval depends on the manner of encoding (process of putting new information into the information processing system). According to the *encoding specificity* hypothesis (Thomson & Tulving, 1970), the manner in which knowledge is encoded determines which retrieval cues will effectively activate that knowledge. The best retrieval occurs when retrieval cues match those present during encoding.

Some experimental evidence supports encoding specificity. When subjects are given category names while they are encoding specific instances of the categories, they recall the instances better if they are given the cate-

---

APPLICATION 6.1: Organizing Information by Networks

Teachers enhance learning when they develop lessons to assist students linking new information with knowledge in memory. Information that is meaningful, elaborated, and organized is more readily integrated into LTM networks.

A teacher planning a botany unit on the reproduction of different species of plants might start by reviewing common plant knowledge that students have stored in their memories (basic structure, conditions necessary for growth). As the teacher introduces new information, students examine familiar live plants that reproduce differently to make the experience more meaningful. Factual information to be learned can be elaborated by providing visual drawings and written details regarding the reproductive processes. For each live plant examined, students can organize the new information by creating outlines or charts to show the means of reproduction.

---

gory names at recall than if not given the names (Klatzky, 1980). A similar benefit is obtained if subjects learn words with associates and then are given the associate names at recall than if not given the associates.

Encoding specificity can be explained in terms of spreading activation among propositional networks. Cues associated with material to be learned are linked in LTM with the material at the time of encoding. During recall, presentation of these cues activates the relevant portions in LTM. In the absence of the same cues, recall depends on subjects' recalling the individual propositions in memory. Because the cues lead to spreading activation (not the individual propositions or concepts), recall is facilitated by presenting the same cues at encoding and recall.

Processing of Declarative Knowledge

Although declarative knowledge often is processed automatically, there is no guarantee that it will be integrated with relevant information in LTM. Meaningfulness, elaboration, and organization enhance the potential for declarative information to be effectively processed.

Meaningfulness. Meaningless information will not activate information in LTM and will be lost unless students rehearse it repeatedly until it becomes established in LTM, perhaps by forming a new propositional network. One also can connect the sounds of new information, which are devoid of meaning, to other similar sounds. The word *constitution*, for example, may be linked phonetically with other uses of *constitution* stored in learners' memories (e.g., Constitution Avenue).

Meaningful information is more likely to be retained because it easily connects to propositional networks. Teachers assist by pointing out connections to students. Not only does meaningfulness promote learning, it also saves time. Propositions in WM take time to process; Simon (1974) estimates that each new piece of information takes 10 seconds to encode (or 6 pieces of information per minute). Even when information is meaningful, much knowledge is lost before it can be encoded. Although every piece of incoming information is not crucially important and some loss usually does not significantly impair learning, students are apt to retain little information even under the best circumstances.

Elaboration. Adding to information being learned, termed *elaboration*, may be in the form of examples, details, inferences, or anything that serves to link new and old information. A learner might elaborate the role of the Vice President in the Senate by thinking through the roll call and, when there is a tie, having the Vice President vote.

Elaboration facilitates learning because it is a form of rehearsal: by keeping information active in WM, elaboration increases the likelihood that information will be permanently stored in LTM. Elaboration also aids learning because it establishes links between old and new information. Students who elaborate the role of the Vice President in the Senate link this new information with what they know about the Senate and the Vice President. Well-linked information in LTM is easier to recall than poorly linked information (Stein et al., 1984).

Although elaboration promotes learning, it also takes time. It takes longer to comprehend sentences requiring elaboration than sentences not requiring elaboration (Haviland & Clark, 1974). For example, the following sentences require drawing an inference that the speaker took her checkbook along: "I went to the grocery store." "I wrote a check for my groceries." The link is clarified in the following sentences: "I took my checkbook with me when I went to the grocery store." "I wrote a check for my groceries." Making explicit links between adjoining propositions assists the latter's encoding and retention.

An important aspect of learning is deciding on the importance of information. Not all learned information needs to be elaborated. Comprehension is aided when students elaborate only the most important aspects of text (Reder, 1979). Elaboration aids retrieval by providing alternate paths along which activation can spread, so that if one path is blocked, others are available (J. Anderson, 1976). Elaboration also provides additional information from which answers can be constructed (Reder, 1982), for example, when students must answer questions with information in a different form from that of the learned material.

In general, almost any type of elaboration is better than none for encoding and retrieving information; however, some types of elaborations are more effective than others. Such activities as taking notes or asking oneself how new information relates to what one knows build propositional networks. Effective elaborations link propositions and stimulate accurate recall. Elaborations not linked well to the content do not aid recall (Mayer, 1984).

Organization.   *Organization* takes place by breaking information into parts and specifying relationships between parts. In studying U.S. government, organization might involve breaking government into three branches (executive, legislative, judicial), breaking each of these into subparts, and so on. Although older students employ organization more often, elementary grade children are capable of using organizational principles (Klatzky, 1980). For example, children studying leaf patterns often organize leaves by size, shape, and edge pattern.

Organization improves retrieval by linking relevant information; when retrieval is cued, spreading activation accesses the relevant propositions in LTM. Teachers routinely organize material, but student-generated organization is also effective for retrieval. Instruction on organizational principles assists learning. Consider a schema for understanding stories with four major attributes: setting, theme, plot, resolution (Rumelhart, 1975, 1977). The setting ("Once upon a time . . . ") places the action in a context. The theme is then introduced, which consists of characters who have certain experiences and goals. The plot traces the actions of the characters to attain their goals. The resolution describes how the goal is reached or how the characters adjust to not attaining the goal. By describing and exemplifying these phases of a story, teachers help students learn to identify them on their own.

MENTAL IMAGERY

Representation of Spatial Information

Mental imagery refers to mental representations of spatial knowledge including physical properties of the objects or events represented (Klatzky, 1980). Recall that visual stimuli attended to are held briefly in veridical form in the sensory register and then are transferred to WM. The term *imagery* suggests that the WM representation preserves some of the physical attributes of the stimulus it represents (E. Gagné, 1985). Images are *analogue representations* that are similar but not identical to their referents (Shepard, 1978).

Imagery has been valued as far back as the time of the ancient Greeks. Plato felt that thoughts and perceptions are impressed on the mind as a block of wax and are remembered as long as the images last (Paivio, 1970).

APPLICATION 6.2: Using Imagery in the Classroom

Imagery can be used to increase student learning. One application involves instructing children on three-dimensional figures (e.g., cubes, spheres, cones) including calculating their volumes. Verbal descriptors and two-dimensional diagrams are also used, but actual models of the figures greatly enhance teaching effectiveness. Allowing students to hold the shapes fosters their understanding of the concept of volume.

Imagery can be applied in a physical education class. For example, when students are learning an exercise routine accompanied by music, the teacher can model in turn each portion of the routine first without music, after which students close their eyes and think about what they observed. The students then perform each part of the routine. Later the teacher can add music to the portions of the routine.

Imagery can also be used to teach language arts. For instance, for a unit involving writing a paragraph that gives directions for performing a task or making something, the teacher could ask students to close their eyes and think about the individual steps (e.g., of making a peanut butter and jelly sandwich). Once students finish imagining the task, they could visualize each step while writing it down.

Art teachers can use imagery to teach students to follow directions. The teacher might give the following directions orally and write them on the board: Close your eyes and visualize on a piece of art paper a design including four circles, three triangles, and two squares, with some of the shapes overlapping one another. While students' eyes are closed, the teacher might ask the following questions to ensure that students are using imagery: How many circles do you see? How many triangles do you see? How many squares do you see? Are any of the shapes touching? Which ones?

Simonides, a Greek poet, believed that images are associative mediators. He devised the *method of loci* as a memory aid. In this method, information to be remembered is paired with locations in a familiar setting (see also section on Information Processing Theory in Chapter 9). Mental imagery also has been influential in discoveries. Shepard (1978) describes Einstein's Gedanken experiment that marked the beginning of the relativistic reformulation of electromagnetic theory. Einstein imagined himself traveling with a beam of light (186,000 miles/second), and what he saw corresponded neither to light nor to anything described by Maxwell's equations in classical electromagnetic theory. Einstein reported that he typically thought in terms of images and only reproduced his thoughts in words and mathematical equations once he conceptualized the situation visually. The German chemist Kekulé supposedly had a dream in which he visualized the structure of benzene, and Watson and Crick apparently used mental rotation to "crack" the genetic code.

In contrast to images, propositions are discrete representations of meaning not resembling their referents in structure. The expression "New York City" no more resembles the actual city than virtually any three words picked at random from a dictionary. An image of New York City containing skyscrapers, stores, people, and traffic is more similar in structure to its referent. The same contrast is evident for events. Compare the sentence, "The black cat walked across the lawn," with an image of this scene.

Mental imagery is a controversial topic (Kosslyn, 1980). A central issue is how closely mental images resemble actual pictures: Do they contain the same details as pictures or are they fuzzy pictures portraying only highlights? As discussed in Chapter 5, the visual pattern of a stimulus is perceived when its features are linked to a LTM representation. This implies that images can only be as clear as the LTM representations (Pylyshyn, 1973). To the extent that mental images are the products of people's perceptions, images are likely to be incomplete representations of stimuli (Klatzky, 1980).

Support for the idea that people use imagery to represent spatial knowledge comes from studies by Shepard (Cooper & Shepard, 1973; Shepard & Cooper, 1983). In one study, subjects were shown pairs of two-dimensional pictures; each picture portrayed a three-dimensional object. The subjects' task was to determine if the two pictures in each pair portrayed the same object. The solution strategy involved mentally rotating one object in each pair until it matched the other object or until the subject decided that no amount of rotation would yield an identical object. Subjects' reaction times were a direct function of the number of mental rotations needed. Although these and other data suggest that people employ images to represent knowledge, they do not directly address the issue of how closely images correspond to actual objects.

To the extent that students use imagery to represent spatial and visual knowledge, imagery seems germane to educational content involving concrete objects. When teaching a unit about different types of rock formations (mountains, plateaus, ridges), an instructor could show pictures of the various formations and ask students to imagine them. In geometry, imagery could be employed when dealing with mental rotations.

Evidence shows that people use imagery to think about abstract dimensions. Kerst and Howard (1977) asked students to compare pairs of cars, countries, and animals on the concrete dimension of size and on an appropriate abstract dimension (e.g., cost, military power, ferocity). The abstract and concrete dimensions yielded similar results: As items became more similar, reaction times increased. For instance, in comparing size, it is easier to compare a bobcat and elephant than a rhinoceros and hippopotamus. It is not clear how subjects imagined abstract dimensions or whether they even used imagery. Perhaps they represented abstract dimensions in terms of propositions, for example, by comparing Russia and Jamaica on military power using the proposition, "Soviet Union is mightier than Jamaica."

Imagery in LTM

Most researchers agree that images are used in WM but disagree whether they are retained in LTM (Kosslyn & Pomerantz, 1977; Pylyshyn, 1973). Paivio's (1971, 1978) *dual-code theory* directly addresses this issue. According to Paivio, LTM has two means of representing knowledge: a *verbal system* incorporating knowledge expressed in language and an *imaginal system* storing visual and spatial information. These systems are interrelated—a verbal code can be converted into an imaginal code and vice versa—but there are important differences. The verbal system is suited for abstract information, whereas the imaginal system is used to represent concrete objects or events. As Paivio (1971) notes,

> Which mode [visual, imaginal] will be functionally dominant in a given situation will depend on the nature and demands of the situation. One of the important determining characteristics, already considered, is the abstractness–concreteness of the situation or task: Imagery is particularly functional when the task is relatively concrete, and verbal processes become increasingly necessary for both the "flights" and the "perchings" of the stream of thought as the task is more abstract. These functional differences are presumably related to the differential availability of images and verbal processes in abstract task situations. (pp. 32–33)

Shepard's experiments support the utility of imagery and offer indirect support for the dual-code theory. Other supporting evidence comes from research showing that when recalling lists of concrete and abstract words, people recall concrete words better than abstract ones (Klatzky, 1980). The dual-code theory's explanation of this finding is that concrete words can be coded verbally and imaginally, whereas abstract words usually are coded only verbally. At recall, people draw on both memory systems for the concrete words, but only the verbal system for the abstract words. Other research on imaginal mnemonic mediators supports the dual-code theory (see Information Processing Theory in Chapter 9).

An opposing view—*unitary theory*—postulates that all information is represented in LTM in verbal codes (propositions). Images in WM are reconstructed from verbal LTM codes. Indirect support for this notion comes from Mandler (Mandler & Johnson, 1976; Mandler & Ritchey, 1977). Mandler found that, as with verbal material, subjects employ schemata while acquiring visual information. Subjects remember scenes better when elements are in a typical pattern; memory is poorer when elements are disorganized. Meaningful organization and elaboration of information into schemata improve memory for scenes much as they do for verbal material. This finding suggests a common process is operating regardless of the form of information presented.

This debate notwithstanding, using concrete materials and pictures enhances memory. Such instructional tools as manipulatives and audiovisual aids facilitate learning. Although concrete devices are undoubtedly more important for young children, who lack the cognitive capability to think in abstract terms, students of all ages benefit from information presented in multiple modes.

Individual Differences

The extent to which people actually use imagery to remember information varies as a function of cognitive development. Kosslyn (1980) proposed that children are more likely to use imagery to remember and recall information than adults, who rely more on propositional representation. Kosslyn gave children and adults such statements as "A cat has claws," and "A rat has fur." The task was to determine validity of the statements. Kosslyn reasoned that adults could respond quicker because they could access the propositional information from LTM, whereas children would have to recall the image of the animal and scan it. To control for adults' better information processing in general, some adult subjects were explicitly asked to scan an image of the animal, whereas others were free to use any strategy. Adults were slower to respond when given the imagery instructions than when free to choose a strategy, but no difference was found for children. These results show that imagery is the strategy used by children even when they are free to do otherwise, but they do not explain whether children cannot use propositional information (because of cognitive limitations) or whether they can but choose not to because they find scanning to be more effective.

The use of imagery by people of any age depends on what is to be imagined. Concrete objects are more easily imagined than abstractions. Another factor that influences use of imagery is one's ability to employ it. *Eidetic imagery*, or photographic memory (Leask, Haber, & Haber, 1969), actually is unlike a photograph; the latter is seen as a whole, whereas eidetic imagery occurs in pieces. People report that an image appears and disappears in segments rather than all at once.

Eidetic imagery is found almost exclusively in children (Gray & Gummerman, 1975), yet it is uncommon even among children (about 5%). Eidetic imagery possibly is lost with development, perhaps because propositional representation replaces the imaginal mode. It also is possible that adults retain the capacity to form clear images but do not routinely do so because their propositional systems can represent more information. Just as memory can be improved, it seems likely that the capacity to form images can be improved, but most of us do not explicitly work to develop our imaginal systems.

PROCEDURAL KNOWLEDGE

Procedural knowledge is knowing how to perform cognitive activities (Anderson, 1990; Paris et al., 1983). Procedural knowledge is important in many aspects of schooling. Students demonstrate procedural knowledge when they correctly solve long division or mathematical word problems, summarize written information, skim passages, and display proper biology laboratory techniques.

Declarative and procedural knowledge interact. While adding fractions, students use procedures (i.e., convert to lowest common denominator, add numerators) and declarative knowledge (addition facts). During reading comprehension, some processes operate as procedures (decoding, monitoring comprehension), whereas others involve only declarative knowledge (word meanings). People typically employ procedures to acquire declarative knowledge, such as mnemonic techniques to remember declarative knowledge (see the section on Information Processing Theory in Chapter 9). Having declarative information is typically a prerequisite for successfully implementing procedures. To solve for square roots, students must know multiplication facts.

Declarative and procedural knowledge are alike in that each varies tremendously in scope. Individuals possess declarative knowledge about the world, themselves, and others. Similarly, they understand procedures for interacting in all aspects of life. Procedural and declarative knowledge are different in that the former *transforms* information. Such declarative knowledge as "2 + 2 = 4" and "Uncle Fred smokes smelly cigars" changes nothing, but applying the long division algorithm to a problem transforms an unsolved problem to a solved one.

Another difference is in speed of processing. Declarative knowledge activation is often slow and conscious. Even assuming people know the answer to a question, they may have to think for some time to answer the question. For example, consider the time needed to answer, "Who was the U.S. President in 1867?" Once procedural knowledge is established in memory, it is processed quickly and often automatically. Skilled readers decode printed text automatically; they do not have to consciously reflect on what they are doing. Once we learn how to multiply, we do not have to think about what steps to follow to solve multiplication problems.

The differences in declarative and procedural knowledge have implications for teaching and learning. Students may have difficulty with a particular content area because they lack domain-specific declarative knowledge or because they do not understand the prerequisite procedures. Discovering which is deficient is a necessary first step for planning remedial instruction. Not only do deficiencies hinder learning, they also produce low self-efficacy. Students who understand how to divide but do not know multiplication facts become demoralized when they consistently arrive at wrong answers.

Classification and Concept Learning

Procedural knowledge is employed in such cognitive activities as identifying pictures, classifying objects, and recognizing concepts and analogies. Consider the following test item:

> Conductor is to orchestra as manager is to
> a. Dugout
> b. Pitchers
> c. Team
> d. Umpires

The procedure is first to determine the relationship of conductor to orchestra and then find that same relationship between manager and _____ . One might think, "A conductor leads the orchestra, which is composed of several musicians. A manager leads the team, which is composed of several players. The correct answer is (c)."

Much learning in and out of school involves concepts. A *concept* is a labeled set of objects, symbols, or events sharing common characteristics (critical attributes). *Concept learning* refers to identifying attributes and generalizing them to new examples, as well as discriminating examples from nonexamples. Concepts, either concrete (e.g., table, chair, cat) or abstract (love, democracy, oneness), involve rules that can be expressed in if-then form. For example, a rule classifying a cat might be as follows: "If it is domesticated, has four legs, fur, whiskers, tail, is relatively small, purrs, and vocalizes 'meow,' then it is a cat." Although there are exceptions to this rule, it will accurately classify cats most of the time. Generalization occurs when the rule is applied to a variety of cats.

Studies by Bruner, Goodnow, and Austin (1956) identified how people learn concepts. The researchers presented subjects with boxes portraying geometrical patterns. Each pattern could be classified using four different attributes: number of stimuli (one, two, three); shape (circle, square, cross); color (red, green, black); and number of borders on the box (one, two, three). The subjects' task was to identify the concept represented in different subsets of the boxes.

The task in such studies is varied to yield different types of concepts. A *conjunctive concept* is represented by two or more features (e.g., two red circles). Other features (number of borders) are not relevant. A *disjunctive concept,* which consists of one of two or more features, is represented by two circles of any color or one red circle. A *relational concept* specifies a relationship between features that must be present. An example of a relational concept is that the number of objects in the figure must outnumber the number of borders; here type of object and color are unimportant.

Subjects in concept learning tasks tend to formulate a hypothesis about the rule underlying the concept. They retain the hypothesis as long as it correctly identifies concepts and nonconcepts; they modify it when it fails. Subjects learn concepts better when they are presented with *positive instances,* or examples of the concept. Learning is much slower when subjects are given *negative instances* (nonexamples). When trying to confirm the rule underlying the concept, subjects prefer to receive positive rather than negative instances (Wason, 1960).

Teaching of Concepts. Tennyson and his colleagues developed a model of concept teaching based on empirical research (Tennyson, 1980, 1981; Tennyson, Steve, & Boutwell, 1975). This model includes the following four steps (Tennyson & Park, 1980):

1. Determining the structure of the concept to include superordinate, coordinate, and subordinate concepts and identifying the critical and variable attributes
2. Defining the concept in terms of the critical attributes and preparing several examples with the critical and variable attributes
3. Arranging the examples in sets based on the attributes and ensuring that the examples have similar variable attributes within any set containing examples from each coordinate concept
4. Ordering and presenting the sets in terms of the divergence and difficulty of the examples and ordering the examples within any set according to the learner's current knowledge

Most concepts can be represented in a hierarchy with *superordinate* and *subordinate concepts.* For any given concept, there may be similar concepts that are at roughly the same level in the hierarchy; these are known as *coordinate concepts.* For example, the concept "domestic cat" has "cat family" and "mammal" as superordinate concepts, the various breeds (shorthair, Siamese) as subordinate concepts, and other members of the cat family (lion, jaguar) as coordinate concepts. Critical attributes (paws, teeth) are those that must be present in examples of the concept; variable attributes (hair length, eye color) can differ between examples. A set comprises examples and nonexamples (dog, squirrel) of the concept.

APPLICATION 6.3: Teaching of Concepts

Concept learning involves identifying attributes, generalizing them to new examples, and discriminating examples from nonexamples. Using superordinate, coordinate, and subordinate concepts and critical and variable attributes to present the concept to be learned should help students clearly define its structure.

A kindergarten teacher presenting a unit instructing students to identify and distinguish shapes (circle, square, rectangle, oval, triangle, diamond) might initially have children group objects alike in shape and identify critical attributes (e.g., a square has four straight sides, the sides are the same size) and variable attributes (squares, rectangles, triangles, and diamonds have straight sides but a different number of sides of different lengths and arranged in different ways). The teacher might then focus on a particular shape by presenting different examples representing each shape so children can compare attributes with those of other shapes. As for content progression, the teacher might introduce shapes familiar to students (circle and square) before moving to less common ones (parallelogram).

Although the concept should be defined with its critical attributes before examples and nonexamples are given, presenting a definition does not ensure students will learn the concept. Examples should differ widely in variable attributes, and nonexamples should differ from examples in a small number of critical attributes at once. This mode of presentation prevents students from overgeneralizing (classifying nonexamples as examples) and undergeneralizing (classifying examples as nonexamples). Pointing out relationships among examples is an effective way to arrange sets to foster generalization.

The optimal number of examples to present depends on such concept characteristics as number of attributes and whether the concept is abstract or concrete. Abstract concepts (love, democracy) usually have fewer perceptible examples than concrete concepts (table, chair), and examples of the former may be difficult for learners to grasp. Concept learning also depends on such learner attributes as age and prior knowledge (Tennyson & Park, 1980). Older students learn better than younger ones, and students with more relevant knowledge outperform those lacking such knowledge.

In teaching concepts, it is helpful to present examples that differ in irrelevant attributes and that have relevant attributes in common so that the latter can be clearly pointed out, along with the irrelevant dimensions. In teaching children the concept of "right triangle," the size is irrelevant, as is the direction it faces. One might present right triangles of various sizes pointing in different directions.

Not only must students learn to generalize right triangles, they must also learn to discriminate them from other triangles. To foster concept discrimination, teachers initially should present negative instances that clearly differ from positive instances. As students' skills develop, they can be taught to make finer discriminations. The following suggestions are helpful in teaching students to generalize and discriminate concepts:

Step	Example
Name concept	Chair
Define concept	Seat with a back for one person
Give relevant attributes	Seat, back
Give irrelevant attributes	Legs, size, color, material
Give examples	Easy chair, high chair, beanbag chair
Give nonexamples	Bench, table, stool

The Tennyson model requires a careful analysis of the taxonomic structure of a concept. Structure is well specified for many concepts (e.g., the animal kingdom), but for many others—especially abstract concepts—the links with higher- and lower-order concepts, as well as with coordinate concepts, are problematic. Future research might attempt to integrate Tennyson's ideas with recent novice-to-expert research by determining the differences in knowledge and strategies between expert and novice concept learners (see the section on Problem Solving in Chapter 7).

Skill Acquisition

Concept learning is a necessary prerequisite for performing cognitive operations. To children unskilled in fractions, the notation $\frac{3}{4} - \frac{1}{2}$ is meaningless. Once they understand this problem involves subtracting fractions, they are ready to learn the algorithm.

Learning of skill procedures often occurs slowly. J. Anderson (1982) discussed how skills are learned. First, learners represent a sequence of actions in terms of declarative knowledge. Each step in the sequence is represented as a proposition. Gradually, learners drop out individual cues and integrate the separate steps into a continuous sequence of actions. For example, children learning to tie a knot are apt initially to perform each step slowly, possibly even verbalizing it aloud. As they become more skillful, tying knots becomes part of a smooth sequence that occurs rapidly and without deliberate, conscious attention.

A major constraint on skill learning is the size limitation of WM. Procedures would be learned quicker if WM could simultaneously hold all the declarative knowledge propositions. Because it cannot, students must combine propositions slowly and periodically stop and think (e.g., "What do I do next?"). There is insufficient space in WM to create large procedures in the early stages of learning. As propositions are combined into small procedures, the latter are stored in WM simultaneously with other propositions. In this fashion, larger procedures are gradually constructed.

These ideas explain why skill learning proceeds faster when students can perform the prerequisite skills. When the latter exist as well-established procedures, they are in WM at the same time as new propositions to be integrated. In learning to solve long division problems, students who know how to multiply simply recall the procedure when necessary; it does not have to be learned along with the other steps in long division.

Because representing skill procedures as pieces of declarative knowledge is essentially a way station along the road to mastery, one might question whether students should memorize the individual steps. The memorized steps will eventually not be used, so time may be better spent allowing students to practice them. Providing students with a list of steps they can refer to as they gradually proceduralize the knowledge facilitates learning and enhances self-efficacy (Schunk, 1989).

In some cases, it is difficult to specify the steps in detail. Thinking creatively is one example. Although creative thinking may not follow the same sequence for each student, teachers can model creative thinking to include such self-questioning as "Are there any other possibilities?" Whenever steps can be specified, teacher demonstrations of the steps, followed by student practice, are effective (Rosenthal & Zimmerman, 1978).

One problem with the learning of procedures is that students might view them as lock-step sequences to be followed regardless of whether they are appropriate. As discussed in Chapter 5, the Gestalt psychologists showed how *functional fixedness*, or an inflexible approach to a problem, hinders problem solving (Duncker, 1945). Adamantly following a sequence while learning it may help acquisition, but students also need to understand the circumstances under which other methods are more efficient.

Practice and Feedback

There is the danger of overlearning skill procedures to the point that alternative, easier procedures are not used. At the same time, no alternatives exist for many of the procedures students learn (decoding words, adding numbers, determining subject–verb agreement). Overlearning these skills to the point of automatic production becomes an asset to students and makes it easier to learn new skills (e.g., drawing inferences, writing term papers) that have these basic skills as prerequisites.

One might argue that it makes little sense to teach problem solving or inference skills to students deficient in basic mathematical facts and decoding, respectively. From an empirical perspective, poor grasp of basic number facts is related to low performance on complex arithmetic tasks (Tait, Hartley, & Anderson, 1973), and slow decoding relates to poor comprehension (Perfetti & Lesgold, 1979). Not only is skill learning affected, but self-efficacy suffers as well.

Practice is essential to instate basic procedural knowledge (Lesgold, 1984). In the early stages of learning, students require corrective feedback highlighting the portions of the procedure they implemented correctly and those requiring modification. It is not unusual for students to learn some parts of a procedure but not others. As students become more skillful, teachers can point out their progress, such as how they are solving more problems correctly or more quickly.

Generalization (transfer) of procedural knowledge occurs when the knowledge is linked in LTM with different content. Transfer is aided by having students apply the procedures to the different forms of content and altering the procedures as necessary. General problem-solving strategies are applicable to different academic content (Chapter 7). Exercises calling for different skills can help finely tune students' applications of skills. Review sheets in arithmetic, for example, might contain addition, subtraction, multiplication, and division of whole numbers, mixed numbers, and fractions.

CONDITIONAL KNOWLEDGE AND METACOGNITION

Conditional Knowledge

Possessing the requisite declarative and procedural knowledge to perform a task does not guarantee students will perform it well. Consider students reading a social studies text. They know what to do (read a passage in the text), and they understand the meanings of vocabulary words (declarative knowledge). They know how to decode, skim, find main ideas, and draw inferences (procedural knowledge). When they start reading, they skim the text. As a consequence, they perform poorly on a subsequent comprehension test.

This type of situation is not uncommon in learning settings. Achievement depends on more than just knowing facts and procedures. Conditional knowledge is understanding when and why to employ forms of declarative and procedural knowledge (Paris et al., 1983, 1984). In the preceding example, conditional knowledge would include knowing when skimming is appropriate. One might skim a newspaper to pick up the gist of the news, but skimming should not be used to comprehend difficult textual material.

Conditional knowledge helps students select and employ declarative and procedural knowledge to fit task goals. To decide to skim a passage and then skim it, students should believe that skimming is appropriate for the task at hand, that is, that skimming has *functional value* because it will allow them to accomplish the task. Learners who do not possess conditional knowledge about when and why skimming is valuable will employ it at inappropriate times. If they believe it is valuable for all reading tasks, they may indiscriminately employ it unless otherwise directed. If they believe it has no value they may never use it unless directed.

Conditional knowledge likely is represented in LTM as propositions in networks and linked with the declarative and procedural knowledge to which it applies. Conditional knowledge is a form of declarative knowledge because it is "knowledge that"; for example, *knowledge that* skimming is valuable to get the gist of a passage and *knowledge that* summarizing text is valuable to derive greater understanding. Conditional knowledge also is included in procedures: Skimming is valuable so long as I can get the gist, but if I find that I am not getting the gist, I should abandon skimming and read more carefully. The three types of knowledge are summarized in Table 6.1 (p. 184).

Conditional knowledge is an integral part of self-regulated learning (Chapter 9). Self-regulated learning requires that students decide which learning strategy to use prior to engaging in a task. While students are engaged in a task, they assess task progress (e.g., their level of comprehension) using the metacognitive processes discussed below. When comprehension problems are detected, students alter their strategy based on conditional knowledge of what might prove more effective.

Metacognition and Learning

The term *metacognition* refers to the deliberate conscious control of one's cognitive activity (Brown, 1980). As Flavell (1985) wrote,

> What is metacognition? It has usually been broadly and rather loosely defined as any knowledge or cognitive activity that takes as its object, or regulates, any aspect of any cognitive enterprise. . . . It is called metacognition because its core meaning is "cognition about cognition." Metacognitive skills are believed to play an important role in many types of cognitive activity, including oral communication of information, oral persuasion, oral comprehension, reading comprehension, writing, language acquisition, perception, attention, memory, problem solving, social cognition, and various forms of self-instruction and self-control. (p. 104)

Metacognition comprises two related sets of skills. First, one must understand *what* skills, strategies, and resources are needed to accomplish

---

APPLICATION 6.4: Metacognition

Teachers can help students develop their metacognitive skills. A teacher working with students on listening comprehension might include such situations as listening to an enjoyable story, a set of explicit directions, and a social studies lecture. For each situation, the teacher could ask students why they would listen in that setting, for example, enjoyment and general theme (stories), specific elements (directions), facts and concepts (social studies). Then the teacher could work with students to develop such listening skills as retelling in their own words, visualizing, and taking notes. To foster conditional knowledge, the teacher can discuss with students the various listening techniques and which seem most appropriate for each situation.

---

a task. Included in this cluster are finding main ideas, rehearsing information, forming associations or images, using memory techniques, organizing material, taking notes or underlining, and using test-taking techniques. Second, one must know *how* and *when* to use these skills and strategies to ensure the task is completed successfully. These monitoring activities include checking one's level of understanding, predicting outcomes, evaluating the effectiveness of one's efforts, planning one's activities, deciding how to budget time, and revising or switching to other activities to overcome difficulties (Baker & Brown, 1984). Collectively, metacognitive activities reflect the systematic application of declarative, procedural, and conditional knowledge to tasks.

Metacognitive skills develop slowly. Young children often are not fully aware of which cognitive processes are involved in various tasks. They may not understand that disorganized passages are harder to comprehend than organized ones or that passages containing unfamiliar material are more difficult than those composed of familiar material (Baker & Brown, 1984). Monitoring activities are employed more often by older children and adults than by young children; however, older children do not always monitor their comprehension and young children are cognitively capable of monitoring their activities on simple problems. In general, learners are more likely to monitor their activities on tasks of intermediate difficulty as opposed to easy tasks (where monitoring may not be necessary) or on very difficult tasks (where one may not know what to do or may quit working).

Metacognitive abilities begin to develop around ages 5 to 7 and continue throughout the time children are in school, although within any age group there is much variability. Preschool children are capable of learning some strategic behaviors (Kail & Hagen, 1982), but as a result of schooling, children develop the awareness they can control what they learn by the

TABLE 6.1
Comparison of types of knowledge.

Type	Knowing	Examples
Declarative	That	Historical dates, number facts, episodes (what happened when), task features (stories have a plot, setting), beliefs ("I'm good in math.")
Procedural	How	Math algorithms, reading strategies (skimming, scanning, summarizing), goals (breaking long-range goals into subgoals)
Conditional	When, why	Skim the newspaper because it gives the gist but doesn't take much time; read texts carefully to gain understanding

strategies they use (Duell, 1986). Flavell and Wellman (1977) hypothesized that children form generalizations concerning how their actions influence the environment; for example, they learn "what works" for them to promote school achievement. This is especially true with memory strategies, perhaps because much school success depends on memorizing information.

Variables Influencing Metacognition

Learners' metacognitive awareness is influenced by variables associated with learners, tasks, and strategies (Duell, 1986; Flavell & Wellman, 1977).

Learner Variables. Learners' developmental changes influence their metacognition. Older children understand their own memory abilities and limitations better than younger children (Flavell, Friedrichs, & Hoyt, 1970). Flavell et al. presented children with study material and told them to study it until they felt they could accurately recall the information. Children aged 7 to 10 were more accurate in judging their readiness to recall than were the children aged 4 to 6. Older children were also more aware that their memory abilities differ from one context to another. Children of the same age showed differences in memory abilities.

Learners' abilities to monitor how well they have done on a memory task also vary. Older children are more accurate in judging whether they have recalled all items they were to recall and whether they can recall information. Wellman (1977) presented children with pictures of objects and asked them to name the objects. If children could not name them, they were asked whether they would recognize the name. Compared with kindergartners, third graders were more accurate at predicting which object names they would be able to recognize.

Task Variables. Knowledge of the relative difficulty of learning and retrieving from memory different types of information is part of metacognitive awareness. Although kindergartners and first graders believe that familiar or easily named items are easier to remember, older children are better at predicting that categorized items are easier to recall than conceptually unrelated items (Duell, 1986). Older children are more likely to believe that organized stories are easier to remember than disorganized pieces of information. With respect to the goal of learning, sixth graders are more likely than second graders to know that one would use different reading strategies depending on whether their goal is to recall a story word for word or in their own words (Myers & Paris, 1978).

Strategy Variables. Metacognition depends on the strategies learners employ. Children as young as ages 3 to 4 can use memory strategies to remember information, but their ability to use strategies improves with development. Older children are able to state more things they can do to help them remember. Regardless of age, children are more likely to think of external things (write a note) than internal ones (think about doing something). Students' use of such memory strategies as rehearsal and elaboration also improves with development.

Even though many students are capable of using metacognitive strategies, they may not be aware of which aid learning and retrieval from LTM and they may not employ those that are helpful (Flavell, 1985). Salatas and Flavell (1976) asked kindergartners, third graders, and college students to recall all list items that exhibit a given property (e.g., are breakable). Even though the young children often reported that it is important to conduct a thorough search for information (Duell, 1986), only the college students spontaneously recalled each item and decided whether it exhibits the given property.

Task, strategy, and learner variables typically interact when students engage in metacognitive activities. Learners consider the type and length of material to be learned (task), the potential strategies to be used (strategy), and their skill at using the various strategies (learner). If learners think that note taking and underlining are good strategies for identifying main points of a technical article and that they are good at underlining but poor at taking notes, they should decide to underline (see discussion of Information Processing Theory in Chapter 9).

Metacognition and Behavior

Understanding which skills and strategies help one learn and remember information is necessary for enhanced achievement but not sufficient. Even students who are aware of what helps them learn do not consistently engage in metacognitive activities. There are different reasons why. In some cases, metacognition may be unnecessary (learning easy material). Learners also might be unwilling to invest the effort to employ metacognitive activities. The latter are tasks in their own right; they take time and effort. Learners may not understand fully that metacognitive strategies improve their performances, or they may believe they do but that other factors, such as time spent in learning or effort expended, are more important for learning (Borkowski & Cavanaugh, 1979; Flavell & Wellman, 1977).

Given that metacognitive activities improve achievement but students may not automatically use them, educators urge that students be taught these activities and encouraged to use them in various contexts. Students need to be taught different activities ranging from those applying to learning in general (e.g., determining the purpose in learning) to those applying to specific situations (underlining important points in text). Although the *what* component of learning is important, so are the *when, where,* and *why* of strategy use. Teaching the former without the latter will only confuse students and could prove demoralizing; students who know what to do but not when, where, or why to do it might hold a low sense of self-efficacy for performing well in school.

Learners often need to be taught basic declarative or procedural knowledge along with metacognitive skills. It is fine to teach students to monitor their understanding of main ideas, but if they do not understand what a main idea is or how to find one, the monitoring is useless. Teachers need to encourage students to employ metacognitive strategies and provide opportunities for them to apply what they have learned outside of the strategy instruction context. Students also need feedback on how well they are applying a strategy and how strategy use improves their performances. A danger of teaching a metacognitive strategy in conjunction with a unit is that students will see the strategy as applying only to similar material, which does not foster transfer. Borkowski and Cavanaugh (1979) recommend teaching strategies using multiple tasks.

SUMMARY

Knowledge is encoded and represented in memory. The most basic form of knowledge is declarative, or knowledge that something is the case. Declarative knowledge is represented as propositions, which are the smallest units of information that can be judged true or false. Propositions are formed according to a set of rules, are stored as units of meaning (not as actual sentences), and are combined to form networks. The larger structures, or schemata, contain knowledge relevant to given topics. Propositions seem to be organized in hierarchical fashion.

SUMMARY

Declarative knowledge is acquired when new information is represented in WM as propositions. Related propositions in LTM are cued and retrieved. New and old propositions are associated in WM, integrated, and stored in LTM. Central to this linking process is the notion of spreading activation. Cued information in LTM activates propositions linked to it. Although activated information stays in LTM unless accessed, it is easier to recall than nonactivated information. Spreading activation also facilitates transfer through links between propositional networks. It may be that the best retrieval occurs when cues match those present during encoding. The encoding, storage, and retrieval of propositions are aided by meaningfulness, elaboration, and organization.

Mental imagery refers to representation of spatial knowledge that includes the physical properties of the objects or events represented. Images are analogue representations: They are similar but not identical to their referents. Researchers argue whether images can only be as complete as the LTM representations of their referents. Although there is evidence that people use imagery in WM, debate has centered on whether LTM contains visual representations. Paivio's dual-code theory postulates two LTM representational systems—verbal and imaginal. The imaginal system primarily stores concrete objects and events, but the two systems are interrelated. Others contend that all LTM representations are verbal codes and that WM images are constructed from those. Developmental evidence shows that children are more likely than adults to represent knowledge as images.

Procedural knowledge is knowledge of how to perform cognitive activities. Whereas declarative knowledge is static, procedural knowledge transforms information. Another difference is in speed of processing. Retrieval of declarative knowledge is often conscious and deliberate; when procedural knowledge is well established, processing is relatively automatic with little conscious involvement. One important class of procedures involves identifying concepts. When learning concepts, people form hypotheses about their attributes and retain the hypotheses so long as they correctly distinguish instances from noninstances.

Procedural knowledge initially may be represented as a series of propositions (declarative knowledge). People gradually drop out individual steps and integrate them into a smooth sequence of actions. The size of WM limits the speed with which procedures are acquired. Practice and feedback are essential for developing automaticity in using procedures.

Conditional knowledge is knowing when and why to employ declarative and procedural knowledge. Simply knowing what to do and how to do it does not produce success. Students also must understand under which conditions knowledge is useful and why performing procedures aid achievement. Conditional knowledge helps students fit declarative and procedural knowledge to task goals. Conditional knowledge likely is stored in LTM as propositions linked with other declarative and procedural knowledge.

Metacognition refers to deliberate conscious control of one's mental activities. Metacognition includes knowledge and monitoring activities designed to ensure that tasks are completed successfully. Although preschoolers are capable of some strategic behaviors, metacognition begins to develop around ages 5 to 7 and continues throughout schooling. One's metacognitive awareness is influenced by task, strategy, and learner variables. Even when learners are capable of monitoring task performances, they do not always do so. Educators have suggested that learners benefit from explicit instruction on metacognitive activities.

Chapter 7

Problem Solving and Domain-Specific Learning

Researchers are increasingly interested in problem solving and learning in content domains. This focus is important, because knowledge about students' problem-solving efforts in content areas has direct relevance to learning and instruction. This chapter examines problem solving and learning in language comprehension, reading, writing, mathematics, and science. Much academic task engagement reflects problem-solving processes. Problem solving is, however, not the only major commonality among the content areas. Other similarities between such tasks as "learning how to play chess, learning how to play the flute, learning mathematics, and learning to read the sprung rhymes in the verse of Gerard Manley Hopkins" (Bruner, 1985, pp. 5–6) are attention, memory, and persistence.

This is not to suggest there is nothing unique about each content area. Bruner (1985) contends that views of learning are not unambiguously right or wrong; rather they can be evaluated only in light of such conditions as the nature of the task to be learned, the type of learning to be accomplished, and the characteristics learners bring to the situation. To investigate academic tasks, many researchers adopt a *novice-to-expert framework:* They (a) identify the skill to be learned, (b) find an expert (i.e., one who performs the skill well) and a novice (one who performs it poorly), and (c) determine how the novice can be moved to the expert level as efficiently as possible. The last step often involves computer simulation to identify substeps leading to skill attainment. Intertask similarities show up in the simulations.

Space limitations preclude providing a comprehensive account of learning in many domains. Interested readers should consult the *Handbook of Research on Teaching* (Wittrock, 1986) for reviews of learning in other areas (e.g., social studies, moral and values education, arts and aesthetics, professional education).

PROBLEM SOLVING

A *problem* is "a situation in which you are trying to reach some goal, and must find a means for getting there" (Chi & Glaser, 1985, p. 229). The problem may be to answer a question, compute a solution, locate an object, secure a job, teach a student, and so on. *Problem solving* refers to people's efforts to achieve a goal for which they do not have an automatic solution.

Regardless of content area and complexity, all problems have certain things in common. Problems have an *initial state*—the problem solver's present status or level of knowledge. Problems have a *goal*—the problem solver's desired attainment. Except for the most trivial, problems require breaking the goal into a series of *subgoals* that, when mastered (usually sequentially), result in goal attainment. Finally, problems require performing *operations* on the initial state and the subgoals, where operations are activities (behavioral, cognitive) that alter the nature of those states (Anderson, 1990; Chi & Glaser, 1985).

Note from the preceding definition that not all learning activities are examples of problem solving. Problem solving technically is not involved when students' skills become so well established that they automatically execute actions to attain goals. As discussed in this chapter, basic skills in different domains do become quite automatic for many students. At the same time, students learn new skills and new uses for previously learned skills, so most school activities involve some degree of problem solving.

Historical Influences

Trial and Error. Problem solving is by no means a new topic. Thorndike's (1913b) early research with cats was concerned with problem solving; the problem for the cat was how to escape from the cage. Thorndike conceived of problem solving as *trial and error.* The animal was capable of performing certain behaviors in the cage. From this repertoire, the animal performed one behavior and experienced the consequences. After a series of random behaviors, the cat made the response that opened the hatch leading to escape. With repeated trials, the cat made fewer errors before performing the escape behavior and the time required to solve the problem diminished. The escape behavior became connected to confinement in the cage.

Trial and error is one means of problem solving, but it is not very effective. Simply performing actions until one "works" wastes time, may never result in a solution, and can have negative effects. In desperation, a teacher might use a trial-and-error approach to cope with student problems; a teacher might try different reading materials with students having difficulty reading until they begin to perform better. This approach is likely to expose such students to materials that prove frustrating and temporarily retard skill development.

Insight. Problem solving often has been viewed as involving *insight*, or the sudden awareness of a likely solution. Wallas (1921) studied great problem solvers and formulated a four-step model as follows:

1. *Preparation:* Learning about the problem and gathering information that might be relevant to its solution
2. *Incubation:* A period of thinking about the problem, which may also include putting the problem aside for a time
3. *Illumination:* A period of insight when a potential solution suddenly comes into awareness
4. *Verification:* Testing the proposed solution to ascertain whether it is correct

Wallas's stages were descriptive and not subjected to empirical verification. Gestalt psychologists also postulated that much human learning is insightful (see the discussion of Historical Perspectives in Chapter 5). Learning involves a change in perception. In the presolution phase, learners think about the ingredients necessary to solve a problem. They integrate these in various ways until the problem is solved. When learners arrive at a solution, they do so suddenly and with insight.

Systematic research on problem solving by apes was conducted by Kohler (1925). In one problem situation (detour), the animal could see the goal but not attain it without turning away and taking an indirect route. For example, the animal might be in a room with a window and see food outside. To reach the goal, the animal must exit the room via a door and proceed down a corridor that led outside. In going from the presolution to the solution phase, the animal might try a number of alternatives before settling on one and employing it. Insight occurred when the animal tested a likely solution.

Wertheimer (1945) distinguished rote memorization from insight in humans. Rote memorization generally is an inefficient method of solving problems, because in most situations there is some organization. Problems are solved by discovering the organization of the situation and the relationship of the individual elements to the problem solution. By arranging and rearranging these elements, learners eventually gain insight into the solution.

Gestalt theory had little to say about how problem-solving strategies are learned. Wertheimer (1945) felt that teachers could aid problem solving by arranging elements of a situation so that students would be more likely to "see" how the parts relate to the whole. Gestalt psychologists did not address how learners could be taught to be more insightful. Although Gestalt psychology offered some interesting ideas, its principles were not directly applicable to classroom learning.

Heuristic. A *heuristic* is a method for solving a problem in which one employs principles (rules of thumb) that usually lead to a solution (Anderson, 1990). Polya (1945/1957) described the following heuristic for problem solving:

> Modern heuristic endeavors to understand the process of solving problems, especially the *mental operations typically useful* in this process. It has various sources of information none of which should be neglected. A serious study of heuristic should take into account both the logical and the psychological background, it should not neglect what . . . older writers . . . have to say about the subject, but it should least neglect unbiased experience. Experience in solving problems and experience in watching other people solving problems must be the basis on which heuristic is built. In this study, we should not neglect any sort of problem, and should find out common features in the way of handling all sorts of problems; we should aim at general features, independent of the subject matter of the problem. The study of heuristic has "practical" aims; a better understanding of the mental operations typically useful in solving problems could exert some good influence on teaching. (pp. 129–130)

Polya's list of problem-solving mental operations is as follows:

1. Understand the problem
2. Devise a plan
3. Carry out the plan
4. Look back

Understanding the problem involves asking such questions as "What is the unknown?" and "What are the data?" It often helps to draw a diagram representing the problem and the given information. In *devising a plan,* one tries to find a connection between the data and the unknown. Breaking the problem into subgoals is useful, as is thinking of a similar problem and how that was solved. The problem may need to be restated. While *carrying out the plan,* it is important to check each step to ensure that it was properly implemented. *Looking back* means examining the solution: Is it correct? Is there another means of attaining it?

More recently, Bransford and Stein (1984) formulated a similar heuristic known as IDEAL:

I = *I*dentify the problem

D = *D*efine and represent the problem

E = *E*xplore possible strategies

A = *A*ct on the strategies

L = *L*ook back and evaluate the effects of your activities

General heuristics are very useful when one is working with unfamiliar content (Andre, 1986). Such heuristics are less efficient when one is working within a familiar domain, because as domain-specific skill develops, students increasingly use established procedural knowledge for that content. General heuristics have an instructional advantage: They can help students become systematic problem solvers. Although the heuristic approach may appear to be inflexible, there actually is flexibility in how steps are carried out. For many students, a heuristic will be more systematic than their present problem-solving approaches and will lead to better solutions.

Information Processing View

In information processing theory, problem solving involves a *problem space* with a beginning state, a goal state, and possible solution paths leading through subgoals and requiring application of operations (Newell & Simon, 1972). The problem solver forms a mental representation of the problem and performs operations to reduce the discrepancy between the beginning and goal states. Operating on the representation to find a solution is known as *search* (Andre, 1986).

The first step in problem solving is to form a *representation.* Similar to Polya's first step, understanding the problem, representation requires translating known information into a model in memory. The internal representation consists of propositions, and possibly images, in STM (short-term memory) or WM (working memory). The problem also can be represented externally on paper, computer screen, chalkboard, and so forth. Information in WM activates related knowledge in LTM (long-term memory), and the solver eventually selects a problem-solving strategy. As people solve problems, they often alter their initial representation and activate new knowledge, especially if their problem solving does not succeed. Thus, problem solving includes evaluating goal progress.

The problem representation determines what knowledge is activated in memory and, consequently, how easy the problem is to solve (Holyoak, 1984). If solvers incorrectly represent the problem by not considering all aspects or by adding too many constraints, the search process is unlikely to identify a correct solution path (Chi & Glaser, 1985). No matter how clearly solvers subsequently reason, they will not reach a correct solution unless they form a

APPLICATION 7.1: Problem Solving

There are various ways to help students improve problem-solving skills. As students solve mathematical word problems, they can state each problem in their own words, draw a sketch, decide what information is relevant, and state the ways they might solve the problem. The following questions focus students' attention on important task aspects and guide their thinking:

1. What information is important?
2. What information is missing?
3. Which formulas are necessary?
4. What is the first thing to do?

Another way to assist students is to encourage them to view a problem from varying perspectives. During an exercise in which high school students categorize wartime figures (e.g., Hitler, Napoleon), they could discuss various ways these figures could be categorized, for example, by personality, political makeup of countries they ruled, goals of the war, and so forth. This exercise illustrates different ways to organize information, which is an aid to problem solving.

Teachers also can teach strategies. In a geography lesson, students might be given the following problem: "Pick a state (not your own) that you believe could attract new residents, and create a poster depicting the

new representation. Not surprisingly, problem-solving training programs typically spend a lot of time on the representation phase (Andre, 1986).

Problem-Solving Strategies

General and specific problem-solving strategies are distinguished as follows: A *general strategy* can be applied to problems regardless of content; a *specific strategy* is useful only in a particular domain. For example, breaking a complex problem into subproblems is a general strategy applicable to such problems as selecting a term paper topic, choosing an academic major, and deciding where to live. Conversely, tests that one might perform to classify laboratory specimens are task-specific.

General strategies are useful when one is working on problems with nonobvious solutions. Useful general strategies are the generate-and-test method, means-ends analysis, analogical analysis, and brainstorming; these are discussed in this section. General strategies are less useful when working with familiar content, because domain-specific strategies (discussed in subsequent sections) can be used.

most important attributes of that state." A working backward strategy could be taught as follows:

- *Goal:* Create a poster depicting state's important attributes
- *Subgoal:* Decide how to portray the attributes in a poster
- *Subgoal:* Decide which attributes to portray
- *Subgoal:* Decide which state to pick
- *Initial subgoal:* Decide which attributes attract new residents

To attain the initial subgoal, students could brainstorm in small groups to determine which factors attract people to a state. They then could conduct library research to check on which states possess these attributes. Students could reconvene to discuss the attributes of different states and decide on one. They then would decide which attributes to portray in the poster and how to portray them, after which they would create their poster and present it to the class.

When students are developing problem-solving skills, teachers might want to give clues rather than answers. A teacher working with younger children on categorizing might give the children a word list of names of animals, colors, and places to live. Children are likely to experience some difficulty categorizing the names. Rather than tell them the answers, the teacher could provide clues as follows: "Think of how the words go together. How are *horse* and *lion* alike? How are *pink* and *house* different?"

Generate-and-Test Method. The *generate-and-test method* generates a possible problem solution and then tests its effectiveness (Chi & Glaser, 1985). This strategy works with problems for which there are multiple solutions preferably ordered in likelihood such that at least one will solve the problem. A familiar example is flipping a light switch and the light does not come on. Possible causes include (1) bulb is burned out, (2) electricity is turned off, (3) switch is faulty, (4) lamp socket is faulty, (5) circuit breaker is tripped, (6) fuse is blown, or (7) wiring has a short. One initially generates and tests the most likely solution (replace the bulb); if this does not solve the problem, one generates and tests another likely solution and so forth. Prior and current knowledge are important to use this method effectively. Prior knowledge establishes the hierarchy of possible solutions, and current knowledge influences solution selection. For example, if the electric company is working in the neighborhood, one might first determine if the power is off.

Means-Ends Analysis. To use *means-ends analysis*, one compares the present situation with the goal and identifies the differences between them

PROBLEM SOLVING AND DOMAIN-SPECIFIC LEARNING

(Resnick, 1985). A subgoal is set to reduce one of the differences. One performs operations to accomplish the subgoal, at which point the process is repeated until the goal is attained.

Means-ends analysis was studied by Newell and Simon (1972), who formulated a computer simulation program called the General Problem Solver (GPS). GPS breaks a problem into subgoals, each representing a difference from the present state. GPS starts with the most important difference and uses operations to eliminate that difference. In some cases, the operations must first eliminate another difference prerequisite to the more important one.

Means-ends analysis is a powerful problem-solving heuristic. When subgoals are properly identified, means-ends analysis is likely to solve the problem. One drawback is that it taxes WM with complex problems, because one may have to keep track of several subgoals. Forgetting a subgoal thwarts problem solution.

Means-ends analysis can proceed from the goal to the initial state or vice versa. In *working backward,* one starts with the goal and asks what subgoals are necessary to accomplish it. One then asks what is necessary to attain these subgoals and so forth, until the initial state is reached. To work backward, therefore, one plans a series of moves, each of which is designed to attain a subgoal. Working backward requires good knowledge in the problem domain to determine goal and subgoal prerequisites.

Working backward is frequently used to prove geometric theorems. One starts by assuming that the theorem is true and then works backward until the postulates are reached. A geometric example is shown in Figure 7.1. The problem is to solve for angle m. Working backward, students realize that they need to determine angle n, because angle $m = 180° - $ angle n (straight line $= 180°$). Continuing to work backward, students understand that because there are intersecting parallel lines, the corresponding angle d on line q equals angle n. Drawing on their geometric knowledge, students determine that angle $d = $ angle a, which is 30°. Thus, angle $n = 30°$, and angle $m = 180° - 30° = 150°$.

Another type of means-ends analysis is *working forward* by starting with the present situation and doing something to alter it. Several alterations usually are necessary to attain the goal. One danger is that working forward sometimes proceeds based on superficial problem analysis. Although each step represents an attempt to attain a necessary subgoal, one can easily proceed off on a tangent or arrive at a dead end. As we see later in this chapter, working forward is generally the strategy followed by expert problem solvers. Working forward also may be the strategy of choice when a fast decision is needed because there is insufficient time to perform a detailed means-ends analysis.

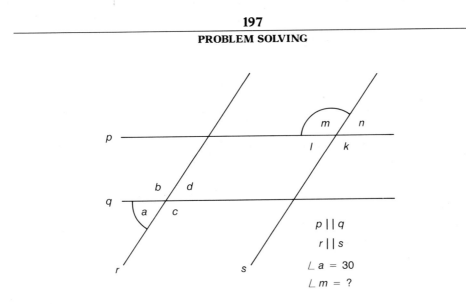

FIGURE 7.1
Means-ends analysis applied to a geometry problem.

Analogical Analysis. Using analogies involves drawing an analogy between the problem situation and a situation with which one is familiar
(Anderson, 1990). One works the problem through the familiar domain and
then relates the solution to the problem situation. From an information
processing perspective, one accesses the familiar domain's network in LTM
and relates it point by point to the problem situation in WM. Successful
application necessitates the familiar situation being similar to the problem
situation. The subgoals in this approach are relating the steps in the familiar domain to those in the problem area. Students often use the analogy
method to solve problems in textbooks. Examples are worked in the text
(familiar domain), then students relate these problem steps to the problems
they must solve.

The power of analogical problem solving was demonstrated by Gick
and Holyoak (1980, 1983). Subjects were presented with a difficult medical
problem and, as an analogy, a solved military problem. Simply giving subjects the analogical problem did not automatically lead them to use it.
However, giving subjects a hint to use the military problem to solve the
medical problem improved problem solving.

Gick and Holyoak also found that giving subjects two analogue stories
led to better problem solving than giving one story. However, having subjects
summarize the analogue story, giving them the principle underlying the
story while they read it, or providing them with a diagram illustrating the
problem solution principle, did not enhance problem solving. These results
suggest that in an unfamiliar domain, students need guidance on how to

employ analogies and that multiple examples increase the likelihood of students linking one to the problem to be solved.

To be maximally effective, analogical problem solving requires good knowledge of the familiar and problem domains. Students have enough difficulty using analogies to solve problems even when the solution strategy is highlighted. With inadequate knowledge, students are unlikely to see the relation between the problem and the analogue. Even assuming good knowledge, the analogy is likely to fail when the familiar and problem domains are conceptually dissimilar. Fighting a battle (the military problem) is similar to fighting a disease (the medical problem), but other analogies (fighting a corporate takeover attempt) might not be.

Analogical problem solving is relevant to teaching and learning. Teachers often have students whose native language is not English. Teaching students in their native language is impossible. Teachers might relate this problem to teaching students who have difficulty learning. With the latter students, teachers would proceed slowly, use concrete experiences whenever possible, and provide much individual instruction. They might try the same tactics with non–English language students, while simultaneously teaching them English words and phrases so they can follow along with the other students in class.

This analogy is appropriate because students with learning problems and students who speak little English have difficulties in the classroom. Other analogies might not be appropriate. Unmotivated students also have learning difficulties. Using them for the analogy, the teacher might offer the non–English speaking students rewards for learning. This solution is apt to be less effective, because the problem with the latter students is instructional, not motivational.

Brainstorming.   *Brainstorming* is useful for formulating possible problem solutions (Osborn, 1963). The steps in brainstorming are as follows (Mayer, 1983):

1. Define the problem
2. Generate as many solutions as possible without evaluating them
3. Decide on criteria for judging potential solutions
4. Use these criteria to select the best solution

As with analogical problem solving, the amount of knowledge one has about the problem domain affects the success of brainstorming, because better domain knowledge allows one to generate more potential solutions and criteria for judging their feasibility. Brainstorming can be used individually, though the group interaction usually leads to more solutions.

Brainstorming lends itself well to many instructional and administrative decisions made in schools. Assume that a new school principal finds low staff morale. Staff members agree that better communication is needed. The grade-level leaders meet with the principal, and the group arrives at the following potential solutions: Hold a weekly meeting with staff, send out a weekly bulletin, post notices on a bulletin board, hold weekly meetings with grade-level leaders (after which they meet with teachers), make announcements over the public address system. The group formulates two criteria: (1) minimally time-consuming for teachers and (2) minimally disrupting to classes. With the criteria in mind, they decide that the principal should send out a weekly bulletin and meet with grade-level leaders as a group. Although these meetings will take time, they will be more focused between the principal and grade-level leaders than between the principal and the entire staff.

Experts and Novices

Research shows that one difference between expert and novice problem solvers involves the demands made on WM. Expert problem solvers do not activate large amounts of potentially relevant information; they identify key features of the problem, relate them to background knowledge, and generate one or a small number of potential solutions (Mayer, 1983). Experts reduce complex problems to manageable size by separating the problem space from the larger task environment, which includes the domain of facts and knowledge within which the problem is embedded (Newell & Simon, 1972). This reduction process retains relevant information, discards irrelevant information, fits within the limits of WM, and is accurate enough to allow a solution. Novice problem solvers, however, often attempt problem solving in piecemeal fashion because of the poorer organization in their memories. In mathematics, novices generate formulas from memory when confronted with word problems. Trying to store excess information in WM clutters their thinking (Resnick, 1985).

Experts and novices also differ in *background knowledge*, not in knowledge of general problem-solving strategies but rather in quality and quantity of *domain-specific knowledge* (Elstein, Shulman, & Sprafka, 1978; Simon, 1979). Experts have more extensive and better-organized LTM structures in their area of expertise (Chi, Feltovich, & Glaser, 1981). The greater amount of knowledge experts can use in solving problems, the more likely they are to solve them and the better their memory organization facilitates efficiency.

Qualitative differences are found in how knowledge is structured in memory (Chi, Glaser, & Rees, 1982). Experts have knowledge more *hierarchically organized*. Chi et al. (1981) had expert and novice problem solvers sort physics textbook problems on any basis they wished. Novices grouped problems according to the type of apparatus employed (e.g., lever, beam), the words used in the problem, or the similarities in visual features. Experts classified problems based on the underlying physics principle needed to solve the problem (e.g., laws of motion, Newton's laws).

Novices typically respond to problems in terms of how they are presented; experts reinterpret problems to reveal an underlying structure, one that most likely matches their own LTM network (Resnick, 1985). Novices attempt to translate the given information directly into formulas and solve for the missing quantities. Rather than generate formulas, experts may initially draw diagrams to clarify the relations among problem aspects. They often construct a new version of the problem. By the time they are ready to perform calculations, they usually have simplified the problem and perform fewer calculations than novices. The differences between novices and experts can be summarized as follows. Compared with novices, experts

- Possess more declarative knowledge
- Have better hierarchical organization of knowledge
- Recognize problem formats more easily
- Monitor their performances more carefully
- Understand better the value of strategy use

Production Systems

The knowledge and heuristics used to solve problems can be collectively represented by the theoretical construct of a production system. A *production system* is a network of condition-action sequences (rules), where the condition is the set of circumstances that activates the system and the action is the set of activities that occurs (Anderson, 1990; Andre, 1986). A production system consists of *if-then statements*. If-statements (the condition) include the goal and test statements; then-statements are the actions. Anderson (1990) cites the following simple production:

> IF   the goal is to drive a standard transmission car
>   and the car is in first gear
>   and the car is going more than 10 miles an hour
> THEN shift the car into second gear. (p. 243)

Productions are forms of procedural knowledge that include the conditions under which they are applicable. Productions are represented in LTM as propositional networks and are acquired in the same fashion as other procedural knowledge. Productions also are organized hierarchically with subordinate and superordinate productions. To solve two equations with two unknowns, one first represents one unknown in terms of the second unknown (subordinate production), after which one solves for the second unknown (production) and uses that value to solve for the first unknown (superordinate production).

Productions can be general or specific. The driving-a-car production is domain-specific. Heuristics are general productions because they are applicable to diverse content. A means-ends analysis is represented as follows (Anderson, 1990):

> IF   the goal is to transform the current state into the goal state
>   and D is the largest difference between the states
> THEN set as subgoals
>   1. To eliminate the difference D
>   2. To convert the resulting state into the goal state. (p. 243)

A second production needs to be employed with the if-statement, "IF the goal is to eliminate the difference D." This sequence continues until the subgoals have been identified at a specific level; then domain-specific rules are applied. In short, general productions are broken down until the level at which domain-specific knowledge is applied. Production systems offer a means of linking general with specific problem-solving procedures.

LANGUAGE COMPREHENSION

Components of Comprehension

Language has been viewed as a central element to understanding the mind. Although humans differ from other animals in many ways, the gap between human language and animal communication systems is tremendous. Language is the principal means of teaching, establishing rules, and transmitting cultural practices.

Although Skinner (1957) explained language in terms of reinforcement contingencies, this view is not accepted by the research community (see the discussion of Basic Processes in Chapter 3). Chomsky (1959) criticized this approach as unsuitable to explain the richness and diversity of natural languages. Most investigators view language as reflecting cognitive processes. Much current research explores language processes in schools to include methods of language instruction.

Language comprises spoken and written communication. Although reading is crucially important in school, children understand spoken language before they learn to read (Calfee & Drum, 1986):

> "By the age of three or four, virtually every child has learned a language." You immediately and properly understand the reference to *spoken language*. The child's linguistic performance matures through adolescence and beyond, but the essential characteristics of adult language appear in the preschooler's speech and comprehension, including a well-developed phonological system, a substantial store of morphemes and rules for adding to that store, a syntax that allows the child to parse and

---

APPLICATION 7.2: Language Comprehension

Students presented with confusing or vague information may misconstrue it or relate it to the wrong context. Teachers need to present clear, concise information and ensure that students have adequate background information to build networks and schemata. For instance, a teacher wants to present a unit on farm life to young children who live in an urban area. Most of the children will have difficulty comprehending the unit because they have not seen a farm or farm animals. The teacher can produce better student understanding by providing farm-related experiences for the children: taking a field trip to a farm; hatching chicken or duck eggs in the classroom; showing films about farm life; and bringing in small farm equipment, seeds, plants, small animals, and photographs. As students become familiar with farms, they will be better able to comprehend spoken and written communications about farms.

> produce the strings of morphemes that relate ideas, and an understanding of the conventions for carrying on a conversation. (p. 806)

There are processes common to spoken and written comprehension. Comprehension of speech is the more basic phenomenon; reading comprehension incorporates additional processes. The underlying theme is that efforts to comprehend spoken and written language represent a problem-solving process involving domain-specific declarative and procedural knowledge (production systems).

Comprehension has three major components: perception, parsing, and utilization (Anderson, 1990). *Perception* involves attending to and recognizing an input; in language comprehension, sound patterns are translated into words in WM. *Parsing* means mentally dividing the sound patterns into units of meaning. *Utilization* refers to what happens to the parsed mental representation—storing it in LTM if it is a learning task, giving an answer if it is a question, asking a question if it is not comprehended. This section addresses parsing and utilization; perception was discussed in Chapter 5 in section on Attention and Sensory Reception.

Parsing

Linguistic research shows that people understand the grammatical rules of their language, even though they usually cannot verbalize them (Clark & Clark, 1977). Beginning with the work of Chomsky (1957), researchers have investigated the role of *deep structures* containing prototypical representations of language structure. The English language contains a deep structure for the pattern "noun1–verb–noun2," which allows us to recognize these patterns in speech and interpret them as, "noun1 did verb to noun2." Deep structures may be represented in LTM as productions (if-then statements). Chomsky postulated that the capacity for acquiring deep structures is innately human, although which structures are acquired depends on the language of one's culture.

Parsing includes more than just fitting language into production systems. When people are exposed to language they construct a mental representation of the situation. They recall from LTM propositional knowledge about the context, into which they integrate new knowledge. *All communication is incomplete.* Speakers do not provide all information relevant to the topic being discussed. Rather, they omit the information listeners are likely to know (Clark & Clark, 1977). For example, assume A meets B, and B remarks, "You won't believe what happened to me at the airport!" A is likely to activate propositional knowledge in LTM about airports. Then B says, "As I was checking my baggage. . . . " To comprehend this statement, A must know that one packs a bag for a trip and checks the bag at the airport. B did not tell A these things but assumed A knows them.

Effective language parsing requires knowledge and inferences (Resnick, 1985). When exposed to verbal communication, individuals access from LTM information about the described situation. This information exists in LTM as propositional networks hierarchically organized as schemata (prototypical versions of situations). Networks allow people to understand incomplete communications. Consider the following sentence: "I went to the grocery store and wrote a check for $10 over the amount." Knowledge that people buy merchandise in grocery stores and that they use checks to pay for it enables listeners to comprehend this sentence. The missing information is filled in with knowledge in memory.

People often misconstrue communications because they fill in missing information with the wrong context. When given a vague passage about four friends getting together for an evening, music students interpreted it as a description of playing music, whereas physical education students described it as an evening of playing cards (Anderson, Reynolds, Schallert, & Goetz, 1977). The interpretative schemata salient in people's minds are used to comprehend problematic passages.

That spoken language is incomplete can be shown by decomposing communications into propositions and identifying how propositions are linked. Consider the following example (Kintsch, 1979):

> The Swazi tribe was at war with a neighboring tribe because of a dispute over some cattle. Among the warriors were two unmarried men named Kakra and his younger brother Gum. Kakra was killed in battle.

Although this passage seems straightforward, a propositional analysis reveals the following 11 distinct propositions:

1. The Swazi tribe was at war.
2. The war was with a neighboring tribe.
3. The war had a cause.
4. The cause was a dispute over some cattle.
5. There were warriors.
6. The warriors were two men.
7. The men were unmarried.
8. The men were named Kakra and Gum.
9. Gum was the younger brother of Kakra.
10. Kakra was killed.
11. The killing was in a battle.

Even this propositional analysis is incomplete. Propositions 1 to 4 link together, as do propositions 5 to 11, but there is a gap between 4 and 5. To supply the missing link, one might have to change proposition 5 to "The dispute involved warriors."

Kintsch and van Dijk (1978) showed that features of communication influence comprehension. Comprehension becomes more difficult when more links are missing and when propositions are further apart (in the sense of requiring inferences to fill in the gaps). When much material has to be inferred, WM easily becomes overloaded and comprehension suffers.

In building representations, people include important information and omit details (Resnick, 1985). These *gist representations* include propositions most germane to comprehension. Readers' ability to make sense of a text depends on what they know about the topic (Chiesi, Spilich, & Voss, 1979; Spilich, Vesonder, Chiesi, & Voss, 1979). When the appropriate network or schema exists in learners' memories, learners employ a production that extracts the most central information to fill the slots in the schema. Comprehension proceeds slowly when a network has to be constructed because it does not exist in LTM.

How schemata are employed is exemplified with stories. Stories have a prototypical schema that includes setting, initiating events, internal responses of characters, goals, attempts to attain goals, outcomes, and reactions (Black, 1984; Rumelhart, 1975, 1977; Stein & Trabasso, 1982). When hearing a story, people recall the story schema and gradually fit information into it. Some categories (e.g., initiating events, goal attempts, consequences) are nearly always included, but others (internal responses of characters) may be omitted (Mandler, 1978; Stein & Glenn, 1979). People recall stories better when events are presented in the expected order rather than in a nonstandard order. When a schema is well established, people rapidly integrate information into it.

Utilization

Utilization refers to what people do with the language communications they receive. For example, if the communication asks a question, listeners retrieve information from LTM to answer it. In a classroom, students link the communication with related information in LTM. Clark and Clark (1977) characterized utilization as follows:

1. On hearing an utterance, listeners identify the speech act, propositional content, and thematic content.
2. They next search memory for information that matches the given information.
3. Finally, depending on the speech act, they deal with the new information:
   a. If the utterance is an assertion, they add the new information to memory.
   b. If the utterance is a yes/no question, they compare the new information with what is in memory and, depending on the match, answer yes or no.
   c. If the utterance is a WH–question, they retrieve the wanted information from memory and compose an answer conveying that information.
   d. If the utterance is a request, they carry out the action necessary to make the new information true. (p. 90)

To properly utilize sentences as speakers intend, listeners must encode three pieces of information: speech act, propositional content, and thematic content. *Speech act* refers to the speaker's purpose in uttering the communication, that is, what the speaker is trying to accomplish with the utterance (Austin, 1962; Searle, 1969). Speakers may be conveying information to listeners, commanding them to do something, requesting information from them, promising them something, and so on. *Propositional content* is information that can be judged true or false. *Thematic content* refers to the context in which the utterance is made. Speakers make assumptions about what listeners know. On hearing an utterance, listeners infer information not explicitly stated but germane to how it is utilized. It is likely that the speech act and propositional and thematic contents are encoded with productions.

Assume that a teacher is giving a history lesson and is questioning students about text material. The teacher asks, "What was Churchill's position during World War II?" The speech act is a request and is signaled by the sentence beginning with a WH word. The propositional content refers to Churchill's position during World War II; it might be represented in memory as follows: Churchill–Prime Minister–Great Britain–World War II.

The thematic content refers to what the teacher left unsaid; the teacher assumes students have heard of Churchill and World War II. The thematic content also includes the classroom question and answer setting. The students understand the teacher will be asking questions for them to answer.

Of special importance for school learning is how students encode assertions. When teachers utter an assertion, they are conveying to students they believe the stated proposition is true. If a teacher says, "Churchill was the Prime Minister of Great Britain during World War II," the teacher is conveying the belief that this assertion is true. Students record the assertion with related information in LTM.

Speakers facilitate the process whereby people relate new assertions with information in LTM by employing the *given-new contract* (Clark & Haviland, 1977). For example,

> The speaker agrees (a) to use given information to refer to information she thinks the listener can uniquely identify from what he already knows and (b) to use new information to refer to information she believes to be true but is not already known to the listener. (Clark & Clark, 1977, p. 92)

The given-new contract says that given information should be readily identifiable and new information should be unknown to the listener. We might think of the given-new contract as a production. In integrating information into memory, listeners identify given information, access it in LTM, and relate new information to it (i.e., store it in the appropriate "slot" in the network). For the given-new contract to enhance utilization, given information must be readily identified by listeners. When given information is not readily available—it is not in listeners' memories or has not been accessed in a long time—using the given-new production is difficult.

READING

As with language comprehension, reading involves perception, parsing, and utilization. The perceptual part of reading (recognizing words) is referred to as *lexical access* or *decoding*. *Comprehension*, or the attachment of meaning to printed information, involves parsing and utilization.

Decoding

Decoding means deciphering printed symbols or making letter-sound correspondences by using a whole-word or a phonetic approach. In the whole-word approach, the printed word is matched to a similar pattern in LTM, which activates the word's meaning for comprehension. This approach relies on pattern recognition procedures; the patterns are in one's sight vocabulary. In the phonetic approach, one sounds out a word by dividing it into syllables and generating corresponding sound patterns. The phonetic patterns activate the word's meaning in memory.

The phonetic and whole-word techniques employ *bottom-up* and *top-down* processes, respectively (Just & Carpenter, 1980; Resnick, 1985). In bottom-up processing, people recognize features of letters, combine letters into syllables, and combine syllables into words. Word recognition precedes meaning. Reading is controlled by the printed input. Less-skilled readers often employ bottom-up processing, and it is used by good readers when they encounter unfamiliar words.

In top-down processing, reading is controlled by such higher-level processes as forming expectations about what will occur and drawing inferences. Readers create a context based on prior knowledge and current information. This context comprises propositional networks and schemata with empty slots. They fill in the required information and confirm or disconfirm hypotheses about what will occur (Frederiksen, 1979). Readers employ production systems to extract the expected information from text. With efficient top-down processing, readers do not encode separate words but rather propositions or larger units.

Examples of top-down and bottom-up processing are shown in Figure 7.2. Assume that a student has been reading a passage about a tall boy. The reader encounters the sentence, "Martin was outside playing _____." Using top-down processing, the reader might expect to find the word *basketball*. With bottom-up processing, the reader would construct the work from individual syllables.

In skilled reading, much information is processed automatically. *Automaticity* of word recognition distinguishes good from poor readers, not whether words are recognized. Automatic processing is important because the WM has a limited capacity (Calfee & Drum, 1986). Readers can rapidly transfer information in WM to LTM and move to new material (Resnick, 1985).

In studies of eye fixations during reading, good readers spend significantly less time on both unfamiliar and familiar words (Just & Carpenter, 1980). The former also sound out unfamiliar words faster than the latter. Good readers tend to parse passages at the end of phrases and sentences; they pause longer there than in the middle. They integrate information at natural break points (units of thought), which helps them draw inferences and construct meaning.

Although speed in reading does not guarantee total comprehension, a positive relationship does exist between decoding speed and comprehension skill (Curtis, 1980). Rapid decoding seems to activate comprehension processes sooner. Thus, one can comprehend more information in less time. Slow decoding takes more time to activate comprehension processes; in the meantime, some information previously decoded is lost from WM and is inaccessible for comprehension.

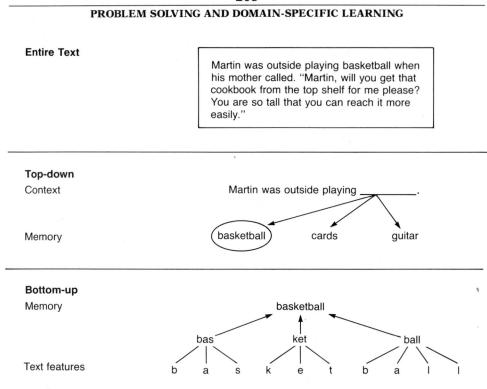

Entire Text

Martin was outside playing basketball when his mother called. "Martin, will you get that cookbook from the top shelf for me please? You are so tall that you can reach it more easily."

Top-down

Context

Martin was outside playing _____ .

Memory

basketball   cards   guitar

Bottom-up

Memory

basketball

bas   ket   ball

Text features

b   a   s   k   e   t   b   a   l   l

FIGURE 7.2
Examples of top-down and bottom-up processing.

Comprehension

Comprehension involves attaching meaning to printed information and us-ing the information for a particular purpose. There are different levels of comprehension (Perfetti, 1985). At an elementary level, readers access a word's meaning as a consequence of decoding. At a higher level, readers move beyond the literal meaning of printed words and engage in such men-tal activities as drawing inferences, deciding on main ideas, inferring the writer's purpose or bias, and anticipating how events will unfold in text.

Once a word is decoded, readers access the meaning stored with the letter-sound correspondence in LTM. Understanding word meanings de-pends on one's store of declarative knowledge. Compared with poor readers, good readers have rich vocabularies and thus have quicker access to word meanings. Speed of access to word meanings bears a positive relationship to reading comprehension (Goldberg, Schwartz, & Stewart, 1977).

Comprehension is influenced by the reading context. Good readers em-ploy top-down processing more than poor readers and are faster in part because they usually rely on context to identify words. Skilled readers also take advantage of word context to parse sentences into natural units, even when punctuation marks are absent. Readers derive contextual cues that signal where units are to be parsed, such as word order, word endings, and punctuation. In the sentence, "The plodols went home," readers will not know the meaning of *plodols* but will surmise that it is a plural noun because it follows *the* in the first position of the sentence and because it ends in *s*.

Literal comprehension is important for reading such texts as a set of directions on how to assemble a bookcase or a restaurant menu. People often find it desirable to go beyond literal meaning to understand better what they are reading. Inferential comprehension is involved in such activities as identifying main ideas, getting the gist, summarizing and integrating information, and drawing conclusions. Inferential comprehension requires mentally linking different ideas in text. Consider the following sentences:

- The Senate failed to ratify the treaty.
- Senator Milhoudy was livid.

These sentences are linked in the sense that both refer to the Senate, but their meanings are not linked with each other. A reader might infer that the reason Senator Milhoudy was livid was because the senator wanted the treaty ratified and voted to ratify it, but the vote failed in the Senate.

Compared with poor readers, skilled readers integrate ideas better within and between sentences (Perfetti & Roth, 1981). For example, skilled readers are quicker to determine a pronoun's referent, whereas poor readers benefit when noun phrases are repeated.

Another inferential comprehension process is *summarization*, or grouping important points into a coherent structure formed by drawing inferences and using words and phrases that signal main ideas (e.g., "in summary") (Kintsch & van Dijk, 1978). Good readers are more proficient at summarizing than poor readers (Meyer, Brandt, & Bluth, 1980). The ability to identify and use structure improves with development.

Compared with poor readers, skilled readers approach texts with knowledge about how they are organized and with a strategy for acquiring information from them to complement the organization. Skilled readers have mental schemata representing prototypical organizations of texts (Meyer, 1975, 1977, 1984). A text may compare and contrast, discuss cause and effect, show how ideas are related, state an idea or principle with examples, or present a problem with solutions. Skilled readers identify the text pattern, access the schema from LTM, and integrate information from text into the appropriate schema slots while reading.

Inferential comprehension also involves *elaboration*, or adding to new knowledge by using one's prior knowledge. Following are some ways to elaborate new knowledge:

- Think of examples of the ideas or principles described
- Anticipate what will happen in the story
- Fill in missing details in text
- Draw an analogy between new material and what is known
- Think about implications of what is stated
- Relate details to main ideas
- Compare ideas to your beliefs

Elaborations help link new information to organizational structures already in memory. Skilled readers are more facile at employing elaborations than poor readers.

Metacognition

Metacognition involves students' understanding and monitoring of reading purposes and strategies (Paris, Wixson, & Palincsar, 1986). (See the discussion under Conditional Knowledge and Metacognition in Chapter 6.) Metacognition includes understanding how and when to use skills and strategies to accomplish tasks. Beginning readers often do not understand the conventions of printed material: One reads words not pictures and (in English) from left to right and top to bottom. Beginning and poorer readers typically do not monitor their comprehension or adjust their strategies accordingly (Baker & Brown, 1984). Older and skilled readers are better at comprehension monitoring than are younger and less-skilled readers, respectively (Paris et al., 1986).

Monitoring involves setting goals, evaluating goal progress, and making necessary corrections (McNeil, 1987). Skilled readers do not approach all reading tasks in identical fashion. They determine their goal: finding main ideas, reading for details, skimming, getting the gist, and so on. They then adopt the strategy they believe will accomplish the goal. When reading skills are highly developed, these processes may occur automatically.

While reading, skilled readers check their progress. If their goal is to locate important ideas and if after reading a few pages they have not located any important ideas, they are apt to reread those pages. If they come across a word they do not understand, they try to determine its meaning from context or consult a dictionary rather than continue reading.

Developmental evidence indicates a trend in greater recognition and correction of comprehension deficiencies (Garner & Reis, 1981). Although younger children recognize comprehension failures less often than older children, younger children who are good comprehenders may recognize a problem but may not employ a strategy to solve it (e.g., rereading). Older children who are good comprehenders recognize problems and employ correction strategies.

READING

Children develop metacognitive abilities through interactions with parents and teachers (Langer & Applebee, 1986). Adults help children solve problems by guiding them through solution steps, reminding them of their goal, and helping them plan how to reach the goal. An effective teaching procedure includes informing children of the goal, making them aware of information relevant to the task, arranging a situation conducive to problem solving, and reminding them of their goal progress (Wertsch, 1979).

Since many children do not use effective strategies, researchers have recommended strategy training programs. These programs generally have been successful in helping students learn strategies and maintain their use over time. Brown and her colleagues advocate strategy training incorporating practice in use of skills, instruction in how to monitor outcomes of one's efforts, and feedback on when and where a strategy may be useful (Brown, 1980; Brown, Palincsar, & Armbruster, 1984).

Palincsar and Brown (1984) identified seventh graders with poor comprehension skills. Students were trained in self-directed summarizing (review), questioning, clarifying, and predicting. Summarizing included stating what had happened in the text and also served as a self-test on the content. Questioning addressed determining what main idea question a teacher or test might ask about that material. Clarifying was used when portions of the text were unclear and students could not adequately summarize. Predicting was used when text cues signaled forthcoming information.

These activities were taught as part of an interactive dialogue between teacher and student known as *reciprocal teaching.* During the lessons, an adult teacher met with two students. Initially the teacher modeled the activities. The teacher and students silently read a passage, after which the teacher asked a question that a teacher or test might ask, summarized the content, clarified troublesome points, and predicted future content. Following the teacher's modeled demonstration, the teacher and students took turns being the teacher. At first, students had difficulty assuming the role of teacher; the teacher often had to construct paraphrases and questions for students. Students became more capable of following the procedure and implementing the four activities.

Compared with a condition in which students receive instruction on locating information in text, reciprocal teaching leads to greater comprehension gains, better maintenance over time, and better generalization to classroom comprehension tests. Students exposed to reciprocal teaching also show greater improvements in quality of summaries and questions asked. The maintenance and generalization results are important because changes brought about by strategy training programs often do not maintain themselves or generalize to other tasks (Borkowski & Cavanaugh, 1979).

The dialogue about the following text occurred between teacher (T) and student (S) early in the training program (Palincsar & Brown, 1984). The text read as follows:

> The snake's skeleton and parts of its body are very flexible—something like a rubber hose with bones. A snake's backbone can have as many as 300 vertebrae, almost ten times as many as a human's. These vertebrae are connected by loose and rubbery tissues that allow easy movement. Because of this bendable, twistable spinal construction, a snake can turn its body in almost any direction at almost any point. (p. 142)

S: Like, if a snake is turning around, he wouldn't break any bones because he is flexible.

T: And the reason he is so flexible is . . .

S: If someone stepped on his tail, he wouldn't be able to move unless he was flexible.

T: O.K. That explains why it would be helpful to be so flexible, but what makes the snake so flexible? I think that is an important part of the summary.

S: So he can move faster?

T: That is another reason for being flexible. Let me do a summary for you. Sara [the student] is right. The most important thing we have learned is that the snake is very flexible. The reason they can bend so easily is that they have so many little bones in their backbones and each of them can move separately, making the snake very flexible. Does that make sense? (p. 142)

The last statement by the teacher is a modeled demonstration of summarization.

Another example of strategy training incorporating metacognitive elements is the Informed Strategies for Learning (ISL) program by Paris and his colleagues (Paris et al., 1984; Paris & Oka, 1986). ISL is based on the premise that reading requires declarative, procedural, and conditional knowledge. The program also attempts to enhance students' self-efficacy for effectively applying strategies. Children are taught such reading skills as understanding goals of reading, elaborating text information, summarizing main points, skimming for meaning, monitoring comprehension while reading, and knowing when and why to implement strategies. Twice a week for 14 weeks, students receive 30-minute lessons on the usefulness of different strategies. Discussions between teacher and students are designed to influence children's beliefs about the efficacy of strategy use. Children exposed to this program typically show gains in awareness of comprehension strategies and monitoring skills, which in turn bear a positive relationship to reading achievement. The program benefits students with high, average, and low reading abilities, which enhances its potential for classroom use.

WRITING

Writing refers to translating ideas into linguistic symbols in print. Compared with reading, less research has been conducted on writing. In part, historical reluctance to investigate writing may have stemmed from its mystique. Many students believe that good writers are born, not made, or that good writing is creative and inspirational—that words flow with little effort. Contemporary research has debunked this myth by showing that good writing, like good reading, good mathematics, and so forth, is essentially a problem-solving process that can be taught (Bereiter, 1980; Flower, 1981; Flower & Hayes, 1980; Scardamalia & Bereiter, 1986).

Early models of writing subdivided it into such stages as prewriting, writing, rewriting (Rohman, 1965). One benefit of these models is that they call attention to different phases of the writing process. Good writers do not simply write down words; they spend much time thinking and organizing their thoughts, as well as rewriting what they have written. At the same time, writing does not seem to be a straightforward, linear process, as conceptualized by stage models. As writers write down words they also are mentally planning, organizing, and revising (Sommers, 1980).

Current writing models examine writers' mental processes as they engage in different aspects of writing (de Beaugrande, 1984). A general research goal is to define expertise. By comparing expert with novice writers, researchers have begun to identify how their mental processes diverge (Bereiter & Scardamalia, 1986). One useful strategy is having writers "think

---

APPLICATION 7.3: Writing

Teachers can incorporate planning, transcribing, and revising activities into lessons. If a teacher wants students to write a paragraph describing their summer vacations, the teacher might have students share what they did during the summer. Following this large-group activity, the teacher and students might jointly develop and edit a paragraph about the teacher's summer vacation. This exercise would emphasize the important elements of a good paragraph and components of the writing process.

Students then could be paired and could share orally with each other some things done during the summer. Sharing helps students generate ideas to use in transcribing. Following this activity, students could list their summer activities on a sheet of paper. For the transcribing, students could use their lists to formulate sentences of a paragraph and could then share their written products with their partners. Partners could provide feedback about clarity and grammar, and students could revise their paragraphs.

aloud" or say aloud everything they think about while writing (Hayes & Flower, 1980). Think-aloud protocols are recorded, transcribed, and analyzed to determine which mental processes are associated with writing expertise defined by external criteria (e.g., writing prizes, high grades in writing courses, extent of professional writing).

This section discusses composition processes that translate one's initial ideas into print and reviewing processes that alter what one originally thought or wrote. These components are not mutually exclusive; writing involves interacting with one's environment rather than proceeding through hard-and-fast stages.

Composition Processes

Flower and Hayes (1980, 1981a; Hayes & Flower, 1980) formulated a problem-solving model in which writing is viewed as a set of thinking processes that writers organize while composing. Writing is goal-directed behavior; writers generate superordinate and subordinate goals incorporating their purposes and alter their goals based on what they learn while writing. Rather than focus on products of writing, Flower and Hayes emphasize processes that writers employ throughout writing. The Flower and Hayes model reflects the general orientation espoused by Newell and Simon (1972). Writers define a problem space and perform operations on their mental representation of the problem to attain their goals (Figure 7.3).

The *rhetorical problem* shown in the figure includes the writer's topic, intended audience, and goals. In school, the rhetorical problem is often well defined; teachers assign a term paper topic, the audience is the teacher, and the goal (e.g., to inform, to persuade) is provided; however, the rhetorical problem is never defined completely by someone other than the writer. Writers interpret problems in their own ways.

The writer's LTM plays a crucial role. Writers differ in their knowledge of the topic, audience, and mechanics of writing (organization, grammar, spelling, punctuation). Writers knowledgeable about their topics include fewer irrelevant statements in their compositions but more auxiliary statements (designed to elaborate upon main points) compared with less-knowledgeable writers (Voss, Vesonder, & Spilich, 1980). Differences in declarative knowledge impact the quality of writing.

Planning (see Figure 7.3) refers to forming an internal representation of knowledge to be used in composing. The internal representation generally is more abstract than the actual writing. Planning includes several subprocesses such as *generating ideas*, that is, retrieving relevant information from memory or other sources. These ideas may be well formed or fragmentary. *Organizing* helps give ideas better meaning by grouping them into superordinate and subordinate roles. Organizing also includes deciding on the flow of the text—what to present first, next, and so on.

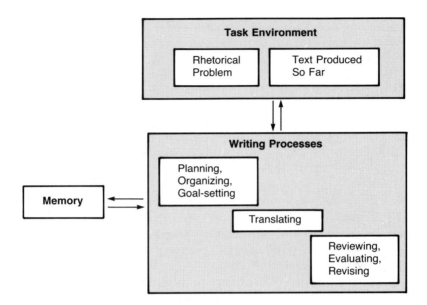

FIGURE 7.3
Process model of writing (*Source:* Adapted from "A Cognitive Process Theory of Writing" by L. Flower and J. R. Hayes, 1981, *College Composition and Communication, 32,* p. 370. Copyright 1981 by the National Council of Teachers of English. Reprinted with permission).

A major subprocess is *goal setting.* Goals are substantive (*what* the writer wants to communicate) and procedural (*how* to communicate, that is, what and how points should be expressed). Good writers often alter their goals based on what they have already produced. Writers have goals in mind prior to writing, but as they proceed, they may realize that a certain goal is not relevant to the composition. New goals are suggested by actual writing.

There are individual differences in planning. Young children produce fewer ideas than older ones (Scardamalia & Bereiter, 1986). Among older students, higher scores on the verbal portion of the Scholastic Aptitude Test (SAT) are associated with greater idea generation (Glynn, Britton, Muth, & Dogan, 1982). Idea generation depends on students' cuing themselves to produce more ideas. Younger children benefit from external cues (e.g., "Can you write some more?"). Older and better writers make greater use of internal prompts. They search relevant topics in LTM and assess knowledge before they begin composing.

Organization is conveyed through cohesion between sentence parts and coherence across sentences. Cohesive devices tie ideas together with pronouns, definite articles, conjunctions, and word meanings. For example, in the following sentences, the referent of *he* is unclear: "Joe and Jim sat together during the game. He left to get some food." Cohesion is obtained as follows: "Joe and Jim sat together during the game. Joe left to get some food." Young children have more difficulty with cohesion, but unskilled writers of any age use cohesion less well. Developmental differences also are found in coherence. Young writers have difficulty linking sentences with one another and with the topic sentence (McCutchen & Perfetti, 1982). Good writers have better coherence than poor writers.

Goals of good and poor writers differ. The primary goal of skilled writers is to communicate meaning. Poor writers often practice "associative writing" (Bereiter, 1980); they put onto paper the contents of LTM relevant to the topic. They may believe the goal of writing is to regurgitate everything one knows about the topic; order is less important than inclusiveness. Another goal of less-skilled writers is to avoid making errors. When asked to critique their own writing, good writers focus on how well they communicated their intentions, whereas poor writers cite surface considerations (spelling, punctuation) more often.

Translation (see Figure 7.3) refers to putting one's ideas into print. For children and inexperienced writers, translating often overburdens the WM. They must keep in mind their goal, the ideas they wish to express, and the necessary organization and mechanics. Good writers concern themselves less with surface features during translation; they focus more on meaning and apparently think they can correct surface problems later. Poor writers concentrate more on surface features and write slower than good writers. Better writers take stylistic and surface considerations into account when they pause during writing. Poorer writers benefit when they read what they have written as they prepare to compose.

A common problem in translation is *writer's block*, or difficulty in beginning to compose. Block may be caused by inadequate knowledge of the topic or by lack of interest. Rose (1980) found that adopting rigid rules for writing can cause block. Writers who believe they must begin with a quote or make four important points may get stuck because they cannot follow these rules.

Reviewing Processes

Reviewing consists of evaluating and revising. Reviewing occurs when writers read what they have written as a precursor to further translation or to systematic evaluation and revision (Flower & Hayes, 1981a; Hayes & Flower, 1980). During reviewing, writers evaluate and modify plans and alter subsequent writing.

Reviewing processes are important because writers typically spend as much as 70% of their writing time pausing (Flower & Hayes, 1981b). Much pause time is spent on sentence-level planning. Writers reread what they have written and decide what to say next. These bottom-up processes construct a composition a section at a time. When such building-up is accomplished with the overall plan in mind, the composition continues to reflect the writers' goals.

Dependence on bottom-up writing is characteristic of poor writers. While pausing, good writers also engage in rhetorical planning not directly linked to what they have produced. This type of planning reflects a top-down view of writing as a problem-solving process; writers have an overall goal that they think of how to attain or that they revise. Abstract planning may include information about content (deciding what topic to discuss) and style (deciding to alter the style by inserting an anecdote). This abstract or whole-text planning subsumes sentence-level planning and is characteristic of mature writers (Bereiter & Scardamalia, 1986).

Elementary school children often recognize when their writing contains problems but do little revising without teacher or peer support (Fitzgerald, 1987). Students benefit from instruction designed to improve the quality of their writing. Fitzgerald and Markham (1987) gave average sixth-grade writers instruction on such revisions as additions, deletions, substitutions, and rearrangements. The teacher explained and modeled each revision strategy, after which students worked in pairs. Instruction improved students' knowledge of revision processes and their actual revisions.

Evaluation skills develop earlier than revision skills. Even fourth graders may not successfully correct writing problems they recognize as often as 70% of the time (Scardamalia & Bereiter, 1983). When children correct problems, differences between good and poor writers become evident. Among fourth- and seventh-grade students, the poor writers revise errors in spelling or punctuation, whereas the better writers revise for stylistic reasons (Birnbaum, 1982).

Older students also sometimes fail to recognize problems in writing. Among high school students, good writers revise more than average writers (Stallard, 1974), and a greater proportion of good writers' revisions involve word choice (meaning). Stallard found these two groups did not differ in spelling, punctuation, or other syntactic revisions.

MATHEMATICS

A distinction is typically made in mathematics between *computation* (use of rules, procedures, and algorithms) and *concepts* (problem solving and use of strategies). Computational and conceptual problems require students to implement productions involving rules and algorithms. The difference between these two categories lies in how explicitly the problem tells students what operations to perform. Consider the following problems:

1. $26 + 42 = ?$
2. $5x + 3y = 19$
   $7x - y = 11$
3. What is the length of the hypotenuse of a right triangle with sides equal to 3 inches and 4 inches?

Although students are not directly told what to do in problems 2 and 3, recognition of the problem format and knowledge of procedures lead them to perform the correct operations.

Now contrast the problems above with the following:

1. A man has 20 coins composed of dimes and quarters. If the quarters were dimes and the dimes were quarters, he would have 90 cents more than he has now. How much money does he have?
2. If it takes twice as long for a passenger train to pass a freight train after it first overtakes it as it takes the two trains to pass when going in opposite directions, how many times faster than the freight train is the passenger train?
3. A hiker can average 2 miles per hour uphill and 6 miles per hour downhill. If she goes uphill and downhill and spends no time at the summit, what will be her average speed for an entire trip?

These problems use mathematical computations no more difficult than those required by the problems in the first set; however, the latter problems do not explicitly tell students what to do. Students must decide how to solve the problem, which involves recognizing the problem format, generating appropriate productions, and performing the computations. This is not to suggest that conceptual expertise is better than computational proficiency; deficiencies in either area cause problems. Understanding how to solve a problem but not being able to perform the computations results in incorrect answers, as does being computationally proficient but not being able to conceptualize problems. Mathematical proficiency requires that computation and problem solving be taught together.

Computation Skills

The earliest computational skill children use is *counting* (Resnick, 1985). Children count objects on their fingers and in their heads using a strategy (Groen & Parkman, 1972). The *sum model* involves setting a hypothetical counter at zero, counting in the first addend in increments of one, and then counting in the second addend to arrive at the answer. A somewhat more efficient strategy is to set the counter at the first addend and then count in the second addend in increments of one. Still more efficient is the *min model:* Set the counter at the larger of the two addends and then count in the smaller addend in increments of one (Romberg & Carpenter, 1986). Children as young as $4\frac{1}{2}$ years have been observed to use the min model, even though they never have been instructed in its use (Groen & Resnick, 1977).

This type of invented procedure is efficient and successful. Children and adults often invent procedures to solve mathematical problems. Errors generally are not random but rather reflect *buggy algorithms,* or systematic mistakes in thinking and reasoning (Brown & Burton, 1978). A common mistake in subtraction is to subtract the smaller number from the larger number in each column, regardless of direction, as follows:

$$
\begin{array}{r} 53 \\ -27 \\ \hline 34 \end{array}
\qquad
\begin{array}{r} 602 \\ -274 \\ \hline 472 \end{array}
$$

Mathematical bugs likely develop when students encounter new problems and incorrectly generalize productions. In subtraction without regrouping, students subtract the smaller number from the larger one column by column, so it is easy to see how they could generalize this procedure to problems requiring regrouping. Rather than cease working problems when they do not know what to do, students modify their rules to fit new problems. Buggy algorithms are durable and can instill in students a false sense of competence, perhaps because their application produces answers.

Another source of computational difficulties is poor declarative knowledge of number facts. Basic addition, subtraction, multiplication, and division facts involving simple numbers are not well established in children's memories. The problem $8 \times 7 = ?$ is a cue to retrieve this fact from LTM. Until facts become established, children count or compute answers.

Problems in computation result from using overly complex but technically correct productions to solve problems. Such procedures produce correct answers, but because they are complex, the risk of computational errors is high. The problem $\frac{256}{5}$ can be solved by the division algorithm or by successively subtracting 5 from 256 and counting the number of subtractions. The latter procedure is correct but inefficient, and there is a high probability of error. One of the goals of computation instruction is for students to become skillful in using efficient procedures.

The model of skill acquisition discussed in Chapter 6 (Procedural Knowledge) is relevant to computational skills (J. Anderson, 1982). Learners initially represent the skill as declarative knowledge in a propositional network. Facts concerning the different steps (e.g., in the algorithm) are committed to memory through mental rehearsal and overt practice. The production that guides performance at this stage is general; for example, "IF the goal is to solve this division problem, THEN apply the method the teacher taught us." Learners then insert the steps they have memorized into this general heuristic. With added practice, the declarative representation changes into a domain-specific procedural representation and eventually becomes automated. At the automatic stage, learners quickly recognize the problem pattern—a division problem, a square root problem—and implement the procedure without much conscious deliberation. As a skill is developed, learners are able to execute it rapidly and achieve greater accuracy in their answers.

Problem-Solving Skills

Mathematical problem solving requires that students first accurately represent the problem to include the given information and the goal and then select and apply a problem-solving production (Mayer, 1985). It often is difficult to translate a problem from its linguistic representation to a mental representation. Translation requires good declarative and procedural knowledge. Solving problem 1 above about the man with 20 coins requires knowledge that dimes and quarters are coins, that a dime is $\frac{1}{10}$ (0.10) of $1, and that a quarter is $\frac{1}{4}$ (0.25) of $1. This declarative knowledge needs to be coupled with procedural understanding that dimes and quarters are variables such that dimes + quarters = 20.

One reason why experts translate problems better is that their knowledge is better organized in LTM; the organization reflects the underlying structure of the subject matter (Romberg & Carpenter, 1986). Experts overlook surface features of a problem and analyze it in terms of the operations required for solution. Novices are swayed more by surface features.

Silver (1981) had students sort mathematical word problems into categories by type. The students' word problem–solving skills were tested. Students were classified as good, average, or poor problem solvers. Good problem solvers organized problems according to the process required for solution; poor problem solvers were more likely to group problems with similar content (e.g., money, trains). For example,

> On a ferry trip, the fare for each adult was 50 cents and for each child was 25 cents. The number of passengers was 30 and the total paid was $12.25. How many adults and how many children were there? (Mayer, 1982).

This problem involves two equations with two unknowns. If x = number of adults and y = number of children, then

$$x + y = 30$$
$$.5x + .25y = 12.25$$

Multiplying the first equation by .5 and subtracting the second equation leaves $.25y = 2.75$, or $y = 11$. Substituting the value of y into the first equation yields $x = 19$. Compared with novices, experts are more likely to classify this problem according to solution process (two equations with two unknowns) rather than surface features (money).

Not only are there differences in problem translation and classification, experts and novices also differ in productions (Greeno, 1980). Novices often adopt a "working backward" strategy: They begin with the goal and work their way back to the givens. This is a powerful problem-solving approach, but it requires that one understand the problem domain sufficiently to know what knowledge is required to attain each subgoal. Working backward is a good general heuristic and is useful in the early stages of learning when learners have acquired some domain knowledge but are not competent enough to recognize problem formats quickly. As domain-specific knowledge is acquired, more powerful problem-solving productions become available (Anderson, 1990).

In contrast to novices, experts often adopt a "working forward" strategy. They identify the problem type and select the appropriate production to solve the problem. Experts develop sophisticated procedural knowledge for classifying mathematical problems according to type. High school algebra problems fall into roughly 20 general categories such as motion, current, coins, and interest/investment (Mayer, 1983). These categories can be aggregated into 6 major groups. For example, the amount-per-time group includes motion, current, and work problems. These problems are solvable with the general formula: amount = rate × time. The development of mathematical problem-solving expertise depends in part on being able to classify a problem into the correct group.

Classification procedures are developed through exposure to instruction and by solving different types of problems. Students initially may apply a working backward approach, but with experience they develop accurate classification procedures. How this novice-to-expert progression occurs is not well understood. Research addressing this progression would have important implications for teaching students to become better problem solvers.

SCIENCE

Much current research in scientific domains compares novices with experts to identify the components of expertise. Researchers also are investigating reasoning processes that students use to evaluate logical arguments.

Domain Knowledge

Experts in scientific domains differ from novices in quantity and organization of knowledge. Experts possess more domain-specific knowledge and are likely to organize it in hierarchies, whereas novices often demonstrate little overlap between scientific concepts.

In the Chi et al. (1981) study, novices classified physics problems based on superficial features (e.g., apparatus); experts classified the problems based on the principle needed to solve the problem. The experts and novices also differed in declarative knowledge memory networks. "Inclined plane," for example, was related in novices' memories with such descriptive terms as *mass, friction,* and, *length.* These descriptors were found in experts' memories, along with principles of mechanics (e.g., conservation of energy, Newton's force laws). Experts had more knowledge (in terms of principles) organized so that descriptors were subordinate to principles.

Novices often use principles erroneously to solve problems. Consider the following example:

> A train is speeding over a bridge that spans a valley. As the train rolls along, a passenger leans out of a window and drops a rock. Where will it land? (McCloskey & Kaiser, 1984)

McCloskey and Kaiser posed the question above to college students. About one-third of the students said the rock would fall straight down. They believed that an object pushed or thrown acquires a force but that an object being carried by a moving vehicle does not acquire a force, so it drops straight down. The analogy the students made was with a person standing still who drops an object, which falls straight down. However, the path of descent of the rock from the moving train is, in fact, parabolic. The idea that objects acquire force is erroneous because objects move in the same direction and at the same speed as their moving carriers. When the rock is dropped, it continues to move forward with the train until the force of gravity pulls it down. Novices overgeneralized their basic knowledge and arrived at an erroneous solution.

Another difference between novices and experts concerns the use of problem-solving strategies (Larkin, 1980; Larkin, McDermott, Simon, & Simon, 1980; White & Tisher, 1986). When confronted with scientific problems, novices often use a means-ends analysis by determining the goal of the problem and deciding which formulas might be useful to reach that goal. They work backward and repeatedly recall formulas containing quantities in the target formula. If they reach a point where they are uncertain how to proceed, they may abandon the problem or attempt to solve it based on their current knowledge.

Experts quickly recognize the problem format, work forward toward intermediate subgoals, and use that information to reach the ultimate goal. Experience in working scientific problems builds knowledge of problem types. Experts often automatically recognize familiar problem features and carry out necessary productions. Even when they are less certain how to solve a problem, experts begin with some information in the problem and work forward to the solution. Notice that the last step experts take is often the novices' first step.

Reasoning

Reasoning refers to the mental processes involved in generating and evaluating logical arguments (Anderson, 1990). Reasoning skills include clarification, basis, inference, and evaluation (Ennis, 1987; Quellmalz, 1987).

Clarification. Clarification requires identifying and formulating questions, analyzing elements, and defining terms. These skills involve determining which elements in a situation are important, what they mean, and how they are related. At times, scientific questions are posed, but at other times students must develop such questions as "What is the problem, hypothesis, or thesis?" Clarification corresponds to the representation phase of problem solving; students define the problem to obtain a clear mental representation. Little productive reasoning occurs without a clear problem statement.

Basis. People's conclusions about a problem are supported by information from personal observations, statements by others, and previous inferences.

APPLICATION 7.4: Reasoning (Clarification)

Teachers can teach students how to ask questions to produce an accurate mental representation of a problem. A teacher gives primary students objects to classify according to shape. The teacher, to help them identify and clarify the problem, can ask some of the following questions:

- What have you been asked to do?
- What items do you have?
- What are some of the shapes you know?
- Does it matter if the items are different colors?
- Does it matter if some of the items are little and some are big?
- Does it matter if some of the items are soft and some are hard?
- What do you think you will do with the items you have?

Students can verbalize what information they need to use and what they are supposed to do with that information. Each time the teacher works with students in solving a problem, the teacher can help them generate questions to determine what information is important for solving the problem.

It is important to judge the credibility of a source. In so doing, one must distinguish between fact, opinion, and reasoned judgment. Assume that a suspect armed with a gun is apprehended near the scene of a murder. That the suspect had a gun when arrested is a fact. Laboratory tests on the gun, the bullets, and the victim lead to the reasoned judgment that the gun was used in the crime. Someone familiar with the case might believe that the suspect is the murderer.

Inference.   Scientific reasoning proceeds inductively or deductively. *Induction* is the process whereby general rules, principles, and concepts are developed from observation and knowledge of specific examples (Pellegrino, 1985). People reason inductively when they extract similarities and differences among specific objects and events and arrive at generalizations, which are tested by applying them to new experiences. Individuals retain their generalizations as long as they are effective, and they modify them when they experience conflicting evidence.

Some of the more common types of tasks used to assess inductive reasoning are classification, concept, and analogy problems. Consider the following analogy (Pellegrino, 1985):

sugar : sweet :: lemon : _____
yellow sour fruit squeeze tea

The appropriate mental operations may be thought of as a type of production system. Initially, one mentally represents critical attributes of each term in the analogy. One activates networks in LTM involving each term, which contain critical attributes of the terms to include subordinate and superordinate concepts. Next, one compares the features of the first pair to determine the link. "Sweet" is a property of sugar that involves taste. One then searches the "lemon" network to determine which of the five features listed corresponds in meaning to "lemon" as "sweet" does to "sugar." Although all five terms are likely to be stored in one's "lemon" network, only "sour" directly involves taste.

Children display basic inductive reasoning ability around age eight. With development, children are able to reason faster and with more complex material. This occurs because children's LTM networks become more complex and better linked, which in turn reduces the burden on WM. To help foster inductive thinking, teachers might use a guided discovery approach in which children learn different examples and try to formulate a general rule. For example, children may collect leaves and based on the collection formulate some general principles involving stems, veins, sizes, and shapes of leaves from different trees. Bruner's (1960) *discovery learning* (discussed in the section on Early Cognitive Perspectives in Chapter 10) can enhance inductive thinking. In this method, the teacher poses a problem for students, such as "Why does metal sink in water but metal ships float?" Rather than telling students how to solve the problem, the teacher provides materials and encourages students to formulate hypotheses and test them as they work on the task.

Deduction is the process whereby one uses a rule or principle to decide whether specific instances logically follow. When individuals reason deductively, they proceed from general concepts (*premises*) to specific instances (*conclusions*) to determine whether the latter follow from the former. A deduction is valid if the premises are true and if the conclusion follows logically from the premises (Johnson-Laird, 1985).

One type of deduction problem is the *three-term series* (Johnson-Laird, 1972). For example,

> If Karen is smarter than Tina, and
>
> If Mary Beth is not as smart as Tina, then
>
> Who is the smartest?

The problem-solving processes employed with this problem are similar to those discussed previously. Initially one forms a mental representation of the problem, such as K > T, MB < T. One then works forward by combining the propositions (K > T > MB) to solve the problem. Developmental factors limit children's proficiency in solving such problems. Children may have difficulty keeping relevant problem information in WM and may not understand the language used to express the relationships.

Another type of deductive reasoning problem is the *syllogism*. Syllogisms are characterized by premises and a conclusion containing the words *all, no,* and *some.* The following are sample premises:

> All university professors are crazy.
>
> Some graduate students are not crazy.
>
> No undergraduate student is crazy.

A sample syllogism is as follows:

> All the students in Ken's class are good in math.
>
> All students who are good in math will attend college.
>
> (Therefore) All the students in Ken's class will attend college.

There is debate about the mental processes people use to solve syllogisms, including whether people represent the information as Venn (circle) diagrams or as strings of propositions (Johnson-Laird, 1985). A production system analysis of syllogisms gives a basic rule: A syllogism is true only if there is no way to interpret the premises to imply the opposite of the conclusion; that is, a syllogism is true unless an exception to the conclusion can be found. Future research needs to examine the types of rules people apply to test whether the premises of a syllogism allow an exception.

Evaluation. Evaluation involves using criteria to judge the adequacy of a problem solution. In evaluating, students address such questions as "Are the data sufficient for the problem?" "Do I need more information?" "Are my conclusions based on facts, opinions, or reasoned judgments?" Evaluation also involves deciding what ought to happen next, that is, formulating hypotheses about future events, assuming that one's problem solving is correct so far.

Metacognitive processes enter into all aspects of scientific reasoning. One needs to monitor one's efforts to ensure that questions are properly posed, that data from adequate sources are available and used to draw inferences, and that relevant criteria are employed in evaluation. Teaching reasoning requires instruction in skills and in metacognitive strategies.

SUMMARY

A problem exists when one is trying to reach a goal but lacks a means for attaining it. Problem solving consists of an initial state, a goal, subgoals, and operations performed to attain the goal and subgoals. Current research examines the mental processes of learners engaged in problem solving and the different way these processes operate in experts and novices.

Problem solving has been viewed as reflecting trial and error (Thorndike), insight (Gestalt), and heuristics. These general approaches can be applied to academic content. As people gain experience in a domain, they acquire knowledge and production systems, or sets of rules to strategically apply to accomplish goals. Problem solving requires that one form a mental representation of the problem and apply a production to solve it. When problems are well defined and potential solutions can be ordered in terms of likelihood, a generate-and-test strategy is useful. For more difficult or less-defined problems, means-ends analysis is used. Means-ends requires establishing subgoals, which can be done by working backward from the goal to the initial state or working forward from the initial state to the goal. Other problem-solving strategies involve analogies and brainstorming.

Research reveals many differences between experts and novices. Experts possess more domain-specific knowledge organized to reflect the underlying structure of the content. Experts form a more accurate problem representation and usually work forward from the givens to reach the goal. Novices often adopt a working backward strategy. Experts and novices do not seem to differ in their knowledge of problem-solving strategies.

Language comprehension requires perception, parsing, and utilization. Language is parsed according to one's deep mental structures. People

SUMMARY

construct a context and fill in the elements as they comprehend them. Experts have more complete mental representations of situations. Utilization requires that listeners determine the function of the communication: to inform, to request, to command, and so forth. Speakers and listeners may operate according to a given-new contract.

Reading involves decoding and comprehension. Decoding proceeds in top-down and bottom-up fashion. Novices use much bottom-up processing, but as skill develops learners construct a mental representation of the context and develop expectations about what will appear in print. Experts rely on top-down processing, much of which occurs automatically. Text is comprehended when it activates meanings in LTM. Inferential comprehension is aided when schemata are activated and learners implement productions to fill in slots with information acquired from text. Metacognitive processes assist students' comprehension. Strategy training helps learners monitor their text understanding.

Writing requires composition and reviewing. Expert writers plan text around a goal of communicating meaning. They generate more ideas and link them better than novices. Experts also keep their goal in mind during reviewing. Novices write by putting down what they can recall about a topic. They focus on what to write next rather than keeping their goal in mind.

Children display early mathematical competence with counting. Computational skills require algorithms and declarative knowledge; deficient procedural or declarative knowledge leads to computational difficulties. Students often overgeneralize procedures, which result in buggy algorithms. In problem solving, students acquire knowledge of problem types through task experience. Experts readily recognize the problem type and apply the appropriate production to solve the problem. They work forward through the solution. Novices work backward by applying formulas that include quantities given in the problem. Similar strategies are employed in science domains. A key skill in reasoning is drawing inferences. Expertise in induction and deduction reflects the application of rule-based productions.

Chapter 8

Motivational Processes

Motivation is the process whereby goal-directed behavior is instigated and sustained. This is a cognitive definition because it postulates that people set goals and engage in cognitive activities (e.g., monitor goal progress) and behaviors (e.g., expend effort) to attain their goals. This definition is consistent with the focus of this book—current learning theory and research. Behavioral views of motivation are reviewed in this chapter, but the bulk of the chapter is devoted to cognitive perspectives.

Motivation, as with learning, is not observed directly but rather inferred from such behavioral indexes as people's verbalizations, task choices, effort expenditure, and persistence. Motivation is an explanatory concept used to understand why people behave as they do.

Although one can learn without being motivated, motivation plays an important role in learning. Students who are motivated to learn attend to instruction and engage in such activities as rehearsing information, relating it to previously acquired knowledge, and asking questions. Rather than quit when they encounter difficult material, motivated students expend greater effort to learn. They choose to work on tasks when they are not required to do so; in their spare time they read books on topics of interest, solve problems and puzzles, and work on special projects. In short, motivation leads students to engage in activities facilitating learning.

Motivation has been discussed in various terms: psychological, instinctual, hedonistic, and physiological. This chapter presents psychological views, reflecting this book's focus but not intending to ignore the validity of other perspectives. Much early work examined the idea that motivation results primarily from *instincts*. Ethologists, for example, based their ideas on Darwin's theory, which postulates that instincts have survival value for organisms. Energy builds within organisms and releases itself in behaviors designed to help the species survive. Others have emphasized the organism's need for *homeostasis*, or optimal levels of physiological states. Still another perspective involved *hedonism*, or the idea that humans seek pleasure and avoid pain. Although each of these views may explain some instances of human motivation, they are inadequate to account for a wide range of motivated activities, especially those that occur in learning contexts. Readers interested in these views should consult other sources (Petri, 1986; Weiner, 1985b).

Physiological research is an active area of current interest. Investigators are examining how changes in brain waves, hormones, and neurochemical activities relate to behavior. This research holds promise for making significant contributions in understanding motivational processes.

From a psychological perspective, motivation has figured prominently in theories of personality and achievement. Some personality theory is discussed in this chapter, but motivation as it relates to achievement is the main focus. A special area of interest is *motivated learning*, or the motivation to acquire skills and strategies, as distinct from motivation to complete activities (Brophy, 1985; Corno & Mandinach, 1983). Motivated learning theories have clear implications for the classroom.

HISTORICAL PERSPECTIVES

Drive Theory

Drive theory was a physiological view that eventually was broadened to include psychological needs. As originally conceptualized (Woodworth, 1918), drives were internal forces that sought to maintain homeostatic body balance. When an organism was deprived of an essential element (e.g., food, air, water), a drive was activated causing the organism to respond. The drive was reduced when the element was obtained.

Much research was conducted with laboratory animals (Richter, 1927; Woodworth & Schlosberg, 1954). The general procedure was to deprive animals of food or water for some time and then to assess their behaviors to get food or water. For example, rats were deprived of food for varying amounts of time and placed in a maze. The time it took them to run to the end to receive food was measured. Not surprisingly, response strength (running speed) varied directly with the number of prior reinforcements and with longer deprivation up to 2 to 3 days, after which it dropped off because the animals became progressively weaker.

The drive concept was broadened by Hull (1943), who postulated physiological deficits to be primary needs instigating drives to reduce the needs. The motivational construct energizing and prompting organisms into action is called *drive* (D). Obtaining reinforcement to satisfy a need is called *drive reduction:*

$$\text{Need} \rightarrow \text{Drive} \rightarrow \text{Behavior}$$

For Hull (1943), motivation was "the initiation of learned, or habitual, patterns of movement or behavior" (p. 226). He believed that innate behaviors usually satisfy primary needs and that learning occurs only when innate behaviors prove ineffective. Learning represents the organism's adaptation to the environment to ensure survival.

Hull also postulated the existence of secondary reinforcers, meaning that much behavior is not oriented toward satisfying primary needs. Stimulus situations (e.g., work to earn money) acquire reinforcing power by being paired with primary reinforcement (money buys food).

Drive theory generated much research as a consequence of Hull's writings (Weiner, 1985b). As an explanation for motivated behavior, drive theory seems best applied to immediate physiological needs: A person lost in a desert is primarily concerned with finding food, water, and shelter, and someone who falls into shark-infested waters, with physical safety.

There are problems with drive theory as an explanation for much human motivation. Needs do not always trigger drives oriented toward need reduction. People hastily finishing an overdue project may experience strong symptoms of hunger, yet they do not stop to eat. Physiological needs are outweighed by the desire to complete an important task. Conversely, drives can exist in the absence of biological needs. A sex drive can lead to promiscuity even though sex is not immediately needed for survival.

Although drive theory may explain some immediate goals, many human behaviors reflect long-term goals: finding a job, obtaining a college degree, or sailing around the world. People are not in a continuously high drive state while pursuing these goals. They typically experience periods of high motivation along with slumps. High drive is not conducive to performance over lengthy periods or on complex tasks (Broadhurst, 1957; Yerkes & Dodson, 1908). Drive theory does not offer an adequate explanation for academic motivation.

Conditioning Theories

Conditioning theories explain motivation in terms of responses elicited by stimuli (classical conditioning) or emitted in the presence of stimuli (operant conditioning). In the *classical conditioning model* (Chapter 2), the motivational properties of a UCS (unconditioned stimulus) are transmitted to the CS (conditioned stimulus) through repeated pairings. Conditioning occurs when the CS elicits a CR (conditioned response) in the absence of the UCS. This is a passive view of motivation because it postulates that once conditioning occurs, the CR is elicited when the CS is presented. As discussed in Chapter 2, conditioning is not an automatic process but rather depends on information conveyed to the individual about the likelihood of the UCS occurring when the CS is presented.

In *operant conditioning*, motivated behavior is an increased rate of responding or a greater likelihood that a response will occur in the presence of a stimulus. Skinner (1953) contended that internal processes accompanying responding are not necessary to explain behavior. Individuals' immediate environment and their history must be examined for the causes of behavior. Labeling a student as "motivated" adds nothing to the explanation of why the student works productively. The student is productive because of prior reinforcement for productive work and because effective reinforcers are presently available in the environment.

There is ample evidence that reinforcers influence what people do; however, it is not reinforcement that affects behavior but rather people's beliefs concerning reinforcement. People engage in activities because they believe they will be reinforced and they value that reinforcement (Bandura, 1986). When reinforcement history conflicts with present beliefs, people act based on their beliefs (Brewer, 1974). By omitting cognitive elements, conditioning theories offer an incomplete account of human motivation.

Cognitive Consistency Theories

Cognitive consistency theories assume that motivation results from relationships between cognitions and behaviors. These theories are homeostatic: When tension occurs among elements there is a need to resolve the problem by making cognitions and behaviors consistent with one another.

Balance Theory. Heider's (1946) *balance theory* postulates that a tendency exists to cognitively balance relations among persons, situations, and events. The basic situation involves three elements, and relations can be positive or negative. Assume the three elements are Janice (teacher), Ashley (student), and chemistry (subject). Balance exists when there is a positive relationship among all elements; Ashley likes Janice, Ashley likes chemistry, Ashley believes Janice likes chemistry. Balance also exists with one positive and two negative relations: Ashley does not like Janice, Ashley does not like chemistry, Ashley believes Janice likes chemistry (Figure 8.1).

Cognitive imbalance exists with one negative and two positive relations (Ashley likes Janice, Ashley does not like chemistry, Ashley believes Janice likes chemistry) and when all relations are negative. Balance theory predicts there is no tendency to change relationships when the triad is balanced, but people will try (cognitively and behaviorally) to resolve con-

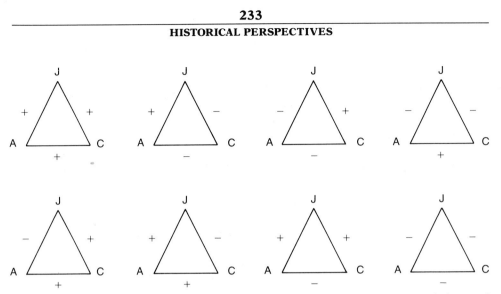

Note: J = Janice (chemistry teacher); A = Ashley (student); C = chemistry. The symbols + and − stand for "likes" and "does not like," respectively, so that the top left balance can be read as follows: Ashley likes Janice; Ashley likes chemistry; Ashley believes Janice likes chemistry.

FIGURE 8.1
Predictions of balance theory.

flicts when imbalance exists. For example, Ashley might decide because she likes Janice and Janice likes chemistry, that maybe chemistry is not so bad after all (i.e., Ashley changes her attitude about chemistry).

That people seek to restore cognitive imbalance is intuitively plausible, but balance theory contains problems. It predicts when people will attempt to restore balance but not *how* they will do it. Ashley might change her attitude toward chemistry, but she also could establish balance by disliking chemistry and Janice. The theory also does not adequately take into account the importance of imbalanced relationships. People care very much when imbalance exists among people and things they value, but they make no effort to restore balance when they care little about the elements.

Cognitive Dissonance Theory. One of the most elegant consistency theories is Festinger's (1957) *cognitive dissonance.* Dissonance theory postulates that individuals attempt to maintain consistent relations among their beliefs, attitudes, opinions, and behaviors. Relations can be *consonant, irrelevant,* or *dissonant.* Two cognitions are consonant if one follows from or fits with the other. The following two cognitions are consonant: "I have to give a speech in Los Angeles tomorrow morning at 9." "I'm flying there today." Many beliefs are irrelevant to one another: "I like chocolate." "There is a hickory tree in my yard." Dissonant cognitions exist when one follows from the opposite of the other. The following cognitions are dissonant because the second follows from the opposite of the first: "I don't like Deborah." "I bought Deborah flowers." Dissonance is tension with drive-like properties leading to reduction. Dissonance should increase as the discrepancy between cognitions increases. Assuming I bought Deborah flowers, the cognition "I hate Deborah" ought to produce more dissonance than "I don't like Deborah."

Cognitive dissonance theory also takes the importance of the cognitions into account. Large discrepancies between trivial cognitions do not cause much dissonance. "Yellow is not my favorite color" and "I drive a yellow car" will not produce much dissonance if car color is not important to me.

Changing a discrepant cognition is one way to reduce dissonance. If I change my belief to "I actually like Deborah," dissonance is reduced. Another way is to qualify cognitions: "The reason I do not like Deborah is because 10 years ago she borrowed $100.00 and never repaid it. But she's changed a lot since then and probably would never do that again." A third way is to downgrade the importance of the cognitions: "It's no big deal that I gave Deborah flowers; I give flowers to lots of people for different reasons." Finally, I can alter my behavior by never giving Deborah flowers again.

Dissonance theory calls attention to how cognitive conflicts can be resolved (Aronson, 1966). The idea that dissonance propels us into action is appealing. Also, by dealing with discrepant cognitions, the theory is not confined to triadic relationships as is balance theory. But dissonance and balance theories share many of the same problems. The dissonance notion is vague and difficult to verify experimentally. To predict whether cognitions will conflict in a given situation is problematic, because they must be salient and important. The theory does not predict which means will be used to reduce dissonance—changing behavior or altering thoughts. These problems suggest that additional factors are needed to explain human motivation.

Maslow's Hierarchy of Needs

Abraham Maslow (1968, 1970) developed a humanistic theory of motivation that emphasizes striving to develop one's full potential. Maslow viewed human behavior in a holistic sense: one's actions are unified by being directed toward goal attainment. One's behaviors could serve several functions simultaneously; for example, socializing at a party could satisfy social and esteem needs. Maslow believed that conditioning theories do not capture the complexity of human behavior. To say that one socializes at a party because one has previously been reinforced for doing so fails to take into account the function of socialization for the individual at the present time.

Most human action represents a striving to satisfy needs. Needs are hierarchical (Figure 8.2). On the hierarchy, lower-order needs have to be satisfied adequately before higher-order needs can influence behavior. Phys-

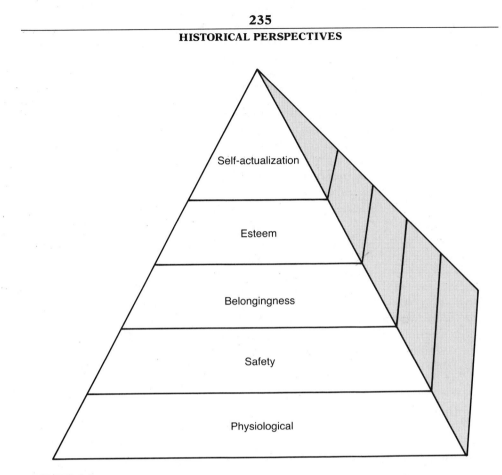

FIGURE 8.2
Maslow's hierarchy of needs (*Source:* "Hierarchy of Needs" from MOTIVATION AND PERSONALITY by Abraham H. Maslow. Copyright © 1954 by Harper & Row, Publishers, Inc. Copyright © 1970 by Abraham H. Maslow. Reprinted by permission of Harper & Row, Publishers, Inc.).

iological needs, the lowest on the hierarchy, concern such necessities as food, air, and water. These needs are satisfied for most people most of the time, but they are prepotent when they are not satisfied. Safety needs, which involve environmental security, dominate during emergencies: People fleeing from rising waters will abandon valuable property to save their lives. People's safety needs are also manifested in such activities as opening bank accounts, securing jobs, and taking out insurance policies (Petri, 1986).

Once physiological and safety needs are adequately met, belongingness (love) needs become important. These needs involve having intimate relationships with others, belonging to groups, and having close friends and acquaintances. A sense of belonging is attained through marriage, personal commitments, volunteer groups, clubs, churches, and the like. Esteem needs comprise self-esteem and esteem from others. These needs manifest them-

---

APPLICATION 8.1: Applying Maslow's Hierarchy

Teachers can use Maslow's hierarchy to understand students and create an environment to enhance learning. It is unrealistic to expect students to show interest in classroom activities if they are suffering from physiological or safety deficiencies. Children who come to school having had no breakfast and with no lunch money will have difficulty focusing on classroom tasks. Teachers can work with counselors, principals, and social workers to assist children's families or to have children approved for free meal programs.

Some students will have difficulty working on tasks with nearby distractions (e.g., movement, noises). Teachers can meet with parents to assess whether home conditions also are disruptive. A disruptive home environment might result in an unfilled safety need—a desire to feel more secure about learning. Teachers can urge parents to provide a favorable home environment for studying. Teachers can ensure there are not many classroom distractions and can teach skills for coping with them (e.g., how to concentrate and to monitor task attention).

---

selves in high achievement, independence, competent work, and recognition from others.

The first four needs are deprivation needs: Their lack of satisfaction produces deficiencies that motivate people to satisfy them. Severe deficiencies could produce mental problems.

> Most neuroses involved, along with other complex determinants, ungratified wishes for safety, for belongingness and identification, for close love relationships and for respect and prestige. (Maslow, 1968, p. 21)

At the highest level is the need for *self-actualization,* or the desire for self-fulfillment, that is, becoming everything one is capable of becoming. Behavior is not motivated by a deficiency but rather by a desire for personal growth (Maslow, 1968):

> Healthy people have sufficiently gratified their basic needs for safety, belongingness, love, respect and self-esteem so that they are motivated primarily by trends to self-actualization [defined as ongoing actualization of potentials, capacities and talents, as fulfillment of mission (or call, fate, destiny, or vocation), as a fuller knowledge of, and acceptance of, the person's own intrinsic nature, as an unceasing trend toward unity, integration or synergy within the person]. (p. 25)

Although most people go beyond the deficiency needs and attempt self-actualization, few people ever fully reach this level—perhaps 1% of the population (Goble, 1970). Self-actualization can be manifested in various ways as follows (Maslow, 1970):

> The specific form that these needs will take will of course vary greatly from person to person. In one individual it may take the form of the desire to be an ideal mother, in another it may be expressed athletically, and in still another it may be expressed in painting pictures or in inventions. At this level, individual differences are greatest. (p. 46)

A strong motive to achieve in or out of school is another manifestation of self-actualization.

Maslow informally studied personal acquaintances and historical figures to determine the characteristics of self-actualized individuals. Some of the major characteristics are an increased perception of reality, acceptance (of self, of others, of nature), spontaneity, problem-centering, detachment and desire for privacy, autonomy and resistance to enculturation, freshness of appreciation and richness of emotional reaction, frequency of peak experiences (loss of self-awareness), and identification with the human species (Maslow, 1968).

Another important characteristic of self-actualized persons is that they focus on important problems, looking outside of themselves to a problem or cause and dedicating their efforts to it. They also display great interest in the means for attaining their goals. The outcome (righting a wrong or solving a problem) is as important as the means to the end (the actual work involved).

Maslow's hierarchy is a useful general guide to understanding behavior. For example, it is unrealistic to expect students to show much interest in school learning if they are suffering from physiological or safety deficiencies. The hierarchy provides teachers with clues concerning why students act as they do. Teachers stress intellectual achievement, but many adolescents are preoccupied with belongingness and esteem.

The hierarchy of needs theory has its own problems. One is conceptual vagueness. For instance, what constitutes a deficiency is not clear. What one person considers a deficiency in some area, another person may not. Another problem is that lower-order needs are not always prepotent. People commonly risk their own safety to rescue others from danger. Third, research on the qualities of self-actualized individuals has yielded mixed results (Petri, 1986). Apparently, self-actualization can take many forms. Despite these problems, the idea that people strive to feel competent and lead self-fulfilling lives is a central notion in many theories of motivation.

ACHIEVEMENT MOTIVATION THEORY

Achievement motivation refers to the striving to perform difficult tasks as well as possible. The achievement motive was identified by Murray (1938), along with other physiological and psychological needs contributing to personality development. Motivation to act presumably results because of a desire to satisfy needs.

Murray (1936) devised the Thematic Apperception Test (TAT) to study personality processes. The TAT is a projective technique that consists of a series of ambiguous pictures for which the subject makes up a story or answers a series of questions. The TAT was adapted by McClelland and his colleagues to assess the achievement motive (McClelland, Atkinson, Clark, & Lowell, 1953). Subjects are shown pictures of individuals in unclear situations and are asked such questions as "What is happening?" "What led up to this situation?" "What is wanted?" "What will happen?" Responses are scored according to various criteria, and subjects are categorized on strength of achievement motive. Although the TAT has been employed in many experimental studies, it suffers from problems including low reliability and correlations with other achievement measures. In recent years, other measures of achievement motivation have been devised (Weiner, 1985b).

Atkinson's Expectancy-Value Theory

A name identified with achievement motivation is John W. Atkinson (Atkinson, 1957; Atkinson & Birch, 1978; Atkinson & Feather, 1966; Atkinson & Raynor, 1974, 1978). Atkinson developed an *expectancy-value theory* of achievement motivation. There are different expectancy-value theories, but the basic idea is that behavior is a function of how much the individuals value a particular reinforcer and their expectation of obtaining that reinforcer as a result of performing that behavior. People make judgments of the likelihood of attaining various goals. They are not motivated to attempt the impossible, so they do not pursue goals perceived as unattainable. Even a positive outcome expectation does not produce action if the goal is not valued. An attractive goal, along with the belief that it is attainable, motivates people to act.

Atkinson postulated that achievement behaviors represent a conflict between approach (hope for success) and avoidance (fear of failure) tendencies. Achievement actions carry with them the possibilities of success and failure. Key concepts are as follows: the tendency to approach an achievement-related goal (T_s), the tendency to avoid failure (T_{af}), and the resultant achievement motivation (T_a). T_s is a function of the motive to succeed (M_s), the subjective probability of success (P_s), and the incentive value of success (I_s):

$$T_s = M_s \times P_s \times I_s$$

Atkinson believed that M_s (achievement motivation) is a stable disposition, or characteristic trait of the individual, to strive for success. P_s (the individual's estimation of how likely goal attainment is) is inversely related to I_s: There is greater incentive to work hard at difficult tasks than at easy tasks. Greater pride is experienced in accomplishing difficult tasks.

APPLICATION 8.2: Fear of Failure and Hope for Success

Atkinson's theory has implications for teaching and learning. If academic work is perceived as too hard, students may not attempt their work or may give up readily because of high fear of failure and low hope for success. Lowering fear of failure and raising hope for success enhance motivation which can be done by conveying positive expectations for learning to students and by structuring tasks so students can successfully complete them with reasonable effort. Also, perceiving academic work as too easy is not beneficial: Higher achieving students may become bored with material they feel is not challenging. If lessons are not planned to meet the varying needs of students, the desired achievement behaviors will not be displayed.

In working on long division, students still having difficulty with multiplication may need to spend the majority of their time learning facts and using manipulatives to reinforce learning of new concepts. Successes on these activities in a nonthreatening classroom environment build hope for success and lower fear of failure. Students who are proficient in multiplication, have mastered the division algorithm and understand the relationship between multiplication and division should not spend lots of class time on review. Instead, they should be given a brief review and then guided into more difficult skills. Thus a degree of challenge is maintained, which enhances achievement motivation.

In similar fashion, the tendency to avoid failure (T_{af}) is a multiplicative function of the motive to avoid failure (M_{af}), the probability of failure (P_f), and the inverse of the incentive value of failure ($-I_f$):

$$T_{af} = M_{af} \times P_f \times (-I_f)$$

The resultant achievement motivation (T_a) is represented as follows:

$$T_a = T_s - T_{af}$$

Notice that simply having a high hope for success does not guarantee achievement behavior, because the strength of the motive to avoid failure must be considered. The best combination to promote achievement behavior is a strong hope for success and a low fear of failure.

One prediction is that students high in resultant achievement motivation will choose tasks that are of intermediate difficulty or that they believe are attainable and will produce a sense of accomplishment. These students should avoid difficult tasks for which successful accomplishment is unlikely, as well as easy tasks for which success, though guaranteed, is meaningless. Students low in resultant achievement motivation are more apt to select either easy or difficult tasks. To accomplish the former, students have to expend little effort to succeed. Although accomplishing the latter seems unlikely, students have an excuse for failure—the task is so difficult that no one can succeed at it. This excuse gives these students a reason for not expending effort, because no amount of effort will produce success.

Research on task difficulty preference as a function of level of achievement motivation has yielded conflicting results (Cooper, 1983; Ray, 1982). Task difficulty was systematically investigated by Kuhl and Blankenship (1979a, 1979b) in situations where individuals repeatedly chose tasks. These researchers assumed that fear of failure would be reduced following task success, so they predicted the tendency to choose easy tasks would diminish over time. This change should be most apparent among subjects for whom $M_{af} > M_s$. Kuhl and Blankenship found a shift toward more difficult tasks for subjects in whom $M_{af} > M_s$, as well as for those in whom $M_s > M_{af}$. There was no support for the notion that this tendency would be greater in the former subjects.

These findings make sense when interpreted differently. Repeated success builds perceptions of competence. People then are more likely to choose difficult tasks because they feel capable of accomplishing them. In short, there undoubtedly are many reasons why people choose to work on easy or difficult tasks, and it seems that achievement motivation theory may have overestimated the influence of strength of the achievement motive.

Achievement motivation theory has generated much research. One problem with a global construct such as the achievement motive is that the latter rarely manifests itself uniformly across different achievement domains. Students typically show greater motivation to perform well in some subjects than in others. Since the achievement motive varies with the domain, how well such a global trait predicts achievement behavior in specific situations is in question.

Familial Influences

It is plausible that achievement motivation would be strongly influenced by factors in children's homes. An early investigation studied parents' interactions with their sons (Rosen & D'Andrade, 1959). Children were given tasks and parents could interact in any fashion. Parents of boys with high achievement motivation interacted more, gave more rewards and punishments, and held higher expectations for their children than parents of boys with low achievement motivation. These authors concluded that parental pressure to perform well is a more important influence on achievement motivation than parental desire for child independence.

Subsequent research has yielded conflicting findings (Weiner, 1985b). Attempts to identify parental behaviors that encourage achievement strivings are complicated because parents display many behaviors with their children. Determining which behaviors are most influential is difficult. For example, parental encouragement to perform well may co-occur with conveying high expectations, giving rewards and punishments, responding with positive affect (warmth, permissiveness), and encouraging independence. These behaviors also are displayed by teachers and significant other persons in the child's life, which complicates determining the familial influence. Another point is that, although parents influence children, children also influence parents (Feld, 1967). Parents help children develop achievement behaviors when they encourage preexisting tendencies in their children; for example, children develop independence through interactions with peers, which then is praised by parents. Additional research is needed on the role of familial antecedents.

Fear of Success

As originally conceptualized by Atkinson and his colleagues, the achievement motive manifests itself in such behaviors as competition, independence, and "moving up the ladder." In Western societies, these behaviors are stereotypically associated with success among men but less so among women. Many men and women view these behaviors as incompatible with the basic notion of femininity. It is not surprising, therefore, that some research shows that Atkinson's theory predicts achievement behaviors better for men than women (Petri, 1986). Due to cultural beliefs and social practices, achievement motivation may be more complex among women.

This notion has been captured in the construct *fear of success,* or the motive to avoid success (M_{as}) (Horner, 1972, 1978). Fear of success is a stable motivational disposition manifested by anxiety that inhibits achievement behavior. Fear of success arises from such anticipated negative consequences of success in competitive achievement situations as rejection by others and loss of one's self-esteem and sense of femininity. Compared with men, women typically experience greater anxiety in competitive activities, including those involving intellectual achievement. The motive presumably is acquired early in life as a function of training in sex role standards (Horner, 1978). There are individual differences in motive strength, with some women being highly debilitated. The motive acts as an inhibitory tendency in achievement situations and can lead women to avoid competitive settings or to perform poorly.

Horner (1978) investigated fear of success by including a verbal item at the end of the TAT. For women, the item was, "After the first term finals Anne finds herself at the top of her medical school class." For men, "John" was substituted for "Anne." Subjects' responses were scored to determine the extent of perceived negative consequences and anxiety as a result of the success. The results showed that 62% of the women expressed fear of success compared with 10% of the men.

Other research has yielded conflicting results (Zuckerman & Wheeler, 1975). Hoffman (1974) found that a greater proportion of men demonstrate fear of success than women. Breedlove and Cicirelli (1974) found that fear of success among women is greater in nontraditional settings (e.g., medical school class) than in traditional ones (elementary education class). These inconsistent findings do not disprove Horner's ideas about fear of success but they question whether fear of success is a stable motive in women. Fear of success is not confined to women. It also may be highly situationally specific and easily affected by task conditions. To the extent that fear of success reflects people's perceptions concerning acceptable behavior, one should expect these perceptions to change as societal traditions change. While the construct is of interest, additional research is needed to determine its theoretical and practical usefulness.

Self-Worth Theory

Atkinson's theory views achievement behavior as resulting from an emotional conflict between hope of success and fear of failure. This notion is intuitively appealing. Thinking about beginning a new job or taking a difficult course produces anticipated satisfaction from being successful as well as anxiety over the possibility of failing. *Self-worth theory* combines this emotional aspect with cognitive factors (Beery, 1975; Covington, 1983; Covington & Beery, 1976).

Self-worth theory assumes that success is valued and that failure, or the belief that one has failed, is to be avoided because failure implies low ability. People want to be viewed as able, but failure creates feelings of unworthiness. To preserve a basic sense of self-worth, individuals must feel able and must demonstrate ability often.

One means of avoiding failure is to pursue easy goals where success is assured. Another means is to cheat, although cheating is problematic; one might copy answers from a student who does poorly on an exam, and there is the possibility one will get caught. Another way to avoid failure is to escape from a negative situation. Students who believe they will fail a course are apt to drop it; those who are failing many courses may quit school.

Ironically, the perception of low ability can be avoided through deliberate failure. One can pursue difficult goals where failure is guaranteed (Covington, 1984). Setting high aspirations is valued in our society, and failure to attain them does not necessarily imply low ability. A related tactic is to blame failure on low effort: One could have succeeded if circumstances had allowed one to expend greater effort. One cannot be faulted for failing an exam that one did not properly study for, especially if one had to work at a job and had inadequate study opportunities.

Expending effort carries risk. High effort that produces success maintains the perception of ability, but high effort that results in failure implies low ability. Low effort also carries risk, because teachers routinely stress effort and criticize students for not expending effort (Weiner & Kukla, 1970). Effort is a "double-edged sword" (Covington & Omelich, 1979). Only the presence of excuses helps students maintain the proper balance. The following are common excuses: "I would have done better had I been able to study more." "I didn't work hard enough" [when in fact the student worked very hard]," "I was unlucky—I studied the wrong material."

Self-worth theory stresses perceptions of ability as the primary influences on motivation. Research shows that perceived ability bears a strong positive relationship to students' expectations for success, motivation, and achievement (Eccles & Wigfield, 1985). Although perceived ability is one influence on motivation, there are other important factors as this chapter makes clear. Self-worth predictions are somewhat constrained by students' developmental level, because older students perceive ability to be a more important influence on achievement than younger students (Harari & Covington, 1981). Nonetheless, self-worth theory illustrates the preoccupation with achievement seen in too many students and its negative consequences.

Task and Ego Involvement

Achievement motivation theories gradually have shifted their focus away from general achievement motives to task-specific beliefs. Self-worth theory reveals that people desire to demonstrate their ability to themselves and others; however, *ability* can have different meanings. Nicholls (1983) proposed that different conceptions of ability lead to different motivated behaviors. *Ego involvement* is a type of self-preoccupation. Ego-involved students desire to avoid looking incompetent. Learning is not valued for itself but only as a means to avoid appearing incapable. In contrast, *task involvement* stresses learning as a goal. Task-involved students "forget about themselves" and focus on task demands: solve the problem, balance the equation, write the book report.

Task and ego involvement reflect different beliefs about ability and effort (Jagacinski & Nicholls, 1984, 1987). Ego-involved students perceive ability as synonymous with capacity. Ability is a relatively fixed quantity assessed by comparisons with others (norms). The role of effort is limited; effort can improve performance only to the limit set by ability. Success achieved with great effort implies high ability only if others require more effort for the same performance or if others perform less well with the same effort. Task-involved students perceive ability as close in meaning to learning; thus, more effort can raise ability. Students feel more competent if they expend more effort to succeed, because learning is an end in itself and implies greater ability. Feelings of competence arise when students' present performance is seen as having improved compared with prior performance.

Ego and task involvement are not fixed characteristics. Nicholls (1983) suggests they are affected by conditions in school. Ego involvement is engendered by competition, which fosters self-evaluation of abilities relative to those of others. Task involvement is promoted under individual learning conditions (students evaluate their own progress relative to how they [not others] performed previously,) and under cooperative learning conditions (students in a group collectively work on tasks). In support of these predictions, Ames (1984) found that students place greater emphasis on ability as a determinant of outcomes in competitive contexts, but they stress the role of effort in noncompetitive (cooperative, individual) situations.

Certain classroom features foster ego involvement (Nicholls, 1979). Students typically compete for teacher attention, privileges, and grades. Elementary students often are grouped for reading and mathematics instruction based on ability differences; secondary students are "tracked." Teacher feedback may unwittingly foster ego involvement (e.g., "Tommy, finish your work; everyone else is done"), as can teacher introductions to a lesson ("This is hard material; some of you may have trouble learning it"). Current research is examining how instructional and social factors affect students' motivational involvement (Ames, 1987; Brophy, 1985).

Achievement Motivation Training

Achievement motivation training has as its goal to help students develop thoughts and behaviors typical of learners high in achievement motivation (de Charms, 1968). De Charms (1976) initially trained teachers, who afterward worked with students. A goal was to help individuals develop personal responsibility for their learning outcomes. Teacher training included self-study of academic motivation, realistic goal setting, development of concrete plans to accomplish goals, and evaluation of goal progress.

Student motivation training was integrated with academic content. Classroom activities included self-study of academic motives, achievement motivation thinking, development of self-concept, realistic goal setting, and personal responsibility training. In one spelling activity designed to teach goal setting, students could choose easy, moderate, or difficult words to learn. To teach personal responsibility, teachers had students write stories about achievement, which were then used in a classroom essay contest. The results showed that training positively affected teachers' and students' motivation. Training halted the trend among low achievers to fall increasingly behind their peers in achievement. It also reduced student absenteeism and tardiness.

It seems imperative to integrate achievement motivation training with regular classroom content, rather than have it as an add-on activity with special content. The danger of the latter approach is that students may not learn how the training applies in regular achievement domains.

Alderman (1985) recommends several useful components of motivation training. One is having teachers assist students in realistic goal setting and having them provide feedback concerning student goal progress. Another aspect is self-study to examine one's motives for learning and to develop personal responsibility. Nicholls's task-/ego-involvement distinction seems useful. Through a series of questions, students examine how they feel about tasks and what they see as their goals (e.g., learning versus pleasing others). Attributional training (discussed in the next section) also is relevant. One means of teaching personal responsibility can be taught by helping students place greater emphasis on effort as a cause of outcomes rather than blame others when they fail or believe they were lucky when they succeed. As students experience successes, they should develop increased self-efficacy for continued learning and consequently take greater control of their learning goals.

Alderman (1985) applied these ideas to a senior high girls physical education class. On the first day of class, students completed a self-evaluation of their health and physical fitness status and competence and interest in various activities, and they set fitness goals. Weekly self-tests were given in different activities (e.g., aerobics, flexibility, strength, posture). At the end of the first grading period, students set goals for the final exam. There were various ways to accomplish the aerobic goal (running, walking, jumping rope). The teacher met with individual students to assess goals and made suggestions if these did not seem realistic. Students established practice schedules of at least three times a week for 9 weeks and kept a record of practices. Following the final exam, students completed a self-evaluation of what they had learned. Alderman noted, "To the instructor, the most striking comment made by students on the final self-evaluation was, 'I learned to set a goal and accomplish it' " (p. 51).

ATTRIBUTION THEORY

Attribution theory explains how people view the causes of their behaviors and those of others. The theory assumes that people are inclined to seek information to form *attributions*, or perceived causes of outcomes. The process of assigning causes is presumably governed by rules, and much attributional research has addressed how rules are used. From a motivational perspective, attributions are important because they influence beliefs, emotions, and behaviors.

Before discussing attributions in achievement settings, relevant background material is presented. Rotter's locus of control and Heider's naive analysis of action incorporate important attributional concepts.

Rotter's Locus of Control

A central idea in many cognitive views of motivation is that people desire control over important aspects of their lives. Rotter's (1954) social learning theory (Chapter 4) was expanded to include the construct of generalized control of reinforcements, or *locus of control* (Rotter, 1966). People differ in whether they believe that outcomes occur independently of how they behave (external control) or that outcomes are highly contingent on their behavior (internal control):

> When a reinforcement is perceived by the subject as following some action of his own but not being entirely contingent upon his action, then, in our culture, it is typically perceived as the result of luck, chance, fate, as under the control of powerful others, or as unpredictable because of the great complexity of the forces surrounding him. When the event is interpreted in this way by an individual, we have labeled this a belief in *external control*. If the person perceived that the event is contingent upon his own behavior or his own relatively permanent characteristics, we have termed this a belief in *internal control*. (Rotter, 1966, p. 1)

Rotter conceptualized locus of control as a generalized expectancy concerning whether responses influence the attainment of outcomes (e.g., successes, rewards), although investigators subsequently noted that locus of control may vary depending on the situation (Phares, 1976). Students who generally believe they have little control over academic successes and failures may feel they can exert much control in a particular class because the teacher and peers are helpful and because they like the instructional content.

Locus of control is important in achievement contexts because one's expectancy beliefs are hypothesized to affect behavior. Students who believe they have control over their successes and failures should be more inclined to engage in academic tasks, to expend effort, and to persist than students who believe their behaviors have little impact on outcomes. In turn, effort and persistence promote achievement (Lefcourt, 1976; Phares, 1976).

Regardless of whether locus of control is a general disposition or is situationally specific, it is a reflection of outcome expectations. Outcome expectations are important determinants of achievement behaviors, but they alone are insufficient (Bandura, 1982b). Students may not work on tasks because they do not expect competent performances to produce results (negative outcome expectation), as might happen if they believe the teacher dislikes them. Positive outcome expectations do not guarantee high motivation; students may believe hard work earns a high grade but will not work hard if they doubt their capability to do so (low self-efficacy). In school, efficacy and outcome expectations usually are related. Students who believe they are capable of performing well (high self-efficacy) expect positive reactions from their teachers following successful performances (positive outcome expectation). Outcomes, in turn, validate one's efficacy because they convey one is capable of succeeding.

Heider's Naive Analysis of Action

The origin of attribution theory is generally ascribed to Heider (1958). Heider referred to his theory as a *naive analysis of action*, where *naive* means that the average individual is uninformed on the objective determinants of behavior. Heider's theory examines how ordinary people view the causes of important events in their lives.

Heider believed that people attribute causes to internal or external factors. He referred to these factors, respectively, as the *effective personal force* and the *effective environmental force*, as follows:

$$outcome = personal\ force + environmental\ force$$

Internal causes are within the individual: needs, wishes, emotions, abilities, intentions, and effort. The personal force is allocated to two factors: *power* and *motivation*. Power refers to abilities and motivation (trying) to intention and exertion:

$$outcome = trying + power + environment$$

Collectively, power and environment constitute the *can* factor, which combined with the *try* factor is used to explain outcomes. One's power (or ability) is relative to the environment. Whether one can swim across a lake depends on one's swimming ability relative to the forces of the lake (current, width, temperature). Similarly, one's success or failure on a test is explained by one's ability relative to the difficulty of the test, along with one's intentions and efforts in studying. Assuming that ability is sufficient to conquer environmental forces, then trying (effort) affects outcomes.

Heider sketched a framework for how people view significant events in their lives; however, this framework provides researchers with few empirically testable hypotheses. Subsequent investigators clarified his ideas and conducted attributional research.

Weiner's Attribution Theory

Causal Factors.   In achievement settings, the search for causes elicits the following types of questions: "Why did I do well (poorly) on my social studies test?'' ''Why did I get an A (D) in biology?'' A series of studies by Weiner and his colleagues provided the empirical base for developing an attributional theory of achievement behavior (Weiner, 1974, 1979, 1985a; Weiner et al., 1971; Weiner, Graham, Taylor, & Meyer, 1983; Weiner & Kukla, 1970).

Guided by Heider's work, Weiner et al. (1971) postulated that students attribute their academic successes and failures to ability, effort, task difficulty, and luck. These authors assumed that these factors were given general weightings and that for any given outcome one or two factors would be perceived as primarily responsible. For example, a student who receives an A on a social studies test might attribute it mostly to ability (''I'm good in social studies'') and effort (''I studied hard for the test''), somewhat to task difficulty (''The test wasn't too hard''), and very little to luck (''I guessed right on a couple of questions''). (See Table 8.1.)

Weiner et al. (1971) did not imply that ability, effort, task difficulty, and luck were the only attributions used by students to explain their successes and failures. Subsequent investigations identified other attributions: other people (teachers, students), mood, fatigue, illness, personality, physical appearance (Frieze, 1980; Frieze, Francis, & Hanusa, 1983). Of the four attributions identified by Weiner et al. (1971), relatively less emphasis is placed on luck. Luck is a more important attribution in games of chance. Frieze et al. (1983) have shown that task conditions are associated with particular attributional patterns. Exams tend to generate effort attributions, whereas art projects are ascribed to ability and effort.

Causal Dimensions. An attributional theory requires that causes be integrated into a framework highlighting their similarities and differences.

TABLE 8.1
Sample attributions for grade on math exam.

Grade	Attribution	Example
High	Ability	I'm good in math.
	Effort	I studied hard for the exam.
	Ability + effort	I'm good in math, and I studied hard for the exam.
	Task (ease)	It was an easy test.
	Luck	I was lucky; I studied the right material for the exam.
Low	Ability	I'm no good in math.
	Effort	I didn't study hard enough.
	Ability + effort	I'm no good in math, and I didn't study hard enough.
	Task (difficulty)	The test was impossible; nobody could have done well.
	Luck	I was unlucky; I studied the wrong material for the exam.

TABLE 8.2
Weiner's model of causal attribution.

	Internal		External	
	Stable	**Unstable**	**Stable**	**Unstable**
Controllable	Typical effort	Immediate effort	Teacher bias	Help from others
Uncontrollable	Ability	Mood	Task difficulty	Luck

Source: Adapted from "A Theory of Motivation for Some Classroom Experiences" by B. Weiner, 1979, *Journal of Educational Psychology, 71,* pp. 3–25. Copyright 1979 by the American Psychological Association. Adapted by permission.

Drawing on the work of Heider (1958) and Rotter (1966), Weiner et al. (1971) originally represented causes along two dimensions: (1) *internal* or *external* to the individual and (2) relatively *stable* or *unstable* over time (Table 8.2). Ability is internal and relatively stable. Effort is internal but unstable; one can alternatively work diligently and lackadaisically. Task difficulty is external and relatively stable because task conditions do not vary much from moment to moment; luck is external and unstable—one can be "lucky" one moment and "unlucky" the next.

Weiner (1979) added a third causal dimension—*controllable* or *uncontrollable* by the individual (Table 8.2). Although effort is generally viewed as internal and unstable (immediate effort), there also is a general effort factor (typical effort): People are characterized as lazy or hard-working. Effort is considered to be controllable; mood factors (to include fatigue and illness) are not. There are some problems with the classification in Table 8.2 (e.g., Can an external factor be controllable?), but it has served as a good framework to guide research and attributional intervention programs.

In forming attributions, people use situational cues, the meanings of which are learned via prior experiences. Salient cues for ability attributions are success attained easily or early in the course of learning, as well as many successes. With motor skills, an important effort cue is physical exertion. On cognitive tasks, effort attributions are credible when we expend mental effort or persist for a long time to succeed. Task difficulty cues include task features; for example, reading passages with fewer words or easier words are indicative of easier tasks than those with more words or more difficult words. Task difficulty also is judged from social norms. If everyone in class fails a test, failure is likely to be attributed to high task difficulty; if everyone makes an A, then success may be attributed to task ease. A prominent cue for luck is random outcomes; how good students are (ability) or how hard they work (effort) has no bearing on whether they succeed.

APPLICATION 8.3: Attributional Feedback

Providing effort attributional feedback to students for their successes promotes achievement expectancies and behaviors, but the feedback must be perceived as credible. With a student who is having difficulty mastering long multiplication problems, the teacher can use past student successes and attributional feedback to build confidence in learning the new task. If the student has mastered addition and multiplication concepts and facts, the teacher might say, "I know this new type of problem looks hard, but you can learn how to work it because you know all the things you need to know. You just need to work hard and you'll do fine."

As the student works, the teacher can interject comments similar to the following: "You're doing well; you completed the first step. I was sure you knew your multiplication facts. Keep working hard." "Wow! Look at that! You added those so quickly. I knew you could do that because you're working hard." "You did it! You got it right because you worked hard."

Attributional Consequences.   Attributions affect students' expectations for subsequent successes, achievement behaviors, and emotional reactions (Weiner, 1979, 1985a). The stability dimension is hypothesized to influence expectancy of success. Assuming that task conditions remain much the same, attributions of success to stable causes (high ability, low task difficulty) should result in higher expectations of future success than attributions to unstable causes (immediate effort, luck). Students may be uncertain whether they can sustain the effort needed to succeed or whether they will be lucky in the future. Failure ascribed to low ability or high task difficulty is apt to result in lower expectations for future success than failure attributed to insufficient effort or bad luck. Students may believe that increased effort will produce more favorable outcomes or that their luck may change in the future.

The locus dimension is hypothesized to influence affective reactions. One experiences greater pride (shame) after succeeding (failing) when outcomes are attributed to internal causes rather than to external ones. Students experience greater pride in their accomplishments when they believe they succeeded on their own (ability, effort) than when they believe external factors were responsible (teacher assistance, easy task).

The controllability dimension has diverse effects (Weiner, 1979). Feelings of control are postulated to increase one's choosing to engage in academic tasks, effort and persistence at difficult tasks, and achievement (Bandura, 1986; Dweck & Bempechat, 1983; Monty & Perlmuter, 1987; Wang, 1983). Students who believe they have little control over academic outcomes hold low expectations for success and display low motivation to succeed (Licht & Kistner, 1986).

Attribution Change Programs

Attribution change programs attempt to enhance motivation by altering students' attributions for successes and failures. It is not unusual for students to experience difficulties when learning new material. Some learners attribute these problems to low ability. Students who believe they lack the requisite ability to perform well may work at tasks in a lackadaisical fashion, which retards skill development.

Researchers have identified students who fit this attributional pattern and have trained them to attribute failure to controllable factors (e.g., low effort, improper strategy use) rather than to low ability. Effort has received special attention; if students believe that they fail because of low ability, they may not expend much effort to succeed. Because effort is under volitional control, training students to believe that prior difficulties resulted from low effort may lead them to expend greater effort with the expectation that it will produce better outcomes.

Dweck (1975) identified children with low expectations for success and whose achievement behaviors deteriorated after they experienced failure (e.g., low effort, lack of persistence). Dweck presented the children with arithmetic problems—some of which were insolvable—to assess the extent of performance decline following failure. Children largely attributed their failures to low ability. During training, children solved problems with a criterion number set for each trial. For some (success-only) children, the criterion was set at or below their capabilities as determined by the pretest. A similar criterion applied on most trials for attribution retraining children, but on some trials the criterion was set beyond their capabilities. When these children failed, they were told they did not try hard enough. On the posttest, success-only children continued to show deterioration in performance following failure, whereas attribution retraining children showed less impairment. Success-only children continued to stress low ability; attribution retraining subjects emphasized low effort.

Dweck did not assess students' expectancies for success, so the effect of attributions on expectancies could not be determined. Other investigations have shown that teaching students to attribute failures to low effort enhances effort attributions, expectancies for success, and achievement behaviors (Andrews & Debus, 1978; Chapin & Dyck, 1976).

Providing effort attributional feedback to students for their successes also affects achievement expectancies and behaviors (Schunk, 1982a; Schunk & Cox, 1986; Schunk & Rice, 1986). Linking children's prior achievements with effort (e.g., "You've been working hard") enhances task motivation, perceived competence, and skill acquisition better than linking their future achievement with effort ("You need to work hard") or not providing effort feedback. To be effective, effort feedback must be perceived as credible by students. Effort is credible when students realistically have to work hard to succeed, as in the early stages of learning.

Effort feedback may be especially useful for students with learning problems. Schunk and Cox (1986) gave learning disabled middle school students subtraction instruction and practice opportunities over sessions. Some students received effort feedback ("You've been working hard") during the first half of the instructional program, others received it during the second half, and subjects in a third condition did not receive effort feedback. Each type of feedback promoted self-efficacy, motivation, and skill acquisition better than no feedback. Feedback during the first half of the program enhanced students' effort attributions for successes. Given students' learning disabilities, effort feedback for early or later successes may have seemed credible.

Young children attribute successes to effort, but around age 9 they begin to exhibit a distinct conception of ability (Nicholls, 1978, 1979; Nicholls & Miller, 1984). Ability attributions become increasingly important, whereas the influence of effort as a causal factor declines (Harari & Covington, 1981). Schunk (1983a) found that ability feedback for prior successes ("You're good at this") enhances perceived competence and skill better than effort feedback or ability + effort (combined) feedback. Children in the latter condition judged effort expenditure greater than ability-only subjects. Children in the combined condition may have discounted some of the ability information in favor of effort. In a follow-up study (Schunk, 1984), ability feedback given when children succeeded early in the course of learning enhanced achievement outcomes better than effort feedback regardless of whether ability feedback was continued during the later stages of learning.

The structure of classroom activities conveys attributional information. When students compete for grades and other rewards, their ability comparisons are heightened. Students successful under competitive conditions emphasize their abilities as contributing to their successes; those who fail believe they lack the requisite ability to succeed. These conditions create an ego-involved motivational state. Students begin to ask themselves, "Am I smart?" (Ames, 1985). In cooperative or individualistic reward structures, ability differences are minimized. Cooperative structures stress student effort when each student has responsibility for some task aspect and when the group is rewarded for its collective performance. In individualistic structures, students compare their present work with their prior performances. Students in individualistic structures focus on their efforts ("Am I trying hard enough?") and on learning strategies for enhancing their achievement ("How can I do this?").

Mixing students having learning problems with normal learners to work on tasks cooperatively is beneficial as long as the group succeeds

(Ames, 1984). Group success enhances self-evaluations of poor performers. Cooperative groups comprising learning disabled and nondisabled students work successfully if students are given prior training on how to work in small groups (Bryan, Cosden, & Pearl, 1982). When group members do not work well together, the performances and self-evaluations of learning disabled and nondisabled students suffer (Licht & Kistner, 1986).

SOCIAL COGNITIVE THEORY

In social cognitive theory, goals and expectations are important learning mechanisms. Bandura (1986) views motivation as goal-directed behavior instigated and sustained by people's expectations concerning the anticipated outcomes of their actions and their self-efficacy for performing those actions.

Goals and Expectations

Goal setting and self-evaluation of goal progress constitute an important motivational mechanism (Bandura, 1977b, 1986). The perceived negative discrepancy between one's goal and present performance creates an inducement for change. As people work toward goals, they note their progress. The perception of progress helps sustain behavior. Goal setting works in conjunction with outcome expectations. People act in ways they believe will help them attain their goals. People's sense of self-efficacy for performing actions to accomplish the goal also is necessary (see the section on Influences on Learning and Performance in Chapter 4). Most school children desire teacher praise (goal) and believe if they can volunteer correct answers they will earn teacher praise (positive outcome expectation). These students may not volunteer answers if they doubt their capabilities to give the correct answers (low self-efficacy).

Unlike conditioning theorists viewing reinforcement as a response strengthener, Bandura (1986) believes that reinforcement informs people about the likely outcomes of behaviors and motivates them to behave in ways they believe will be followed by positive consequences. People form expectations based on their experiences; however, another important source of motivation is observation of models.

Social Comparisons

Social comparison is the process of comparing ourselves with others. Festinger (1954) hypothesized that when objective standards of behavior are unclear or unavailable, people evaluate their abilities and opinions through comparisons with others. He also noted that the most accurate self-evalu-

APPLICATION 8.4: Social Comparisons

Teachers can use social comparisons as a motivation tool for improving behavior and effort in completing assigned tasks. Assume that a teacher is working with students grouped by reading ability. Complimenting students for appropriate displays of behavior emphasizes expected behaviors and instills students' self-efficacy for performing accordingly. Note the following examples of effective compliments: "I really like the way Johnny is sitting quietly and waiting for all of us to finish reading." "I like the way Susan read that sentence clearly so we could hear her." Observing student successes leads other students to believe they are capable of succeeding. A teacher might ask a student to go to the chalkboard and match contractions with the original words. Since the students in the group have similar abilities, the successes of the student at the board should raise self-efficacy in the others.

Teachers should be judicious in their use of social comparisons. Students who serve as models must succeed and be perceived by others as similar in important attributes. If models are perceived as dissimilar (especially in underlying abilities) or if they fail, social comparisons will not exert positive motivational effects on observers.

ations derive from comparisons with those similar in the ability or characteristic being evaluated. The more alike observers are to models, the greater is the probability that similar actions by observers are socially appropriate and will produce comparable results (Schunk, 1987).

The motivational effects of vicarious consequences depend in part on self-efficacy. Observing similar others succeed raises observers' self-efficacy and motivates them to try the task because they are apt to believe that if others can succeed, they will too. Observing similar others fail can lead people to believe they also lack the competencies to succeed, which dissuades them from attempting the behavior. Similarity may be especially influential in situations where individuals have experienced difficulties and possess self-doubts about performing well.

Developmental Considerations. The ability to use comparative information depends on higher levels of cognitive development and on experience in making comparative evaluations (Veroff, 1969). Festinger's hypothesis may not apply to children younger than age 5 or 6, because they tend not to relate two or more elements in thought and are egocentric in that the "self" dominates their cognitive focus (Higgins, 1981). This does not mean that young children cannot evaluate themselves relative to others; rather, they may not automatically do so. Children show increasing interest in comparative information in elementary school, and by fourth grade they regularly use this information to form self-evaluations of competence (Ruble, Boggiano, Feldman, & Loebl, 1980; Ruble, Feldman, & Boggiano, 1976).

The meaning and function of comparative information in children's lives change with their development, especially after they enter school. Preschoolers actively compare at an overt level (e.g., amount of reward). Other social comparisons involve how one is similar to and different from others, and competition is based on a desire to be better than others without involving self-evaluation (e.g., "I'm the general; that's higher than the captain") (Mosatche & Bragioner, 1981). Later social comparisons shift to a concern for how to perform a task (Ruble, 1983). First graders engage in peer comparisons, but they often do that to obtain correct answers from peers. Providing comparative information to young children increases motivation, but for practical reasons. Direct adult evaluation of children's capabilities (e.g., "You can do better") is more influential on children's self-evaluations than comparative information.

Motivated Learning

Motivated learning refers to motivation to acquire skills and strategies rather than to perform tasks (Corno & Mandinach, 1983; Schunk, 1989). At the start of an activity, students differ in how efficacious they feel about learning. Students derive cues conveying how well they are learning, which they use to appraise their self-efficacy for continued learning.

Efficacy Cues. Performance outcomes (successes, failures), attributions, persuader credibility, and bodily symptoms are influential cues. Successes raise students' self-efficacy and failures lower it, but an occasional failure (success) after many successes (failures) may not have much impact. Early learning is often fraught with failures, and the perception of progress promotes efficacy. Students' self-efficacy may not be aided much if they believe their progress is slow or their skills have stabilized at low levels.

Success achieved with great effort should raise efficacy less than if minimal effort is required, because the former implies that skills are not well developed. Learners' self-efficacy remains high as long as they believe they can maintain the level of effort needed to succeed. As students develop skills, ability attributions for successes enhance their efficacy better than effort attributions.

Persuader credibility is important because students may experience higher efficacy when told they are capable of learning by a trustworthy source (e.g., the teacher), whereas they may discount the advice of less credible sources. Students also may discount otherwise credible sources if they believe the sources do not understand the task demands (e.g., difficult for students to comprehend) or the effect of contextual factors (e.g., too many distractions).

Bodily symptoms serve as physiological cues for appraising efficacy. Sweating and trembling may signal that students are not capable of learning. Students who notice they are reacting in less-agitated fashion to academic tasks may feel more efficacious about learning.

Educational Practices. Educational practices convey information to students about how well they are learning by making cues salient. Students use these cues to assess self-efficacy for continued learning (Schunk, 1989). The *purpose of instruction* refers to the uses students will make of the material to be learned. These uses influence efficacy and motivation. When teachers announce that material will be on a test, students who have performed poorly on tests may experience anxiety, which could lead to low efficacy. Also relevant is *content difficulty.* Subject matter perceived as difficult to learn may lead to low efficacy for learning. Many students have qualms about solving fraction problems and reducing answers to lowest common denominators. Those who believe they are competent in the component skills (multiplication, division) feel more efficacious about learning than students who doubt their capabilities.

The type of *cognitive processing* required affects self-efficacy. Students who have difficulty processing information required by a task may conclude they have low ability and may feel less certain about learning than those who believe they can process the material. Students perceive learning from TV easier than learning from print and hold higher self-efficacy about and invest less mental effort in the former type of learning than the latter (Salomon, 1984). For learning from written materials, higher self-efficacy is associated with greater expended effort.

Much classroom learning depends on applying cognitive strategies (see the section on Information Processing Theory in Chapter 9). *Strategy training* fosters efficacy for learning. Believing that one understands and can effectively apply a strategy leads to a greater sense of control over learning outcomes, which promotes efficacy. *Instructional presentation* should affect efficacy for learning. Teachers who present material in a fashion students comprehend are apt to engender high efficacy for learning. When assessing self-efficacy, students take into account how well they learn from various instructional methods. If they believe they learn well from lectures and the teacher lectures a lot, they should feel more efficacious about learning than students who believe they learn best from small-group discussions. Even how the teacher opens the lesson may affect efficacy (Brophy, 1985). Teachers may cue positive (negative) expectations by asserting that students will enjoy (will not enjoy) the task and do well (poorly) on it. To the extent that students view the teacher as a credible judge of their capabilities, these statements should have different effects on efficacy.

The role of *performance feedback* is minimal when students derive their own feedback (e.g., mathematical exercises in which students check answers). When students cannot determine whether they are learning, teacher feedback highlighting progress (e.g., "That's right; you're getting better at this") ought to be beneficial.

Models are important influences on students' self-efficacy. Although students attend to and emulate teachers despite dissimilarity in attributes and competence, observation of successful peers exerts beneficial effects on efficacy, especially among low achievers who doubt they can attain the teacher's level of competence (Schunk, 1989). Remedial students may not feel highly efficacious about learning by observing a flawless teacher model, whereas they should feel more capable of learning when they observe peers.

As a result of *goal setting*, students may experience a sense of efficacy that is substantiated as they observe goal progress. Progress is easy to gauge with short-term and specific goals (Bandura & Schunk, 1981). Although students initially may doubt their capabilities to attain goals they believe are difficult, these goals build high efficacy because they offer more information about learning capabilities than easier goals.

Rewards are likely to enhance efficacy when they are tied to students' accomplishments. Telling students they can earn rewards based on what they accomplish instills a sense of efficacy for performing well, which is validated as they work at the task and note their progress. Receipt of the reward further validates efficacy because it symbolizes progress. When teachers reward students for time spent working regardless of performance, rewards may convey negative efficacy information. Students might infer they are not expected to learn much because they lack the ability.

Attributional feedback, or linking students' successes and failures with causes, is a highly persuasive source of efficacy information. The key is to ensure that learners view the feedback as credible. Providing ability feedback ("You're good at this") when students have to struggle to succeed does not raise students' self-efficacy for learning.

LEARNED HELPLESSNESS

Learned helplessness refers to a psychological state involving a disturbance in motivation, cognitive processes, and emotions due to previously experienced uncontrollability (Maier & Seligman, 1976; Seligman, 1975). Learned helplessness results from perceived independence between responses and outcomes. Helplessness was identified in laboratory studies in which dogs given inescapable shocks were moved to another location where they could avoid shocks by jumping a hurdle. The prior inescapable shocks conditioned the dogs; they made little attempt to escape in the new setting but rather passively endured the shock. Dogs not previously exposed to inescapable shock easily learned to escape.

One manifestation of helplessness is passivity. People may do nothing when they believe they have no control over a situation. Passivity does not depend on the outcome; uncontrollable rewards produce *learned laziness* (Engberg, Hansen, Welker, & Thomas, 1972). Helplessness also retards learning. Organisms exposed to uncontrollable situations may never learn adaptive responses or may learn them slower than organisms not exposed to uncontrollability. Helplessness has emotional manifestations. Prior uncontrollable situations may initially make one respond more aggressively, but eventually behavior becomes less assertive.

Learned helplessness has been applied in diverse clinical contexts (Fincham & Cain, 1986). Seligman (1975) proposed helplessness as an explanation for human reactive depression, or depression brought about by sudden and dramatic changes in one's life (e.g., death of loved one, divorce, loss of job). Although people often feel helpless in these situations, many depressed individuals blame themselves for the negative events in their lives. They believe, for example, they were fired because they continually were late to work but that they easily could have arrived at work a few minutes earlier each day. Feeling personally responsible for negative events is incompatible with the notion that helplessness results from perceived lack of control.

Seligman's original model of learned helplessness was reformulated to incorporate an attributional perspective (Abramson, Seligman, & Teasdale, 1978). The reformulated model postulates that people's explanations (attributions) for outcomes influence future expectancies of outcomes and reactions to them. Explanations vary along three dimensions: stable–unstable, global–specific, and internal–external. One who attributes negative outcomes to stable causes is likely to expect bad events in the future, which may produce helplessness. Causes can impact many areas of one's life (global) or only one area (specific). Students may believe they lack ability in all school subjects or only in one subject. Global attributions are more likely to produce helplessness. Causes for negative events may be internal, that is, reside within the individual (low intelligence), or external, that is, in the environment (teacher gives unfair tests). Internal attributions are apt to result in helplessness. Collectively, people who are most prone to helplessness are those who typically explain negative events with internal, global, and stable attributions (failure in school due to low intelligence).

Students with Learning Problems

The learned helplessness construct is applicable to many students with learning problems who enter a vicious cycle in which negative beliefs reciprocally interact with academic failures (Licht & Kistner, 1986). For various reasons, students fail in school, and they begin to doubt their learning capabilities and view academic successes as uncontrollable. These beliefs produce frustration and giving up readily on tasks. Lack of effort and persistence contributes to further failures, which reinforce negative beliefs.

Eventually, students interpret their successes as externally caused: The task was easy; they were lucky; the teacher helped them. They attribute failures to low ability—an internal, global, stable attribution—which negatively affects self-efficacy, motivation, and achievement (Nolen-Hoeksema, Girgus, & Seligman, 1986).

Compared with normal learners, students with learning problems hold lower expectations for success, judge themselves lower in ability, and place greater emphasis on lack of ability as a cause of failure (Boersma & Chapman, 1981; Butkowsky & Willows, 1980; Palmer, Drummond, Tollison, & Zinkgraff, 1982). Such students often do not stress low effort as a cause of failure (Andrews & Debus, 1978; Dweck, 1975; Pearl, Bryan, & Donohue, 1980). They give up readily when they encounter difficulties, cite uncontrollable causes for successes and failures, and hold low perceptions of internal control over outcomes (Johnson, 1981; Licht & Kistner, 1986). Students even may generalize these negative beliefs to situations in which they previously have not failed.

Dweck integrated the learned helplessness construct into a model of achievement motivation (Dweck, 1986; Dweck & Leggett, 1988). Helpless students are characterized by ego involvement. Their school goals are to complete tasks and avoid negative judgments of their competence. They believe that intelligence is a fixed quantity. They avoid challenges, display low persistence in the face of difficulty, hold low perceptions of their capabilities, and often demonstrate anxiety while engaged in tasks (Diener & Dweck, 1978, 1980). In contrast, mastery oriented students display a task-involved achievement pattern. They believe intelligence can be improved, and their school goals are to learn and become more competent. They hold high perceptions of their learning capabilities, frequently seek challenges, and persist at difficult tasks.

Mastery-oriented and helpless students do not differ in intellectual ability. Although helpless students often possess cognitive skill deficits, these alone do not cause failure. Not all students with learning problems enter this cycle; some continue to feel confident and display positive attributional patterns. One factor that may be important is frequency of failure: Students who fail in many school subjects are especially susceptible. Reading deficits are particularly influential, presumably because reading pervades the curriculum. Reading deficits can promote negative beliefs in areas that involve little or no reading (e.g., math) (Licht & Kistner, 1986). Variables associated with the instructional environment prevent students with learning problems from entering this cycle or help them overcome it (Friedman & Medway, 1987). Attributional feedback can alter students' maladaptive achievement beliefs and behaviors. Teachers also need to give students tasks they can accomplish and feedback highlighting progress toward learning goals (Schunk, 1989).

INTRINSIC MOTIVATION

Different theories postulate that motivation arises in part from a desire to effectively control one's environment. This desire has been labeled *mastery, competence, effectance,* or *intrinsic motivation.* Although there are differences in theoretical perspectives, the different theories agree that intrinsic motivation involves task engagement for no obvious reward except for the activity itself (Deci, 1975).

Theoretical Perspectives

In a seminal paper, White (1959) defined *effectance motivation* as follows:

> ... fitness or ability, and the suggested synonyms capability, capacity, efficiency, proficiency, and skill. It is therefore a suitable word to describe such things as grasping and exploring, crawling and walking, attention and perception, language and thinking, manipulating and changing the surroundings, all of which promote an effective—a competent—interaction with the environment. The behavior . . . is directed, selective, and persistent, and it is continued not because it serves primary drives, which indeed it cannot serve until it is almost perfected, but because it satisfies an intrinsic need to deal with the environment. (pp. 317–318)

Effectance motivation is seen in young children as they interact with environmental aspects catching their attention. A youngster may reach out and grab an object, turn it over, and push it away in an effort to control it. Effectance motivation is undifferentiated in young children; it is directed

---

APPLICATION 8.5: Intrinsic Motivation

Intrinsic motivation focuses on control and competence. Individuals develop perceived competence by mastering difficult situations. If teachers are helping slower students complete assigned tasks in an allotted time, they may begin by offering a reward (extrinsic motivator) and work toward building student pride in their accomplishments (intrinsic motivator). Initially teachers might reward students for increased output with time on the computer, verbal praise, or special notes home to parents. Gradually teachers could reward intermittently and then decrease it to allow students to focus more on their accomplishments. The ability to complete tasks in the appropriate time span provides students with information about their capabilities and their ability to control situations. When pride from successfully completing tasks becomes a reward, students are intrinsically motivated to continue to display the new behavior.

toward all aspects of the environment. With development, motivation becomes increasingly specialized. Once children enter school, they manifest effectance motivation in achievement behaviors in various school subjects.

Effectance motivation arises when biological motives are satisfied; it also facilitates future need satisfaction. Taking the top off of a jar initially satisfies the effectance motive, but in so doing the child learns there are cookies in the jar. This knowledge is used in the future to satisfy hunger.

Investigators have postulated that intrinsic motivation is related to an inherent need for a moderate amount of environmental stimulation. Hunt (1963) argued that exploratory behaviors and curiosity are intrinsically motivated and result from incongruity between prior experiences and new information. People extract information from the environment and compare it to internal representations. When incongruity exists between the input and internal knowledge or expectation, people become intrinsically motivated to reduce the incongruity. Hunt postulated that people require an optimal level of incongruity. When deprived of that level, they seek situations that provide it. Too much incongruity proves frustrating and triggers a drive to reduce frustration. Although Hunt's views have intuitive merit, they have been criticized because the term *optimal level of incongruity* is vague and it is not clear how much incongruity is required to trigger motivation (Deci, 1975).

In related fashion, Berlyne (1960) hypothesized that an optimal level of physiological incongruity (stimulation to the nervous system) is necessary. Berlyne's "arousal potential" may be interpreted as being approximately equivalent on a physiological level to Hunt's psychological incongruity.

Deci proposed a theory of intrinsic motivation emphasizing control and competence (Deci, 1975, 1980; Deci & Porac, 1978). Intrinsic motivation generates behaviors that seek to control one's environment and that convey a sense of competence. Some behaviors increase environmental stimulation, whereas others are oriented toward conquering challenges. Humans develop perceived competence by mastering difficult situations.

People cognitively represent anticipated outcomes. Individuals choose to engage in activities that appear challenging and attainable. While engaged in these activities, people derive competence information based on the success of their interactions. The resultant feelings of competence are a type of intrinsic reward.

Theoretical debate exists over whether intrinsic motivation represents a need state seeking satisfaction or a cognitive state represented by incongruity, challenge, desire for competence information, and seeking control. One need not choose sides in this debate to accept the basic premise that people seek to control important aspects of their lives.

Overjustification and Reward

When people are intrinsically motivated they engage in an activity as an end in itself. In contrast, extrinsic motivation involves engaging in an activity for reasons external to the task. This activity is a means to some end: an object, a grade, feedback or praise, or being able to engage in another activity. Students are extrinsically motivated if they try to perform well in school primarily to please their parents, earn high grades, or receive teacher approval.

Intrinsic reasons for working on a task are internal to the task. The reward comes from working on the task; the task is both the means and the end. The rewards for intrinsic motivation may be feelings of competence and control, self-satisfaction, task success, or pride in one's work.

One can engage in an activity for both intrinsic and extrinsic reasons. Many students like to feel competent in school and experience pride for a job done well, but they also desire teacher praise and good grades. Rewards are not inherently extrinsically motivating. Deci (1975) contended that rewards have an informational and a controlling aspect. Reward systems may be primarily structured to convey information about one's capabilities or to control one's behavior, and the relative salience of each (information or control) influences one's subsequent behavior. A salient informational aspect indicating successful performance should promote feelings of competence, whereas a salient controlling aspect can lead to perceptions of the reward as the cause of the behavior.

For example, suppose a teacher implements a reward system in which the more work students accomplish, the more points they earn. Although students will want to work to earn points (because the points can be exchanged for privileges), the points convey information about their capabilities: The more points students earn, the more work they have accomplished. As points accumulate, students are apt to believe they are becoming more competent. In contrast, if points are given simply for time spent on a task, the task may be viewed primarily as a means to an end. The points convey nothing about capabilities; students are likely to view the rewards as controlling their task engagement.

Lepper postulated that the perception of reward influences students' intrinsic motivation (Lepper, 1983; Lepper & Greene, 1978). One's motivation is largely a function of one's perceptions for engaging in the task. When external constraints are salient, unambiguous, and sufficient to explain the behavior, individuals attribute their behaviors to those constraints. If external constraints are viewed as weak, unclear, or psychologically insufficient to account for their behavior, people are likely to attribute their actions to their desires or personal dispositions.

In a classic experiment (Lepper, Greene, & Nisbett, 1973), preschoolers were observed during free play. Those who spent a lot of time drawing were selected for the study and assigned to one of three conditions. In the expected award group, children were offered a good player certificate if they drew a picture. Unexpected award subjects were not offered the certificate, but unexpectedly received it after they drew a picture. No award subjects were not offered the award and did not receive it. Two weeks later children were again observed during free play.

The expected award children engaged in drawing for a significantly shorter time following the experiment than they had prior to the study, whereas the other two conditions showed no significant change. Expected award children spent less time drawing following the study compared with the other conditions. It was not the reward itself that was important, rather the contingency. Lepper et al. (1973) postulated the *overjustification hypothesis:* Engagement in an intrinsically interesting activity under conditions that make it salient as a means to an end (reward) decreases subsequent interest in that activity. The overjustification hypothesis has been supported in experimental investigations with different tasks and subjects of all ages (Lepper & Greene, 1978).

Rewards need not have detrimental effects on performance. Rewards can help develop skills and interest when they are informative of one's capabilities. Offering children rewards based on the amount of work they accomplish during an instructional program increases self-efficacy, motivation, and skill acquisition, compared with offering rewards merely for task participation or not offering rewards (Schunk, 1983d). During a subtraction instruction program, Bandura and Schunk (1981) found that higher self-efficacy related positively to the amount of intrinsic interest children subsequently showed in solving arithmetic problems.

SUMMARY

Motivation refers to the process whereby goal-directed behavior is instigated and sustained. Some important early views on motivation were drive theory, operant conditioning, cognitive consistency theories, and Maslow's need hierarchy. Each of these contributed to the understanding of motivation, but none seems adequate to explain human motivated behavior. Most current theories view motivation as reflecting cognitive processes, though these theories differ in the importance ascribed to various cognitive constructs.

Atkinson's achievement motivation theory postulated that need for achievement is a general motive leading individuals to perform their best in achievement contexts. Achievement behavior represents an emotional conflict between hope for success and fear of failure. Horner broadened the theory to include fear of success. More recently, Nicholls and others postulated that achievement motivation reflects students' perceptions of ability and their goals in achievement settings. The self-worth theory of Covington and his colleagues hypothesized that achievement behavior is a function of students' efforts to preserve the perception of high ability among themselves and others.

Attribution theory, a systematic cognitive view of motivation, incorporates Rotter's locus of control and many elements of Heider's naive analysis of action. Weiner's attribution theory, which is relevant in achievement settings, categorized attributions along three dimensions: internal–external, stable–unstable, and controllable–uncontrollable. Attributions are important because they affect achievement beliefs, emotions, and behaviors. Attributional change programs attempt to alter students' dysfunctional attributions for failure, such as from low ability or insufficient effort. Attributional feedback for prior successes improves students' self-efficacy, motivation, and skill acquisition.

Social cognitive theory views motivation as resulting from goals and expectations. People set goals and act in ways they believe will help them attain their goals. By comparing present performance to the goal and noting progress, people experience a sense of efficacy for improvement. Motivation depends on believing that one will achieve desired outcomes from given behaviors (positive outcome expectations) and that one is capable of performing or learning to perform those behaviors (high self-efficacy). Social comparisons with others are important sources of information to form outcome and efficacy expectations.

Many cognitive theories stress people's desire to exert control over important aspects of their lives. Seligman noted that when people perceive independence between responses and outcomes, learned helplessness manifests itself in motivational, learning, and emotional deficits. The learned helplessness notion is applicable to many students with learning problems who display negative attributional patterns and low self-efficacy in their learning capabilities.

Intrinsic motivation is interest in engaging in an activity for its own sake. Intrinsically interesting activities are ends in themselves, in contrast to extrinsically motivated actions, which are means to some end. Young children have intrinsic motivation to understand and control their environments, which becomes more specialized with development and progression in school. Many theorists hypothesize that intrinsic motivation depends on individuals' needs for optimal levels of psychological or physiological incongruity. Much research has addressed the effect of rewards on intrinsic motivation. Offering rewards for task engagement decreases intrinsic motivation when rewards are seen as controlling behavior. Rewards given contingent on one's level of performance are informative of capabilities and foster students' self-efficacy, interest, and skill acquisition.

Chapter 9

Self-Regulated Learning

Self-regulated learning research began as an outgrowth of psychological investigations into self-control and the development of self-regulatory processes (Zimmerman, 1989). Although theoretical traditions differ in their definitions, most stress that *self-regulated learning* refers to the process whereby students personally activate and sustain cognitions and behaviors systematically oriented toward the attainment of academic learning goals (Zimmerman, 1986). Cognitive researchers emphasize such mental activities as attention, rehearsal, use of learning strategies, and comprehension monitoring, along with such beliefs as self-efficacy, outcome expectations, and value of learning (Schunk, 1986). Behavioral researchers focus on overt responses involved in self-monitoring, self-instruction, and self-reinforcement.

Regardless of theoretical tradition, self-regulated learning fits well with the notion that students contribute actively to their learning goals and are not passive recipients of information. Researchers of different traditions postulate that self-regulated learning involves learners having a purpose or goal and employing goal-directed actions. Different theories also hypothesize that students monitor their behaviors while learning and adjust them to ensure success. Theories differ in the mechanisms postulated to underlie students' use of cognitive and behavioral processes to regulate their activities.

Early research in self-regulation was conducted primarily in therapeutic contexts. Subjects were drawn from diverse populations: adults and children, normal and retarded, workers and supervisors (Bandura, 1986; Karoly & Kanfer, 1982). In a typical study, subjects were taught ways to alter dysfunctional behaviors. Research addressed such areas as aggressive and disruptive behaviors, addictions, sexual disorders, interpersonal skills, educational problems, and supervisory skills (Mace & West, 1986).

This chapter focuses on self-regulation during academic skill learning in and out of school. Different theoretical approaches are reviewed: reinforcement, cognitive-developmental, social cognitive, and information processing. The chapter concludes with a discussion of *learning strategies*, or systematic plans used by students to regulate their academic work and to increase their skills.

REINFORCEMENT THEORY

The reinforcement theory view of self-regulated behavior derives primarily from the work of Skinner (Mace, Belfiore, & Shea, 1989). Recall from Chapter 3 that operant behavior is emitted in the presence of discriminative stimuli. Whether behavior becomes more or less probable depends on its consequences: Behaviors reinforced become more probable; those punished become less probable. Teacher praise given to a student contingent on a high test score may increase the student's studying for exams; teacher criticism contingent on a student's disruptive behavior may decrease the likelihood of disruptive behavior.

Reinforcement theorists have studied how individuals establish discriminative stimuli and reinforcement contingencies (Brigham, 1982). Self-regulated behavior involves choosing among alternative courses of action (Mace et al., 1989), typically by deferring an immediate reinforcer in favor of a different, and usually greater, future reinforcer (Rachlin, 1974). For example, a student who stays home on Friday night to study for an exam instead of going out on a date and a student who keeps working on an academic task despite taunting peers nearby are deferring immediate reinforcement, as is John in the next example.

John is having difficulty studying. Despite good intentions, he spends an insufficient amount of time studying and is easily distracted. A key to changing his behavior is to establish discriminative stimuli (cues) for studying. With the assistance of his high school counselor, John establishes a definite time and place for studying (7 p.m. to 9 p.m. in his room with one 10-minute break). To eliminate distracting cues, John agrees not to talk on the phone or to play his TV, stereo, radio, or tape recorder. For reinforcement, John will award himself one point for each night he successfully accomplishes his routine. When he receives 10 points, he will take a night off.

In the reinforcement view, one decides which behaviors are to be regulated, establishes discriminative stimuli for their occurrence, evaluates performance in terms of whether it matches the standard, and administers reinforcement. The three key subprocesses are self-monitoring, self-instruction, and self-reinforcement.

Self-Monitoring

Self-monitoring refers to deliberate attention to some aspect of one's behavior; it is often accompanied by recording its frequency or intensity (Mace & Kratochwill, 1988). People cannot regulate their actions if they are not aware of what they do. Behaviors can be assessed on such dimensions as quality, rate, quantity, and originality. While writing a term paper, students may periodically assess their work to determine whether it states important ideas, whether it will be finished by the due date, whether it will be long enough, and whether it integrates their ideas in unusual fashion. Self-monitoring is applicable to such diverse areas as motor skill performances (how fast one runs the 100-meter dash), artistic efforts (how original are one's pen and ink drawings), and social behaviors (how comfortable one feels while attending social functions).

APPLICATION 9.1: Self-Monitoring

Self-monitoring makes students aware of existing behaviors and assists in evaluating and improving them. In a special education self-contained or resource room, self-monitoring could help students improve on-task behavior, particularly if it is coupled with goal setting. The teacher could create individual charts divided into small blocks representing a short time period (e.g., 10 minutes). Once students are working independently at their seats or work stations, a soft bell could be sounded every 10 minutes. When the bell sounds, students could record on their charts what they are doing—writing, reading, daydreaming, or doodling. The teacher could help each student set individual goals related to the number of on-task behaviors expected in a day, which would be increased as the student's behavior improves.

In regular classrooms, teachers need to be careful about how they indicate time periods to self-monitoring students. Using a bell would disrupt other students and draw embarrassing attention to the students having difficulty. Teachers might seat self-monitoring students close to them and gently tap the students' desks at the end of each time period or otherwise quietly indicate its end.

Different methods are used to self-monitor one's behavior, and training generally is necessary (Ollendick & Hersen, 1984; Shapiro, 1987). Methods include narrations, frequency counts, duration measures, time sampling measures, behavior ratings, and behavioral traces and archival records (Mace et al., 1989). *Narrations* are written accounts of a person's behavior and the context in which it occurs. Narrations can range from very detailed to open-ended (Bell & Low, 1977). *Frequency counts* are used to self-record instances of specific behaviors during a given time period (e.g., number of times a student turns around in the seat during a 30-minute seatwork exercise). *Duration measures* record the amount of time a behavior occurs during a given period (e.g., number of minutes a student studies during a 30-minute period). *Time sampling measures* divide a period into shorter intervals and record how often a behavior occurs during each interval. A 30-minute study period might be divided into six 5-minute periods, and for each of the 5-minute periods, students record whether they studied the entire time. *Behavior ratings* require estimates of how often a behavior occurs during a given time period—always, sometimes, never, and so on. *Behavioral traces and archival records* are permanent records that exist independently of other assessments (e.g., number of worksheets completed, number of problems solved correctly).

In the absence of self-recording, selective memory comes into play, and one's observations may not faithfully reflect one's behaviors. Self-recording often yields surprising results. Students having difficulties studying should keep a written record of their activities. They may learn they are wasting over 50% of their study time on nonacademic tasks.

Two important criteria for self-monitoring are regularity and proximity (Bandura, 1986). *Regularity* means observing behavior on a continual basis instead of intermittently; one keeps a daily record rather than recording behavior one day per week. Nonregular observation yields misleading results. *Proximity* means that behavior is observed close in time to its occurrence rather than long after it occurs. One needs to write down what one does at the time rather than wait until the end of the day to reconstruct events.

Self-monitoring methods place responsibility for behavioral assessment on the student. These methods often lead to significant behavioral improvements, a process known as *reactivity*. Self-monitored responses are consequences of behaviors, and like other consequences, they affect future responding. The self-recordings are immediate responses mediating the relationship of preceding behavior to longer-term consequences (Mace & West, 1986; Nelson & Hayes, 1981). Students who monitor completion of workbook pages provide themselves with immediate reinforcers that mediate the link between seatwork and such distant consequences as teacher praise and good grades.

REINFORCEMENT THEORY

Research supports the effectiveness of self-monitoring. Sagotsky, Patterson, and Lepper (1978) had children periodically monitor their performances during mathematics sessions and record whether they were working on the appropriate instructional materials. Other students set daily performance goals for themselves, and students in a third condition received self-monitoring and goal setting. Self-monitoring increased time on task and mathematical achievement, whereas goal setting had minimal effects. For goal setting to affect performance, students initially may need training on how to set challenging but attainable goals.

Schunk (1983c) provided subtraction instruction and practice to children who failed to master subtraction operations in their classrooms. One group (self-monitoring) reviewed their work at the end of each instructional session and recorded the number of workbook pages they completed. A second group (external monitoring) had their work reviewed at the end of each session by an adult who recorded the number of pages completed. No monitoring children received the instructional program but were not monitored or told to monitor their work.

The self- and external monitoring conditions in teaching subtraction led to higher self-efficacy, skill, and persistence, compared with the no monitoring condition. The effects of the two monitoring conditions were comparable. The benefits of monitoring did not depend on children's performances during the instructional sessions, because the three treatment conditions did not differ in amount of work completed. Monitoring of progress, rather than the agent, enhanced children's perceptions of their learning progress and self-efficacy.

Self-Instruction

Self-instruction refers to discriminative stimuli that set the occasion for responses leading to reinforcement (Mace et al., 1989). Self-instruction should not be confused with Meichenbaum's (1977) self-instructional training procedure (discussed in the section on Modeling Processes in Chapter 4). One type of self-regulatory instruction involves arranging the environment to produce discriminative stimuli. Students who realize that they need to review class notes the next day might write themselves a reminder before going to bed. The written reminder serves as a cue to review, which makes reinforcement (good grade on a quiz) more likely. Another type of self-instruction takes the form of statements (rules) that serve as discriminative stimuli to guide behavior. This type of self-instruction is included in Meichenbaum's procedure.

Strategy instruction is an effective means of enhancing comprehension and self-efficacy among poor readers. Schunk and Rice (1986, 1987) taught remedial readers to use the following self-instruction strategy for working on reading comprehension passages:

> What do I have to do?
> 1. Read the questions.
> 2. Read the passage to find out what it is mostly about.
> 3. Think about what the details have in common.
> 4. Think about what would make a good title.
> 5. Reread the story if I don't know the answer to a question. (1987, pp. 290–291)

Children verbalized the individual steps prior to applying them to passages.

Self-instructional statements have been employed in various domains to teach academic, social, and motor skills. These statements are especially useful for students with cognitive deficits who may also suffer from attention disorders. Verbalizing statements keeps them focused on a task. A self-instruction procedure used to improve a learning disabled student's handwriting was as follows (Kosiewicz, Hallahan, Lloyd, & Graves, 1982):

> 1. Say aloud the word to be written.
> 2. Say the first syllable.
> 3. Name each of the letters in that syllable three times.
> 4. Repeat each letter as it is written down.
> 5. Repeat steps 2 through 4 for each succeeding syllable.

This sequence appeared on a card on the student's desk. During training, the student was praised for completion of the steps. Once the student learned the procedure, praise was discontinued and the sequence was maintained by the consequence of better handwriting.

Self-Reinforcement

Self-reinforcement refers to the process whereby individuals, after performing a response, receive a reinforcing stimulus that increases the likelihood of future responding (Mace et al., 1989). As discussed in Chapter 3, a reinforcer is defined on the basis of its effects. To illustrate, assume that a student named Mitch is on a point system whereby he awards himself one point for each page he reads in his geography book. He keeps a record each week, and if his week's points exceed by 5% his previous week's points, he is allowed 30 minutes of free time on Friday. Whether this arrangement functions as a self-reinforcement system cannot be determined until it is known whether he regularly earns the free time. If he does, that is, if his average performance increases as the semester proceeds, his academic behaviors are being regulated by the reinforcement contingencies.

Much research shows that reinforcement contingencies improve academic performance (Bandura, 1986), but it is unclear whether self-reinforcement is more effective than externally administered reinforcement (e.g., by the teacher). Self-reinforcement studies suffer from many problems and experimental confounds (Martin, 1980). In academic settings, a frequent problem is that the reinforcement contingency is part of a context that includes instruction and classroom rules. Students do not work on materials when they choose but rather when told to do so by the teacher. Students may stay on task because of the teacher's direction rather than reinforcement.

Self-reinforcement has been praised as an effective component of self-regulated behavior (O'Leary & Dubey, 1979), but methodological problems and inconsistent findings question its benefits (Brigham, 1982). Although self-reinforcement may enhance behavioral maintenance over time, self-reinforcement seems less important than reinforcement in general during the acquisition of self-regulatory skills.

COGNITIVE-DEVELOPMENTAL THEORY

Private Speech

Cognitive-developmental theory establishes a strong link between private speech and the development of self-regulation (Harris, 1982). *Private speech* refers to the set of speech phenomena that has a self-regulatory function but that is not socially communicative (Fuson, 1979). The historical impetus derives in part from work by Pavlov (1927). Recall from Chapter 2 that Pavlov distinguished between the *first* (perceptual) and *second* (linguistic) signal systems. Pavlov realized that animal conditioning data do not completely generalize to humans; human conditioning often occurs abruptly (few pairings of conditioned stimulus and unconditioned stimulus) in contrast to the multiple pairings required with animals. Pavlov believed that conditioning differences between humans and animals are largely due to the human capacity for language, which mediates the relationship between stimuli and perception. Stimuli do not produce conditioning automatically; people interpret stimuli in light of their prior experiences. Although Pavlov did not conduct research on the second signal system, subsequent investigations have validated his beliefs that human conditioning is complex and language plays a mediational role.

The Soviet psychologist Luria (1961) focused on the child's transition from the first to the second signal system. Luria postulated three stages in the development of verbal control of motor behavior. Initially, the speech of others is primarily responsible for directing the child's behavior (ages 1 ½ to 2 ½). During the second stage (ages 3 to 4), the child's overt verbalizations initiate motor behaviors but do not necessarily inhibit them. In the third stage, the child's private speech becomes capable of initiating, directing, and inhibiting motor behaviors (ages 4 ½ to 5 ½). Luria believed this private, self-regulatory speech directs behavior through neurophysiological mechanisms.

The mediational and self-directing role of the second signal system is embodied in the Soviet psychologist Vygotsky's theory. Vygotsky (1962) believed private speech helps develop thought by organizing behavior. Children employ private speech to understand situations and surmount difficulties. Private speech develops from the child's interactions in the social environment. As children's language facility develops, words spoken by others acquire meaning independent of their phonological and syntactical qualities. Children internalize word meanings and use them to direct their behaviors.

Vygotsky hypothesized that private speech follows a curvilinear developmental pattern: Overt verbalization (thinking aloud) increases until ages 6 to 7, after which it declines and becomes primarily covert by ages 8 to 10. However, overt verbalization can occur at any age when people encounter obstacles. Research shows that although the amount of private speech decreases from about ages 4 or 5 to 8, the proportion of private speech that is self-regulating increases with age (Fuson, 1979). In the typical investigation, the actual amount of private speech is small, and many children do not verbalize. The developmental pattern of private speech seems more complex than originally hypothesized by Vygotsky.

Production, Mediational, and Continued-Use Deficiencies

Many investigations have explored factors responsible for children not using private speech when it would be desirable to do so. A distinction is drawn between production and mediational deficiencies in spontaneous use of private speech (Flavell, Beach, & Chinsky, 1966; Reese, 1962). A *production deficiency* is failure to generate task-relevant verbalizations (e.g., rules, strategies, information to be remembered) when they could improve performance. A *mediational deficiency* occurs when task-relevant verbalizations are produced but do not affect subsequent behaviors (Fuson, 1979; Paris, 1978).

Young children produce verbalizations that do not necessarily mediate performance. Children eventually develop the ability for verbalizations to mediate performance but may not produce relevant verbalizations at appropriate times. With development, children learn to verbalize when it might benefit performance. This developmental model pertains better to situations requiring relatively simple types of verbal self-regulation (e.g., rote rehearsal) than to those calling for more complex verbalizations, in which production and mediational deficiencies may coexist and may not follow a simple progression (Fuson, 1979).

Recent research demonstrates that once children are trained to produce verbalizations to aid performance, they often discontinue use of private speech when no longer required to verbalize (Schunk, 1986). A *continued-use deficiency* arises because of inadequate understanding of the strategy, as might occur when students receive too little instruction and practice using the strategy (Borkowski & Cavanaugh, 1979). To remedy this problem, teachers need to provide repeated instruction and practice with spaced review sessions. A continued-use deficiency also might arise when students associate the strategy with the training context and do not understand how to transfer it to other tasks. Use of multiple tasks during training helps students understand strategy generalizability. Strategies often need to be modified to apply to different tasks. When slight modifications prove troublesome, students benefit from explicit training on strategy modification.

Continued-use deficiencies can also be caused by learners not understanding that use of private speech benefits their performances. They might believe that verbal self-regulation is useful, but that it is not as important for success as such factors as time available or effort expended (Fabricius & Hagen, 1984). To promote maintenance of self-regulators, researchers suggest providing learners with *strategy value information,* or information that links strategy use with improved performance (Baker & Brown, 1984; Paris et al., 1983; Schunk & Rice, 1987). Some ways to convey strategy value are to instruct students to use the strategy because it will help them perform better, to inform them that strategy use benefited other students, and to provide feedback linking strategy use with better performance (Brown, 1980). There is evidence that strategy value information enhances performance, continued strategy use, and strategy transfer to other tasks (Kramer & Engle, 1981; Lodico, Ghatala, Levin, Pressley, & Bell, 1983; Paris, Newman, & McVey, 1982; Ringel & Springer, 1980).

Strategy value information also raises efficacy, which promotes performance through increased effort and persistence (Schunk & Rice, 1987). Students who benefit most from strategy training are those who work at tasks in nonsystematic fashion and who possess doubts about their academic capabilities (Licht & Kistner, 1986). Strategy value information implicitly conveys to students that they are capable of learning and successfully applying the strategy, which engenders a sense of control over learning outcomes and which enhances efficacy for skill improvement.

Verbalization and Achievement

Verbalization of rules, procedures, and strategies can improve student learning. Meichenbaum's (1977, 1986) self-instructional training procedure recreates the overt-to-covert developmental progression of private speech.

APPLICATION 9.2: Self-Talk

A teacher might use verbalization (self-talk) in a special education resource room or at a work station separated from other students in a regular classroom to assist students having difficulty attending to material and mastering skills. Verbalization could be beneficial for students learning to solve long division problems who cannot remember the steps to complete the procedure. The teacher might work individually with the students by verbalizing and applying the following steps:

> Will (number) go into (number)? Divide. Multiply: (number) times (number) is (number). Put down the answer. Subtract: (number) minus (number) is (number). Bring down the next number. Repeat steps.

Use of self-talk helps students stay on task and builds their confidence in systematically working through the long process. Once they begin to grasp the content, it is to their advantage to fade verbalizations to a covert level so they can work more rapidly.

Types of statements modeled are as follows: problem definition ("What is it I have to do?"), focusing of attention ("I need to pay attention to what I'm doing"), planning and response guidance ("I need to work carefully"), self-reinforcement ("I'm doing fine"), self-evaluation ("Am I doing things in the right order?"), and coping statements ("I need to try again when I don't get it right"). Self-instructional training has been used to teach learners cognitive and motor skills, and it can create a positive task outlook and foster perseverance in the face of difficulties (Meichenbaum & Asarnow, 1979).

Verbalization is most beneficial for students who typically perform in a deficient manner (Denney, 1975; Denney & Turner, 1979). Benefits have been obtained with children who do not spontaneously rehearse material to be learned, impulsive subjects, learning disabled and retarded students, and remedial learners (Schunk, 1986). Verbalization helps students with learning problems work at tasks in a systematic manner (Hallahan et al., 1983). It forces students to attend to tasks and to rehearse material, which enhance learning. Verbalization does not facilitate learning when children can handle task demands adequately. Because verbalization constitutes an additional task, it can distract children from the task at hand.

Research has identified the conditions under which verbalization promotes performance. Denney (1975) modeled a performance strategy for 6-, 8-, and 10-year-old normal learners on a 20-question task. The 8- and 10-year-olds who verbalized the model's strategy as they performed the task fared no better than children who did not verbalize. Verbalization interfered with the performance of 6-year-olds. Children verbalized specific statements (e.g., "Find the right picture in the fewest questions"); apparently performing this additional task proved too distracting for the youngest children. Denney and Turner (1979) found that among normal learners ranging in age from 3 to 10 years, the addition of verbalization to a strategy modeling treatment resulted in no benefits on cognitive tasks compared with modeling alone. Subjects constructed their own verbalizations, which might have been less distracting than Denney's (1975) specific statements. Coates and Hartup (1969) found that 7-year-olds who verbalized a model's actions during exposure did not subsequently produce them better than children who passively observed the behaviors. The children regulated their attention and cognitively processed the model's actions without verbalizing.

Berk (1986) studied first- and third-graders' spontaneous private speech. Task-relevant overt speech was negatively related to and faded verbalization (whispers, lip movements, muttering) was positively related to mathematical performance. These results were obtained for first graders of high intelligence and third graders of average intelligence; among third graders of high intelligence, overt and faded speech showed no relationship to achievement. For the latter students, the most effective self-guiding speech apparently is internalized.

Keeney, Cannizzo, and Flavell (1967) pretested 6- and 7-year-olds on a serial recall task and identified those who failed to rehearse prior to recall. After these children were trained to rehearse, their recall matched that of spontaneous rehearsers. Asarnow and Meichenbaum (1979) identified kindergartners who did not spontaneously rehearse on a serial recall test. Some were trained to use a rehearsal strategy similar to that of Keeney et al. (1967), whereas others received self-instructional training. Both treatments facilitated recall relative to a control condition, but the self-instructional treatment was more effective. Taylor and his colleagues (Taylor, Josberger, & Whitely, 1973; Whitely & Taylor, 1973) found that educable mentally retarded children who were trained to generate elaborations between word associate pairs recalled more associates if they verbalized their elaborations than if they did not. In the Coates and Hartup (1969) study, 4-year-olds who verbalized a model's actions as they were being performed later reproduced them better than children who merely observed the model. Schunk (1982b) instructed students deficient in division skills. Some students verbalized explicit statements (e.g., "check," "multiply," "copy"), others constructed their own verbalizations, a third group verbalized the statements and their own verbalizations, and students in a fourth condition did not verbalize. Self-constructed verbalizations—alone or combined with the statements—led to the highest division skill.

In summary, verbalization is likely to promote student achievement if it is relevant to the task and does not interfere with performance. A greater proportion of task-relevant statements produces better cognitive skill learning (Schunk & Gunn, 1986). Private speech follows the overt-to-covert developmental cycle, and speech becomes internalized earlier in students with higher intelligence (Berk, 1986; Frauenglass & Diaz, 1985). Allowing students to construct their verbalizations—possibly in conjunction with verbalizing steps in a strategy—is more beneficial than limiting verbalizing to specific statements. Overt verbalization should eventually be faded to whispering or lip movements and then to a covert level.

These results do not imply that all students should verbalize while learning, which would distract many students. Verbalization could be incorporated into instruction for students having difficulties learning. A teacher or classroom aide could work with such students individually or in groups, which would not disrupt other class members.

SOCIAL COGNITIVE THEORY

Social cognitive theory views self-regulation as comprising three subprocesses: self-observation, self-judgment, and self-reaction (Bandura, 1986; Kanfer & Gaelick, 1986) (Table 9.1). Students enter learning activities with such goals as acquiring knowledge and problem-solving strategies, finishing workbook pages, and completing science experiments. With these goals in mind, students observe, judge, and react to their perceived progress. These subprocesses are not mutually exclusive but rather interact.

Self-Observation

People judge observed aspects of their behavior against certain standards and react positively or negatively. People's evaluations and reactions set the stage for additional observations of the same behavioral aspects or others. These subprocesses also do not operate independently of the environment

TABLE 9.1
Bandura's subprocesses of self-regulated learning.

Self-Observation	Self-Judgment	Self-Reaction
Regularity	Types of standards	Evaluative motivators
Proximity	Goal properties	Tangible motivators
Self-recording	Goal importance	
	Attributions	

Source: From Albert Bandura, SOCIAL FOUNDATIONS OF THOUGHT & ACTION, © 1986, p. 337. Adapted by permission of Prentice Hall, Inc., Englewood Cliffs, N.J.

(Zimmerman, 1986). Students who judge their learning progress as inadequate may react by asking for teacher assistance, which alters their environment. In turn, teachers may instruct students in a more efficient strategy, which students then use on their own. That environmental influences (e.g., teachers) can assist the development of self-regulation is important, because educators are increasingly advocating training students in self-regulation (Paris et al., 1983; Zimmerman, 1985).

The observation subprocess is conceptually similar to self-monitoring (discussed earlier). Self-monitoring usually is insufficient to regulate one's behavior. Standards of goal attainment and criteria in assessing goal progress are necessary.

Self-Judgment

Self-judgment refers to comparing one's present performance level with one's goal. Self-judgments are affected by the type of standards employed, properties of the goal, importance of goal attainment, and performance attributions.

Self-Evaluative Standards. Learning goals may be cast as absolute or normative standards. *Absolute standards* are fixed; *normative standards* are based on performances of others. Students whose goal is to complete six workbook pages in 30 minutes gauge their progress against this absolute standard. Grading systems often are based on absolute standards (e.g., A = 90–100, B = 80–89).

Normative standards often are acquired by observing models (Bandura, 1986). Social comparison of one's performances with those of others is an important source for determining the appropriateness of behaviors and for evaluating one's performances (Veroff, 1969). When absolute standards are nonexistent or ambiguous, social comparison becomes more probable (Festinger, 1954). Students have numerous opportunities to compare their work with that of their peers. Absolute and normative standards often are employed in concert, as when students have 30 minutes to complete six pages and compare their progress with peers to gauge who will be the first to finish.

Standards inform and motivate. Comparing one's performance with standards is informative of goal progress. Students who complete three pages in 10 minutes realize they finished half of the work in less than half of the time. The belief that they are making progress enhances their self-efficacy, which sustains their motivation to complete the task. Similar others, rather than those much higher or lower in ability, offer the best basis for comparison, because students are apt to believe that if others can succeed, they will too (Schunk, 1987).

Schunk (1983b) compared the effects of social comparative information with those of goal setting (discussed below) during a division training program. Half of the children were given performance goals during each instructional session; the other half were advised to work productively. Within each goal condition, half of the subjects were told the number of problems other similar children had completed (which matched the session goal) to convey that goals were attainable; the other half were not given comparative information. Goals enhanced self-efficacy; comparative information promoted motivation. Subjects who received both goals and comparative information demonstrated the most learning.

An important means of students acquiring self-evaluative standards is through observation of models. Bandura and Kupers (1964) exposed children to a peer or adult demonstrating stringent or lenient standards while playing a bowling game. Children exposed to high-standard models were more likely to reward themselves for high scores and less likely to reward themselves for lower scores compared with subjects assigned to the low-standard condition. Adult models produced stronger effects than peers. Davidson and Smith (1982) had children observe a superior adult, equal peer, or inferior younger child set stringent or lenient standards while performing a task. Children who observed a lenient model rewarded themselves more often for lower scores than those who observed a stringent model. Children's self-reward standards were lower than those of the adult, equal to those of the peer, and higher than those of the younger child. Model-observer similarity in age might have led children to believe that what was appropriate for the peer was appropriate for them. On ability-related tasks, children take relative estimates of ability into account in formulating standards.

Observation of models affects children's self-efficacy and achievement behaviors. Zimmerman and Ringle (1981) exposed children to an adult model who unsuccessfully attempted to solve a wire puzzle for a long (short) period and who verbalized statements of confidence (pessimism). Children who observed a pessimistic model persist for a long time lowered their efficacy judgments. Perceived similarity to models is especially influential when observers experience difficulties and possess self-doubts about performing well (Schunk & Hanson, 1985; Schunk et al., 1987).

Goal Properties. Recall from Chapter 4 that specific, proximal, and difficult but attainable goals enhance motivation, self-efficacy, and skill acquisition (Bandura, 1982b; Bandura & Schunk, 1981; Gaa, 1973; Rosswork, 1977; Schunk, 1983b). Regardless of goal properties, goals do not enhance performance unless individuals commit to attempting them.

Goal setting is influential with long-term tasks. Many students have initial doubts about writing a good term paper. Teachers can assist by

APPLICATION 9.3: Goal Setting

Goal setting is beneficial in teaching students how to complete long-term tasks. Many students have doubts about completing a science project that includes a display and a research paper. Teachers can assist by breaking the assignment into short-term goals. If students have a six-week period to complete the project, their first task might be to choose a topic by doing research on various topics. The teacher might allow one week for research, after which students would submit their topics with a brief explanation of their selections. The second week could be spent in more specific research and in developing an outline for the paper. After the outlines were submitted and feedback from the teacher was received, students would have two weeks to work on the the initial drafts of their papers and to draw a sketch of the items to be included in their displays. The teacher would review their progress and provide feedback. Students could revise papers and develop displays during the final two weeks.

When long-term projects are broken into subtasks, students are apt to believe they can accomplish the subtasks and that subtask attainment will help them attain the overall goal. Students who have difficulty completing a particular subtask can be given assistance to ensure task accomplishment.

breaking the task into short-term goals (e.g., selecting a topic, conducting background research, writing an outline). Learners are apt to believe they can accomplish the subtasks, and attainment of each subtask develops their self-efficacy for producing a good term paper.

Allowing students to set learning goals enhances goal commitment (Locke et al., 1981) and promotes self-efficacy. Schunk (1985) gave learning disabled children subtraction instruction. Some children set performance goals each session, others were assigned comparable goals, and others received instruction but no goals. Self-set goals led to higher expectancies of goal attainment compared with goals set by others. Self-set goals also produced the highest self-efficacy and greatest skill acquisition.

Importance of Goal Attainment. Self-judgments are affected by the importance of goal attainment. When individuals care little about how they perform, they may not assess their performance or expend effort to improve it (Bandura, 1986). Progress judgments are made for valued goals. Occasionally, goals that originally hold little value become more important when people receive feedback indicating they are becoming skillful. Novice piano players initially may hold ill-defined goals for themselves (e.g., play better). As their skill develops, people begin to set specific goals (learn to play a particular piece) and judge progress relative to these goals.

Performance Attributions.   Attributions (see the discussion of Attribution Theory in Chapter 8), along with goal progress judgments, have influence on performance expectancies, motivation, achievement, and affective reactions. Students who believe they are not making good goal progress may attribute their performances to low ability, which negatively impacts expectancies and behaviors. Students who attribute poor progress to lackadaisical effort or an inadequate learning strategy may believe they will perform better if they work harder or switch to a different strategy (Schunk, 1989). With respect to affective reactions, people take more pride in their accomplishments when they attribute them to ability and effort than to external causes (Weiner, 1985a). People are more self-critical when they believe that they failed due to personal reasons rather than to circumstances beyond their control.

Attributional feedback enhances students' self-regulated learning (Schunk, 1989). Being told that one can achieve more through harder work motivates one to do so, because it conveys that one is capable (Andrews & Debus, 1978; Dweck, 1975). Providing effort feedback for prior successes supports students' perceptions of their progress, sustains their motivation, and increases their efficacy for further learning (Schunk, 1982a; Schunk & Cox, 1986).

The timing of attributional feedback may be important. Early task successes constitute a prominent cue for forming ability attributions. Feedback linking early successes with ability (e.g., "That's correct; you're good at this") should enhance learning efficacy. Many times, however, effort feedback for early successes is more credible, because when students lack skills they have to expend effort to succeed. As students develop skills, ability feedback better enhances self-efficacy (Schunk, 1983a).

Self-Reaction

Evaluative Motivators.   Self-reactions to goal progress motivate behavior (Bandura, 1986). The belief that one is making acceptable progress, along with the anticipated satisfaction of accomplishing the goal, enhances self-efficacy and sustains motivation. Negative evaluations do not decrease motivation if individuals believe they are capable of improving (Schunk, 1989). If students believe they have been lackadaisical but can progress with enhanced effort, they are apt to feel efficacious and redouble their efforts. Motivation is not enhanced if students believe they lack the ability to succeed no matter how much they try (Schunk, 1982a).

Instructions to people to respond evaluatively to their performances promote motivation; people who think they can perform better persist longer and expend greater effort (Kanfer & Gaelick, 1986). Perceived progress is relative to one's goals; the same level of performance can be evaluated positively, neutrally, or negatively. Some students are content with performing at a B level in a course, whereas others are satisfied only with an A. Assuming that people feel capable of improving, higher goals lead to greater effort and persistence than lower goals (Bandura & Cervone, 1983).

Tangible Motivators. People routinely make such rewards as work breaks, new clothes, and nights on the town contingent on task progress or goal attainment. Social cognitive theory postulates that anticipated consequences—not the consequences themselves—enhance motivation (Bandura, 1986). Grades are given at the end of courses, yet students typically set subgoals for accomplishing their work and reward and punish themselves accordingly.

Tangible consequences also affect students' self-efficacy. External rewards enhance efficacy when they are tied to students' accomplishments. Telling students they will earn rewards based on what they accomplish instills a sense of efficacy for learning (Schunk, 1989). Self-efficacy is validated as students work on a task and note their progress. Receipt of the reward further validates efficacy, because it symbolizes progress. Rewards not tied to performances may convey negative efficacy information; students might infer they are not expected to learn much because they are not capable (Schunk, 1983d).

INFORMATION PROCESSING THEORY
Model of Self-Regulation

Recall from Chapters 5 through 7 that information processing theories view learning as the encoding of information (propositional networks) in long-term memory (LTM). Learners activate relevant portions of LTM and relate new knowledge to existing information in working memory (WM). Organized and meaningful information is easier to integrate with existing knowledge and more likely to be remembered.

From an information processing perspective, self-regulation is roughly synonymous with metacognitive awareness (Gitomer & Glaser, 1987). This awareness includes knowledge of the task—what is to be learned, and when and how it is to be learned—as well as self-knowledge of personal capabilities, interests, and attitudes. Self-regulated learning requires that learners have a sound knowledge base comprising task demands, personal qualities, and strategies for completing the task.

Metacognitive awareness also includes procedural knowledge or productions, which regulate learning of the material by monitoring one's level of learning, deciding when to take a different task approach, and assessing readiness for a test. Self-regulatory (metacognitive) activities are types of control processes (see Information Processing System in Chapter 5) under the direction of the learner. They facilitate processing and movement of information through the system.

The basic (superordinate) unit of self-regulation may be a problem-solving production system, where the problem is to reach the goal and the monitoring function is to check each step to ascertain whether the learner is making goal progress. This system compares the present situation against a standard and attempts to reduce discrepancies. An early formulation was Miller, Galanter, and Pribham's (1960) TOTE model (Test–Operate–Test–Exit). In the initial test phase, a present situation is compared against a standard. If they are the same, no further action is required. If they do not match, control is switched to the operate function to change behavior in order to resolve the discrepancy. One perceives a new state of affairs, which is compared with the standard during the second test phase. Assuming these match, one exits the model. If they do not match, further behavioral changes and comparisons are necessary.

To illustrate, assume that Lisa is reading her economics text and stops periodically to summarize what she has read. She recalls information from LTM pertaining to what she has read and compares the information to her internal standard of an adequate summary. This standard also may be a production characterized by rules (e.g., be precise, include information on all topics covered, be certain of accuracy) developed through experiences in summarizing. Assuming that her summary matches her standard, she continues reading. If they do not match, Lisa evaluates where the problem lies (in her understanding of the second paragraph) and executes a correction strategy (rereads the second paragraph).

Information processing models differ, but two central features are (1) comparisons of present activity against standards and (2) steps taken to resolve discrepancies (Carver & Scheier, 1982). A key aspect of these models is knowledge of learning strategies including their procedures and conditional knowledge of when and why to employ the strategies.

Learning Strategies

Learning strategies are plans oriented toward successful task performance, or production systems to reduce the discrepancy between learners' present knowledge and their learning goal. Strategies include such activities as selecting and organizing information, rehearsing material to be learned, relating new material to information in memory, and enhancing meaningfulness of material. Strategies also include techniques to create and maintain a positive learning climate, for example, ways to overcome test anxiety, to enhance self-efficacy, and to develop positive outcome expectations and attitudes (Weinstein & Mayer, 1986). Strategies produce self-regulated learning because they give learners better control over information processing (Rigney, 1978).

From an information processing perspective, learning (or encoding) involves integrating new material into LTM networks in meaningful fashion. To encode information, learners initially attend to relevant task information and transfer it from the sensory register to WM. Learners also activate related knowledge in LTM. In WM, learners build connections (links) between new information and prior knowledge and integrate these links into LTM networks. Learning strategies assist encoding in each of these phases.

The steps in formulating and implementing a learning strategy are as follows:

Step	Learner Tasks
1. Analyze	Identify learning goal, important task aspects, relevant personal characteristics, and potentially useful learning tactics.
2. Plan	Formulate plan: "Given this task _____ to be done _____ according to these criteria _____ , and given these personal characteristics _____ , I should use these techniques _____ ."
3. Implement	Employ tactics to enhance learning and memory.
4. Monitor	Assess goal progress to determine how well tactics are working.
5. Modify	Change nothing if assessment is positive; modify the plan if progress is deemed inadequate.
6. Metacognitive knowledge	Guide operation of steps. (Snowman, 1986)

Initially learners *analyze* an activity or situation by determining the following: the goal of the activity, the aspects of the situation relevant to that goal, the important personal characteristics, and the potentially useful learning procedures. Learners then develop the strategy or *plan* by thinking along the following lines: "Given this task to be accomplished at this time and place according to these criteria and given these personal characteristics, I should use these procedures to accomplish the goal" (paraphrased from Snowman, 1986). The specific procedures included in strategies to attain goals are *learning tactics*. Learners next *implement* the procedures, *monitor* their goal progress, and *modify* the strategy when the procedures are not producing goal progress. Guiding the implementation of these steps is *metacognitive knowledge*, which involves knowing that one must carry out the steps, why they are important, and when and how to perform them.

Learning Tactics

As previously noted, *learning tactics* are specific procedures included in strategies to attain goals. The categories of learning tactics shown in Table

---

APPLICATION 9.4: Learning Tactics

Learning tactics are useful at all grade levels. An elementary teacher might use rhyming schemes or catchy songs to teach the alphabet. By using familiar words, teachers can assist students in learning the directions north, south, east, and west (e.g., the first letters in *west* and *east* spell *we*).

At the junior or senior high school level, teachers may help students as they study for a unit test in history by showing them ways to organize material to be studied—the text, class notes, and supplementary readings. Teachers could show students how to create new notes that integrate material from the various sources. Teachers also could demonstrate how to create a time line and could incorporate all related material to provide a sequenced list of events covered in the unit.

9.2 are interdependent (Weinstein & Mayer, 1986). For example, tactics that elaborate information often rehearse and organize it. Tactics that organize information also may relieve one's stress about learning and help one cope with anxiety. Tactics are not equally appropriate with all types of tasks. Rehearsal may be the tactic of choice when one must memorize simple facts, but an organizational tactic is more appropriate for comprehension.

Rehearsal Tactics. Repeating information verbatim, underlining, and summarizing are forms of *rehearsal tactics. Repeating information* to oneself—aloud, subvocally (whispering), or covertly—is a rehearsal tactic commonly used on tasks requiring rote memorization. For example, to learn the names of the 50 state capitals, students might rehearse the name of each state followed by the name of its capital. Rehearsal also is used to memorize lines to a song or poem and to learn English translations of foreign language words.

Rehearsal tactics that rotely repeat information do not link information with what one already knows. Nor does rehearsal organize information in hierarchical or other fashion. As a consequence, rehearsed information is not stored in any meaningful sense in LTM, and retrieval after some time is often difficult.

Rehearsal is useful for complex learning but involves more than merely repeating information. One useful rehearsal tactic is *underlining (highlighting)* important points in text. This method, which is popular among high school and college students, improves learning if employed judiciously (Snowman, 1986). When too much material is underlined, underlining loses its effectiveness because less-important material is underlined along with more-important ideas. Underlined material should represent points most relevant to learning goals.

TABLE 9.2
Learning tactics.

Category	Types
Rehearsal	Repeating information verbatim Underlining Summarizing
Elaboration	Using imagery Using mnemonics: acronym, sentence, narrative story, pegword, method of loci, keyword Questioning Note taking
Organization	Using mnemonics Grouping Outlining Mapping
Comprehension monitoring	Self-questioning Rereading Checking consistencies Paraphrasing
Affective	Coping with anxiety Having positive beliefs: self-efficacy, outcome expectations, attitudes Creating a productive environment Managing time

Source: Adapted from Weinstein & Mayer, 1986.

Summarizing is another popular rehearsal tactic. Summaries (oral or written) require that students put into their own words the main ideas expressed in the text. As with underlining, summarizing loses its effectiveness if too much information is included (Snowman, 1986). Limiting the length of students' summaries forces them to identify main ideas.

The reciprocal teaching method of Palincsar and Brown (1984) includes summarization as a means for promoting reading comprehension (Chapter 7). Reciprocal teaching is based on Vygotsky's (1978) *zone of proximal development,* or the amount of learning possible by a student given the proper instructional conditions. Instruction begins with the teacher performing the activity, after which students and teacher perform together. Students gradually assume more responsibility and teach one another.

Palincsar and Brown taught children to summarize, question, clarify, and predict. Children periodically summarized what they read in the passage, asked teacher-type questions about main ideas, clarified unclear portions of text, and predicted what would happen next. It should be noted that these tactics are not unique to reading comprehension instruction; they also are good problem-solving tactics to use with science, mathematics, and social studies (Calfee & Drum, 1986).

Elaboration Tactics.   *Elaboration tactics* (imagery, mnemonics, questioning, and note taking) expand information by adding something to make learning more meaningful. *Imagery* is an elaboration tactic that adds a mental picture. Consider the definition of a turnip ("a biennial plant of the mustard family with edible hairy leaves and a roundish, light-colored fleshy root used as a vegetable"). One could memorize this definition through rote rehearsal or elaborate it by looking at a picture of a turnip and forming a mental image to link with the definition.

   Mnemonics are popular elaboration tactics (Weinstein, 1978). Mnemonics make information meaningful by relating it to what one knows. There are various types of mnemonics (Table 9.2). *Acronyms* combine the first letters of the material to be remembered into a meaningful word. HOMES is an acronym for the five Great Lakes (Huron, Ontario, Michigan, Erie, Superior); ROY G. BIV for the colors of the spectrum (Red, Orange, Yellow, Green, Blue, Indigo, Violet). *Sentence* mnemonics use the first letters of the material to be learned as the first letters of words in a sentence, as follows: "Every Good Boy Does Fine" for the notes on the musical staff (E, G, B, D, F); and "My Very Educated Mother Just Served Us Nine Pizzas" for the order of the planets (Mercury, Venus, Earth, Mars, Jupiter, Saturn, Uranus, Neptune, Pluto). It is possible to combine material to be remembered into a paragraph or *narrative story*. This method might be useful with long lists of material (e.g., 50 state capitals). Student-generated acronyms, sentences, and stories are as effective as those supplied by others (Snowman, 1986).

   The *pegword* method requires that learners first memorize a set of objects rhyming with integer names: one–bun, two–shoe, three–tree, four–door, five–hive, six–sticks, seven–heaven, eight–gate, nine–wine, ten–hen. Then the learner generates an image of each item to be learned and links it with the corresponding object image. For instance, Joan needs to buy some items at the grocery store (butter, milk, apples). She might imagine a buttered bun, milk in a shoe, and apples growing on a tree. To recall the shopping list, she recalls the rhyming scheme and its paired associates. Successful use of this technique requires that learners know the rhyming scheme by heart.

   To use the *method of loci*, learners first imagine a familiar scene, such as a room in their house. Then they take a mental walk around the room and stop at each prominent object. Each new item to be learned is paired mentally with one object in the room. Assuming that the room contains (in order) a table, a lamp, and a stereo, and using the grocery list example above, Joan might first imagine butter on the table, a milky-colored lamp, and apples on top of the stereo. To recall the grocery list, she mentally retraces the path around the room and recalls the appropriate object at each stop.

The *keyword* method was developed by Atkinson and his colleagues for learning foreign language vocabulary words (Atkinson, 1975; Atkinson & Raugh, 1975). For example, *pato* (pronounced "pot-o") is a Spanish word meaning "duck." Learners initially think of an English word (*pot*) that sounds like the foreign word (*pato*). Then they link an image of a pot with the English translation of the foreign word ("duck"); for example, a duck with a pot on its head. When the learners encounter *pato*, they recall the image of a duck with a pot on its head. Although the keyword method has been employed effectively with various types of academic content (Pressley, Levin, & Delaney, 1982), its success with young children often requires supplying them with the keyword and the picture incorporating the keyword and its English translation.

Mnemonic techniques incorporate several valid learning principles including rehearsal and relating new information to prior knowledge. Informal evidence indicates that most students have favored memorization techniques, many of which employ mnemonics. Experiments in which recall of information by students instructed in a mnemonic tactic is compared with recalled information of students not given a memory technique generally indicate that learning is enhanced when students are instructed in mnemonics (Weinstein, 1978). One important qualification is that students understand how to use the tactic. Proper use often requires training.

Elaboration tactics also are useful with complex learning tasks. Another elaboration tactic, called *questioning*, requires that learners stop periodically as they read text and ask themselves questions. To address higher-order learning outcomes, learners might ask, "How does this information relate to what the author discussed in the preceding section?" (synthesis) or "How can this idea be applied in a school setting?" (application).

One might intuitively think that questioning would improve comprehension, but research has not yielded strong support for its effects (Snowman, 1986). For questioning to be effective, the questions must reflect the types of desired learning outcomes. Questioning will not aid comprehension if students' questions address low-level, factual knowledge. Unfortunately, most research studies have used relatively brief passages of less than 1,500 words. With older students, questioning would seem to be most useful with longer passages. Among elementary children, rereading or reviewing (rehearsing) material is equally effective. This may be due to children's limited knowledge of how to construct good questions.

Note taking, another elaboration tactic, requires learners to construct meaningful paraphrases of the most important ideas expressed in text. Note taking is similar to summarizing except that the former is not limited to immediately available information. While taking notes, students might integrate new textual material with other information in personally meaningful ways. For note taking to be effective, the notes must not reflect verbatim textual information. Simply copying material is a form of rehearsal and may improve recall, but it is not elaboration. Note taking is not rote copying; the intent is to elaborate (integrate and apply) information. Students generally need to be taught how to take good notes for this tactic to be effective. Note taking is most effective when the notes include content highly relevant to the learning goals. Notes that are too lengthy include less-relevant material.

Organization Tactics. The different types of organization tactics are mnemonics, grouping, outlining, and mapping. *Mnemonics* elaborate information and organize it in meaningful fashion. Acronyms, for example, organize information into a meaningful word. Organization can be achieved by *grouping* information before using rehearsal or mnemonics. If students are learning various mammal names, they first might group the names into common families (apes, cats, etc.) and then rehearse or use a mnemonic. Organization imposed by learners is an effective aid to recall; learners first recall the organizational scheme and then the individual components (Weinstein & Mayer, 1986).

Organizational tactics are useful with complex material. One popular tactic is *outlining*, which requires that learners establish headings. Outlining improves comprehension, but as with other learning tactics, students usually require training in constructing a good outline. One way to teach outlining is to use a text with headings that are set off from the text or that appear in the margins, along with embedded (boldface or italic) headings interspersed throughout the text. Another way is to have students identify topic sentences and points that relate to each sentence. Simply telling students to outline a passage does not facilitate learning if students do not understand the procedure.

Mapping is an organizational tactic that improves learners' awareness of text structure. Mapping involves identifying important ideas and specifying their interrelationship. Concepts or ideas are identified, categorized, and related to one another. The exact nature of the map varies depending on the content and types of relationships to be specified. The following method describes how to teach mapping: (1) Discuss how different sentences in a paragraph relate to one another by giving the categories into which sentences will fit: main idea, example, comparison/contrast, temporal relationship, and inference. (2) Model the application of this categorization with sample paragraphs. (3) Give students guided practice on categorizing sentences and on explaining the reasons for their choices. (4) Have students practice independently on paragraphs. Once students acquire these basic skills, more complex textual material can be used (multiple paragraphs, short sections of stories or chapters) with new categories introduced as needed (e.g., transition) (McNeil, 1987).

A map is conceptually akin to a propositional network, because mapping involves creating a hierarchy in which main ideas or superordinate concepts are listed at the top, followed by supporting points, examples, and subordinate concepts. Branching off from the main hierarchy are lines to related points, such as might be used if a concept is being contrasted with related concepts. A sample map is shown in Figure 9.1.

Research indicates differential effectiveness for mapping as a means of improving comprehension (Snowman, 1986). The skill to discern some relationships is learned easily (main idea–example) and that to discern others is more difficult to acquire (cause–effect). Students often have difficulty linking ideas between sections or paragraphs. In training students to

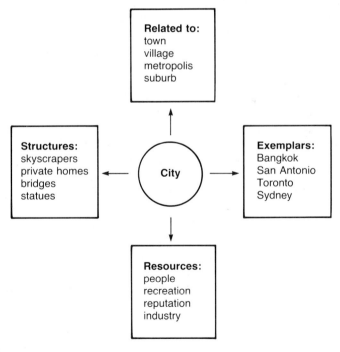

FIGURE 9.1
Cognitive map for "city."

construct maps, it is helpful to have them first map each section or paragraph separately and then have them link maps. Mapping is especially effective with low-ability students who have trouble integrating ideas (Holley, Dansereau, McDonald, Garland, & Collins, 1979).

Comprehension Monitoring Tactics. *Comprehension monitoring* tactics help learners to determine whether they are properly applying declarative and procedural knowledge to material to be learned, to evaluate whether they understand the material, to decide whether their strategy is effective or whether a better strategy is needed, and to know why strategy use will improve learning. Teaching students comprehension monitoring is a central component of strategy training programs (Baker & Brown, 1984; Borkowski & Cavanaugh, 1979; Paris et al., 1983). Self-questioning, rereading, checking consistencies, and paraphrasing are monitoring tactics.

Some textual material periodically provides students with questions about content. Students who answer these questions as they read the material are engaging in *self-questioning*. When questions are not provided, students need to generate their own. As a means of training students to ask questions, teachers can instruct students to periodically stop while reading and ask themselves a series of questions (i.e., who, what, when, where, why, how).

Rereading is often accomplished in conjunction with self-questioning; when students cannot answer questions about the text or otherwise doubt their understanding, these cues prompt them to reread. *Checking for consistencies* involves determining whether the text is internally consistent, that is, whether parts of the text contradict others and whether conclusions drawn follow from what has been discussed. The reader's belief that textual material is inconsistent serves as a cue for rereading to determine whether the author is inconsistent or whether the reader has failed to comprehend the content. Students who periodically stop and *paraphrase* material are checking their level of understanding. Being able to paraphrase is a cue that rereading is necessary (Paris & Oka, 1986).

A useful method to teach comprehension monitoring is Meichenbaum's (1986) self-instructional training (see section on Modeling Processes in Chapter 4). Cognitive modeling portrays a systematic approach to comprehension, along with self-statements to check one's understanding and take corrective action as necessary. While presenting comprehension instruction to elementary remedial readers, a teacher might verbalize the following (Meichenbaum & Asarnow, 1979):

> Well, I've learned three big things to keep in mind before I read a story and while I read it. One is to ask myself what the main idea of the story is. What is the story about? A second is to learn important details of the story as I go along. The order of the main events or their sequence is an especially important detail. A third is to know how the characters feel

and why. So, get the main idea. Watch sequences. And learn how the characters feel and why. (p. 17)

Students are taught to verbalize such statements and gradually fade them to a covert level. To remind learners what to think about, teachers might display key ideas on a poster board (e.g., get the main idea, watch sequences, learn how the characters feel and why).

Affective Tactics. *Affective tactics* create a favorable psychological climate for learning (Weinstein & Mayer, 1986). These tactics address coping with anxiety, developing positive beliefs (self-efficacy, outcome expectations, attitudes), setting work goals, establishing a regular time and place for studying, and minimizing distractions (setting such rules as no talking on the phone and no TV or stereo playing).

Affective tactics help learners focus and maintain attention on important task aspects, manage time effectively, and minimize anxiety. Self-verbalization helps keep students' attention on the academic task. At the outset of an academic activity, students might think to themselves, "This might be tough. I need to pay close attention to the teacher." If they notice their attention is waning, they might think, "Stop thinking about _____ . I need to concentrate on what the teacher is saying."

Goal setting is an effective time management tactic. Learners who set overall learning goals and subdivide them into short-term goals are self-regulating their efforts by evaluating goal progress. In goal setting, students set time limits for the accomplishment of subgoals. The belief that they are making progress instills in them efficacy for learning (Schunk, 1989).

Anxiety about tests, grades, and failure interferes with learning. Students who ruminate about potential failure waste time and strengthen doubts about their capabilities. Anxiety-reduction programs employ systematic desensitization, modeling, and guided self-talk. Models verbalize positive achievement beliefs ("I know that if I work hard, I can do well on the test") rather than dysfunctional beliefs ("I can't pass the test"). Coping models, who initially are anxious but display productive learning tactics and persist until they perform better, are important therapeutic agents of change (Goldfried, Linehan, & Smith, 1978).

For students who have difficulties taking tests, a specific program to teach test-taking skills may prove beneficial (Kirkland & Hollandsworth, 1980). These programs typically teach students to subdivide the test, to establish time limits for each part, and not to spend too long on any one question. To conquer negative thoughts while taking a test, students are taught relaxation techniques and ways to refocus attention on test items. Test performance and beliefs exert reciprocal effects. Experiencing some test success creates a sense of efficacy for performing well, which leads to more productive studying and better performance.

Academic Studying

Strategies have been applied to foster self-regulated learning during academic studying. Dansereau and his colleagues developed a strategy training program to teach learning tactics to college students (Dansereau, 1978; Dansereau et al., 1979). The authors distinguished *primary* strategies, or those applied directly to the content, from *support* strategies used by learners to create and maintain a favorable psychological climate for learning. The latter include affective tactics and techniques for monitoring and correcting ongoing primary strategies (comprehension monitoring tactics).

Effective studying requires that students comprehend, retain, retrieve, and use information. These are the primary elements of the *SQ3R method:* Survey–Question–Read–Recite (Recall)–Review (Robinson, 1946). When students use the SQ3R method, they first survey a text chapter by reading headings and boldface (italics) print, after which they develop questions. Learners then read the text while keeping the questions in mind. Following the reading, students close the book and recall what they have read. They then open the book and review the material.

In Dansereau's program, students comprehend material by highlighting important ideas, recall material without referring to text, digest and expand the information, and review it. Expanding information means relating it to other information in LTM by creating links between memory networks. Students are trained to ask themselves questions similar to the following: "Imagine you could talk to the author; what questions would you ask? What criticisms would you raise?" "How can the material be applied?" "How could you make the material more understandable and interesting to other students?"

Dansereau's learning strategy program moves beyond the SQ3R method, because it includes such support strategies as goal setting, concentration management, and monitoring and diagnosing. Students learn to set daily, weekly, and longer-term goals by establishing schedules in a workbook. Learners monitor progress and adjust their work or goals as necessary if their performance does not match expectations. Concentration management is developed by helping students deal with frustration, anxiety, and anger. Use of self-talk is encouraged, and desensitization can be used in which anxiety-provoking situations are imagined while the student is relaxed. Monitoring and diagnosing require that students determine in advance where they will stop in the text to assess their level of comprehension. As they reach each stop point, they assess understanding and take corrective action (e.g., rereading) as needed. Evaluations of the strategy training show that it improves academic behaviors and attitudes (Dansereau et al., 1979).

Dansereau (1988) modified this strategy training program for use in cooperative learning dyads. Each member of the pair takes turns reading about 500 words of a 2,500-word passage. One member then serves as recaller and orally summarizes what was read; the other listens, corrects errors in recall, and elaborates knowledge by adding imagery and links to prior knowledge. Initial research by Dansereau and others shows that this cooperative arrangement facilitates learning and transfer better than individual learning.

SUMMARY

Self-regulated learning refers to the process whereby students personally activate and sustain cognitions and behaviors systematically oriented toward the attainment of learning goals. Cognitive activities include attending to instruction, processing and integrating knowledge, and rehearsing information to be remembered, along with developing self-efficacy, positive outcome expectations and attitudes, and value of learning. Although self-regulated learning is a new topic, it fits well with the notion that students contribute actively to their learning goals.

Different theoretical perspectives have been applied to self-regulated learning. Reinforcement theorists study how individuals establish discriminative stimuli and reinforcement contingencies. Self-regulated behavior involves choosing among alternative courses of action. Key subprocesses are self-monitoring, self-instruction, and self-reinforcement. Research shows that people can be trained to arrange their discriminative stimuli, to establish consequences, and to administer rewards and punishments.

Cognitive-developmental theory establishes a strong link between the development of self-regulation and private speech, or speech having a self-regulatory function but not socially communicative. Vygotsky believed that private speech develops thought by organizing behavior. Children employ private speech to understand situations and surmount difficulties. Vygotsky hypothesized that private speech becomes covert with development, although overt verbalization can occur at any age when people encounter obstacles. Inadequte use of private speech to regulate behavior might reflect a production, mediational, or continued-use deficiency. Self-instructional training is useful for helping children verbally self-regulate the performances.

Social cognitive theory views self-regulation as comprising self-observation, self-judgment, and self-reaction. Students enter learning activities with such goals as acquiring knowledge and problem-solving strategies, finishing workbook pages, and completing science experiments. Learners observe, judge, and react to their perceived goal progress. People's self-judgments about their acceptable progress are subjective; the same level of progress can be judged adequate or inadequate by different individuals. The following factors affect judgements: type of standards (absolute, normative), goal properties, importance of goal attainment, and performance attributions. Self-reactions to goal progress exert motivational effects on behavior. The belief that one is making acceptable progress enhances self-efficacy for continued improvement. Perceived progress and anticipated satisfaction of goal accomplishment sustain motivation.

From an information processing perspective, self-regulation is somewhat synonymous with metacognitive awareness that includes task and personal knowledge. Self-regulated learning requires that learners have knowledge about task demands, their personal qualities, and strategies for completing the task. Metacognitive awareness also includes procedural knowledge, or productions, which regulate learning of material, monitor one's level of learning, indicate when to take a different task approach, and assess test readiness. The basic (superordinate) unit of self-regulation may be a problem-solving production system, in which the problem is to reach the goal and the monitoring's function is to check each step to ascertain whether the learner is making goal progress. This system compares a present situation against a standard and attempts to reduce discrepancies.

Learning strategies are plans oriented toward successful academic task performance (goal attainment). Strategies include such activities as selecting and organizing information, rehearsing material to be learned, relating new material to information stored in memory, enhancing the meaningfulness of material, and creating and maintaining a positive learning climate (ways to overcome test anxiety and to enhance self-efficacy, outcome expectations, and attitudes). To formulate a learning strategy, learners analyze the situation and their personal characteristics, devise a plan to accomplish the learning goal, implement the plan, monitor progress, and modify the plan as necessary. Metacognitive knowledge guides the operation of these steps.

Learners select learning tactics they believe will help them attain their goals. Common tactics involve rehearsal, elaboration, and organization. Mnemonics are tactics that make verbal information meaningful. With complex learning, helpful tactics include underlining, summarizing, questioning, note taking, and mapping. Other learning tactics are comprehension monitoring and creating a positive affective climate for learning. Monitoring tactics include periodic self-questioning and rereading as necessary; affective tactics set goals, create a productive work environment, and reduce anxiety.

Simply knowing how to use strategies does not guarantee students will use them when not required to do so. Learners need to be taught to use learning strategies. Strategy training is often incorporated in programs designed to enhance academic studying. Regardless of the domain, an important aspect of training is providing students with strategy value information linking improved performance with strategy use. The belief that one can effectively apply a strategy to improve one's performance strengthens self-efficacy for learning, which enhances motivation and skill development.

Chapter 10

Learning and Instruction

This chapter addresses instructional theory and research as they relate to school learning. Instructional theory historically was concerned with the design of instruction and included such topics as behavioral objectives and programmed learning (Pintrich et al., 1986). As the influence of behaviorism declined, researchers began to study the impact of learner, instructional, and contextual variables on one another and on learning in educational contexts. Current instructional research also investigates such topics as the influence of instructional variables on learners' cognitions, the role of individual differences in learning, and the impact of motivational variables on learning (Wittrock, 1978).

Two early cognitive perspectives on instruction—Bruner's discovery learning and Ausubel's meaningful reception learning—are discussed first, followed by Gagné's conditions of learning. Other theoretical views are presented, along with research on classroom teaching. Learner characteristics are addressed in the sections on learning styles and adapting instruction. The chapter concludes with an examination of the role of computers in teaching and learning. An exhaustive review of instructional theory and research is beyond the scope of this chapter; interested readers should consult Gagné and Dick (1983) and Pintrich et al. (1986).

EARLY COGNITIVE PERSPECTIVES

Bruner's Theory of Cognitive Growth

Cognitive Growth and Knowledge Representation. Jerome Bruner, a developmental psychologist, formulated a theory of cognitive growth that postulates: "The development of human intellectual functioning from infancy to such perfection as it may reach is shaped by a series of technological advances in the use of mind" (Bruner, 1964, p. 1). These technological advances depend on increasing language facility and exposure to systematic instruction (Bruner, 1966). As children develop, their actions are constrained less by immediate stimuli. Cognitive processes (thoughts, beliefs) mediate the relationship between stimulus and response so that learners might maintain the same response in a changing environment or perform different responses in the same environment, depending on what they feel is adaptive.

There are three ways to represent knowledge, which emerge in a developmental sequence: enactive, iconic, and symbolic (Bruner, 1964; Bruner, Olver, & Greenfield, 1966). *Enactive representation* involves motor responses, or ways to manipulate the environment. Such actions as riding a bicycle and tying a knot are represented largely in muscular actions. Actions prompted by stimuli define the latter. To a toddler, a ball (stimulus) is represented as something to throw and bounce (actions).

Iconic representation refers to action-free mental images. Children acquire the capability to think about objects that are not physically present. They mentally transform objects and think about their properties separately from what actions can be performed with the objects. Iconic representation allows one to recognize objects when they are changed in minor ways (e.g., mountains with and without snow at the top).

Symbolic representation uses symbol systems to encode knowledge. Prominent symbol systems are language and mathematical notation. Such systems allow one to understand abstract concepts (e.g., the x variable in $3x - 5 = 10$) and to alter symbolic information as a result of verbal instruction. Symbolic systems represent knowledge with remote and arbitrary features. The word *Philadelphia* looks no more like the city than a nonsense syllable (Bruner, 1964).

The symbolic mode is the last to develop and quickly becomes the preferred mode, although one maintains the capability to represent knowledge in the enactive and iconic modes. One might experience the "feel" of a tennis ball, form a mental picture of it, and describe it in words. The primary advantage of the symbolic mode is that it allows learners to represent and transform knowledge with greater flexibility and power than is possible with the other modes (Bruner, 1964).

Spiral Curriculum. That knowledge can be represented in different ways suggests that teachers vary instructional presentations depending on learners' developmental levels. Before children can comprehend abstract mathematical notation, they are exposed to mathematical operations represented enactively (with blocks) and iconically (in pictures). Bruner emphasized teaching as a means of enhancing cognitive development. To say that teachers cannot teach a particular concept because students will not understand it really is saying that students will not understand the concept the way teachers plan to teach it. Instruction needs to be matched to children's cognitive capabilities.

Bruner (1960) is well known for his controversial proposition that any content can be taught in meaningful fashion to learners of any age:

> Experience over the past decade points to the fact that our schools may be wasting precious years by postponing the teaching of many important subjects on the ground that they are too difficult. . . . The foundations of any subject may be taught to anybody at any age in some form. . . . The basic ideas that lie at the heart of all science and mathematics and the basic themes that give form to life and literature are as simple as they are powerful. To be in command of these basic ideas, to use them effectively, requires a continual deepening of one's understanding of them that comes from learning to use them in progressively more complex forms. It is only when such basic ideas are put in formalized terms as equations or elaborated verbal concepts that they are out of reach of the young child, if he has not first understood them intuitively and had a chance to try them out on his own. (pp. 12–13)

Bruner's point in the extract above has been misunderstood to mean that learners at any age can be taught anything. Bruner was recommending that content be "revisited," that is, concepts initially taught to children in a simple fashion (so children will understand them) can be presented in more complex fashion to older children. In literature, children can understand the concepts of "comedy" and "tragedy" even though they cannot verbally describe them well. With development, students read comedies and tragedies, write term papers on these subjects, and so forth. Students should address topics at increasing levels of complexity as they move through the curriculum, rather than encountering a topic only once.

Discovery Learning. *Discovery learning* refers to obtaining knowledge for oneself (Bruner, 1961). It involves formulating and testing hypotheses rather than simply reading or listening to teacher presentations. Discovery is a type of inductive reasoning, because students move from studying specific examples to formulating general rules, concepts, and principles. A presumed benefit of discovery is that it promotes meaningful learning.

Discovery is *not* simply letting students do what they want. Discovery is best handled as a "directed" activity: Teachers arrange activities that

APPLICATION 10.1: Discovery Learning

Learning becomes more meaningful when students explore their learning environments rather than listen passively to teachers. Teachers might use guided discovery to help elementary children learn animal groups (e.g., mammals, birds, reptiles). Rather than providing students with the basic animal groups and examples for each, the teacher could ask students to provide the names of types of animals. Then the students and teacher could classify the animals by examining their similarities and differences. Category labels could be assigned once classifications are made. This teaching approach is guided by the teacher to ensure classifications are proper, but students are active contributors as they discover the similarities and differences of animals.

students search, manipulate, explore, and investigate. Students learn new knowledge relevant to the domain and such general problem-solving skills as formulating rules, testing hypotheses, and gathering information (Bruner, 1961):

> Let it be clear what the act of discovery entails. It is rarely . . . that new facts are "discovered" in the sense of being encountered as Newton suggested in the form of islands of truth in an uncharted sea of ignorance. Or if they appear to be discovered in this way, it is almost always thanks to some happy hypotheses about where to navigate. Discovery, like surprise, favors the well prepared mind. . . . Discovery, whether by a school-boy going it on his own or by a scientist cultivating the growing edge of his field, is in its essence a matter of rearranging or transforming evidence in such a way that one is enabled to go beyond the evidence so reassembled to additional new insights. (p. 22)

Discoveries usually are not lucky occurrences. Students require background preparation (the well-prepared mind requires declarative, procedural, and conditional knowledge). Once students possess prerequisite knowledge, careful structuring of material allows students to discover important principles.

Student involvement is encouraged by presenting questions, problems, or puzzling situations that students must resolve. Learners are encouraged to make intuitive guesses when they are uncertain. In leading a class discussion, teachers could ask questions that have no readily available answers and tell students that their answers will not be graded. Discoveries are not limited to activities within school. In studying a unit on ecology, students could discover why animals of a given species live in certain areas and not in others. Students might seek answers in classroom work stations, in the school library, and on or off the school grounds. Teachers provide structure by posing questions and giving suggestions on how to search for answers.

Greater teacher structure is beneficial when students are not familiar with the discovery procedure or require extensive background knowledge.

Discovery learning seems more appropriate for some types of learning than for others. It may not be too useful with well-structured content easily presented by teachers. Students could discover which historical events occurred in which years, but this is trivial learning. If they discover the wrong answers, time would be wasted in reteaching the content. Establishing discovery situations (e.g., growing plants) often takes time and experiments might not work. Discovery seems especially useful with problem-solving activities, in which students are motivated to learn and possess the requisite skills. Types of discovery learning situations that occur commonly in schools are role playing, independent or group projects, and computer simulations (discussed later).

Ausubel's Meaningful Reception Learning

Meaningfulness and Expository Teaching. In contrast to Bruner, David Ausubel (1963, 1968; Ausubel & Robinson, 1969) presented a theory of *meaningful reception learning.* Ausubel (1968) contended,

> The acquisition of subject-matter knowledge is primarily a manifestation of reception learning. That is, the principal content of what is to be learned is typically presented to the learner in more or less final form. Under these circumstances, the learner is simply required to comprehend the material and to incorporate it into his cognitive structure so that it is available for either reproduction, related learning, or problem solving at some future date. (p. 83)

Ausubel advocated using *expository teaching* that presents information to students in organized and meaningful fashion. He believed that the notion of expository teaching is often misunderstood:

> Few pedagogic devices in our time have been repudiated more unequivocally by educational theorists than the method of expository verbal instruction. It is fashionable in many quarters to characterize verbal learning as parrot-like recitation and rote memorization of isolated facts, and to dismiss it disdainfully as an archaic remnant of discredited educational tradition. (Ausubel, 1968, pp. 83–84)

The primary type of learning that occurs in classrooms is fundamentally different from associative and paired-associate learning. Meaningful learning refers to the learning of ideas, concepts, and principles by relating new information to knowledge in memory (Ausubel, 1977; Faw & Waller, 1976). Learning is meaningful when new material bears a nonarbitrary relation to relevant concepts in long-term memory (LTM); that is, new material expands, modifies, or elaborates information in memory. Meaningfulness also depends on such personal variables as age, background experiences, socioeconomic status, and educational background. In any class, whether students find learning meaningful will depend on their prior experiences.

The Ausubel model advocates a deductive strategy to teach interrelated content with general ideas presented initially, followed by specific points. This model requires that teachers help students break ideas into smaller, related points and relate new ideas to similar content in memory. From an information processing perspective, the aims of the model are to expand propositional networks in memory by adding knowledge and to establish links between networks.

Ausubel's model requires much teacher-student interaction. Teachers verbally present new material, but student responses are continually solicited. Lessons must be well organized. Concepts being taught are exemplified in diverse ways by being built on one another so that students possess the requisite knowledge to benefit from the teaching.

Advance Organizers. A device that helps connect new material with prior learning is the *advance organizer.* Advance organizers are broad statements presented at the outset of lessons. Organizers direct students' attention to important concepts in material to be learned, highlight interrelationships among ideas presented, and link new material to what students know (Eggen, Kauchak, & Harder, 1979; Faw & Waller, 1976). It is assumed that learners' cognitive structures are hierarchically organized so that inclusive concepts subsume subordinate ones. Organizers provide information at high levels in hierarchies.

Organizers can be expository or comparative. *Expository organizers* provide students with new knowledge needed to comprehend the lesson. Expository organizers include concept definitions and generalizations. *Concept definitions* state the concept, a superordinate concept, and characteristics of the concept (Eggen at al., 1979). In presenting the concept of "warm-blooded animal," a teacher might define it (i.e., animal whose internal body temperature remains relatively constant), relate it to superordinate concepts (animal kingdom), and give its characteristics (birds, mammals) (see the section on Procedural Knowledge in Chapter 6). A *generalization* is a broad statement of a general principle from which hypotheses or specific ideas are drawn. A generalization appropriate for the study of terrain would be, "Less vegetation grows at higher elevations." Teachers can present examples of generalizations and ask students to think of others.

Comparative organizers introduce new material by drawing analogies with familiar material. Comparative organizers activate and link networks in students' long-term memories. If a teacher is giving a unit on the body's circulatory system to students who already have studied communication

---

APPLICATION 10.2: Advance Organizers

Advance organizers help students connect new material with prior learning. A middle school teacher might employ the organizer approach in a geography class. The teacher might begin a lesson on landforms (surfaces with characteristic shapes and compositions) by reviewing the definition and components of geography concepts previously discussed. The teacher could put the following points on the board to show that geography is composed of three major components (Eggen et al., 1979):

- Elements of the physical environment
- Human beings and the physical environment
- Different world regions and their ability to support human beings

The teacher could focus on elements of the physical environment and then move to landforms. The teacher could discuss types of landforms (e.g., plateaus, mountains, hills) by showing mock-ups and asking students to identify key features of each landform. This deductive approach gives students an overall framework or outline into which they can integrate new knowledge about the components.

---

systems, the teacher might relate the circulatory and communication systems with such relevant concepts as the source, medium, and target. For comparative organizers to be effective, students must have a good understanding of the material used as the basis for the analogy. Learners also must perceive the analogy easily. Difficulty perceiving analogous relationships impedes learning.

Research by Ausubel showed that organizers promote learning (Ausubel, 1978), although others found conflicting results (Barnes & Clawson, 1975). Organizers seem most effective with lessons designed to teach relationships among concepts (Mayer, 1984). If teachers stretch an analogy too far, students may not understand the connection. Organizers also are effective with difficult academic content when an analogy with familiar content is appropriate (Faw & Waller, 1976).

Another consideration is learner developmental level. Organizers operate at general, abstract levels. They require students to relate ideas mentally, which is beyond the capacity of young children. This deductive teaching approach works better with students in at least upper elementary grades (Luiten, Ames, & Ackerson, 1980).

There is evidence that organizers aid transfer. Mayer (1979) reports research with college students who had no computer programming experience. Students were given programming materials to study; one group was given a conceptual model as an organizer, whereas the other group received the same materials without the model. The advance organizer group performed better on posttest items requiring transfer of learning to items different from those discussed in the instructional material. Organizers may help students relate new material to a broader set of experiences, which facilitates transfer.

GAGNÉ'S CONDITIONS OF LEARNING

Robert Gagné's (1985) instructional theory concerns the *conditions of learning,* or the circumstances that prevail when learning occurs. Two issues must be addressed to apply the theory. The first issue is to specify the type of learning outcome. Gagné identified five major types of learning outcomes (discussed below). The second issue is to determine the events of learning, or factors that make a difference in instruction. Events are internal and external: Internal events include personal dispositions and cognitive processes; external events are instructional and are deliberately planned and arranged to promote learning. These issues are considered in turn.

Learning Outcomes

Gagné (1984) contended that learning is complex and that learners acquire capabilities that manifest themselves in different outcomes. Outcomes are distinct when different types of information processing are required for learning and when different types of performances are made possible by learning. The five types of learning outcomes are intellectual skills, verbal information, cognitive strategies, motor skills, and attitudes.

Intellectual skills include rules, procedures, and concepts. In previous chapters, intellectual skills are referred to as forms of procedural knowledge or production systems. This type of knowledge is employed in speaking, writing, reading, solving mathematical problems, and applying scientific principles to problems.

Verbal information, or declarative knowledge, is knowledge "that" something is the case. It is verbal because it is displayed verbally (in speaking or writing). Verbal information involves facts or meaningfully connected prose recalled verbatim (e.g., words to a poem or the "Star Spangled Banner"). Schemata, or organized networks of facts and events, are forms of verbal information.

Cognitive strategies are executive control processes. They include such information processing skills as attending to new information, deciding to rehearse information, elaborating, and using LTM retrieval strategies. The problem-solving strategies discussed in Chapter 7 are examples of strategies.

Motor skills are developed through gradual improvements in the quality (smoothness, timing) of movements attained through practice. Whereas intellectual skills can be acquired abruptly, motor skills develop gradually with continued practice. Intellectual skill development does not compare with the refinements in smoothness and timing found in motor skill learning. Even practice conditions differ: Intellectual skills are practiced with different examples, whereas motor skill practice involves repetition of the same muscular movements.

Attitudes are internal beliefs that influence personal actions reflecting such characteristics as generosity, honesty, and commitment to healthy living. Attitudes are inferred because they cannot be observed directly. Attitudes are learned, though unlike the preceding outcomes, they are not learned directly. Teachers can arrange proper conditions for learning intellectual skills, verbal information, cognitive strategies, and motor skills. Gagné believes that attitudes are learned indirectly through one's experiences and exposures to live and symbolic (televised, videotaped) models.

Learning Events

The five types of learning outcomes given above are distinguished in terms of their conditions of learning. There are internal conditions (prerequisite skills, cognitive processing requirements) and external conditions (environmental stimuli that support the learner's cognitive processes). One must specify as completely as possible both types of conditions when designing instruction to produce desired outcomes.

Internal conditions are learners' present capabilities, which are stored as knowledge in memory. Gagné operates within an information processing framework in which instructional cues from teachers and materials activate relevant knowledge in LTM (Gagné & Glaser, 1987). Internal conditions are important for designing learning hierarchies and instruction.

External conditions differ as a function of the learning outcome and the internal conditions. To teach students a classroom rule, a teacher might inform them of the rule and write it on the chalkboard. To teach students a strategy for checking their comprehension, a teacher might demonstrate the strategy and give students practice using it and feedback on its effectiveness. Proficient readers would be instructed differently from those with decoding problems. Each phase of instruction would be subject to alteration as a function of learning outcome and internal conditions.

Learning Hierarchies

Learning hierarchies are organized sets of intellectual skills. The highest element in a hierarchy is the *target skill*. To devise a hierarchy, one begins at the top and asks what skills the learner must perform prior to learning the target skill, or what skills are immediate prerequisites for the target skill. Then one asks the same question for each prerequisite skill, and so on down the hierarchy until one arrives at the skills the learner presently can perform (Merrill, 1987). A sample learning hierarchy is portrayed in Figure 10.1.

Hierarchies are not linear orderings of skills. One often must apply two or more prerequisite skills to learn a higher-order skill, where neither of the prerequisites is dependent on the other. Nor are higher-order skills necessarily more difficult to learn than lower-order ones. Some prerequisites may be difficult to acquire; once learners have mastered the lower-order skills, learning a higher-order one may seem easier.

Learning Phases

Instruction is a set of external events designed to facilitate internal learning processes. There are nine phases in learning, which can be conveniently grouped in the following three categories (R. Gagné, 1985):

Category	Phase
Preparation for learning	1. Attending
	2. Expectancy
	3. Retrieval
Acquisition and performance	4. Selective perception
	5. Semantic encoding
	6. Retrieval and responding
	7. Reinforcement
Transfer of learning	8. Cueing retrieval
	9. Generalizability

Preparation for learning includes introductory learning activities. *Attending* means learners focus on stimuli relevant to material to be learned (audio-visuals, written materials, teacher-modeled behaviors). The learner's *expectancy* orients the learner to the goal (learn a motor skill, learn to reduce fractions). During *retrieval* of relevant information from LTM, learners activate the portions relevant to the topic studied (Gagné & Dick, 1983).

The main phases of learning are *acquisition and performance. Selective perception* means that relevant stimulus features are recognized by the sensory register and are transferred to WM for processing. *Semantic encoding* is the process whereby new knowledge is transferred to LTM. During *retrieval and responding*, learners retrieve new information from memory and make a response demonstrating learning. *Reinforcement* refers to feedback that confirms the accuracy of learners' responses and that provides corrective information as necessary.

GAGNÉ'S CONDITIONS OF LEARNING

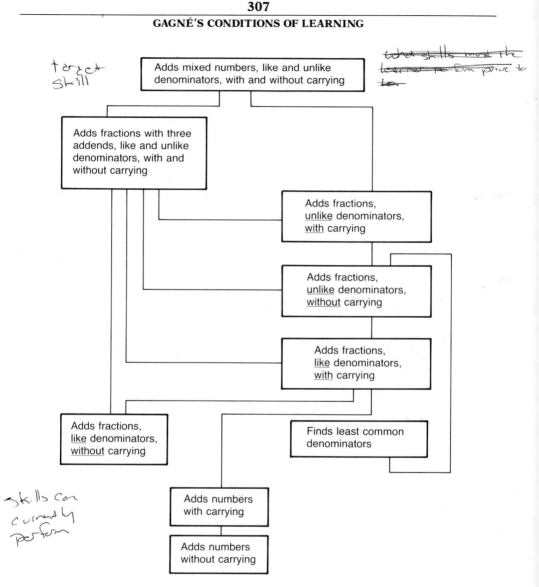

[handwritten annotations: "target skill" (left of top box); "what skills must the learner perform prior to..." (upper right); "skills can currently perform" (lower left)]

FIGURE 10.1
Sample learning hierarchy.

Transfer of learning phases include cueing retrieval and generalizability. In *cueing retrieval,* cues are provided to learners signaling that previous knowledge is applicable in that situation. When solving word problems, the teacher might inform learners that their knowledge of right triangles is applicable. *Generalizability* is enhanced by providing learners the opportunity to practice skills with different content and under different circumstances (homework, spaced review sessions).

These nine phases are equally applicable for the five types of learning outcomes. Gagné and Briggs (1979) have specified types of instructional events that might accompany each phase, as follows:

Phase	Instructional Event
1. Attending	Informs class that it is time to begin
2. Expectancy	Informs class of lesson objective and type and quantity of performance to be expected
3. Retrieval	Asks class to recall subordinate concepts and rules
4. Selective perception	Presents examples of new concept or rule
5. Semantic encoding	Provides cues for how to remember information
6. Retrieval and responding	Asks students to apply concept or rule to new examples
7. Reinforcement	Confirms accuracy of students' learning
8. Cueing retrieval	Gives short quiz on new material
9. Generalizability	Provides special reviews

Instructional events enhancing each phase depend on the type of outcome. Instruction proceeds differently for intellectual skills than for verbal information.

OTHER INSTRUCTIONAL THEORIES

Gagné's ideas represent a systematic combination of learning and instruction principles. There are many other instructional theories that are less elaborate but also incorporate learning principles and specify instructional conditions to optimize learning, retention, and transfer. Some of these perspectives are discussed below.

Carroll's Time Model

Carroll (1963, 1965) formulated a model of school learning that places primary emphasis on the amount of time spent learning. The model assumes that learning tasks can be specified clearly and that reliable means exist for determining whether students have learned the tasks.

The central premise is that learners successfully learn to the extent that they spend the amount of time they need to learn. *Time* means academically engaged time, that is, time spent paying attention and trying to learn. Within this framework, Carroll postulated factors that influence how much time is needed for learning and how much time is actually spent learning.

Time Needed for Learning.   One influence on this factor is *aptitude for learning the task.* Learning aptitude depends on amount of prior task-relevant learning and on such personal characteristics as abilities and attitudes. A second, related factor is ability to understand instruction. This variable interacts with instructional method; for example, some learners comprehend verbal instruction well, whereas others benefit more from visual presentations.

Quality of instruction refers to how well the task is organized and presented to learners. Quality includes what learners are told about what they will learn and how they will learn it, the extent to which they have adequate contact with the learning materials, and how much prerequisite knowledge is acquired prior to learning the task. The lower the quality of instruction, the more time learners require to learn.

Time Spent in Learning.   *Time allowed for learning* is one influence on this factor. The school curriculum includes so much content that time allotted for a particular type of learning is less than optimal for some students. Teachers usually present material to the entire class at once. Students who have difficulty grasping material need additional, remedial instruction. In some cases, students are ability grouped, and the amount of time devoted to different content varies depending on the ease with which students learn.

A second influence on the time-spent-in-learning factor is *time the learner is willing to spend learning.* Even when learners are given ample time to learn, they may not spend that time working productively. Whether due to low interest, high perceived task difficulty, or other factors, students may be unwilling to persist at a task for the amount of time they require to learn. Motivational factors are important influences on learning. Carroll incorporated these factors into a formula to estimate the degree of learning for any student on a given task:

$$\text{degree of learning} = \text{time spent/time needed}$$

Ideally, students spend as much time as they need to learn (degree of learning = 1.0), but learners typically spend either more time (degree of learning > 1.0) or less time (degree of learning < 1.0) than they require.

Carroll's model highlights the importance of academic engaged time required for learning and the factors influencing time spent and time needed to learn. It does not offer specific prescriptions for how to correct inadequate student learning. The model incorporates valid psychological principles, but only at a general level as instructional or motivational factors. Greater specificity is provided by mastery learning researchers, who have systematically investigated the time variable.

Bloom's Mastery Learning

Carroll's model predicts that if students vary in aptitude for learning a subject and if all are given the same amount and type of instruction, they will differ in achievement. If the amount and type of instruction are varied depending on student individual differences, each student has the potential to demonstrate mastery; the positive relationship between aptitude and achievement will disappear because all students will demonstrate equal achievement regardless of aptitudes.

These ideas form the basis of *mastery learning* (Bloom, 1976; Bloom, Hastings, & Madaus, 1971). Mastery learning incorporates Carroll's ideas into a systematic instructional plan that includes defining mastery, planning for mastery, teaching for mastery, and grading for mastery (Block & Burns, 1977).

To *define mastery,* teachers prepare a set of objectives and a final (summative) exam. Level of mastery is established (e.g., where A students typically perform under traditional instruction). Teachers break the course into learning units mapped against course objectives.

Planning for mastery means teachers plan instructional procedures for themselves and students to include corrective feedback procedures (formative evaluation). Such evaluation typically is in the form of unit mastery tests where mastery is set at a given level (e.g., 90%). Corrective instruction—used with students who fail to master aspects of the unit's objectives—is given in small-group study sessions, individual tutorials, and supplemental materials.

At the outset of *teaching for mastery,* teachers orient students to the mastery procedures and provide instruction using the entire class, small groups, or individual seatwork activities. Teachers give the formative test and certify which students achieve mastery. Students who fall short might work in small groups reviewing troublesome material, often with the aid of peer tutors who have mastered the material. Students are given time to work on remedial materials, along with homework.

Grading for mastery includes a summative (end-of-course) test. Student scores at or above the course mastery performance level receive A's; lower scores are graded accordingly. Mastery learning has been most frequently applied at the elementary and secondary school levels, although Keller's Personalized System of Instruction has seen widespread application at colleges and universities (see the section on Instruction in Chapter 3).

The emphasis on student abilities as determinants of learning may seem uninteresting given that abilities generally do not change much as a result of instructional interventions. Bloom (1976) also stressed the *alterable variables* of schooling: cognitive entry behaviors (student skills and cognitive processing strategies at the outset of instruction), affective character-

APPLICATION 10.3: Mastery Learning

A mastery learning approach can be very beneficial in certain learning environments. For example, in a remedial reading group for secondary students, a well-organized mastery learning program would allow students to progress at their own rates. Students motivated to make rapid progress are not slowed down by this type of instruction, as might happen if they are placed in a traditional learning format designed for slow learners. Whether teachers use existing mastery learning reading programs or develop their own, the key is to include a progression of activities from less to more difficult. The program should have checkpoints at which the students interact with the teacher so that their progress is evaluated and reteaching or special assistance is provided if needed.

The mastery approach also can build students' self-efficacy for learning. As they note their progress in completing units, they are apt to believe they are capable of further learning. Enhancing self-efficacy is particularly important with remedial learners, who have encountered school failures and doubt their capabilities to learn.

istics (interest, motivation), and specific factors influencing the quality of instruction (student participation, type of corrective feedback). These variables can be improved with brief interventions.

Reviews of the effect of mastery learning on student achievement are mixed. Block and Burns (1977) generally found mastery learning more effective than traditional forms of instruction, whereas Bangert, Kulik, and Kulik (1983) found weaker support. Bangert et al. noted that mastery-based instruction is more effective at the college level than at lower levels. Its effectiveness undoubtedly depends on the proper instructional conditions (planning, teaching, grading) being established.

Students participating in mastery instruction often spend more time in learning compared with traditional classroom peers (Block & Burns, 1977). Given that time is at a premium in schools, much mastery work—especially remedial efforts—must be accomplished outside of regular school hours. There is no evidence that mastery-based instruction improves such affective outcomes as interest in and attitudes toward the subject matter.

An important premise of mastery learning is that individual differences in student learning decrease over time. L. Anderson (1976) found that when remedial students gain experience with mastery instruction, they gradually require less extra time to attain mastery because their entry-level skills have improved. These results imply cumulative benefits of mastery learning. This point requires further research, but has important instructional implications.

Case's Developmental Model

Case (1978a, 1978b, 1981) described cognitive development as the acquisition of efficient strategies for processing information. Development produces an increase in the size of WM. As strategies become more efficient (automatic), less WM space is consumed, which leaves extra space available for acquiring new strategies.

Case emphasized instruction to help students process information more automatically. One first identifies the learning goal and the steps through which learners must proceed to reach the goal. Instructional designers follow a *novice-to-expert* approach by comparing the performances and reported thoughts of experts with those of novices. Instruction is designed to include exercises demonstrating to students inadequacies of their less-efficient task approaches. During instruction, demands on WM are reduced by not presenting too much new material at once and by breaking each complex step into simpler steps. This process is illustrated with missing addend problems of the form $4 + \underline{} = 7$ (Case, 1978b). The required steps are as follows:

1. Read symbols from left to right
2. Note that quantity to be found is one of the two addends
3. Decide that the known addend must be subtracted from the known total
4. Note and store value of the given addend
5. Note and store value of the total
6. Perform the subtraction (p. 214)

Children commonly make two types of strategy errors in solving the problem given above: (1) They give either 4 or 7 as the answer, seemingly by (a) looking at the symbols and reading one of them, and (b) copying this symbol as the answer; and (2) they add the two given numbers to get 11 by performing the following strategy:

1. Looking at and storing the first symbol
2. Counting out that many (on fingers)
3. Looking at and storing the second symbol
4. Counting out that many
5. Counting out total number
6. Writing this number as the answer

To show children that their strategies are incorrect, one might use faces. A full face is placed on one side of an equal sign, and a half face on the other. Children see that these faces are not the same. Then a full face is portrayed on one side of the equal sign and two half faces on the other side, where one half face has markings on it and the other is blank. Children fill in the markings on the blank half to make it the same as the full face. Eventually numerical symbols are introduced to replace the faces.

Case's model is similar to Gagné's in assessing the learners' initial states of knowledge and specifying learning goals and a sequence of steps to move learners from novices to experts. One difference lies in organization of steps. Gagné specified component intellectual skills to be mastered before learners acquire the target skill; Case emphasized strategies learners use. Case also stressed minimizing WM demands and designing instruction to show learners the problems with their present approaches.

Case (1978a) cited evidence showing that the preceding method is more effective than either structured practice or traditional instruction. One drawback is that the cost is high in terms of time necessary for the diagnostic, analytic, and planning aspects. Case recommended its use with mentally handicapped and remedial students because they tend to use inefficient strategies and have WM limitations. For any learner, this model seems appropriate with difficult tasks and when objectives and solution strategies are clearly specified.

Collins's Inquiry Teaching

Collins (1977; Collins & Stevens, 1983) formulated a theory of instruction using the Socratic teaching method. The goals are to have students reason, derive general principles, and apply them to new situations. Appropriate learning outcomes include formulating and testing hypotheses, differentiating necessary from sufficient conditions, making predictions, and determining when more information is needed to make predictions.

The theory is particularly useful for developing an intelligent computer-assisted instruction (CAI) system. The actual implementation is one of intelligent one-to-one tutoring. The tutor repeatedly questions the student. Questions are guided by such rules as, "Ask about a known case," "Pick a counterexample for an insufficient factor," "Pose a misleading question," and "Question a prediction made without enough information" (Collins, 1977). Rule-generated questions help students formulate general principles and apply them to specific problems.

The following is a sample dialogue between teacher (T) and student (S) on the topic of population density (the rules being applied are in parentheses) (Collins, 1977):

T: In Northern Africa is there a large population density there? (Rule 9: Pick a case with an extreme wrong value.)
S: In Northern Africa? I think there is.
T: Well there is in the Nile valley, but elsewhere there is not. Do you have any idea why not? (Rule 12: Probe for a necessary factor.)

S: Because it's not good for cultivating purposes?
T: It's not good for agriculture?
S: Yeah.
T: And do you know why? (Rule 4: Ask for prior factors.)
S: Why?
T: Why is the farming at a disadvantage?
S: Because it's dry.
T: Right. (p. 353)

The instructional approach above has limited classroom implementation potential because it is intended to be a plan for constructing CAI systems, which are not generally found in schools. Its applicability is further limited because it represents a tutoring (one-to-one) system. Persons who serve as tutors require extensive training to pose appropriate questions in response to a student's level of thinking. With some modification, this approach is applicable with small groups of students.

Research is needed to specify the conditions under which inquiry teaching is beneficial. Good content-area knowledge is a prerequisite for problem-solving skills. Students with basic knowledge deficiencies are not likely to function well under an inquiry system designed to teach reasoning and application of principles. There undoubtedly are other student characteristics (age, abilities) that predict success under this model. Research also is needed on whether skills and strategies acquired through inquiry teaching transfer to other domains (Gagné & Dick, 1983).

Merrill's Instructional Quality Profile

The Instructional Quality Profile (IQP) is a prescriptive model that specifies procedures for analyzing quality of instruction with respect to instructional objectives and test items (Merrill, Reigeluth, & Faust, 1979; Merrill, Richards, Schmidt, & Wood, 1977). *Instructional quality* refers to "the degree to which instruction is effective, efficient, and appealing—that is, the degree to which it works in cost-effectively promoting student performance on a posttest and student affect toward learning" (Merrill et al., 1979, p. 165).

The IQP is used to analyze the quality of instruction in the following six areas, shown with questions they address:

Area	Question Addressed
Purpose-objective consistency	Is substance of the objectives consistent with purpose of the course?
Objective adequacy	Does objective contain characteristics that make it useful for guiding design of test items and instructional presentations?

Objective-test consistency	Are test items consistent with justified objectives?
Test adequacy	Do test items have characteristics necessary to ensure they will adequately test the objectives with which they are consistent?
Test-presentation consistency	Do instructional presentations provide information necessary for students to learn how to perform as required by the test?
Presentation adequacy	Have students been provided with complete, concise, easily studied, adequately illustrated, and sufficiently elaborated presentation to enable them to acquire desired performance efficiently? (Merrill et al., 1979)

The model is prescriptive in that it details what one should do to obtain desired outcomes. Although the learning principles in the IQP are valid, their links to instruction often are not clear. Instructional principles tend to read like a checklist and readers must decide on their validity.

Outcomes deal with facts, concepts, procedures, and principles. There are three major task levels: remember an instance, remember a generality, use a generality. Application of task levels to content types yields 10 cells (listed in parentheses): Remember an instance (fact, concept, procedure, principle), remember a generality (concept, procedure, principle), use a generality (concept, procedure, principle). Instructional presentations are judged adequate based on which strategies are employed. Some appropriate strategy components are the following (Merrill et al., 1979):

1. *Feedback:* Give information on which answer is correct and why
2. *Isolation:* Separate critical information from other information and clearly label it as such
3. *Helps:* Add information to presentations to assist students in developing mastery (mnemonics, algorithms, attention-focusing devices)
4. *Sampling:* Provide an adequate number of instances and practice items
5. *Divergence:* Provide instances and practice items that can differ in various ways
6. *Difficulty level:* Use a range of difficulty levels from easy to difficult
7. *Matching:* Match instances with noninstances on common properties (but not relevant to learning the concept or principle)

The IQP specifies precisely how to design instruction and tests consistent with purpose and objectives. It operates on a micro level, that is, it deals with content within a broader unit. Reigeluth has extended this idea to a macro level, or ways to organize topics within larger (course) units (Reigeluth, 1979; Reigeluth & Curtis, 1987; Reigeluth, Merrill, & Bunderson, 1978). This Elaboration Theory of Instruction contains points of overlap with the IQP, but one distinctive feature is the former's emphasis on "zooming." One begins with a general view of the content and moves to specific details, returning later to the general view (review, practice). This idea is similar to Ausubel's notion of presenting advance organizers and then specifics of instruction. From an information processing perspective, zooming activates a context in LTM, where new information is integrated into the slots.

Reigeluth's model also incorporates the learning hierarchy notion. In designing instruction, the initial step is to use task analysis to determine skills to be taught and the order in which to teach them. Content is assigned to different lessons, and instruction is designed for each lesson in the proper skill sequence. Elaboration Theory is prescriptive and contains many valid learning principles; as with those of the IQP, however, they often are not firmly linked with the instructional prescriptions.

RESEARCH ON TEACHING

Much research has investigated how teaching practices affect student achievement. In several large-scale studies, some teachers were trained to implement specific instructional procedures, whereas others taught in their regular manner. Not surprisingly, these studies generally showed that trained teachers produce higher achievement (Brophy & Good, 1986). Rosenshine and Stevens (1986) summarized how successful instructors teach well-structured material, as follows:

1. Begin lesson with brief review of prior prerequisite learning
2. Provide short statement of objectives
3. Present material in short steps with student practice after each step
4. Give clear explanations and demonstrations
5. Provide for much student practice of new learning
6. Ask questions and check for understanding by all students
7. Monitor students during guided practice
8. Provide feedback and corrective instruction as necessary
9. Give clear directions for seatwork; monitor as necessary

These suggestions link with learning theory and research (Winne, 1985). Given that WM has a limited capacity, teachers need to ensure that they do not present too much new information at once or require unduly complex cognitive processing by students. One means of assisting students to integrate new information into LTM networks is to cue relevant prior information from memory by reviewing it during a lesson overview. When skills are well established, many aspects of skilled performance occur automatically (e.g., decoding in good readers). Automaticity is facilitated by student practice so that students eventually execute mental processes with little effort (Rosenshine & Stevens, 1986).

By integrating learning research with research on teaching, one can say that teaching practices facilitate learning if they

1. Break material to be learned into small steps
2. Give learners practice on each step before introducing complexity
3. Assist encoding by relating new information to prior knowledge
4. Give additional practice to facilitate automatic processing

This instructional approach works best with well-structured content taught step by step (factual knowledge, mathematical algorithms, mechanics of writing letters, English grammar). The approach is not as applicable with less-structured content (composition writing, discussions of social issues). In applying this approach, one must also take the students' level of development into account. Breaking material into small steps is important for young children, students of any age during the early stages of learning, and students with learning problems. How much practice students require also depends on age; younger students usually require more overt practice than older learners who can rehearse information better.

Teaching Functions

Rosenshine and Stevens (1986) developed the following list of six teaching functions based on information processing research and research on teaching:

1. Review and check previous day's work; reteach if necessary
2. Present new material
3. Give students guided practice; check for understanding
4. Offer feedback; reteach if necessary
5. Give students independent practice
6. Review at spaced intervals (weekly, monthly)

These steps are typically contained in instructional models (Hunter, 1982). One research challenge is to explore links between teaching practices and learning principles, especially those involving learners' cognitive processes (Winne, 1985). For example, during the lesson focus phase, teachers cue knowledge and relate it to the lesson purpose. Learning research suggests that cued information is activated in students' memories and that links are formed with the lesson content.

Another research challenge is to determine ways to implement steps of effective instructional models. Independent practice, for example, might be accomplished by students working alone or in small groups. Research on cooperative learning shows that small groups operate best when each member is responsible for some aspect of the task (Slavin, 1983). Research might determine how to subdivide tasks during independent practice to facilitate learning and a sense of accomplishment among group members.

LEARNER CHARACTERISTICS

Instructional theories provide for tailoring instruction to fit learner differences. Much instructional research has explored the role of *aptitude-treatment interactions* (ATIs). *Aptitudes* are such student characteristics as abilities, attitudes, personality variables, and demographic factors (e.g., age, sex, ethnic background). *Treatments* are forms of instruction or sets of conditions associated with instruction. ATI research examines how individual differences in aptitudes predict students' responses to forms of instruction. Although there is a wealth of evidence for ATIs, many findings are questionable because they have not been replicated in subsequent studies (Cronbach & Snow, 1977). Another problem is that complex interactions involving three or more variables are difficult to interpret, which precludes implications for teaching. Currently, many researchers interested in learner characteristics are exploring cognitive styles and ways of adapting instruction to fit student differences.

Cognitive Styles

Cognitive styles are stable individual variations in perceiving, organizing, processing, and remembering information (Shipman & Shipman, 1985; Sigel & Brodzinsky, 1977). Because these consistent individual variations are thought to be general in nature, they presumably affect performances on different tasks. Cognitive styles are types of information processing habits; they are not synonymous with abilities. Abilities refer to capacities to execute skills; cognitive styles involve ways of processing information. There are different types of cognitive styles (Messick, 1976). In addition to those discussed in this section, other styles include leveling or sharpening (blurring or accentuating differences among stimuli), risk taking or cautiousness (high or low willingness to take chances to achieve goals), and sensory modality preference (enactive or kinesthetic, iconic or visual, symbolic or auditory).

Cognitive styles are important because they provide information about the nature of cognitive development. One also can relate cognitive styles to larger behavioral patterns to study personality development. Educators

APPLICATION 10.4: Global and Analytical Cognitive Styles

Secondary teachers can take cognitive style differences into account in lesson planning. In teaching a unit on the Civil War, the teacher could emphasize both global and analytical styles by discussing overall themes and underlying causes of the war (e.g., slavery, economy) and by creating lists of important events and characters (e.g., Lincoln, Lee, Battle of Fredericksburg, Appomattox). Student activities can include discussions of important issues underlying the war (global style) and making timelines showing dates of important battles and other activities (analytical style). If teachers only stress one type of cognitive style, students who process information differently may doubt their ability to understand material, which will negatively impact self-efficacy and motivation for learning.

investigate styles to devise complementary learning environments and to teach students more adaptive styles to enhance learning and motivation.

This section discusses three cognitive styles that have substantial research bases and educational implications: (1) field dependence and independence, (2) categorization, and (3) cognitive tempo.

Field Dependence and Independence. Also called *global and analytical functioning,* the term *field dependence and independence* refers to the extent one is dependent on or distracted by the context in which a stimulus or event occurs (Sigel & Brodzinsky, 1977). The construct was identified and principally researched by Witkin and his colleagues (Witkin, 1969; Witkin, Moore, Goodenough, & Cox, 1977). Various measures determine reliance on perceptual context. One is the Rod-and-Frame test, in which the individual attempts to align in an upright position a tilted luminous rod inside a tilted luminous frame, inside a dark room with no other perceptual cues. Field independence originally was defined as the ability to align the rod upright by making use only of an internal standard of upright. Other measures are the Embedded Figures test, in which one attempts to locate a simpler figure embedded within a more complex design, and the Body Adjustment test, in which the individual sits in a tilted chair in a tilted room and attempts to align the chair upright. Subjects who can easily locate figures and align themselves upright are classified as field independent.

Young children are field dependent, but an increase in field independence begins during preschool and extends into adolescence. Children's individual preferences remain reasonably consistent over time (Sigel & Brodzinsky, 1977). The data are less clear on sex differences. Although some data suggest older male students are more field independent than older female students, research on young children shows that girls are more field independent than boys. It is not clear whether these differences reflect cognitive style or some other construct that contributes to test performance (e.g., activity–passivity).

Witkin et al. (1977) noted that field dependent and independent learners do not differ in learning ability, but they do in response to learning environments and content. Because field dependent persons may be more sensitive to and attend more carefully to aspects of the social environment, they are better at learning material with social content; however, field independent learners can easily learn such content when it is brought to their attention. Field dependent learners seem sensitive to social reinforcement (e.g., teacher praise) and criticism. Field independent persons are more likely to impose structure when material lacks organization; field dependent learners consider material as it is. With poorly structured material, field dependent learners may be at a disadvantage. Field dependent learners use salient features of situations in learning, whereas field independent learners also consider less-salient cues. The latter students may be at an advantage with concept learning, when relevant and irrelevant attributes are contrasted.

These differences suggest ways for teachers to alter instructional methods. If field dependent learners miss nonprominent cues, teachers need to highlight cues to use in distinguishing relevant features of concepts. This may be especially important with beginning readers, who need to focus on relevant letter features. There is evidence that field dependent learners have more trouble during early stages of reading (Sunshine & DiVesta, 1976).

Categorization Style. *Categorization style* refers to criteria used to perceive objects as similar to one another (Sigel & Brodzinsky, 1977). Style is assessed with a grouping task where one must group objects on the basis of perceived similarity. This is not a cut-and-dried task, because there are many ways to categorize objects. From a collection of pictures of animals, one might select a cat, dog, and rabbit and give as the reason for the grouping that they are mammals, have fur, run, and so forth. Categorization style reveals information about how the individual prefers to organize information.

Three types of categorization styles are relational, descriptive, and categorical (Kagan, Moss, & Sigel, 1960). A *relational* (or *contextual*) style links items on a theme or function (spatial, temporal); a *descriptive* (or *analytic*) style involves grouping by similarity according to some detail or physical attribute; a *categorical* (or *inferential*) style classifies objects as instances of a superordinate concept. In the preceding example, "mammals," "fur," and "run" reflect categorical, descriptive, and relational styles, respectively.

Preschoolers' categorizations tend to be descriptive; however, relational responses of the thematic type also are prevalent (Sigel & Brodzinsky,

1977). There is a developmental trend toward greater use of descriptive and categorical classifications, along with a decrease in relational responses.

Style is related to academic achievement, but the causal direction is unclear (Shipman & Shipman, 1985). Perceiving analytic relations is necessary for reading (e.g., fine discriminations); however, it is not just the ability to make such discriminations that is important but also the types of discriminations made. The latter are taught to students. Style and achievement may reciprocally influence each other.

Cognitive Tempo. *Cognitive* (or *response*) *tempo* has been extensively researched by Kagan and his associates (Kagan, 1966; Kagan, Pearson, & Welch, 1966). Kagan was investigating styles of categorization when he observed that some children responded rapidly and that others were more thoughtful and took their time. Cognitive tempo refers to the willingness "to pause and reflect upon the accuracy of hypotheses and solutions in a situation of response uncertainty" (Shipman & Shipman, 1985, p. 251).

Kagan developed a measure—the Matching Familiar Figures (MFF) test—for use with children. The MFF is a 12-item match-to-standard test in which a standard figure is shown with six possible matches, one of which is a perfect match. The dependent variables are mean latency time to the first response on each item and total errors across all items. Reflective children score above the median on time but below the median on errors, whereas impulsive children show the opposite pattern. There are two other groups of children: fast-accurate (below the median on both measures) and slow-inaccurate (above the median on both measures).

Children become more reflective with development, particularly in the early school years (Sigel & Brodzinsky, 1977). Evidence suggests different rates of development for boys and girls, with girls showing greater reflectivity at an earlier age. There is a moderate positive correlation between scores over a 2-year period, which indicates reasonable stability (Brodzinsky, 1982; Messer, 1970).

Differences in tempo are unrelated to intelligence scores but do relate to school achievement. Messer (1970) found that children not passed to the next grade were more impulsive than peers passed to the next grade. Reflective children perform better on moderately difficult perceptual and conceptual problem-solving tasks and make more mature judgments on concept attainment and analogical reasoning tasks (Shipman & Shipman, 1985). Reflectivity also bears a positive relationship to prose reading, serial recall, and spatial perspective taking (Sigel & Brodzinsky, 1977). Impulsive children often are judged less attentive and more disruptive than reflective children.

Given the educational relevance of cognitive tempo, many have suggested training children to be less impulsive. The Meichenbaum and Goodman (1971) study (see Modeling Processes in Chapter 4) found that self-instructional training decreased errors among impulsive children. Modeled demonstrations of reflective cognitive style, combined with student practice and feedback, seem important as a means of change.

Adapting Instruction

In an ideal instructional system, the instructional conditions match the learners' characteristics. Unfortunately, this match rarely occurs. Learners often must adapt to changes in such instructional conditions as content difficulty and teaching methods. Self-regulated learning (Chapter 9) concerns itself with learner adaptation to changing instructional conditions.

Conversely, instructional conditions can be tailored to individual differences: At the onset of the instructional activity, equal learning opportunities can be provided for all students despite individual differences (Corno & Snow, 1986). Macroadaptation occurs at the system or course level; microadaptation at the lesson or segment level.

Macroadaptation. Most macroadaptation occurs at the course rather than at the system level. The most widespread example is college courses using the Keller Plan (see the section on Instruction in Chapter 3). By allowing students to proceed at their own pace and recycle through material as needed, such courses take into account individual differences in learning ability. Mastery learning programs at the elementary and secondary levels attempt the same.

Two other macro-level adaptive programs are Individually Guided Education (IGE) and the Adaptive Learning Environments Model (ALEM). Under an IGE program, a school determines instructional objectives for each student based on aptitude profiles (e.g., reading, mathematics, motivation). Instruction is varied along different dimensions: teacher attention and guidance, amount of time spent interacting with other students and forms of media, and amount of instruction provided in whole-class and small-group settings (Corno & Snow, 1986). Repeated formative evaluations show how well each student has mastered the objectives, and remedial instruction is given as necessary (Klausmeier, Rossmiller, & Saily, 1977).

ALEM is designed for elementary students (Wang, 1980). Student assignments in reading and mathematics are individualized according to assessments of entry-level competencies. Quantity and quality of instruction are varied depending on student abilities. ALEM makes use of parent involvement programs, team teaching, and student learning groups.

Microadaptation. Individual teachers make adaptations with their students during lessons. Teachers routinely provide remedial instruction to students who have difficulty grasping new material. Teachers control many aspects of the instructional environment, which can be tailored to individual differences. These aspects include organizational structure (whole-class, small-group, individual), regular and supplementary materials, use of media, type of feedback, and type of material presented (tactile, auditory, visual). Students also work on computer programs that offer additional instruction and practice. These individual adaptations often are not systematically applied but rather made spontaneously, depending on how students react to material. In systematic applications, teachers use measures of ability and motivation during instructional planning to tailor instruction to individual differences (Corno & Snow, 1986).

COMPUTER LEARNING

Students spend the majority of their learning time in traditional instructional formats, but computers increasingly are being incorporated into curricula. Educators debate future uses for computers in education, but it seems likely that computers will increase in prevalence (Bork, 1984).

One educational concern is computer literacy (Seidel, Anderson, & Hunter, 1982). At a general level, *computer literacy* means, "The minimum knowledge, know-how, familiarity, capabilities, abilities, and so forth, about computers essential for a person to function well in the contemporary world" (Bork, 1985, p. 33). On a more specific level, computer literacy can refer to: (a) ability to control and program a computer; (b) ability to employ preprogrammed computer packages for personal, academic, or business uses; (c) knowing about available hardware and software packages; or (d) understanding how computers affect individuals, nations, and the world at large. Which definition one embraces depends on experiences and needs, but it seems valuable to understand the uses to which computers can be put.

Computer literacy and computer learning do not constitute theories of learning or instruction, but computers play a role in teaching and learning. We might ask, for example, whether computers improve school achievement more than traditional instruction or whether working on computers (e.g., programming) helps develop thinking or problem-solving skills better than other activities.

Taylor (1980) identified three roles for computers in education: tutor, tool, and tutee. The computer as tutor presents material to be learned or reviewed, along with evaluative feedback, and decides what material to present next. The tool role is found in word processing, data analysis, and record keeping. Computers function as tutees when they are instructed what to do (i.e., are programmed) by students. The tool function is useful, but the tutor and tutee roles have greater relevance to teaching and learning. The latter roles are covered in the next two sections, followed by a discussion of the future of computer learning.

Computers as Tutors

The computer functions as tutor in *computer-based* (or *computer-assisted*) *instruction* (CBI or CAI). CBI was discussed in Chapter 3 in the context of operant conditioning. CBI has most commonly been employed for drill and tutorials (O'Shea & Self, 1983). Drill programs are easy to write; because they review information, the student proceeds in linear fashion. Tutorials are interactive; they present information and feedback to students and respond based on students' answers. Branching programs are examples of tutorials (see the section on Instruction in Chapter 3).

Other instructional uses of CBI are simulations and games. Simulations represent real or imaginary situations that cannot be brought into the learning setting. Examples are programs simulating the flights of aircraft, underwater expeditions, and life in a fictional city. Games are designed to create an enjoyable learning context by linking material with a sport, adventure, or fantasy. Games can emphasize thinking skills and problem solving but also can be used to teach specific content (e.g., basketball game to teach fractions).

Studies investigating CBI in college courses yield beneficial effects on students' achievement and attitudes (Kulik, Kulik, & Cohen, 1980). Several CBI features are firmly grounded in learning theory and research (Lepper, 1985). Computers command the students' attention and provide immediate response feedback. Feedback can be of a type often not given in the classroom, such as how students' present performances compare with their prior performances (to show progress in learning). Computers also individualize content and rate of presentation.

Simulations and games also impact learning via motivational enhancement value (Lepper, 1985). Motivational inducement is greater when there is an "endogenous" (natural) relation between the content and the means ("special effects") used by the game or simulation to present the content. Fractions are endogenously related to a basketball game when students are asked to determine how much of the court is covered by players dribbling down the floor. From an information processing perspective, an endogenous relationship enhances meaningfulness and thereby coding and storage in LTM. In many games and simulations, however, the relation between content and means is arbitrary, as when a correct response by a student to a verbal item produces fantasy elements (e.g., cartoon characters). When the relation is arbitrary, computers do not produce better learning than traditional instruction, although the former may be more interesting.

Aside from interest value, another advantage of CBI is that many programs allow personalization; students enter information about themselves, parents, and friends, which is then included in the instructional presenta-

APPLICATION 10.5: Computer Tutorials

Although students spend the majority of their learning time in traditional settings, computers can be incorporated into the instructional program to enhance learning. In a resource classroom for students with learning problems, a teacher might use a tutorial program to teach and reinforce multiplication facts. To be effective, the program should incorporate the following features:

1. Present multiplication facts for the student to answer with the facts progressing from the 1-tables to the 9-tables
2. Personalize instruction for the student, using the student's name when feedback is given on the accuracy of answers
3. Keep track of the student's progression to provide review when required and to move to the next level when the student attains mastery
4. Review problems missed at the end of each exercise
5. Provide the student with feedback on number of correct and incorrect responses for each exercise and on overall progress through the multiplication tables

tion. Personalization can produce higher achievement than other formats (Anand & Ross, 1987; Ross, McCormick, Krisak, & Anand, 1985). Anand and Ross (1987) gave elementary school children instruction in dividing fractions according to one of three problem formats (abstract, concrete, personalized), shown with sample problems:

> (Abstract) There are 3 objects. Each is cut in half. In all, how many pieces would there be? (Concrete) Billy had 3 candy bars. He cut each one of them in half. In all, how many pieces of candy did Billy have? (Personalized for student named Joseph) Joseph's teacher, Mrs. Williams, surprised him on December 15 when she presented Joseph with 3 candy bars. Joseph cut each one of them in half so that he could share the birthday gift with his friends. In all, how many pieces of candy did Joseph have? (pp. 73–74)

The personalization format led to better learning and transfer than the abstract format and to more positive attitudes toward instruction than the concrete format. Personalizing instruction may improve meaningfulness and allow easy integration into LTM networks.

Computers also are beneficial in teaching problem solving. Woodward, Carnine, and Gersten (1988) found that the addition of computer simulations to structured teaching produced problem-solving gains for special education high school students compared with traditional instruction alone. The authors noted, however, that the mechanism producing these results is unclear and the results may not generalize to stand-alone computer simulations.

From the preceding evidence, one might conclude that computers often enhance learning compared with traditional instruction. However, comparisons of computer learning with conventional instruction often present misleading results. Research shows that no one medium is consistently superior to others, regardless of content, learners, or setting (Clark & Salomon, 1986). Many computer studies suffer from methodological problems involving inadequate comparison groups and the introduction of novelty (Clark, 1983). When computer learning shows advantages over traditional instruction, it may be because computers allow for better prepared instructional materials and for the implementation of more effective instructional design strategies. The computer is not a cause of learning but rather a *medium* for applying principles of effective instruction and learning.

Clark and Salomon (1986) recommended that researchers determine the conditions under which computers facilitate instruction and learning. The history of educational reform is littered with examples of changes being adopted before there was clear evidence of their effectiveness. The use of computers should depend on the learning goals. Though computers have the potential to foster different learning goals, they may not be the medium of choice for promoting student interaction through peer teaching, group discussions, or cooperative learning. Even when their use is warranted, they have some disadvantages. Computers do not allow for much incidental learning, as when a teacher or student mentions in class an anecdote related to the material being studied. Computer programs also need to be supplemented to relate material to current events; after students work through a program on the history and geography of a world region, the teacher and students could discuss the current political unrest in the area. There is promising evidence that computers can enhance learning, but more research evaluating CBI's effectiveness is necessary.

Computers as Tutees

In its role as tutee, the computer assists students learning to program. Programming knowledge helps prepare students for jobs and higher education (Coburn et al., 1985). Programming also presumably can aid the development of students' intellectual abilities—thinking, reasoning, and problem solving. Specifically, computers may teach thinking and problem-solving skills in ways not possible with standard educational curricula (Lepper, 1985). Different aspects of the computer environment make it unique. Learning to program helps one acquire such general problem-solving skills as formalizing a conceptual model, breaking a larger problem into subproblems, employing a flow chart to determine alternatives, and isolating and correcting conceptual and computational errors (debugging). Computers also allow students to engage in hypothetical thinking and to test their ideas with simulations. In an ecology unit, for example, one could vary the composition of flora in a particular habitat to determine which environments are favorable for given animal species. Another advantage is that programming exposes children to concepts ordinarily associated with higher-level mathematics (variables, geometric functions), which, to use Bruner's (1960) expression, can be "revisited" periodically during schooling.

A leading proponent of the preceding position is Seymour Papert. In his book *Mindstorms* (1980), Papert described the Logo philosophy and programming language. Logo is a language explicitly designed for children. In the activity of "turtle geometry," children create unusual geometric designs and cartoon drawings by using a small number of simple commands (e.g., "forward," "back," "left turn"). The effects provide children with immediate feedback of efforts to control the environment. In addition, children form commands by using subroutines, or sets of commands that produce given configurations. Rather than simply giving the computer a list of instructions, learners combine standard commands with their unique ones.

Research evidence is mixed regarding whether computer programming develops thinking skills (Lepper, 1985). Although critics argue that programming results in no benefits on cognitive measures, positive effects were obtained by Clements and Gullo (1984). Six-year-olds were assigned to a programming group or a CBI condition and participated in two 40-minute sessions for 12 weeks. The programming group received training on Logo; the CBI group worked on commercial software dealing with reading and mathematics. On a posttest, the programming condition scored higher on measures of reflectivity (cognitive style), divergent thinking (fluency, originality), and metacognition (awareness of comprehension failure). Subsequent research found advantages for programming on measures of social behaviors while children worked in pairs during problem solving (conflict resolution, self-directed work, rule determination), but found no advantage for programming on reading or mathematics achievement tests (Clements, 1986; Clements & Nastasi, 1988). Perhaps, as Lepper suggested, effects are not as robust as proponents claim nor as transitory as critics contend.

Future Directions

The field of computer learning is rapidly changing, and research will accelerate in the future. Though advances are likely in many areas, two seem particularly germane to human learning. As technology becomes more sophisticated, computers will offer more instructional possibilities. A second area involves artificial intelligence, which may provide insight into human thinking and problem-solving processes. These are discussed in turn.

Technology.   In their brief history, computers have progressed from large, costly, relatively inefficient units to smaller, more powerful and cost-effective ones. Technological advances will continue, especially in peripheral devices (or peripherals). *Peripherals* are components that exist outside of the computer system and include input devices, printers, mice, joysticks, and interfaces (Hannafin & Peck, 1988).

One class of peripherals comprises *input devices* that send responses to computers. The standard input device is the keyboard, which is similar to a standard typewriter keyboard with some additional keys. Advantages of keyboards are low cost and flexibility—students can use them to enter letters, numbers, words, and other information into the computer. Specialty keys allow students to execute such functions as deleting or moving information. Keyboards also have disadvantages. Students who cannot type have difficulty entering information and responding to questions, which slows their rate of learning. Younger and handicapped students often have difficulties with keyboards.

Several options now exist for ways to enter information without keyboards, and future refinements are likely. Alternatives include touch screens, light pens, mice, graphics tablets, joysticks, and voice recognition devices (Hannafin & Peck, 1988). *Touch screens* allow students to respond by touching the appropriate place on the screen (e.g., correct answer in multiple-choice item). *Light pens* reflect the same principle except that students touch the screen with a pen rather than their fingers. *Mice* are pointing devices connected to computers such that as they are moved across a desk, the signals translate into movement on the screen. *Graphics tablets* are kept next to the computer; students make drawings on the tablets, the drawings are transferred to the computer. *Joysticks* are control sticks that when moved change the position of the cursor (position indicator) or another object on the screen. *Voice recognition devices* are microphones that accept voice signals as input.

Output devices transmitting information from the computer to the student constitute another class of peripherals. Standard output devices are video displays and printers. Resolution of video displays has been a problem, but high-quality displays are available today. Future advances are likely to include better graphics and color displays. Progress also can be expected in voice synthesis (where the computer "talks" to the student) and in digitized audio (which presents as part of a CBI program audio input stored on disks).

Technological progress is likely in the capabilities of computers to interface with other media. Video and audio tapes and disks, along with slide projectors, have been connected with computers for instructional purposes (Hannafin & Peck, 1988). During videotape or videodisk instruction, computers control the instructional program and produce text and graphics while the video player produces the video and audio effects. Videotapes and -disks resolve problems with video or audio quality that might result from computers alone. Tapes also capitalize on benefits from portraying modeled demonstrations by teachers or other students. In particular, viewing peers acquiring skills can raise self-efficacy in observers, which positively impacts motivation and skill development (Schunk, 1987).

There are some problems with interactive video. Interactive capabilities are expensive to develop and produce. Costs may prohibit many school systems from purchasing components. Interactive video may require additional instruction time because programs present more material and allow for more student responding. Compared with video alone, students might demonstrate higher achievement with interactive video, but if the latter requires more instruction time, there is no advantage in the amount learned per unit of time (Schaffer & Hannafin, 1986). Though future developments may enhance portability, at present such interactive systems are bulky and require a permanent work station. Interactive video seems most useful when quality of learning is more important than time spent.

Another area of technological progress is in *microcomputer networking*. Networks connect microcomputers to one another and to central peripherals (e.g., printers, storage devices). Networking allows schools in a district to be connected with one another and with devices in- and outside of the district. Networking offers several advantages. Students have easy access to computers in their schools. Computer processing takes place in the microcomputer rather than in larger (mainframe) computers. Microcomputers are portable; permanent work stations are not required. Centralized peripheral devices help contain costs. One disadvantage is that if the system becomes excessively large it may require full-time supervision.

Artificial Intelligence. *Artificial intelligence* (AI) refers to computer programs that simulate human abilities to infer, evaluate, reason, solve problems, understand speech, and learn (Trappl, 1985). The term was coined by John McCarthy in 1956 as a conference theme. Other terms found in the literature (e.g., machine intelligence, intelligent CAI) are roughly synonymous.

There are three important aspects or goals of AI. Computers can be programmed to behave in an intelligent manner. These *expert systems* are increasingly used to solve problems and provide instruction in various domains. A second aspect involves programming computers to simulate human learning and other thought processes with the goal of understanding the operation of the mind. The third aspect (robotics) investigates how machines can be programmed to perform tasks. These are discussed below.

Expert systems are large computer programs that make available the knowledge and problem-solving processes of one or more experts (Fischler & Firschein, 1987; Trappl, 1985). Analogous to human consultants, expert systems have been applied to such diverse fields as medicine, chemistry, electronics, and law (Shallis, 1984). Expert systems have a vast knowledge base consisting of declarative knowledge (facts) and procedural knowledge (system of rules used to draw inferences). There is an interface that poses questions to users and gives recommendations or solutions. A common application of expert systems is to teach by providing expertise to students (Park, Perez, & Seidel, 1987). Instruction often employs guided discovery; students formulate and test hypotheses and experience consequences.

Future developments include expert systems being applied to a wider array of domains (Self, 1988). One challenge is to improve systems' capabilities to understand natural languages, especially speech. Though expert systems can perform pattern recognition tasks, most of these tasks involve only visual stimuli. At present, machines can be programmed to understand a particular human voice; this capability must be expanded for machines to function with different users. This type of advance also will enhance the use of expert systems by individuals with visual handicaps.

Another goal of artificial intelligence is to understand human thought processes. This application involves programming computers with some knowledge and rules that allow them to alter and acquire new knowledge and rules based on experiences (Shallis, 1984). In concept learning, for example, a computer might be programmed with an elementary rule and then be exposed to instances and noninstances of the concept. The program modifies itself by storing the new information in memory and altering its rule. Learning also can occur from exposure to case histories. A computer can be programmed with facts and case histories of a disease. As the computer analyzes these histories, it alters its memory to incorporate the etiology, symptoms, and course of the disease. When the computer acquires an extensive knowledge base for a particular disease, it can diagnose future cases with precision.

Technological progress is likely by the inclusion of more content areas, as well as in the area of information processing. Computers are built to process information sequentially; however, humans can process information in parallel (e.g., think of one thing while attending to something else). In a computer, parallel processing could occur by initially dividing a task into subgoals and then assigning subgoals to different processors that are linked.

This type of computer activity might provide insight into how pieces of information become linked in thought to provide integrated knowledge.

A third goal is to explore ways to program machines to perform tasks (*robotics*). Robots often conjure up images of humanlike forms in science fiction novels, but most robots in use today are boxes with mechanical arms and grippers or normal looking machines (e.g., forklift trucks) without operators. Robots contain sensors that detect light, pressure, sound, and distances, which provide feedback on location of the robot relative to aspects of its environment. Mechanical hands, arms, wheels, and other devices are used to operate on the environment. The computer may be inside the robot or a mainframe computer linked to the robot by electric wire, cable, or radio. The typical robots used in industrial contexts can move freely but cannot think or reason. Robots are insensitive to adverse working conditions involving noise, dust, and dangers; they also do not become ill, desire long lunch breaks, or complain about working conditions. Future research is likely to focus on making them more economical to build and operate and more able to perform additional repetitious tasks (Shallis, 1984).

SUMMARY

Instructional theory historically involved the design of instruction, but with the decline of behaviorism, the focus has broadened to studying how learner, instructional, and contextual variables impact one another and influence what students learn in educational contexts. Current instructional research investigates the influence of instructional variables on learners' cognitions, the role of individual differences in learning, and the impact of motivational variables on learning.

Bruner's view of instruction emphasized cognitive growth through use of language and exposure to systematic instruction. Knowledge can be represented enactively (action), iconically (images), and symbolically (language, symbol systems). Bruner believes the essentials of any subject can be taught in meaningful fashion to learners of different ages. Rather than teach particular content once, Bruner recommended revisiting the curriculum, or teaching the same content in different ways depending on students' developmental levels. Meaningful learning occurs when students explore their environments. Discovery learning is obtaining knowledge for oneself through forming and testing hypotheses. Discovery learning is a type of inductive reasoning process that proceeds best when directed by teachers who arrange activities for students to search, manipulate, and explore. Discovery is not letting students do what they want. Discovery works best with motivated students who possess relevant background knowledge and with content that lends itself to problem solving.

A different view of instruction was advanced by Ausubel. Meaningful reception learning of facts, concepts, and principles occurs by relating new information to knowledge in memory. Ausubel recommended expository teaching: Information should be presented to learners in organized fashion or in a form they easily can incorporate into memory. In this deductive teaching approach, the key is to build hierarchical structures in memory in which more general concepts subsume specific ideas. To make learning meaningful, advance organizers are used to introduce lessons. Advance organizers are broad statements presented at the outset. Organizers direct students' attention to important material, highlight interrelationships between ideas, and link material to what students know. Research shows that organizers facilitate learning and transfer; they are most effective with older students and with lessons designed to teach students relationships among concepts.

Gagné postulated an instructional theory emphasizing the conditions of learning, or the circumstances that prevail when learning occurs. It is necessary to consider the type of learning outcome and the events of learning. There are five types of learning outcomes: intellectual skills, verbal information, cognitive strategies, motor skills, and attitudes. Events of learning are factors that make a difference in instruction. Internal events are learners' present capabilities, personal dispositions, and ways of processing information. External events are instructional factors (material, mode of presentation) that support students while they are learning. In designing instruction for intellectual skills, it is helpful to employ a learning hierarchy specifying component skills and prerequisites. The Gagné–Briggs model is a systematic approach to instruction. Objectives are defined at the system, course, and lesson levels. Nine phases of learning are grouped into preparation for learning, acquisition and performance, and transfer of learning.

Other theoretical perspectives on instruction include Time Model (Carroll), Mastery Learning (Bloom), Developmental Model (Case), Inquiry Teaching (Collins), and Instructional Quality Profile (Merrill, Reigeluth). Research on teaching has identified teaching behaviors that promote student learning. An effective instructional model includes such components as specifying learning goals, explaining and demonstrating concepts, monitoring student guided practice, having students practice independently, and arranging spaced reviews of material.

Instructional models provide for tailoring instruction to individual differences. Important individual differences are found in cognitive styles (stable variations in perceiving, organizing, processing, and remembering information). Cognitive styles are not synonymous with abilities but are general and affect performance on different tasks. Three styles are field dependence and independence, categorization style, and cognitive tempo.

SUMMARY

Styles serve as bases for adapting instruction to individual differences. The goal is to provide equal learning opportunities to all students despite initial differences. Macroadaptations are made at the system or course level; microadaptations at the lesson or segment level. Adaptations involve how material is presented, which learning aids are employed, how learners are grouped for instruction, and what feedback is provided.

Computers increasingly are found in educational settings. A primary concern is computer literacy, or minimal knowledge required to function in the contemporary world. Computers serve as tools, tutors, and tutees. The tool role (word processing, record keeping) is practical, but less educationally relevant than the other functions. Computers serve as tutors when they present material to be learned, provide learners with feedback, and decide what to present next. Types of computer-based instruction (CBI) are drill and practice, tutorials, games, and simulations. In college courses, CBI is associated with positive effects on student achievement and attitudes. Simulations and games also enhance learning through their motivational value, but only when there is a natural relation between the content and the means of presentation. Computers function as tutees when they are instructed what to do, or programmed, by students. Programming may help teach thinking and problem-solving skills. Research evidence is mixed; although benefits on cognitive style, metacognition, and creativity have been obtained, critics argue that programming does not relate to gains in student achievement. Future developments in computer learning include technological progress and research on artificial intelligence.

Glossary

Achievement Motivation The striving to perform difficult tasks as well as possible.

Act A class of movements that produces an outcome.

Adapting Instruction Tailoring instructional conditions at the system, course, or individual class level to suit important individual differences to ensure equal learning opportunities for all students.

Advance Organizer Device that helps connect new material with prior learning, usually with a broad statement presented at the outset of a lesson.

Affective Learning Tactic Specific procedure included in a learning strategy to create a favorable psychological climate for learning by helping the learner cope with anxiety, develop positive beliefs, set work goals, establish a place and time for working, or minimize distractions.

All-or-None Learning View that a response is learned by proceeding from zero or low strength to full strength rapidly (during one trial).

Analogical Problem Solving Problem-solving strategy in which one draws an analogy between the problem situation and a situation with which one is familiar, works through the problem in the familiar domain, and relates the solution to the problem situation.

Aptitude-Treatment Interaction Differential response to variations in instruction depending on learner characteristics.

Artificial Intelligence Programming computers to engage in such human activities as thinking, using language, and solving problems.

Associative Shifting Process of changing behavior whereby responses made to a particular stimulus eventually are made to an entirely different stimulus if, on repeated trials, the stimulus is altered slightly.

Associative Structure Means of representing information in long-term memory; bits of information that occur close together in time or that otherwise are associated are stored together such that when one is remembered the other also is remembered.

Attention The process of selecting some environmental inputs for further information processing.

Attribution Perceived cause of an outcome.

Attribution Retraining Intervention strategy aimed at altering students' attributional beliefs, usually from dysfunctional attributions (e.g., failure attributed to low ability) to those conducive to motivation (failure attributed to low effort).

Autoshaping An organism's efforts to shape its own behaviors to obtain reinforcement.

Behavior Modification (Therapy) Systematic application of behavioral learning principles to facilitate adaptive behaviors.

Behavior Potential The probability that an individual will act in a given fashion relative to alternative behaviors.

Behavioral Objective Statement describing the behaviors a student will perform as a result of instruction, the conditions under which behaviors will be performed, and the criteria for assessing behaviors to determine whether the objective has been accomplished.

Behavioral Theory Theory that views learning as a change in the form or frequency of behavior as a consequence of environmental events.

Bottom-Up Processing Pattern recognition of visual stimuli that proceeds from analysis of features to building a meaningful representation.

Brainstorming Problem-solving strategy that comprises defining the problem, generating possible solutions, deciding on criteria to use in judging solutions, and applying criteria to select the best solution.

Branching Program Programmed instructional materials that students complete in different sequences depending on how well they perform.

Buggy Algorithm An incorrect rule for solving a mathematical problem.

Categorical Clustering Recalling items in groups based on similar meaning or membership in the same category.

Categorization Style Cognitive style referring to the criteria used to perceive objects as similar to one another.

Chaining The linking of three-term contingencies such that each response alters the environment and that the altered condition serves as a stimulus for the next response.

Classical Conditioning   Descriptive term for Pavlov's theory in which a neutral stimulus becomes conditioned to elicit a response through repeated pairing with an unconditioned stimulus.

Cognitive Behavior Modification   Behavior modification techniques that incorporate learners' thoughts (overt and covert) as discriminative and reinforcing stimuli.

Cognitive Dissonance   Mental tension that is produced by conflicting cognitions and that has drive-like properties leading to reduction.

Cognitive Map   Internal plan comprising expectancies of which actions are required to attain one's goal.

Cognitive Modeling   Modeled explanation and demonstration incorporating verbalizations of the model's thoughts and reasons for performing given actions.

Cognitive (Response) Tempo   Cognitive style referring to the willingness to pause and reflect on the accuracy of information in a situation of response uncertainty.

Cognitive Style   Stable variation among learners in ways of perceiving, organizing, processing, and remembering information.

Cognitive Theory   Theory that views learning as the acquisition of knowledge and cognitive structures due to information processing.

Comparative Organizer   Type of advance organizer that introduces new material by drawing an analogy with familiar material.

Comprehension   Attaching meaning to verbal (printed or spoken) information and using it for a particular purpose.

Comprehension Monitoring   Cognitive activity directed toward determining whether one is properly applying knowledge to material to be learned, evaluating whether one understands the material, deciding that the strategy is effective or that a better strategy is needed, and knowing why strategy use improves learning. Monitoring tactics include self-questioning, rereading, paraphrasing, and checking consistencies.

Computer-Based (-Assisted) Instruction   Interactive instruction in which the computer provides information and feedback to students and receives student input.

Computer Learning   Learning that occurs with the aid of a computer.

Computer Literacy   The minimum knowledge of computers and capabilities to operate them needed to function well in the contemporary world.

Concept   Labeled set of objects, symbols, or events sharing common characteristics (critical attributes).

Concept Learning   Identifying attributes, generalizing them to new examples, and discriminating examples from nonexamples.

Conditional Knowledge   Knowledge of when to employ forms of declarative and procedural knowledge and why it is important to do so.

Conditioned Response   The response elicited by a conditioned stimulus.

Conditioned Stimulus   A stimulus that, when repeatedly paired with an unconditioned stimulus, elicits a response similar to the unconditioned response.

Conditions of Learning   Circumstances that prevail when learning occurs and that include internal conditions (prerequisite skills and cognitive processing requirements of the learner) and external conditions (environmental stimuli that support the learner's cognitive processes).

Connectionism   Descriptive term for Thorndike's theory postulating learning as the forming of connections between sensory experiences (perceptions of stimuli or events) and neural impulses that manifest themselves behaviorally.

Contiguity   The basic principle of Guthrie's theory, which refers to a pairing close in time of a response with a stimulus or situation.

Contingency Contract   Written or oral agreement between teacher and student specifying what work the student must accomplish to earn a particular reinforcer.

Continued-Use Deficiency   Discontinuing use of task-facilitating private speech when no longer required to use it.

Continuous Reinforcement   Reinforcement for every response.

Control (Executive) Processes   Cognitive activities that regulate the flow of information through the processing system.

Coping Model   Model who initially demonstrates the typical fears and deficiencies of observers but gradually demonstrates improved performance and self-confidence in his or her capabilities.

Correlational Research   A study in which an investigator explores naturally existing relations among variables.

Declarative Knowledge   Knowledge that something is the case; knowledge of facts, beliefs, organized passages, and events of a story.

Decoding   Deciphering printed symbols or making letter-sound correspondences.

Discovery Learning   A type of inductive reasoning in which one obtains knowledge by formulating and testing hypotheses rather than by reading or listening to presentations.

Discrimination   Responding differently depending on the stimulus.

Discriminative Stimulus   The stimulus to which the organism responds in the operant model of conditioning.

Drive   Motivational construct that energizes the organism and propels it into action.

Dual-Code Theory   The view that long-term memory represents knowledge with a verbal system that includes knowledge expressed in language and an imaginal system that stores visual and spatial information.

Dual-Memory Model of Information Processing *See* Two-Store (Dual-Memory) Model of Information Processing.

Efficacy Expectations *See* Self-Efficacy.

Ego Involvement Conception of ability characterized by self-preoccupation, a desire to avoid looking incompetent, and viewing learning as a means to avoid looking incapable.

Eidetic Imagery Photographic memory in which an image appears and disappears in segments.

Elaboration The process of expanding upon new information by adding to it or linking it to what one already knows.

Elaboration Theory of Instruction Means of presenting instruction in which one begins with a general view of the content, moves to specific details, and returns later to the general view with review and practice.

Empiricism The idea that experience is the only source of knowledge.

Enactive Representation Representing knowledge through motor responses.

Encoding The process of putting new, incoming information into the information processing system and preparing it for storage in long-term memory.

Encoding Specificity The idea that retrieval of information from long-term memory is maximized when retrieval cues match those present during encoding.

Episodic Memory Memory of particular times, places, persons, and events that is personal and autobiographical.

Epistemology Study of the origin, nature, limits, and methods of knowledge.

Executive Processes *See* Control (Executive) Processes.

Expectancy-Value Theory Psychological theory postulating that behavior is a function of how much one values a particular outcome and one's expectation of obtaining that outcome as a result of performing that behavior.

Experimental Research A study in which an investigator systematically varies conditions (independent variables) and observes changes in outcomes (dependent variables).

Expert System Computers that are programmed with a large knowledge base and that behave in an intelligent manner by solving problems and providing instruction.

Expository Organizer Type of advance organizer that introduces new material with concept definitions and generalizations.

Expository Teaching Deductive teaching strategy in which material is presented to students in an organized and meaningful fashion with general ideas followed by specific points.

Extinction Decrease in intensity and disappearance of a conditioned response due to repeated presentations of the conditioned stimulus without the unconditioned stimulus.

Fatigue Method of Behavioral Change Altering behavior by transforming the cue for engaging in the behavior into a cue for avoiding it.

Fear of Failure The tendency to avoid an achievement goal that derives from one's belief concerning the anticipated negative consequences of failing.

Fear of Success The tendency to avoid succeeding at an achievement task that derives from anxiety and the anticipated negative consequences of succeeding (e.g., social rejection).

Feature Analysis View of perception postulating that people learn the critical features of stimuli, which are stored in long-term memory as images or verbal codes and compared with environmental inputs.

Field Dependence and Independence Cognitive style referring to the extent that one is dependent on or distracted by the context in which a stimulus or event occurs. Also called Global and Analytical Functioning.

Field Expectancy Perceived relation between two stimuli or between a stimulus, response, and stimulus.

First Signal System Environmental events that can become conditioned stimuli.

Forgetting Loss of information from memory or inability to recall information due to interference or improper retrieval cues.

Fractional Antedating Goal Reaction A part of the full goal response elicited by stimuli leading up to the goal.

Free Recall Recalling stimuli in any order.

Functional Fixedness Failure to perceive different uses for objects or new configurations of elements in a situation.

Functionalism School of thought postulating that mental processes and behaviors of living organisms help them adapt to their environments.

Generalization Occurrence of a response to a new stimulus or in a situation other than that present during original learning.

Generalized Reinforcer A secondary reinforcer that becomes paired with more than one primary or secondary reinforcer.

Generate-and-Test Problem-solving strategy in which one generates a possible problem solution and tests its effectiveness.

Gestalt Principles *Figure-ground relationship:* A perceptual field comprises a figure against a background. *Proximity:* Elements in a perceptual field are viewed as belonging together according to their closeness in space or time. *Similarity:* Perceptual field elements similar in such respects as size or color are viewed as belonging together. *Common* *direction:* Elements of a perceptual field appearing to constitute a pattern or flow in the same direction are perceived as a figure. *Simplicity:* People organize perceptual fields in simple, regular features. *Closure:* People fill in incomplete patterns or experiences.

Gestalt Psychology   Psychological theory of perception and learning stressing the organization of sensory experiences.

Given-New Contract   Implicit agreement between speaker and listener in which speaker mentally identifies information that is known (given) and unknown (new) to the listener and communicates new information by referring when necessary to given information.

Global (Analytical) Functioning   *See* Field Dependence (Independence).

Goal   What one is consciously trying to accomplish.

Goal-Gradient Hypothesis   The closer fractional antedating goal reactions are to the primary reinforcement, the more strongly they become conditioned.

Goal Setting   Establishing a standard or objective to serve as the aim of one's actions.

Habit-Family Hierarchy   The multiple ways of reaching a goal ordered in likelihood.

Habit Strength   The strength of the association between a stimulus and response.

Heuristic   A method for solving problems in which one employs principles (rules of thumb) that usually lead to a solution.

Higher-Order Conditioning   Use of a conditioned stimulus to condition a new, neutral stimulus by pairing the two stimuli.

Homeostasis   Optimal levels of physiological states.

Hope for Success   The tendency to approach an achievement goal that derives from one's subjective estimate of the likelihood of succeeding.

Human Subject   Living individual about whom an investigator conducting research obtains data through intervention or interaction with the individual or through identifiable, private information.

Hypothesis   Assumption that can be empirically tested.

Iconic Representation   Representing knowledge with mental images.

Identical Elements   View of transfer postulating that application of a response in a situation other than the one in which it was learned depends on the number of features (stimuli) common to the two situations.

Incompatible Response Method of Behavioral Change   Altering behavior by pairing the cue for the undesired behavior with a response incompatible with (i.e., that cannot be performed at the same time as) the undesired response.

Incremental Learning   View that learning becomes established gradually through repeated performances.

Informed Consent   The knowing, legally effective approval to participate in a research study given by an individual or the individual's legally authorized representative under circumstances that provide the prospective subject or representative sufficient opportunity to consider whether to participate and that minimize the possibility of coercion or undue influence.

Inhibition   In Pavlov's theory, a type of neural excitation that works antagonistically to an excitation producing conditioning and that diminishes the conditioned response in intensity or extinguishes it. In Hull's theory, an intervening variable that causes organisms not to respond.

Inhibition/Disinhibition   Strengthening/weakening of inhibitions over behaviors previously learned, which results from observing consequences of the behaviors performed by models.

Inquiry Teaching   Socratic teaching method in which learners formulate and test hypotheses, differentiate necessary from sufficient conditions, make predictions, and decide when more information is needed.

Insight   A sudden perception, awareness of a solution, or transformation from an unlearned to a learned state.

Instinctual Drift   Gradual change in an organism's learned behavior in the direction of instinctive patterns.

Instructional Quality   The degree to which instruction is effective, efficient, appealing, and economical in promoting student performance and attitude toward learning.

Intermittent Reinforcement   Some but not all responses are reinforced.

Interval Schedule   Reinforcement is contingent on the first response being made after a specific time period.

Intervening Variable   Theoretical construct that mediates the relationship between a stimulus and response.

Intrinsic Motivation   Engaging in a task for no obvious reward except for the activity itself; presumably arises as a function of one's desire to effectively control one's environment.

Introspection   Type of self-analysis in which individuals verbally report their immediate perceptions following exposure to objects or events.

Keller Plan (Personalized System of Instruction)   Instructional program incorporating student self-pacing, mastery learning, and self-study of materials.

Keyword Method   Mnemonic device in which one generates an image of a word sounding like the item to be learned and links that image with the meaning of the item to be learned.

Latent Learning Learning that occurs from environmental interactions in the absence of a goal or reinforcement.

Law of Disuse That part of the Law of Exercise postulating that the strength of a connection between a situation and response is decreased when the connection is not made over a period of time.

Law of Effect The strength of a connection is influenced by the consequences of performing the response in the situation: Satisfying consequences strengthen a connection; annoying consequences weaken a connection. Subsequently modified by Thorndike to state that annoying consequences do not weaken connections.

Law of Exercise Learning (unlearning) occurs through repetition (nonrepetition) of a response. Subsequently discarded by Thorndike.

Law of Readiness When an organism is prepared to act, to do so is satisfying and not to do so is annoying. When an organism is not prepared to act, to force it to act is annoying.

Law of Use That part of the Law of Exercise postulating that the strength of a connection between a situation and response is increased when the connection is made.

Learned Helplessness Psychological state involving a disturbance in motivation, cognition, and emotions due to previously experienced uncontrollability.

Learning An enduring change in behavior or in the capacity to behave in a given fashion resulting from practice or other forms of experience.

Learning Hierarchy Organized set of intellectual skills.

Learning Strategy Systematic plan oriented toward regulating academic work and producing successful task performance.

Learning Tactic Specific procedure included in a learning strategy to be used to attain a learning goal. Tactics include rehearsal, underlining, summarizing, elaboration, mnemonics, questioning, note taking, organizing, outlining, mapping, and comprehension monitoring.

Levels of Processing Conceptualization of memory according to the type of processing that information receives rather than the processing's location.

Linear Program Programmed instructional materials that all students complete in the same sequence.

Locus of Control Motivational concept referring to generalized control over outcomes; individuals may believe that outcomes occur independently of how they act (external control) or are highly contingent on their actions (internal control).

Long-Term Memory Stage of information processing corresponding to the permanent repository of knowledge.

GLOSSARY

Mand Verbal response under the control of conditions associated with deprivation or aversive stimulation and reinforced when fulfilled by a listener.

Mapping Learning tactic in which one identifies important ideas and specifies their interrelationship.

Mastery Learning A systematic instructional plan that has as its objective students demonstrating high achievement and that includes the components of defining mastery, planning for mastery, teaching for mastery, and grading for mastery.

Mastery Model Model who demonstrates faultless performance and high self-confidence throughout the modeled sequence.

Matched-Dependent Behavior Behavior matched to (the same as) that of the model and dependent on (elicited by) the model's action.

Meaningful Reception Learning Learning of ideas, concepts, and principles that occurs when material is presented in final form and related to students' prior knowledge.

Means-Ends Analysis Problem-solving strategy in which one compares the present situation with the goal to identify the differences between them, sets a subgoal to reduce one of the differences, performs operations to reach the subgoal, and repeats the process until the goal is attained.

Mediational Deficiency When task-relevant verbalizations are produced but do not affect subsequent behaviors.

Mental Discipline The idea that learning certain subjects in school enhances mental functioning better than does studying other subjects.

Mental Imagery Mental representation of spatial knowledge that includes physical properties of the object or event represented.

Metacognition Deliberate conscious control of one's cognitive activities.

Method of Loci Mnemonic technique in which information to be remembered is paired with locations in a familiar setting.

Mnemonic Device A type of learning tactic that makes to-be-learned material meaningful by relating it to information that one already knows.

Modeling Behavioral, cognitive, and affective changes deriving from observing one or more models.

Molar Behavior A large sequence of behavior that is goal-directed.

Motivated Learning Motivation to acquire skills and strategies rather than to merely complete activities.

Motivation The process whereby goal-directed behavior is instigated and sustained.

Movement Discrete behavior that results from muscle contractions.

Negative Reinforcer A stimulus that, when removed by a response, increases the future likelihood of the response occurring in that situation.

Network A set of interrelated propositions in long-term memory.

Networking Computers in various locations connected to one another and to central peripheral devices.

Nonsense Syllable Three-letter (consonant-vowel-consonant) nonword combination.

Novice-to-Expert Approach to Learning Means of analyzing learning by comparing behaviors and reported thoughts of experts with those of novices and deciding on an efficient means of moving novices to the expert level.

Observational Learning Display of a new pattern of behavior by one who observes a model; prior to the modeling, the behavior has a zero probability of occurrence by the observer even with motivational inducements in effect.

Operant Behavior Behavior that produces an effect on the environment.

Operant Conditioning Presenting reinforcement contingent on a response emitted in the presence of a stimulus to increase the rate or likelihood of occurrence of the response.

Operational Definition Definition of a phenomenon in terms of the operations or procedures used to measure it.

Oscillation Moment-to-moment fluctuations in the likelihood of behavior around a mean value.

Outcome Expectation Belief concerning the anticipated outcome of actions.

Overjustification Decrease in intrinsic interest in an activity subsequent to engaging in it under conditions that make task engagement salient as a means to some end (e.g., reward).

Paired-Associate Recall Recalling the response of a stimulus-response item when presented with the stimulus.

Parsing Mentally dividing perceived sound patterns into units of meaning.

Participant Modeling Therapeutic treatment comprising modeled demonstrations, joint performance between client and therapist, gradual withdrawal of performance aids, and individual mastery performance by the client.

Pattern Recognition (Perception) Process of assigning meaning to an environmental input received via the senses.

Pegword Method Mnemonic tactic in which the learner memorizes a set of objects rhyming with integer names (e.g., one is a bun, two is a shoe, etc.), generates an image of each item to be learned, and links it with the corresponding object image. During recall, the learner recalls the rhyming scheme with its associated links.

Peripherals (Peripheral Devices) Components that exist outside of the computer system (e.g., printers, mice, joysticks, interfaces).

Phi Phenomenon Perceptual phenomenon of apparent motion caused by lights flashing on and off at short intervals.

Positive Reinforcer A stimulus that, when presented following a response, increases the future likelihood of the response occurring in that situation.

Premack Principle The opportunity to engage in a more-valued activity reinforces engaging in a less-valued activity.

Primary Reinforcement Behavioral consequence that satisfies a biological need.

Private Speech The set of speech phenomena that has a self-regulatory function but is not socially communicative.

Proactive Interference Old learning makes new learning more difficult.

Problem A situation in which one is trying to reach a goal and must find a means of attaining it.

Problem Solving One's efforts to achieve a goal for which one does not have an automatic solution.

Problem Space The problem-solving context that comprises a beginning state, a goal state, and possible solution paths leading through subgoals and requiring application of operations.

Procedural Knowledge Knowledge of how to do something: employ algorithms and rules, identify concepts, and solve problems.

Production Deficiency The failure to generate task-relevant verbalizations when they could improve performance.

Production System Memory network of condition-action sequences (rules), where the condition is the set of circumstances that activates the system and the action is the set of activities that occurs.

Programmed Instruction Instructional materials developed in accordance with behavioral learning principles.

Proposition The smallest unit of information that can be judged true or false.

Prototype Abstract form stored in memory that contains the basic ingredients of a stimulus and is compared with an environmental input during perception.

Punishment Withdrawal of a positive reinforcer or presentation of a negative reinforcer contingent on a response, which decreases the future likelihood of the response being made in the presence of the stimulus.

Purposive Behaviorism Descriptive term for Tolman's theory emphasizing the study of large sequences of (molar) goal-directed behaviors.

Rationalism The idea that knowledge derives from reason without the aid of the senses.

Ratio Schedule Reinforcement is contingent on the number of responses.

Reaction Potential Probability that a learned response will be made in a situation.

GLOSSARY

Reciprocal Teaching Interactive dialogue between teacher and students in which teacher initially models activities, after which teacher and students take turns being the teacher.

Rehearsal Repeating information to oneself aloud or subvocally.

Reinforcement Any stimulus or event that leads to response strengthening.

Reinforcement Value How much an individual values a particular outcome relative to other potential outcomes.

Reinforcing Stimulus The stimulus in the operant model of conditioning that is presented contingent on a response and increases the probability that the response will be emitted in the future in the presence of the discriminative stimulus.

Research Systematic investigation designed to develop or contribute to generalizable knowledge.

Response Facilitation Previously learned behaviors of observers prompted by the actions of models.

Response Tempo *See* Cognitive (Response) Tempo.

Retroactive Interference New learning makes recall of old knowledge more difficult.

Rhetorical Problem The problem space in writing, which includes the writer's topic, intended audience, and goals.

Robotics Programming machines to perform manual tasks.

Savings Score Time or trials necessary for relearning as a percentage of time or trials required for original learning.

Schema A cognitive structure that organizes large amounts of information into a meaningful system.

Secondary Reinforcement Behavioral consequence that becomes reinforcing by being paired with primary reinforcement.

Second Signal System Words and other features of language that are used by humans to communicate and that can become conditioned stimuli.

Self-Actualization The desire for self-fulfillment or for becoming everything one is capable of becoming; the highest level in Maslow's hierarchy of needs.

Self-Efficacy (Efficacy Expectations) Personal beliefs concerning one's capabilities to organize and implement actions necessary to perform behaviors at designated levels.

Self-Instruction In a learning setting, discriminative stimuli that are produced by the individual and that set the occasion for responses leading to reinforcement.

Self-Instructional Training Training procedure that comprises cognitive modeling, overt guidance, overt self-guidance, faded overt self-guidance, and covert self-instruction.

Self-Judgment Comparing one's present performance level with one's goal.

Self-Modeling Changes in behaviors, thoughts, and affects that derive from observing one's own performances.

Self-Monitoring (-Observation, -Recording) Deliberate attention to some aspect of one's behavior, often accompanied by recording its frequency or intensity.

Self-Regulated Learning (Self-Regulation) The process whereby students personally activate and sustain behaviors, cognitions, and affects that are systematically oriented toward the attainment of learning goals.

Self-Reinforcement (-Reaction) The process whereby individuals, after performing a response, arrange to receive reinforcement that increases the likelihood of future responding; changes in one's beliefs and behaviors after judging performance against a goal.

Semantic Memory Memory of general information and concepts available in the environment and not tied to a particular individual or context.

Sensory Register State of information processing concerned with receiving inputs, holding them briefly in sensory form, and transferring them to working memory.

Serial Recall Recalling stimuli in the order in which they are presented.

Shaping Differential reinforcement of successive approximations to the desired rate or form of behavior.

Short-Term (Working) Memory Information processing stage corresponding to awareness, or what one is conscious of at a given moment.

Social Comparison Process of comparing one's beliefs and behaviors with those of others.

Speech Act The speaker's purpose in uttering a communication, or what a speaker is trying to accomplish with the utterance.

Spiral Curriculum Building on prior knowledge by presenting the same topics at increasing levels of complexity as students move through the curriculum.

Spontaneous Recovery Sudden recurrence of the conditioned response following presentation of the conditioned stimulus after a time lapse in which the conditioned stimulus is not presented.

Spreading Activation Activation in long-term memory of propositions that are associatively linked with material presently in one's working memory.

SQ3R Method Method of studying text that stands for Survey–Question–Read–Recite–Review.

Stimulus-Response (S-R) Theory Learning theory emphasizing associations between stimuli and responses.

Strategy Value Information Information linking strategy use with improved performance.

Structuralism School of thought postulating that the mind is composed of associations of ideas and that studying the complexities of the mind requires breaking associations into single ideas.

Superstitious Behavior Behavior conditioned accidentally and not instrumental in producing a response.

Symbolic Representation Representing knowledge with symbol systems (e.g., language, mathematical notation).

Systematic Desensitization Therapeutic procedure used to extinguish fears by pairing threatening stimuli with cues for relaxation.

Tact Verbal response under the discriminative control of an object or event and reinforced by a listener when it correctly names the object or event.

Task Involvement Conception of ability characterized by viewing learning as a goal by itself and focusing on task demands rather than on oneself.

Template Matching Theory of perception postulating that people store templates (miniature copies of stimuli) in memory and compare these templates with environmental stimuli during perception.

Theory Scientifically acceptable set of principles offered to explain a phenomenon.

Three-Term Contingency The basic operant model of conditioning: A discriminative stimulus sets the occasion for a response to be emitted, which is followed by a reinforcing stimulus.

Threshold Method of Behavioral Change Altering behavior by introducing the cue for the undesired response at a low level and gradually increasing its magnitude until it is presented at full strength.

Time Needed for Learning Amount of academically engaged time required by a student to learn a task.

Time Spent in Learning Amount of academically engaged time expended to learn.

Top-Down Processing Pattern recognition of stimuli that occurs by forming a meaningful representation of the context, developing expectations of what will occur, and comparing features of stimuli to expectations to confirm or disconfirm one's expectations.

Transfer Application of skills or knowledge in new ways or situations.

Triadic Reciprocality Reciprocal interactions among behaviors, environmental variables, and cognitions and other personal factors.

Two-Store (Dual-Memory) Model of Information Processing Conceptualization of memory as involving stages of processing and having two primary areas for storing information (short- and long-term memory).

Unconditioned Response The response elicited by an unconditioned stimulus.

Unconditioned Stimulus A stimulus that when presented elicits a natural response from the organism.

Unitary Theory The view that all information is represented in long-term memory in verbal codes.

Unlearning   *See* Extinction.

Utilization   The use made of parsed sound patterns (e.g., store in memory, respond if a question, seek additional information).

Verbal Behavior   Vocal responses shaped and maintained by the actions of other persons.

Work Backward   Problem-solving strategy in which one starts with the goal and asks which subgoals are necessary to accomplish it, what is necessary to accomplish these subgoals, and so forth until the beginning state is reached.

Work Forward   Problem-solving strategy in which one starts with the beginning problem state and decides how to alter it to progress toward the goal.

Working Memory   *See* Short-Term (Working) Memory.

Zone of Proximal Development   The amount of learning possible by a student given the proper instructional conditions.

Bibliography

Abramson, L. Y., Seligman, M. E. P., & Teasdale, J. D. (1978). Learned helplessness in humans: Critique and reformulation. *Journal of Abnormal Psychology, 87,* 49–74.

Akamatsu, T. J., & Thelen, M. H. (1974). A review of the literature on observer characteristics and imitation. *Developmental Psychology, 10,* 38–47.

Alderman, M. K. (1985). Achievement motivation and the preservice teacher. In M. K. Alderman & M. W. Cohen (Eds.), *Motivation theory and practice for preservice teachers* (pp. 37–51). Washington, DC: ERIC Clearinghouse on Teacher Education.

American Psychological Association (1982). *Ethical principles in the conduct of research with human participants.* Washington, DC: Author.

Ames, C. (1984). Competitive, cooperative, and individualistic goal structures: A cognitive-motivational analysis. In R. Ames & C. Ames (Eds.), *Research on motivation in education* (Vol. 1, pp. 177–208). New York: Academic Press.

Ames, C. (1985). Attributions and cognitions in motivation theory. In M. K. Alderman & M. W. Cohen (Eds.), *Motivation theory and practice for preservice teachers* (pp. 16–21). Washington, DC: ERIC Clearinghouse on Teacher Education.

Ames, C. (1987). The enhancement of student motivation. In M. L. Maehr & D. A. Kleiber (Eds.), *Advances in motivation and achievement* (Vol. 5, pp. 123–148). Greenwich, CT: JAI Press.

Anand, P. G., & Ross, S. M. (1987). Using computer-assisted instruction to personalize arithmetic materials for elementary school children. *Journal of Educational Psychology, 79,* 72–78.

Anderson, J. R. (1976). *Language, memory, and thought.* Hillsdale, NJ: Erlbaum.

Anderson, J. R. (1980). Concepts, propositions, and schemata: What are the cognitive units? In J. H. Flowers (Ed.), *Nebraska Symposium on Motivation, 1980* (Vol. 28, pp. 121–162). Lincoln, NE: University of Nebraska Press.

Anderson, J. R. (1982). Acquisition of cognitive skill. *Psychological Review, 89,* 369–406.

Anderson, J. R. (1983). A spreading activation theory of memory. *Journal of Verbal Learning and Verbal Behavior, 22,* 261–295.

Anderson, J. R. (1984). Spreading activation. In J. R. Anderson & S. M. Kosslyn (Eds.), *Tutorials in learning and memory: Essays in honor of Gordon Bower* (pp. 61–90). San Francisco: Freeman.

Anderson, J. R. (1990). *Cognitive psychology and its implications* (3rd ed.). New York: Freeman.

Anderson, L. W. (1976). An empirical investigation of individual differences in time to learn. *Journal of Educational Psychology, 68,* 226–233.

Anderson, R. C. (1982). Allocation of attention during reading. In A. Flammer & W. Kintsch (Eds.), *Discourse processing* (pp. 292–305). Amsterdam: North Holland Publishing Company.

Anderson, R. C., & Pichert, J. W. (1978). Recall of previously unrecallable information following a shift in perspective. *Journal of Verbal Learning and Verbal Behavior, 17,* 1–12.

Anderson, R. C., Reynolds, R. E., Schallert, D. L., & Goetz, T. E. (1977). Frameworks for comprehending discourse. *American Educational Research Journal, 14,* 367–381.

Andre, T. (1986). Problem solving and education. In G. D. Phye & T. Andre (Eds.), *Cognitive classroom learning: Understanding, thinking, and problem solving* (pp. 169–204). Orlando: Academic Press.

Andrews, G. R., & Debus, R. L. (1978). Persistence and the causal perception of failure: Modifying cognitive attributions. *Journal of Educational Psychology, 70,* 154–166.

Angell, J. R. (1907). The province of functional psychology. *Psychological Review, 14,* 61–91.

Aronson, E. (1966). The psychology of insufficient justification: An analysis of some conflicting data. In S. Feldman (Ed.), *Cognitive consistency: Motivational antecedents and behavioral consequences* (pp. 109–133). New York: Academic Press.

Asarnow, J. R., & Meichenbaum, D. (1979). Verbal rehearsal and serial recall: The mediational training of kindergarten children. *Child Development, 50,* 1173–1177.

Atkinson, J. W. (1957). Motivational determinants of risk-taking behavior. *Psychological Review, 64,* 359–372.

Atkinson, J. W., & Birch, D. (1978). *Introduction to motivation* (2nd ed.). New York: D. Van Nostrand.

Atkinson, J. W., & Feather, N. T. (1966). *A theory of achievement motivation.* New York: Wiley.

Atkinson, J. W., & Raynor, J. O. (1974). *Motivation and achievement.* Washington, DC: Hemisphere.

BIBLIOGRAPHY

Atkinson, J. W., & Raynor, J. O. (1978). *Personality, motivation, and achievement.* Washington, DC: Hemisphere.

Atkinson, R. C. (1975). Mnemotechnics in second-language learning. *American Psychologist, 30,* 828–921.

Atkinson, R. C., & Raugh, M. R. (1975). An application of the mnemonic keyword method to the acquisition of a Russian vocabulary. *Journal of Experimental Psychology: Human Learning and Memory, 104,* 126–133.

Atkinson, R. C., & Shiffrin, R. M. (1968). Human memory: A proposed system and its control processes. In K. W. Spence & J. T. Spence (Eds.), *The psychology of learning and motivation: Advances in research and theory* (Vol. 2, pp. 89–195). New York: Academic Press.

Atkinson, R. C., & Shiffrin, R. M. (1971). The control of short-term memory. *Scientific American, 225,* 82–90.

Austin, J. L. (1962). *How to do things with words.* Oxford, England: Oxford University Press.

Ausubel, D. P. (1963). *The psychology of meaningful verbal learning: An introduction to school learning.* New York: Grune & Stratton.

Ausubel, D. P. (1968). *Educational psychology: A cognitive view.* New York: Holt, Rinehart & Winston.

Ausubel, D. P. (1977). The facilitation of meaningful verbal learning in the classroom. *Educational Psychologist, 12,* 162–178.

Ausubel, D. P. (1978). In defense of advance organizers: A reply to the critics. *Review of Educational Research, 48,* 251–257.

Ausubel, D. P., & Robinson, F. G. (1969). *School learning: An introduction to educational psychology.* New York: Holt, Rinehart & Winston.

Ayllon, T., & Azrin, N. (1968). *The token economy: A motivational system for therapy and rehabilitation.* New York: Appleton-Century-Crofts.

Baddeley, A. D. (1978). The trouble with levels: A reexamination of Craik and Lockhart's framework for memory research. *Psychological Review, 85,* 139–152.

Baker, L., & Brown, A. L. (1984). Metacognitive skills and reading. In P. D. Pearson (Ed.), *Handbook of reading research* (pp. 353–394). New York: Longman.

Bandura, A. (1969). *Principles of behavior modification.* New York: Holt, Rinehart & Winston.

Bandura, A. (1973). *Aggression: A social learning analysis.* Englewood Cliffs, NJ: Prentice-Hall.

Bandura, A. (1977a). Self-efficacy: Toward a unifying theory of behavioral change. *Psychological Review, 84,* 191–215.

Bandura, A. (1977b). *Social learning theory.* Englewood Cliffs, NJ: Prentice-Hall.

Bandura, A. (1978). The self system in reciprocal determinism. *American Psychologist, 33,* 344–358.

Bandura, A. (1981). Self-referent thought: A developmental analysis of self-efficacy. In J. H. Flavell & L. Ross (Eds.), *Social cognitive development: Frontiers and possible futures* (pp. 200–239). Cambridge, England: Cambridge University Press.

Bandura, A. (1982a). The self and mechanisms of agency. In J. Suls (Ed.), *Psychological perspectives on the self* (Vol. 1, pp. 3–39). Hillsdale, NJ: Erlbaum.

BIBLIOGRAPHY

Bandura, A. (1982b). Self-efficacy mechanism in human agency. *American Psychologist, 37,* 122–147.

Bandura, A. (1986). *Social foundations of thought and action: A social cognitive theory.* Englewood Cliffs, NJ: Prentice Hall.

Bandura, A., & Adams, N. E. (1977). Analysis of self-efficacy theory of behavioral change. *Cognitive Therapy and Research, 1,* 287–308.

Bandura, A., Adams, N. E., & Beyer, J. (1977). Cognitive processes mediating behavioral change. *Journal of Personality and Social Psychology, 35,* 125–139.

Bandura, A., & Cervone, D. (1983). Self-evaluative and self-efficacy mechanisms governing the motivational effects of goal systems. *Journal of Personality and Social Psychology, 45,* 1017–1028.

Bandura, A., & Harris, M. B. (1966). Modification of syntactic style. *Journal of Experimental Child Psychology, 4,* 341–352.

Bandura, A., & Jeffery, R. W. (1973). Role of symbolic coding and rehearsal processes in observational learning. *Journal of Personality and Social Psychology, 26,* 122–130.

Bandura, A., & Kupers, C. J. (1964). Transmission of patterns of self-reinforcement through modeling. *Journal of Abnormal and Social Psychology, 69,* 1–9.

Bandura, A., Ross, D., & Ross, S. A. (1963). Imitation of film-mediated aggressive models. *Journal of Abnormal and Social Psychology, 66,* 3–11.

Bandura, A., & Schunk, D. H. (1981). Cultivating competence, self-efficacy, and intrinsic interest through proximal self-motivation. *Journal of Personality and Social Psychology, 41,* 586–598.

Bandura, A., & Walters, R. H. (1963). *Social learning and personality development.* New York: Holt, Rinehart & Winston.

Bangert, R. L., Kulik, J. A., & Kulik, C. C. (1983). Individualized systems of instruction in secondary schools. *Review of Educational Research, 53,* 143–158.

Barnes, B. R., & Clawson, E. U. (1975). Do advance organizers facilitate learning? Recommendations for further research based on an analysis of 32 studies. *Review of Educational Research, 45,* 637–659.

Bartlett, F. C. (1932). *Remembering: A study in experimental and social psychology.* Cambridge, England: Cambridge University Press.

Becker, W. C. (1971). *Parents are teachers: A child management program.* Champaign, IL: Research Press.

Beery, R. (1975). Fear of failure in the student experience. *Personnel and Guidance Journal, 54,* 190–203.

Bell, D. R., & Low, R. M. (1977). *Observing and recording children's behavior.* Richland, WA: Performance Associates.

Bereiter, C. (1980). Development in writing. In L. W. Gregg & E. R. Steinberg (Eds.), *Cognitive processes in writing* (pp. 73–93). Hillsdale, NJ: Erlbaum.

Bereiter, C., & Scardamalia, M. (1986). Levels of inquiry into the nature of expertise in writing. In E. Z. Rothkopf (Ed.), *Review of research in education* (Vol. 13, pp. 259–282). Washington, DC: American Educational Research Association.

Berger, S. M. (1977). Social comparison, modeling, and perseverance. In J. M. Suls & R. L. Miller (Eds.), *Social comparison processes: Theoretical and empirical perspectives* (pp. 209–234). Washington, DC: Hemisphere.

BIBLIOGRAPHY

Berk, L. E. (1986). Relationship of elementary school children's private speech to behavioral accompaniment to task, attention, and task performance. *Developmental Psychology, 22,* 671–680.

Berlyne, D. E. (1960). *Conflict, arousal, and curiosity.* New York: McGraw-Hill.

Bilodeau, E. A. (1966). *Acquisition of skill.* New York: Academic Press.

Birnbaum, J. C. (1982). The reading and composing behaviors of selected fourth- and seventh-grade students. *Research in the Teaching of English, 16,* 241–260.

Black, J. B. (1984). Understanding and remembering stories. In J. R. Anderson & S. M. Kosslyn (Eds.), *Tutorials in learning and memory: Essays in honor of Gordon Bower* (pp. 235–255). San Francisco: Freeman.

Block, J. H., & Burns, R. B. (1977). Mastery learning. In L. S. Shulman (Ed.), *Review of research in education* (Vol. 4, pp. 3–49). Itasca, IL: Peacock.

Bloom, B. S. (1976). *Human characteristics and school learning.* New York: McGraw-Hill.

Bloom, B. S., Hastings, J. T., & Madaus, G. F. (1971). *Handbook on formative and summative evaluation of student learning.* New York: McGraw-Hill.

Bobrow, D. G., & Norman, D. A. (1975). Some principles of memory schemata. In D. G. Bobrow & A. Collins (Eds.), *Representation and understanding* (pp. 131–150). New York: Academic Press.

Boersma, F. J., & Chapman, J. W. (1981). Academic self-concept, achievement expectations, and locus of control in elementary learning-disabled children. *Canadian Journal of Behavioural Science, 13,* 349–358.

Bolles, R. C. (1972). Reinforcement, expectancy, and learning. *Psychological Review, 79,* 394–409.

Bork, A. (1984). Computers in education today—and some possible futures. *Phi Delta Kappan, 66,* 239–243.

Bork, A. (1985). *Personal computers for education.* New York: Harper & Row.

Borkowski, J. G., & Cavanaugh, J. C. (1979). Maintenance and generalization of skills and strategies by the retarded. In N. R. Ellis (Ed.), *Handbook of mental deficiency, psychological theory and research* (2nd ed., pp. 569–617). Hillsdale, NJ: Erlbaum.

Bousfield, W. A. (1953). The occurrence of clustering in the recall of randomly arranged associates. *Journal of General Psychology, 49,* 229–240.

Bousfield, W. A., & Cohen, B. H. (1953). The effects of reinforcement on the occurrence of clustering in the recall of randomly arranged associates. *Journal of Psychology, 36,* 67–81.

Bower, G. H. (1970). Organizational factors in memory. *Cognitive Psychology, 1,* 18–46.

Bransford, J. D., & Stein, B. S. (1984). *The IDEAL problem solver: A guide for improving thinking, learning, and creativity.* New York: Freeman.

Bransford, J. D., Stein, B. S., Vye, N. J., Franks, J. J., Auble, P. M., Mezynski, K. J., & Perfetto, G. A. (1982). Differences in approaches to learning: An overview. *Journal of Experimental Psychology: General, 111,* 390–398.

Breedlove, C. J., & Cicirelli, V. G. (1974). Women's fear of success in relation to personal characteristics and type of occupation. *Journal of Psychology, 86,* 181–190.

Breland, K., & Breland, M. (1961). The misbehavior of organisms. *American Psychologist, 16,* 681–684.

BIBLIOGRAPHY

Brewer, W. F. (1974). There is no convincing evidence for operant or classical conditioning in adult humans. In W. B. Weimer & D. S. Palermo (Eds.), *Cognition and the symbolic processes* (pp. 1–42). Hillsdale, NJ: Erlbaum.

Brewer, W. F., & Treyens, J. C. (1981). Role of schemata in memory for places. *Cognitive Psychology, 13,* 207–230.

Brigham, T. A. (1982). Self-management: A radical behavioral perspective. In P. Karoly & F. H. Kanfer (Eds.), *Self-management and behavior change: From theory to practice* (pp. 32–59). New York: Pergamon.

Broadbent, D. E. (1958). *Perception and communication.* London: Pergamon.

Broadhurst, P. L. (1957). Emotionality and the Yerkes-Dodson Law. *Journal of Experimental Psychology, 54,* 345–352.

Brodzinsky, D. M. (1982). Relationship between cognitive style and cognitive development: A 2-year longitudinal study. *Developmental Psychology, 18,* 617–626.

Brophy, J. E. (1985). Teacher-student interaction. In J. B. Dusek (Ed.), *Teacher expectancies* (pp. 303–328). Hillsdale, NJ: Erlbaum.

Brophy, J. E., & Good, T. L. (1986). Teacher behavior and student achievement. In M. C. Wittrock (Ed.), *Handbook of research on teaching* (3rd ed., pp. 328–375). New York: Macmillan.

Brown, A. L. (1980). Metacognitive development and reading. In R. J. Spiro, B. C. Bruce, & W. F. Brewer (Eds.), *Theoretical issues in reading comprehension* (pp. 453–481). Hillsdale, NJ: Erlbaum.

Brown, A. L., Palincsar, A. S., & Armbruster, B. B. (1984). Instructing comprehension-fostering activities in interactive learning situations. In H. Mandl, N. L. Stein, & T. Trabasso (Eds.), *Learning and comprehension of text* (pp. 255–286). Hillsdale, NJ: Erlbaum.

Brown, I., Jr., & Inouye, D. K. (1978). Learned helplessness through modeling: The role of perceived similarity in competence. *Journal of Personality and Social Psychology, 36,* 900–908.

Brown, J. S., & Burton, R. R. (1978). Diagnostic models for procedural bugs in basic mathematical skills. *Cognitive Science, 2,* 155–192.

Brown, P. L., & Jenkins, H. M. (1968). Auto-shaping of the pigeon's key-peck. *Journal of the Experimental Analysis of Behavior, 11,* 1–8.

Bruner, J. S. (1960). *The process of education.* New York: Vintage.

Bruner, J. S. (1961). The act of discovery. *Harvard Educational Review, 31,* 21–32.

Bruner, J. S. (1964). The course of cognitive growth. *American Psychologist, 19,* 1–15.

Bruner, J. S. (1966). *Toward a theory of instruction.* New York: Norton.

Bruner, J. S. (1985). Models of the learner. *Educational Researcher, 14*(6), 5–8.

Bruner, J. S., Goodnow, J., & Austin, G. A. (1956). *A study of thinking.* New York: Wiley.

Bruner, J. S., Olver, R. R., & Greenfield, P. M. (1966). *Studies in cognitive growth.* New York: Wiley.

Bryan, J. H., & Bryan, T. H. (1983). The social life of the learning disabled youngster. In J. D. McKinney & L. Feagans (Eds.), *Current topics in learning disabilities* (Vol. 1, pp. 57–85). Norwood, NJ: Ablex.

Bryan, T., Cosden, M., & Pearl, R. (1982). The effects of cooperative goal structures and cooperative models on LD and NLD students. *Learning Disability Quarterly, 5,* 415–421.

BIBLIOGRAPHY

Butkowsky, I. S., & Willows, D. M. (1980). Cognitive-motivational characteristics of children varying in reading ability: Evidence for learned helplessness in poor readers. *Journal of Educational Psychology, 72,* 408–422.

Calfee, R. (1981). Cognitive psychology and educational practice. In D. C. Berliner (Ed.), *Review of research in education* (Vol. 9, pp. 3–73). Washington, DC: American Educational Research Association.

Calfee, R., & Drum, P. (1986). Research on teaching reading. In M. C. Wittrock (Ed.), *Handbook of research on teaching* (3rd ed., pp. 804–849). New York: Macmillan.

Carroll, J. B. (1963). A model of school learning. *Teachers College Record, 64,* 723–733.

Carroll, J. B. (1965). School learning over the long haul. In J. D. Krumboltz (Ed.), *Learning and the educational process* (pp. 249–269). Chicago: Rand McNally.

Carroll, W. R., & Bandura, A. (1982). The role of visual monitoring in observational learning of action patterns: Making the unobservable observable. *Journal of Motor Behavior, 14,* 153–167.

Carver, C. S., & Scheier, M. F. (1982). An information processing perspective on self-management. In P. Karoly & F. H. Kanfer (Eds.), *Self-management and behavior change: From theory to practice* (pp. 93–128). New York: Pergamon.

Case, R. (1978a). A developmentally based theory and technology of instruction. *Review of Educational Research, 48,* 439–463.

Case, R. (1978b). Piaget and beyond: Toward a developmentally based theory and technology of instruction. In R. Glaser (Ed.), *Advances in instructional psychology* (Vol. 1, pp. 167–228). Hillsdale, NJ: Erlbaum.

Case, R. (1981). Intellectual development: A systematic reinterpretation. In F. H. Farley & N. J. Gordon (Eds.), *Psychology and education: The state of the union* (pp. 142–177). Berkeley, CA: McCutchan.

Chapin, M., & Dyck, D. G. (1976). Persistence in children's reading behavior as a function of N length and attribution retraining. *Journal of Abnormal Psychology, 85,* 511–515.

Cherry, E. C. (1953). Some experiments on the recognition of speech with one and two ears. *Journal of the Acoustical Society of America, 25,* 975–979.

Chi, M. T. H., Feltovich, P. J., & Glaser, R. (1981). Categorization and representation of physics problems by experts and novices. *Cognitive Science, 5,* 121–152.

Chi, M. T. H., & Glaser, R. (1985). Problem-solving ability. In R. J. Sternberg (Ed.), *Human abilities: An information-processing approach* (pp. 227–250). New York: Freeman.

Chi, M. T. H., Glaser, R., & Rees, E. (1982). Expertise in problem solving. In R. J. Sternberg (Ed.), *Advances in the psychology of human intelligence* (Vol. 1, pp. 7–75). Hillsdale, NJ: Erlbaum.

Chiesi, H. L., Spilich, G. J., & Voss, J. R. (1979). Acquisition of domain-related information in relation to high and low domain knowledge. *Journal of Verbal Learning and Verbal Behavior, 18,* 257–274.

Chomsky, N. (1957). *Syntactic Structures.* The Hague: Mouton.

Chomsky, N. (1959). Review of Verbal Behavior by B. F. Skinner. *Language, 35,* 26–58.

Clark, H. H., & Clark, E. V. (1977). *Psychology and language: An introduction to psycholinguistics.* New York: Harcourt Brace Jovanovich.

Clark, H. H., & Haviland, S. E. (1977). Psychological processes as linguistic explanation. In R. O. Freedle (Ed.), *Discourse production and comprehension* (pp. 1–40). Norwood, NJ: Ablex.

Clark, R. E. (1983). Reconsidering research on learning from media. *Review of Educational Research, 53,* 445–459.

Clark, R. E., & Salomon, G. (1986). Media in teaching. In M. C. Wittrock (Ed.), *Handbook of research on teaching* (3rd ed., pp. 464–478). New York: Macmillan.

Clements, D. H. (1986). Effects of Logo and CAI environments on cognition and creativity. *Journal of Educational Psychology, 78,* 309–318.

Clements, D. H., & Gullo, D. F. (1984). Effects of computer programming on young children's cognition. *Journal of Educational Psychology, 76,* 1051–1058.

Clements, D. H., & Nastasi, B. K. (1988). Social and cognitive interactions in educational computer environments. *American Educational Research Journal, 25,* 87–106.

Coates, B., & Hartup, W. W. (1969). Age and verbalization in observational learning. *Developmental Psychology, 1,* 556–562.

Coburn, P., Kelman, P., Roberts, N., Snyder, T. F. F., Watt, D. H., & Weiner, C. (1985). *Practical guide to computers in education* (2nd ed.). Reading, MA: Addison-Wesley.

Cofer, C. N., Bruce, D. R., & Reicher, G. M. (1966). Clustering in free recall as a function of certain methodological variations. *Journal of Experimental Psychology, 71,* 858–866.

Collins, A. (1977). Processes in acquiring knowledge. In R. C. Anderson, R. J. Spiro, & W. E. Montague (Eds.), *Schooling and the acquisition of knowledge* (pp. 339–363). Hillsdale, NJ: Erlbaum.

Collins, A., & Loftus, E. F. (1975). A spreading-activation theory of semantic processing. *Psychological Review, 82,* 407–428.

Collins, A., & Quillian, M. R. (1969). Retrieval time from semantic memory. *Journal of Verbal Learning and Verbal Behavior, 8,* 240–247.

Collins, A., & Stevens, A. L. (1983). A cognitive theory of inquiry teaching. In C. M. Reigeluth (Ed.), *Instructional-design theories and models: An overview of their current status* (pp. 247–278). Hillsdale, NJ: Erlbaum.

Collins, J. L. (1982, March). *Self-efficacy and ability in achievement behavior.* Paper presented at the annual meeting of the American Educational Research Association, New York.

Cooper, A. J. R., & Monk, A. (1976). Learning for recall and learning for recognition. In J. Brown (Ed.), *Recall and recognition* (pp. 131–156). London: Wiley.

Cooper, L. A., & Shepard, R. N. (1973). Chronometric studies of the rotation of mental images. In W. G. Chase (Ed.), *Visual information processing* (pp. 95–176). New York: Academic Press.

Cooper, W. H. (1983). An achievement motivation nomological network. *Journal of Personality and Social Psychology, 44,* 841–861.

Corno, L., & Mandinach, E. B. (1983). The role of cognitive engagement in classroom learning and motivation. *Educational Psychologist, 18,* 88–108.

Corno, L., & Snow, R. E. (1986). Adapting teaching to individual differences among learners. In M. C. Wittrock (Ed.), *Handbook of research on teaching* (3rd ed., pp. 605–629). New York: Macmillan.

BIBLIOGRAPHY

Covington, M. V. (1983). Motivated cognitions. In S. G. Paris, G. M. Olson, & H. W. Stevenson (Eds.), *Learning and motivation in the classroom* (pp. 139–164). Hillsdale, NJ: Erlbaum.

Covington, M. V. (1984). The self-worth theory of achievement motivation: Findings and implications. *Elementary School Journal, 85,* 5–20.

Covington, M. V., & Beery, R. G. (1976). *Self-worth and school learning.* New York: Holt, Rinehart & Winston.

Covington, M. V., & Omelich, C. L. (1979). Effort: The double-edged sword in school achievement. *Journal of Educational Psychology, 71,* 688–700.

Craik, F. I. M. (1979). Human memory. *Annual Review of Psychology, 30,* 63–102.

Craik, F. I. M., & Lockhart, R. S. (1972). Levels of processing: A framework for memory research. *Journal of Verbal Learning and Verbal Behavior, 11,* 671–684.

Craik, F. I. M., & Tulving, E. (1975). Depth of processing and the retention of words in episodic memory. *Journal of Experimental Psychology: General, 104,* 268–294.

Crespi, L. P. (1942). Quantitative variation of incentive and performance in the white rat. *American Journal of Psychology, 55,* 467–517.

Cronbach, L. J., & Snow, R. E. (1977). *Aptitudes and instructional methods.* New York: Irvington/Naiburg.

Crouse, J. H. (1971). Retroactive interference in reading prose materials. *Journal of Educational Psychology, 52,* 39–44.

Cuny, H. (1965). *Pavlov: The man and his theories* (P. Evans, Trans.). New York: Paul S. Eriksson, Inc.

Curtis, M. E. (1980). Development of components of reading skill. *Journal of Educational Psychology, 72,* 656–669.

Dansereau, D. F. (1978). The development of a learning strategies curriculum. In H. F. O'Neil, Jr. (Ed.), *Learning strategies* (pp. 1–29). New York: Academic Press.

Dansereau, D. F. (1988). Cooperative learning strategies. In C. E. Weinstein, E. T. Goetz, & P. A. Alexander (Eds.), *Learning and study strategies: Issues in assessment, instruction, and evaluation* (pp. 103–120). San Diego: Academic Press.

Dansereau, D. F., McDonald, B. A., Collins, K. W., Garland, J., Holley, C. D., Diekhoff, G. M., & Evans, S. H. (1979). Evaluation of a learning strategy system. In H. F. O'Neil, Jr., & C. D. Spielberger (Eds.), *Cognitive and affective learning strategies* (pp. 3–43). New York: Academic Press.

Darwin, C. J., Turvey, M. T., & Crowder, R. G. (1972). An auditory analogue of the Sperling partial report procedure: Evidence for brief auditory storage. *Cognitive Psychology, 3,* 255–267.

Davidson, E. S., & Smith, W. P. (1982). Imitation, social comparison, and self-reward. *Child Development, 53,* 928–932.

de Beaugrande, R. (1984). *Text production: Toward a science of composition.* Norwood, NJ: Ablex.

de Charms, R. (1968). *Personal causation: The internal affective determinants of behavior.* New York: Academic Press.

de Charms, R. (1976). *Enhancing motivation: Change in the classroom.* New York: Irvington.

Deci, E. L. (1975). *Intrinsic motivation.* New York: Plenum.

Deci, E. L. (1980). *The psychology of self-determination.* Lexington, MA: D. C. Heath.

BIBLIOGRAPHY

Deci, E. L., & Porac, J. (1978). Cognitive evaluation theory and the study of human motivation. In M. R. Lepper & D. Greene (Eds.), *The hidden costs of reward: New perspectives on the psychology of human motivation* (pp. 149–176). Hillsdale, NJ: Erlbaum.

Denney, D. R. (1975). The effects of exemplary and cognitive models and self-rehearsal on children's interrogative strategies. *Journal of Experimental Child Psychology, 19*, 476–488.

Denney, N. W., & Turner, M. C. (1979). Facilitating cognitive performance in children: A comparison of strategy modeling and strategy modeling with overt self-verbalization. *Journal of Experimental Child Psychology, 28*, 119–131.

Dewey, J. (1896). The reflex arc concept in psychology. *Psychological Review, 3*, 357–370.

Dewey, J. (1900). Psychology and social practice. *Psychological Review, 7*, 105–124.

Diener, C. I., & Dweck, C. S. (1978). An analysis of learned helplessness: Continuous changes in performance, strategy, and achievement cognitions following failure. *Journal of Personality and Social Psychology, 36*, 451–462.

Diener, C. I., & Dweck, C. S. (1980). An analysis of learned helplessness: II. The processing of success. *Journal of Personality and Social Psychology, 39*, 940–952.

Dollard, J., & Miller, N. E. (1950). *Personality and psychotherapy.* New York: McGraw-Hill.

Dowrick, P. W. (1983). Self-modelling. In P. W. Dowrick & S. J. Biggs (Eds.), *Using video: Psychological and social applications* (pp. 105–124). Chichester, England: Wiley.

Duchastel, P. (1979). Learning objectives and the organization of prose. *Journal of Educational Psychology, 71*, 100–106.

Dushastel, P., & Brown, B. R. (1974). Incidental and relevant learning with instructional objectives. *Journal of Educational Psychology, 66*, 481–485.

Duell, O. K. (1986). Metacognitive skills. In G. D. Phye & T. Andre (Eds.), *Cognitive classroom learning: Understanding, thinking, and problem solving* (pp. 205–242). Orlando: Academic Press.

Duncker, K. (1945). On problem-solving (L. S. Lees, Trans.). *Psychological Monographs, 58*(5, Whole No. 270).

Dunham, P. (1977). The nature of reinforcing stimuli. In W. K. Honig & J. E. R. Staddon (Eds.), *Handbook of operant behavior* (pp. 98–124). Englewood Cliffs, NJ: Prentice-Hall.

Dweck, C. S. (1975). The role of expectations and attributions in the alleviation of learned helplessness. *Journal of Personality and Social Psychology, 31*, 674–685.

Dweck, C. S. (1986). Motivational processes affecting learning. *American Psychologist, 41*, 1040–1048.

Dweck, C. S., & Bempechat, J. (1983). Children's theories of intelligence: Consequences for learning. In S. G. Paris, G. M. Olson, & H. W. Stevenson (Eds.), *Learning and motivation in the classroom* (pp. 239–256). Hillsdale, NJ: Erlbaum.

Dweck, C. S., & Leggett, E. L. (1988). A social-cognitive approach to motivation and personality. *Psychological Review, 95*, 256–272.

BIBLIOGRAPHY

Ebbinghaus, H. (1964). *Memory: A contribution to experimental psychology* (H. A. Ruger & C. E. Bussenius, Trans.). New York: Dover. (Original work published 1885)

Eccles, J., & Wigfield, A. (1985). Teacher expectations and student motivation. In J. B. Dusek (Ed.), *Teacher expectancies* (pp. 185–226). Hillsdale, NJ: Erlbaum.

Eggen, P. D., Kauchak, D. P., & Harder, R. J. (1979). *Strategies for teachers: Information processing models in the classroom.* Englewood Cliffs, NJ: Prentice-Hall.

Egger, M. D., & Miller, N. E. (1963). When is a reward reinforcing? An experimental study of the information hypothesis. *Journal of Comparative and Physiological Psychology, 56,* 132–137.

Ellis, S., & Rogoff, B. (1982). The strategies and efficacy of child versus adult teachers. *Child Development, 53,* 730–735.

Elstein, A. S., Shulman, L. S., & Sprafka, S. A. (1978). *Medical problem solving.* Cambridge, MA: Harvard University Press.

Engberg, L. A., Hansen, G., Welker, R. L., & Thomas, D. (1972). Acquisition of key-pecking via autoshaping as a function of prior experience: Learned laziness? *Science, 178,* 1002–1004.

Ennis, R. H. (1987). A taxonomy of critical thinking dispositions and abilities. In J. B. Baron & R. J. Sternberg (Eds.), *Teaching thinking skills: Theory and practice* (pp. 9–26). New York: Freeman.

Estes, W. K. (1944). An experimental study of punishment. *Psychological Monographs, 57*(263).

Estes, W. K. (1970). *Learning theory and mental development.* New York: Academic Press.

Fabricius, W. V., & Hagen, J. W. (1984). Use of causal attributions about recall performance to assess metamemory and predict strategic memory behavior in young children. *Developmental Psychology, 20,* 975–987.

Faw, H. W., & Waller, T. G. (1976). Mathemagenic behaviours and efficiency in learning from prose materials: Review, critique and recommendations. *Review of Educational Research, 46,* 691–720.

Feld, S. (1967). Longitudinal study of the origins of achievement strivings. *Journal of Personality and Social Psychology, 7,* 408–414.

Ferster, C. S., & Skinner, B. F. (1957). *Schedules of reinforcement.* New York: Appleton-Century-Crofts.

Festinger, L. (1954). A theory of social comparison processes. *Human Relations, 7,* 117–140.

Festinger, L. (1957). *A theory of cognitive dissonance.* Stanford, CA: Stanford University Press.

Fincham, F. D., & Cain, K. M. (1986). Learned helplessness in humans: A developmental analysis. *Developmental Review, 6,* 301–333.

Fischler, M. A., & Firschein, O. (1987). *Intelligence: The eye, the brain, and the computer.* Reading, MA: Addison-Wesley.

Fish, M. C., & Pervan, R. (1985). Self-instruction training: A potential tool for school psychologists. *Psychology in the Schools, 22,* 83–92.

Fitts, P. M., & Posner, M. I. (1967). *Human performance.* Belmont, CA: Brooks/Cole.

Fitzgerald, J. (1987). Research on revision in writing. *Review of Educational Research, 57,* 481–506.

Fitzgerald, J., & Markham, L. (1987). Teaching children about revision in writing. *Cognition and Instruction, 4,* 3–24.

Flavell, J. H. (1985). *Cognitive development* (2nd ed.). Englewood Cliffs, NJ: Prentice-Hall.

Flavell, J. H., Beach, D. R., & Chinsky, J. M. (1966). Spontaneous verbal rehearsal in a memory task as a function of age. *Child Development, 37,* 283–299.

Flavell, J. H., Friedrichs, A. G., & Hoyt, J. D. (1970). Developmental changes in memorization processes. *Cognitive Psychology, 1,* 324–340.

Flavell, J. H., & Wellman, H. M. (1977). Metamemory. In R. B. Kail, Jr., & J. W. Hagen (Eds.), *Perspectives on the development of memory and cognition* (pp. 3–33). Hillsdale, NJ: Erlbaum.

Flower, L. (1981). *Problem-solving strategies for writing.* New York: Harcourt Brace Jovanovich.

Flower, L., & Hayes, J. R. (1980). The dynamics of composing: Making plans and juggling constraints. In L. W. Gregg & E. R. Steinberg (Eds.), *Cognitive processes in writing* (pp. 31–50). Hillsdale, NJ: Erlbaum.

Flower, L., & Hayes, J. R. (1981a). A cognitive process theory of writing. *College Composition and Communication, 32,* 365–387.

Flower, L., & Hayes, J. R. (1981b). The pregnant pause: An inquiry into the nature of planning. *Research in the Teaching of English, 15,* 229–243.

Franks, J. J., & Bransford, J. D. (1971). Abstraction of visual patterns. *Journal of Experimental Psychology, 90,* 65–74.

Frauenglass, M. H., & Diaz, R. M. (1985). Self-regulatory functions of children's private speech: A critical analysis of recent challenges to Vygotsky's theory. *Developmental Psychology, 21,* 357–364.

Frederiksen, C. H. (1979). Discourse comprehension and early reading. In L. B. Resnick & P. A. Weaver (Eds.), *Theory and practice of early reading* (Vol. 1, pp. 155–186). Hillsdale, NJ: Erlbaum.

Friedman, D. E., & Medway, F. J. (1987). Effects of varying performance sets and outcome on the expectations, attributions, and persistence of boys with learning disabilities. *Journal of Learning Disabilities, 20,* 312–316.

Frieze, I. H. (1980). Beliefs about success and failure in the classroom. In J. H. McMillan (Ed.), *The social psychology of school learning* (pp. 39–78). New York: Academic Press.

Frieze, I. H., Francis, W. D., & Hanusa, B. H. (1983). Defining success in classroom settings. In J. M. Levine & M. C. Wang (Eds.), *Teacher and student perceptions: Implications for learning* (pp. 3–28). Hillsdale, NJ: Erlbaum.

Frolov, Y. P. (1937). *Pavlov and his school* (C. P. Dutt, Trans.). New York: Oxford University Press.

Fuhrer, M. J., & Baer, P. E. (1965). Differential classical conditioning: Verbalization of stimulus contingencies. *Science, 150,* 1479–1481.

Fuson, K. C. (1979). The development of self-regulating aspects of speech: A review. In G. Zivin (Ed.), *The development of self-regulation through private speech* (pp. 135–217). New York: Wiley.

BIBLIOGRAPHY

Gaa, J. P. (1973). Effects of individual goal-setting conferences on achievement, attitudes, and goal-setting behavior. *Journal of Experimental Education, 42,* 22–28.

Gaa, J. P. (1979). The effects of individual goal-setting conferences on academic achievement and modification of locus of control orientation. *Psychology in the Schools, 16,* 591–597.

Gagné, E. D. (1985). *The cognitive psychology of school learning.* Boston: Little, Brown & Company.

Gagné, R. M. (1984). Learning outcomes and their effects: Useful categories of human performance. *American Psychologist, 39,* 377–385.

Gagné, R. M. (1985). *The conditions of learning* (4th ed.). New York: Holt, Rinehart & Winston.

Gagné, R. M., & Briggs, L. J. (1979). *Principles of instructional design* (2nd ed.). New York: Holt, Rinehart & Winston.

Gagné, R. M., & Dick, W. (1983). Instructional psychology. *Annual Review of Psychology, 34,* 261–295.

Gagné, R. M., & Glaser, R. (1987). Foundations in learning research. In R. M. Gagné (Ed.), *Instructional technology: Foundations* (pp. 49–83). Hillsdale, NJ: Erlbaum.

Garcia, J., & Garcia y Robertson, R. (1985). Evolution of learning mechanisms. In B. L. Hammonds (Ed.), *Psychology and learning: Master lecture series* (Vol. 4, pp. 191–243). Washington, DC: American Psychological Association.

Garcia, J., & Koelling, R. A. (1966). Relation of cue to consequence in avoidance learning. *Psychonomic Science, 4,* 123–124.

Garner, R., & Reis, R. (1981). Monitoring and resolving comprehension obstacles: An investigation of spontaneous text lookbacks among upper-grade good and poor comprehenders. *Reading Research Quarterly, 16,* 569–582.

Gick, M. L., & Holyoak, K. J. (1980). Analogical problem solving. *Cognitive Psychology, 12,* 306–355.

Gick, M. L., & Holyoak, K. J. (1983). Schema induction and analogical transfer. *Cognitive Psychology, 15,* 1–38.

Gitomer, D. H., & Glaser, R. (1987). If you don't know it work on it: Knowledge, self-regulation and instruction. In R. E. Snow & M. J. Farr (Eds.), *Aptitude, learning, and instruction* (Vol. 3, pp. 301–325). Hillsdale, NJ: Erlbaum.

Glover, J. A., Plake, B. S., Roberts, B., Zimmer, J. W., & Palmere, M. (1981). Distinctiveness of encoding: The effects of paraphrasing and drawing inferences on memory from prose. *Journal of Educational Psychology, 73,* 736–744.

Glynn, S. M., Britton, B. K., Muth, K. D., & Dogan, N. (1982). Writing and revising persuasive documents. *Journal of Educational Psychology, 74,* 557–567.

Goble, F. G. (1970). *The third force: The psychology of Abraham Maslow.* New York: Grossman.

Goldberg, R. A., Schwartz, S., & Stewart, M. (1977). Individual differences in cognitive processes. *Journal of Educational Psychology, 69,* 9–14.

Goldfried, M. R., Linehan, M. M., & Smith, J. L. (1978). Reduction of test anxiety through cognitive restructuring. *Journal of Consulting and Clinical Psychology, 46,* 32–39.

Gollub, L. (1977). Conditioned reinforcement: Schedule effects. In W. K. Honig & J. E. R. Staddon (Eds.), *Handbook of operant behavior* (pp. 288–312). Englewood Cliffs, NJ: Prentice-Hall.

Good, T. L., & Brophy, J. E. (1984). *Looking in classrooms* (3rd ed.). New York: Harper & Row.

Grabe, M. (1986). Attentional processes in education. In G. D. Phye & T. Andre (Eds.), *Cognitive classroom learning: Understanding, thinking, and problem solving* (pp. 49–82). Orlando: Academic Press.

Gray, C. R., & Gummerman, K. (1975). The enigmatic eidetic image: A critical examination of methods, data, and theories. *Psychological Bulletin, 82,* 383–407.

Greeno, J. G. (1980). Trends in the theory of knowledge for problem solving. In D. Tuma & F. Reif (Eds.), *Problem solving and education: Issues in teaching and research* (pp. 9–23). Hillsdale, NJ: Erlbaum.

Groen, G., & Parkman, J. M. (1972). A chronometric analysis of simple addition. *Psychological Review, 79,* 329–343.

Groen, G., & Resnick, L. B. (1977). Can preschool children invent additional algorithms? *Journal of Educational Psychology, 69,* 645–652.

Guthrie, E. R. (1930). Conditioning as a principle of learning. *Psychological Review, 37,* 412–428.

Guthrie, E. R. (1938). *The psychology of human conflict.* New York: Harper & Brothers.

Guthrie, E. R. (1940). Association and the law of effect. *Psychological Review, 47,* 127–148.

Guthrie, E. R. (1942). Conditioning: A theory of learning in terms of stimulus, response, and association. In N. B. Henry (Ed.), *The psychology of learning: The forty-first yearbook of the National Society for the Study of Education* (Part II, pp. 17–60). Chicago: University of Chicago Press.

Guthrie, E. R. (1952). *The psychology of learning* (Rev. ed.). New York: Harper & Brothers.

Guthrie, E. R. (1959). Association by contiguity. In S. Koch (Ed.), *Psychology: A study of a science* (Vol. 2, pp. 158–195). New York: McGraw-Hill.

Guthrie, E. R., & Horton, G. P. (1946). *Cats in a puzzle box.* New York: Rinehart & Company.

Hallahan, D. P., Kneedler, R. D., & Lloyd, J. W. (1983). Cognitive behavior modification techniques for learning disabled children: Self-instruction and self-monitoring. In J. D. McKinney & L. Feagans (Eds.), *Current topics in learning disabilities* (Vol. 1, pp. 207–244). Norwood, NJ: Ablex.

Hamilton, R. J. (1985). A framework for the evaluation of the effectiveness of adjunct questions and objectives. *Review of Educational Research, 55,* 47–85.

Hannafin, M. J., & Peck, K. L. (1988). *The design, development, and evaluation of instructional software.* New York: Macmillan.

Harari, O., & Covington, M. V. (1981). Reactions to achievement behavior from a teacher and student perspective: A developmental analysis. *American Educational Research Journal, 18,* 15–28.

Harlow, H. F., & Harlow, M. K. (1966). Learning to love. *American Scientist, 54,* 244–272.

BIBLIOGRAPHY

Harris, B. (1979). Whatever happened to Little Albert? *American Psychologist, 34,* 151–160.

Harris, K. R. (1982). Cognitive-behavior modification: Application with exceptional students. *Focus on Exceptional Children, 15,* 1–16.

Hartup, W. W., & Lougee, M. D. (1975). Peers as models. *School Psychology Digest, 4,* 11–21.

Haviland, S. E., & Clark, H. H. (1974). What's new? Acquiring new information as a process in comprehension. *Journal of Verbal Learning and Verbal Behavior, 13,* 512–521.

Hayes, J. R., & Flower, L. (1980). Identifying the organization of writing processes. In L. W. Gregg & E. R. Steinberg (Eds.), *Cognitive processes in writing* (pp. 3–30). Hillsdale, NJ: Erlbaum.

Hayes-Roth, B., & Thorndyke, P. W. (1979). Integration of knowledge from text. *Journal of Verbal Learning and Verbal Behavior, 18,* 91–108.

Heidbreder, E. (1933). *Seven psychologies.* New York: Appleton-Century-Crofts.

Heider, F. (1946). Attitudes and cognitive organization. *Journal of Psychology, 21,* 107–112.

Heider, F. (1958). The psychology of interpersonal relations. New York: Wiley.

Higgins, E. T. (1981). Role taking and social judgment: Alternative developmental perspectives and processes. In J. H. Flavell & L. Ross (Eds.), *Social cognitive development: Frontiers and possible futures* (pp. 119–153). Cambridge, England: Cambridge University Press.

Hoffman, L. W. (1974). Fear of success in males and females: 1965 and 1971. *Journal of Consulting and Clinical Psychology, 42,* 353–358.

Holland, J. G., & Skinner, B. F. (1961). *The analysis of behavior.* New York: McGraw-Hill.

Holley, C. D., Dansereau, D. F., McDonald, B. A., Garland, J. C., & Collins, K. W. (1979). Evaluation of a hierarchical mapping technique as an aid to prose processing. *Contemporary Educational Psychology, 4,* 227–237.

Holyoak, K. J. (1984). Mental models in problem solving. In J. R. Anderson & S. M. Kosslyn (Eds.), *Tutorials in learning and memory: Essays in honor of Gordon Bower* (pp. 193–218). San Francisco: Freeman.

Homme, L., Csanyi, A. P., Gonzales, M. A., & Rechs, J. R. (1970). *How to use contingency contracting in the classroom.* Champaign, IL: Research Press.

Horner, M. S. (1972). Toward an understanding of achievement-related conflicts in women. *Journal of Social Issues, 28,* 157–175.

Horner, M. S. (1978). The measurement and behavioral implications of fear of success in women. In J. W. Atkinson & J. O. Raynor (Eds.), *Personality, motivation, and achievement* (pp. 41–70). Washington, DC: Hemisphere.

Hosford, R. E. (1981). Self-as-a-model: A cognitive social learning technique. *The Counseling Psychologist, 9*(1), 45–62.

Hull, C. L. (1932). The goal gradient hypothesis and maze learning. *Psychological Review, 39,* 25–43.

Hull, C. L. (1935). The conflicting psychologies of learning—A way out. *Psychological Review, 42,* 491–516.

Hull, C. L. (1937). Mind, mechanism, and adaptive behavior. *Psychological Review, 44,* 1–32.

BIBLIOGRAPHY

Hull, C. L. (1943). *Principles of behavior: An introduction to behavior theory.* New York: Appleton-Century-Crofts.

Hull, C. L. (1951). *Essentials of behavior.* New Haven, CT: Yale University Press.

Hull, C. L. (1952). *A behavior system: An introduction to behavior theory concerning the individual organism.* New Haven, CT: Yale University Press.

Hull, C. L., Hovland, C. I., Ross, R. T., Hall, M., Perkins, D. T., & Fitch, F. B. (1940). *Mathematico-deductive theory of rote learning: A study in scientific methodology.* New Haven, CT: Yale University Press.

Humphrey, G. (1921). Imitation and the conditioned reflex. *Pedagogical Seminary, 28,* 1–21.

Humphreys, L. G. (1939a). Acquisition and extinction of verbal expectations in a situation analogous to conditioning. *Journal of Experimental Psychology, 25,* 294–301.

Humphreys, L. G. (1939b). The effect of random alternation of reinforcement on the acquisition and extinction of conditioned eyelid reactions. *Journal of Experimental Psychology, 25,* 141–158.

Hunt, J. McV. (1963). Motivation inherent in information processing and action. In O. J. Harvey (Ed.), *Motivation and social interaction* (pp. 35–94). New York: Ronald.

Hunter, M. (1982). *Mastery teaching.* El Segundo, CA: TIP Publications.

Jacoby, L. L., Bartz, W. H., & Evans, J. D. (1978). A functional approach to levels of processing. *Journal of Experimental Psychology: Human Learning and Memory, 4,* 331–346.

Jagacinski, C. M., & Nicholls, J. G. (1984). Conceptions of ability and related affects in task involvement and ego involvement. *Journal of Educational Psychology, 76,* 909–919.

Jagacinski, C. M., & Nicholls, J. G. (1987). Competence and affect in task involvement and ego involvement: The impact of social comparison information. *Journal of Educational Psychology, 79,* 107–114.

James, W. (1890). *The principles of psychology* (Vols. I & II). New York: Henry Holt.

James, W. (1892). *Psychology: Briefer course.* New York: Henry Holt.

Johnson, D. S. (1981). Naturally acquired learned helplessness: The relationship of school failure to achievement behavior, attributions, and self-concept. *Journal of Educational Psychology, 73,* 174–180.

Johnson-Laird, P. N. (1972). The three-term series problem. *Cognition, 1,* 57–82.

Johnson-Laird, P. N. (1985). Deductive reasoning ability. In R. J. Sternberg (Ed.), *Human abilities: An information-processing approach* (pp. 173–194). New York: Freeman.

Just, M. A., & Carpenter, P. A. (1980). A theory of reading: From eye fixations to comprehension. *Psychological Review, 87,* 329–354.

Kagan, J. (1966). Reflection-impulsivity: The generality and dynamics of conceptual tempo. *Journal of Abnormal Psychology, 71,* 17–24.

Kagan, J., Moss, H. A., & Sigel, I. E. (1960). Conceptual style and the use of affect labels. *Merrill-Palmer Quarterly, 6,* 261–278.

Kagan, J., Pearson, L., & Welch, L. (1966). Modifiability of an impulsive tempo. *Journal of Educational Psychology, 57,* 359–365.

Kail, R. B., Jr., & Hagen, J. W. (1982). Memory in childhood. In B. B. Wolman (Ed.), *Handbook of developmental psychology* (pp. 350–366). Englewood Cliffs, NJ: Prentice-Hall.

Kanfer, F. H., & Gaelick, L. (1986). Self-management methods. In F. H. Kanfer & A. P. Goldstein (Eds.), *Helping people change: A textbook of methods* (3rd ed., pp. 283–345). New York: Pergamon.

Kardash, C. A. M., Royer, J. M., & Greene, B. A. (1988). Effects of schemata on both encoding and retrieval of information from prose. *Journal of Educational Psychology, 80,* 324–329.

Karoly, P., & Harris, A. (1986). Operant methods. In F. H. Kanfer & A. P. Goldstein (Eds.), *Helping people change: A textbook of methods* (3rd ed., pp. 111–144). New York: Pergamon.

Karoly, P., & Kanfer, F. H. (1982). *Self-management and behavior change: From theory to practice.* New York: Pergamon.

Katona, G. (1940). *Organizing and memorizing.* New York: Columbia University Press.

Keeney, T. J., Cannizzo, S. R., & Flavell, J. H. (1967). Spontaneous and induced verbal rehearsal in a recall task. *Child Development, 38,* 953–966.

Keller, F. S. (1966). A personal course in psychology. In R. Ulrich, T. Stachnik, & J. Mabry (Eds.), *Control of human behavior* (pp. 91–93). Glenview, IL: Scott, Foresman & Company.

Keller, F. S. (1968). Good-bye, teacher. . . . *Journal of Applied Behavior Analysis, 1,* 79–89.

Keller, F. S. (1977). *Summers and sabbaticals: Selected papers on psychology and education.* Champaign, IL: Research Press.

Keller, F. S., & Ribes-Inesta, E. (1974). *Behavior modification: Applications to education.* New York: Academic Press.

Keller, F. S., & Schoenfeld, W. N. (1950). *Principles of psychology: A systematic text in the science of behavior.* New York: Appleton-Century-Crofts.

Keller, F. S., & Sherman, J. G. (1974). *The Keller Plan handbook.* Menlo Park, CA: W. A. Benjamin.

Kerst, S. M., & Howard, J. H., Jr. (1977). Mental comparisons for ordered information on abstract and concrete dimensions. *Memory & Cognition, 5,* 227–234.

Kintsch, W. (1974). *The representation of meaning in memory.* Hillsdale, NJ: Erlbaum.

Kintsch, W. (1979). On modeling comprehension. *Educational Psychologist, 14,* 3–14.

Kintsch, W., & van Dijk, T. A. (1978). Toward a model of text comprehension and production. *Psychological Review, 85,* 363–394.

Kirkland, K., & Hollandsworth, J. G. (1980). Effective test taking: Skills-acquisition versus anxiety-reduction techniques. *Journal of Consulting and Clinical Psychology, 48,* 431–439.

Klatzky, R. L. (1980). *Human memory: Structures and processes* (2nd ed.). New York: Freeman.

Klausmeier, H. J., Rossmiller, R. A., & Saily, M. (1977). *Individually guided elementary education: Concepts and practices.* New York: Academic Press.

Koch, S. (1954). Clark L. Hull. In W. K. Estes et al. (Eds.), *Modern learning theory* (pp. 1–176). New York: Appleton-Century-Crofts.

Koffka, K. (1922). Perception: An introduction to the Gestalt-theorie. *Psychological Bulletin, 19,* 531–585.

BIBLIOGRAPHY

Koffka, K. (1924). *The growth of the mind* (R. M. Ogden, Trans.). London: Kegan Paul, Trench, Trubner.

Koffka, K. (1926). Mental development. In C. Murchison (Ed.), *Psychologies of 1925* (pp. 129–143). Worcester, MA: Clark University Press.

Kohler, W. (1925). *The mentality of apes* (E. Winter, Trans.). New York: Harcourt, Brace & World.

Kohler, W. (1926). An aspect of Gestalt psychology. In C. Murchinson (Ed.), *Psychologies of 1925* (pp. 163–195). Worcester, MA: Clark University Press.

Kohler, W. (1947). *Gestalt psychology: An introduction to new concepts in modern psychology.* New York: Liveright. (Reprinted 1959, New American Library, New York)

Kosiewicz, M. M., Hallahan, D. P., Lloyd, J., & Graves, A. W. (1982). Effects of self-instruction and self-correction procedures on handwriting performance. *Learning Disability Quarterly, 5*, 71–78.

Kosslyn, S. M. (1980). *Image and mind.* Cambridge, MA: Harvard University Press.

Kosslyn, S. M. (1984). Mental representation. In J. R. Anderson & S. M. Kosslyn (Eds.), *Tutorials in learning and memory: Essays in honor of Gordon Bower* (pp. 91–117). San Francisco: Freeman.

Kosslyn, S. M., & Pomerantz, J. P. (1977). Imagery, propositions, and the form of internal representations. *Cognitive Psychology, 9*, 52–76.

Kramer, J. J., & Engle, R. W. (1981). Teaching awareness of strategic behavior in combination with strategy training: Effects on children's memory performance. *Journal of Experimental Child Psychology, 32*, 513–530.

Kuhl, J., & Blankenship, V. (1979a). Behavioral change in a constant environment: Shift to more difficult tasks with constant probability of success. *Journal of Personality and Social Psychology, 37*, 549–561.

Kuhl, J., & Blankenship, V. (1979b). The dynamic theory of achievement motivation: From episodic to dynamic thinking. *Psychological Review, 86*, 141–151.

Kulik, J. A., Kulik, C. C., & Cohen, P. A. (1979). A meta-analysis of outcome studies of Keller's Personalized System of Instruction. *American Psychologist, 34*, 307–318.

Kulik, J. A., Kulik, C. C., & Cohen, P. A. (1980). Effectiveness of computer-based college teaching: A meta-analysis of findings. *Review of Educational Research, 50*, 525–544.

Lange, P. C. (1972). What's the score on: Programmed instruction? *Today's Education, 61*, 59.

Langer, J. A., & Applebee, A. N. (1986). Reading and writing instruction: Toward a theory of teaching and learning. In E. Z. Rothkopf (Ed.), *Review of research in education* (Vol. 13, pp. 171–194). Washington, DC: American Educational Research Association.

Larkin, J. H. (1980). Teaching problem solving in physics: The psychological laboratory and the practical classroom. In D. Tuma & F. Reif (Eds.), *Problem solving and education: Issues in teaching and research* (pp. 111–125). Hillsdale, NJ: Erlbaum.

Larkin, J. H., McDermott, J., Simon, D. P., & Simon, H. A. (1980). Models of competence in solving physics problems. *Cognitive Science, 4*, 317–345.

Leask, J., Haber, R. N., & Haber, R. B. (1969). Eidetic imagery in children: II. Longitudinal and experimental results. *Psychonomic Monograph Supplement, 3* (3, Whole No. 35).

Leeper, R. (1935). A study of a neglected portion of the field of learning—The development of sensory organization. *Pedagogical Seminary and Journal of Genetic Psychology, 46,* 41–75.

Lefcourt, H. M. (1976). *Locus of control: Current trends in theory and research.* Hillsdale, NJ: Erlbaum.

Lenneberg, E. H. (1967). *The biological foundations of language.* New York: Wiley.

Lepper, M. R. (1983). Extrinsic reward and intrinsic motivation: Implications for the classroom. In J. M. Levine & M. C. Wang (Eds.), *Teacher and student perceptions: Implications for learning* (pp. 281–317). Hillsdale, NJ: Erlbaum.

Lepper, M. R. (1985). Microcomputers in education: Motivational and social issues. *American Psychologist, 40,* 1–18.

Lepper, M. R., & Greene, D. (1978). Overjustification research and beyond: Toward a means-ends analysis of intrinsic and extrinsic motivation. In M. R. Lepper & D. Greene (Eds.), *The hidden costs of reward: New perspectives on the psychology of human motivation* (pp. 109–148). Hillsdale, NJ: Erlbaum.

Lepper, M. R., Greene, D., & Nisbett, R. E. (1973). Undermining children's intrinsic interest with extrinsic rewards: A test of the "overjustification" hypothesis. *Journal of Personality and Social Psychology, 28,* 129–137.

Lesgold, A. M. (1984). Acquiring expertise. In J. R. Anderson & S. M. Kosslyn (Eds.), *Tutorials in learning and memory: Essays in honor of Gordon Bower* (pp. 31–60). San Francisco: Freeman.

Licht, B. G., & Kistner, J. A. (1986). Motivational problems of learning-disabled children: Individual differences and their implications for treatment. In J. K. Torgesen & B. W. L. Wong (Eds.), *Psychological and educational perspectives on learning disabilities* (pp. 225–255). Orlando: Academic Press.

Lindsay, P. H., & Norman, D. A. (1977). *Human information processing* (2nd ed.). New York: Academic Press.

Locke, E. A., Shaw, K. N., Saari, L. M., & Latham, G. P. (1981). Goal setting and task performance: 1969–1980. *Psychological Bulletin, 90,* 125–152.

Lockhart, R. S., Craik, F. I. M., & Jacoby, L. (1976). Depth of processing, recognition and recall. In J. Brown (Ed.), *Recall and recognition* (pp. 75–102). London: Wiley.

Lodico, M. G., Ghatala, E. S., Levin, J. R., Pressley, M., & Bell, J. A. (1983). The effects of strategy-monitoring training on children's selection of effective memory strategies. *Journal of Experimental Child Psychology, 35,* 263–277.

Logan, F. A. (1959). The Hull-Spence approach. In S. Koch (Ed.), *Psychology: A study of a science* (Vol. 2, pp. 293–358). New York: McGraw-Hill.

Logan, F. A. (1976). *Fundamentals of learning and motivation* (2nd ed.). Dubuque, IA: William C. Brown Company.

Lovaas, O. I. (1977). *The autistic child: Language development through behavior modification.* New York: Irvington.

Luchins, A. S. (1942). Mechanization in problem solving: The effect of Einstellung. *Psychological Monographs, 54*(6, Whole No. 248).

Luiten, J., Ames, W., & Ackerson, G. (1980). A meta-analysis of the effects of advance organizers on learning and retention. *American Educational Research Journal, 17,* 211–218.

Luria, A. R. (1961). *The role of speech in the regulation of normal and abnormal behavior* (J. Tizard, Trans.). New York: Liveright.

MacCorquodale, K. (1970). On Chomsky's review of Skinner's Verbal Behavior. *Journal of the Experimental Analysis of Behavior, 13,* 83–99.

MacCorquodale, K., & Meehl, P. E. (1954). Edward C. Tolman. In W. K. Estes et al. (Eds.), *Modern learning theory* (pp. 177–266). New York: Appleton-Century-Crofts.

Mace, F. C., Belfiore, P. J., & Shea, M. C. (1989). Operant theory and research on self-regulation. In B. J. Zimmerman & D. H. Schunk (Eds.), *Self-regulated learning and academic achievement: Theory, research, and practice* (pp. 27–50). New York: Springer-Verlag.

Mace, F. C., & Kratochwill, T. R. (1988). Self-monitoring: Applications and issues. In J. Witt, S. Elliott, & F. Gresham (Eds.), *Handbook of behavior therapy in education* (pp. 489–502). New York: Pergamon.

Mace, F. C., & West, B. J. (1986). Unresolved theoretical issues in self-management: Implications for research and practice. *Professional School Psychology, 1,* 149–163.

Mager, R. (1962). *Preparing instructional objectives.* Palo Alto, CA: Fearon.

Maier, S. F., & Seligman, M. E. P. (1976). Learned helplessness: Theory and evidence. *Journal of Experimental Psychology, 105,* 3–46.

Mandler, J. M. (1978). A code in the node: The use of a story schema in retrieval. *Discourse Processes, 1,* 14–35.

Mandler, J. M., & Johnson, N. S. (1976). Some of the thousand words a picture is worth. *Journal of Experimental Psychology: Human Learning and Memory, 2,* 529–540.

Mandler, J. M., & Ritchey, G. H. (1977). Long-term memory for pictures. *Journal of Experimental Psychology: Human Learning and Memory, 3,* 386–396.

Martin, J. (1980). External versus self-reinforcement: A review of methodological and theoretical issues. *Canadian Journal of Behavioural Science, 12,* 111–125.

Maslow, A. H. (1968). *Toward a psychology of being* (2nd ed.). New York: Van Nostrand Reinhold.

Maslow, A. H. (1970). *Motivation and personality* (2nd ed.). New York: Harper & Row.

Mayer, R. E. (1979). Can advance organizers influence meaningful learning? *Review of Educational Research, 49,* 371–383.

Mayer, R. E. (1982). Memory for algebra story problems. *Journal of Educational Psychology, 74,* 199–216.

Mayer, R. E. (1983). *Thinking, problem solving, cognition.* New York: Freeman.

Mayer, R. E. (1984). Aids to text comprehension. *Educational Psychologist, 19,* 30–42.

Mayer, R. E. (1985). Mathematical ability. In R. J. Sternberg (Ed.), *Human abilities: An information-processing approach* (pp. 127–150). New York: Freeman.

McClelland, D. C., Atkinson, J. W., Clark, R. A., & Lowell, E. L. (1953). *The achievement motive.* New York: Appleton-Century-Crofts.

McCloskey, M., & Kaiser, M. (1984). The impetus impulse: A medieval theory of motion lives on in the minds of children. *The Sciences, 24,* 40–45.

McCutchen, D., & Perfetti, C. A. (1982). Coherence and connectedness in the development of discourse production. *Text, 2,* 113–139.

McDougall, W. (1926). *An introduction to social psychology* (Rev. ed.). Boston: John W. Luce.

McNeil, J. D. (1987). *Reading comprehension: New directions for classroom practice* (2nd ed.). Glenview, IL: Scott, Foresman & Company.

Meichenbaum, D. (1977). *Cognitive behavior modification: An integrative approach.* New York: Plenum.

Meichenbaum, D. (1986). Cognitive behavior modification. In F. H. Kanfer & A. P. Goldstein (Eds.), *Helping people change: A textbook of methods* (3rd ed., pp. 346–380). New York: Pergamon.

Meichenbaum, D., & Asarnow, J. (1979). Cognitive-behavior modification and metacognitive development: Implications for the classroom. In P. C. Kendall & S. D. Hollon (Eds.), *Cognitive behavioral interventions: Theory, research, and procedures* (pp. 11–35). New York: Academic Press.

Meichenbaum, D., & Goodman, J. (1971). Training impulsive children to talk to themselves: A means of developing self-control. *Journal of Abnormal Psychology, 77,* 115–126.

Merrill, M. D., Reigeluth, C. M., & Faust, G. W. (1979). The Instructional Quality Profile: A curriculum evaluation and design tool. In H. F. O'Neil, Jr. (Ed.), *Procedures for instructional systems development* (pp. 165–204). New York: Academic Press.

Merrill, M. D., Richards, R. E., Schmidt, R. V., & Wood, N. D. (1977). *The instructional strategy diagnostic profile: Training manual.* San Diego: Courseware, Inc.

Merrill, P. F. (1987). Job and task analysis. In R. M. Gagné (Ed.), *Instructional technology: Foundations* (pp. 141–173). Hillsdale, NJ: Erlbaum.

Messer, S. (1970). Reflection-impulsivity: Stability and school failure. *Journal of Educational Psychology, 61,* 487–490.

Messick, S. (1976). *Individuality in learning: Implications of cognitive styles and creativity for human development.* San Francisco: Jossey-Bass.

Meyer, B. J. F. (1975). *The organization of prose and its effects on memory.* Amsterdam: North-Holland Publishing.

Meyer, B. J. F. (1977). The structure of prose: Effects on learning and memory and implications for educational practice. In R. C. Anderson, R. J. Spiro, & W. E. Montague (Eds.), *Schooling and the acquisition of knowledge* (pp. 179–200). Hillsdale, NJ: Erlbaum.

Meyer, B. J. F. (1984). Text dimensions and cognitive processing. In H. Mandl, N. L. Stein, & T. Trabasso (Eds.), *Learning and comprehension of text* (pp. 3–47). Hillsdale, NJ: Erlbaum.

Meyer, B. J. F., Brandt, D. M., & Bluth, G. J. (1980). Use of the top-level structure in text: Key for reading comprehension of ninth-grade students. *Reading Research Quarterly, 16,* 72–103.

Meyer, D. E., & Schvaneveldt, R. W. (1971). Facilitation in recognizing pairs of words: Evidence of a dependence between retrieval operations. *Journal of Experimental Psychology, 90,* 227–234.

BIBLIOGRAPHY

Miller, G. A. (1956). The magical number seven, plus or minus two: Some limits on our capacity for processing information. *Psychological Review, 63,* 81–97.

Miller, G. A., Galanter, E., & Pribham, K. H. (1960). *Plans and the structure of behavior.* New York: Holt, Rinehart & Winston.

Miller, N. E., & Dollard, J. (1941). *Social learning and imitation.* New Haven, CT: Yale University Press.

Monty, R. A., & Perlmuter, L. C. (1987). Choice, control, and motivation in the young and aged. In M. L. Maehr & D. A. Kleiber (Eds.), *Advances in motivation and achievement* (Vol. 5, pp. 99–122). Greenwich, CT: JAI Press.

Moray, N., Bates, A., & Barnett, T. (1965). Experiments on the four-eared man. *Journal of the Acoustical Society of America, 38,* 196–201.

Morris, C. D., Bransford, J. D., & Franks, J. J. (1977). Levels of processing versus transfer-appropriate processing. *Journal of Verbal Learning and Verbal Behavior, 16,* 519–533.

Morse, W. H., & Kelleher, R. T. (1977). Determinants of reinforcement and punishment. In W. K. Honig & J. E. R. Staddon (Eds.), *Handbook of operant behavior* (pp. 174–200). Englewood Cliffs, NJ: Prentice-Hall.

Mosatche, H. S., & Bragonier, P. (1981). An observational study of social comparison in preschoolers. *Child Development, 52,* 376–378.

Moscovitch, M., & Craik, F. I. M. (1976). Depth of processing, retrieval cues, and uniqueness of encoding as factors in recall. *Journal of Verbal Learning and Verbal Behavior, 15,* 447–458.

Mueller, C. G. (1979). Some origins of psychology as science. *Annual Review of Psychology, 30,* 9–29.

Mueller, C. G., & Schoenfeld, W. N. (1954). Edwin R. Guthrie. In W. K. Estes et al. (Eds.), *Modern learning theory* (pp. 345–379). New York: Appleton-Century-Crofts.

Murray, H. A. (1936). Techniques for a systematic investigation of fantasy. *Journal of Psychology, 3,* 115–143.

Murray, H. A. (1938). *Explorations in personality.* New York: Oxford University Press.

Muth, K. D., Glynn, S. M., Britton, B. K., & Graves, M. F. (1988). Thinking out loud while studying text: Rehearsing key ideas. *Journal of Educational Psychology, 80,* 315–318.

Myers, M., II, & Paris, S. G. (1978). Children's metacognitive knowledge about reading. *Journal of Educational Psychology, 70,* 680–690.

Neisser, U. (1967). *Cognitive psychology.* Englewood Cliffs, NJ: Prentice-Hall.

Nelson, R. O., & Hayes, S. C. (1981). Theoretical explanations for reactivity in self-monitoring. *Behavior Modification, 5,* 3–14.

Nelson, T. O. (1977). Repetition and depth of processing. *Journal of Verbal Learning and Verbal Behavior, 16,* 151–171.

Newell, A., & Simon, H. A. (1972). *Human problem solving.* Englewood Cliffs, NJ: Prentice-Hall.

Nicholls, J. G. (1978). The development of the concepts of effort and ability, perception of academic attainment, and the understanding that difficult tasks require more ability. *Child Development, 49,* 800–814.

Nicholls, J. G. (1979). Development of perception of own attainment and causal attribution for success and failure in reading. *Journal of Educational Psychology, 71*, 94–99.

Nicholls, J. G. (1983). Conceptions of ability and achievement motivation: A theory and its implications for education. In S. G. Paris, G. M. Olson, & H. W. Stevenson (Eds.), *Learning and motivation in the classroom* (pp. 211–237). Hillsdale, NJ: Erlbaum.

Nicholls, J. G., & Miller, A. T. (1984). Reasoning about the ability of self and others: A developmental study. *Child Development, 55*, 1990–1999.

Nolen-Hoeksema, S., Girgus, J. S., & Seligman, M. E. P. (1986). Learned helplessness in children: A longitudinal study of depression, achievement, and explanatory style. *Journal of Personality and Social Psychology, 51*, 435–442.

Norman, D. A. (1976). *Memory and attention: An introduction to human information processing* (2nd ed.). New York: Wiley.

Norman, D. A., & Rumelhart, D. E. (1975). *Explorations in cognition.* San Francisco: Freeman.

O'Day, E. F., Kulhavy, R. W., Anderson, W., & Malczynski, R. J. (1971). *Programmed instruction: Techniques and trends.* New York: Appleton-Century-Crofts.

O'Leary, K. D., & Drabman, R. (1971). Token reinforcement programs in the classroom: A review. *Psychological Bulletin, 75*, 379–398.

O'Leary, S. G., & Dubey, D. R. (1979). Applications of self-control procedures by children: A review. *Journal of Applied Behavior Analysis, 12*, 449–466.

Ollendick, T. H., & Hersen, M. (1984). *Child behavioral assessment: Principles and procedures.* New York: Pergamon.

Osborn, A. F. (1963). *Applied imagination.* New York: Scribner's.

O'Shea, T., & Self, J. (1983). *Learning and teaching with computers: Artificial intelligence in education.* Englewood Cliffs, NJ: Prentice-Hall.

Paivio, A. (1970). On the functional significance of imagery. *Psychological Bulletin, 73*, 385–392.

Paivio, A. (1971). *Imagery and verbal processes.* New York: Holt, Rinehart & Winston.

Paivio, A. (1978). Mental comparisons involving abstract attributes. *Memory & Cognition, 6*, 199–208.

Palincsar, A. S., & Brown, A. L. (1984). Reciprocal teaching of comprehension-fostering and comprehension-monitoring activities. *Cognition and Instruction, 1*, 117–175.

Palmer, D. J., Drummond, F., Tollison, P., & Zinkgraff, S. (1982). An attributional investigation of performance outcomes for learning-disabled and normal-achieving pupils. *Journal of Special Education, 16*, 207–219.

Papert, S. (1980). *Mindstorms: Children, computers, and powerful ideas.* New York: Basic Books.

Paris, S. G. (1978). Coordination of means and goals in the development of mnemonic skills. In P. A. Ornstein (Ed.), *Memory development in children* (pp. 259–273). Hillsdale, NJ: Erlbaum.

Paris, S. G., Cross, D. R., & Lipson, M. Y. (1984). Informed strategies for learning: A program to improve children's reading awareness and comprehension. *Journal of Educational Psychology, 76,* 1239–1252.

Paris, S. G., Lipson, M. Y., & Wixson, K. K. (1983). Becoming a strategic reader. *Contemporary Educational Psychology, 8,* 293–316.

Paris, S. G., Newman, R. S., & McVey, K. A. (1982). Learning the functional significance of mnemonic actions: A microgenetic study of strategy acquisition. *Journal of Experimental Child Psychology, 34,* 490–509.

Paris, S. G., & Oka, E. R. (1986). Children's reading strategies, metacognition, and motivation. *Developmental Review, 6,* 25–56.

Paris, S. G., Wixson, K. K., & Palincsar, A. S. (1986). Instructional approaches to reading comprehension. In E. Z. Rothkopf (Ed.), *Review of research in education* (Vol. 13, pp. 91–128). Washington, DC: American Educational Research Association.

Park, O., Perez, R. S., & Seidel, R. J. (1987). Intelligent CAI: Old wine in new bottles, or a new vintage? In G. Kearsley (Ed.), *Artificial intelligence and instruction: Applications and methods* (pp. 11–45). Reading, MA: Addison-Wesley.

Pavlov, I. P. (1927). *Conditioned reflexes* (G. V. Anrep, Trans.). London: Oxford University Press.

Pavlov, I. P. (1928). *Lectures on conditioned reflexes* (W. H. Gantt, Trans.). New York: International Publishers.

Pavlov, I. P. (1932a). Neuroses in man and animals. *Journal of the American Medical Association, 99,* 1012–1013.

Pavlov, I. P. (1932b). The reply of a physiologist to psychologists. *Psychological Review, 39,* 91–127.

Pavlov, I. P. (1934). An attempt at a physiological interpretation of obsessional neurosis and paranoia. *Journal of Mental Science, 80,* 187–197.

Pearl, R. A., Bryan, T., & Donahue, M. (1980). Learning disabled children's attributions for success and failure. *Learning Disability Quarterly, 3,* 3–9.

Pellegrino, J. W. (1985). Inductive reasoning ability. In R. J. Sternberg (Ed.), *Human abilities: An information-processing approach* (pp. 195–225). New York: Freeman.

Perfetti, C. A. (1985). Reading ability. In R. J. Sternberg (Ed.), *Human abilities: An information-processing approach* (pp. 59–81). New York: Freeman.

Perfetti, C. A., & Lesgold, A. M. (1979). Coding and comprehension in skilled reading and implications for reading instruction. In L. B. Resnick & P. A. Weaver (Eds.), *Theory and practice of early reading* (pp. 57–84). Hillsdale, NJ: Erlbaum.

Perfetti, C. A., & Roth, S. (1981). Some of the interactive processes in reading and their role in reading skill. In A. M. Lesgold & C. A. Perfetti (Eds.), *Interactive processes in reading* (pp. 269–297). Hillsdale, NJ: Erlbaum.

Perry, D. G., & Bussey, K. (1979). The social learning theory of sex differences: Imitation is alive and well. *Journal of Personality and Social Psychology, 37,* 1699–1712.

Peterson, L. R., & Peterson, M. J. (1959). Short-term retention of individual verbal items. *Journal of Experimental Psychology, 58,* 193–198.

Petri, H. L. (1986). *Motivation: Theory and research* (2nd ed.). Belmont, CA: Wadsworth.

BIBLIOGRAPHY

Phares, E. J. (1976). *Locus of control in personality.* Morristown, NJ: General Learning Press.
Piaget, J. (1962). *Play, dreams and imitation.* New York: Norton.
Pintrich, P. R., Cross, D. R., Kozma, R. B., & McKeachie, W. J. (1986). Instructional psychology. *Annual Review of Psychology, 37,* 611–651.
Plato (1965). *Plato's Meno: Text and criticism* (A. Sesonske & N. Fleming, Eds.). Belmont, CA: Wadsworth.
Polya, G. (1945). *How to solve it.* Princeton, NJ: Princeton University Press. (Reprinted 1957, Doubleday, Garden City, NY)
Posner, M. I., & Keele, S. W. (1968). On the genesis of abstract ideas. *Journal of Experimental Psychology, 77,* 353–363.
Postman, L. (1961). The present status of interference theory. In C. N. Cofer (Ed.), *Verbal learning and verbal behavior* (pp. 152–179). New York: McGraw-Hill.
Postman, L., & Stark, K. (1969). Role of response availability in transfer and interference. *Journal of Experimental Psychology, 79,* 168–177.
Premack, D. (1962). Reversibility of the reinforcement relation. *Science, 136,* 255–257.
Premack, D. (1971). Catching up with common sense or two sides of a generalization: Reinforcement and punishment. In R. Glaser (Ed.), *The nature of reinforcement* (pp. 121–150). New York: Academic Press.
Pressley, M., Levin, J. R., & Delaney, H. D. (1982). The mnemonic keyword method. *Review of Educational Research, 52,* 61–91.
Pylyshyn, Z. W. (1973). What the mind's eye tells the mind's brain: A critique of mental imagery. *Psychological Bulletin, 80,* 1–24.

Quellmalz, E. S. (1987). Developing reasoning skills. In J. B. Baron & R. J. Sternberg (Eds.), *Teaching thinking skills: Theory and practice* (pp. 86–105). New York: Freeman.
Quillian, M. R. (1969). The teachable language comprehender: A simulation program and theory of language. *Communications of the Association for Computing Machinery, 12,* 459–476.

Rachlin, H. (1974). Self-control. *Behaviorism, 2,* 94–107.
Ramsel, D., & Grabe, M. (1983). Attentional allocation and performance in goal-directed reading: Age differences in reading flexibility. *Journal of Reading Behavior, 15,* 55–65.
Ray, J. J. (1982). Achievement motivation and preferred probability of success. *Journal of Social Psychology, 116,* 255–261.
Reder, L. M. (1979). The role of elaborations in memory for prose. *Cognitive Psychology, 11,* 221–234.
Reder, L. M. (1982). Plausibility judgment versus fact retrieval: Alternative strategies for sentence verification. *Psychological Review, 89,* 250–280.
Reese, H. W. (1962). Verbal mediation as a function of age level. *Psychological Bulletin, 59,* 501–509.
Reigeluth, C. M. (1979). In search of a better way to organize instruction: The elaboration theory. *Journal of Instructional Development, 2*(3), 8–15.

BIBLIOGRAPHY

Reigeluth, C. M., & Curtis, R. V. (1987). Learning situations and instructional models. In R. M. Gagné (Ed.), *Instructional technology: Foundations* (pp. 175–206). Hillsdale, NJ: Erlbaum.

Reigeluth, C. M., Merrill, M. D., & Bunderson, C. V. (1978). The structure of subject-matter content and its instructional design implications. *Instructional Science, 7*, 107–126.

Rescorla, R. A. (1972). Informational variables in conditioning. In G. H. Bower (Ed.), *The psychology of learning and motivation* (Vol. 6, pp. 1–46). New York: Academic Press.

Rescorla, R. A. (1976). Pavlovian excitatory and inhibitory conditioning. In W. K. Estes (Ed.), *Handbook of learning and cognitive processes* (Vol. 2, pp. 7–35). Hillsdale, NJ: Erlbaum.

Rescorla, R. A. (1987). A Pavlovian analysis of goal-directed behavior. *American Psychologist, 42*, 119–129.

Resnick, L. B. (1981). Instructional psychology. *Annual Review of Psychology, 32*, 659–704.

Resnick, L. B. (1985). Cognition and instruction: Recent theories of human competence. In B. L. Hammonds (Ed.), *Psychology and learning: The master lecture series* (Vol. 4, pp. 127–186). Washington, DC: American Psychological Association.

Reynolds, R., & Anderson, R. (1982). Influence of questions on the allocation of attention during reading. *Journal of Educational Psychology, 74*, 623–632.

Richter, C. P. (1927). Animal behavior and internal drives. *Quarterly Review of Biology, 2*, 307–343.

Rigney, J. W. (1978). Learning strategies: A theoretical perspective. In H. F. O'Neil, Jr. (Ed.), *Learning strategies* (pp. 165–205). New York: Academic Press.

Rilling, M. (1977). Stimulus control and inhibitory processes. In W. K. Honig & J. E. R. Staddon (Eds.), *Handbook of operant behavior* (pp. 432–480). Englewood Cliffs, NJ: Prentice-Hall.

Ringel, B. A., & Springer, C. J. (1980). On knowing how well one is remembering: The persistence of strategy use during transfer. *Journal of Experimental Child Psychology, 29*, 322–333.

Robin, A. L. (1976). Behavioral instruction in the college classroom. *Review of Educational Research, 46*, 313–354.

Robinson, F. P. (1946). *Effective study*. New York: Harper.

Rohman, D. G. (1965). Pre-writing: The stages of discovery in the writing process. *College Composition and Communication, 16*, 106–112.

Romberg, T. A., & Carpenter, T. P. (1986). Research on teaching and learning mathematics: Two disciplines of scientific inquiry. In M. C. Wittrock (Ed.), *Handbook of research on teaching* (3rd ed., pp. 850–873). New York: Macmillan.

Rose, M. (1980). Rigid rules, inflexible plans, and the stifling of language: A cognitivist analysis of writer's block. *College Composition and Communication, 31*, 389–401.

Rosen, B., & D'Andrade, R. C. (1959). The psychosocial origins of achievement motivation. *Sociometry, 22*, 185–218.

Rosenshine, B., & Stevens, R. (1986). Teaching functions. In M. C. Wittrock (Ed.), *Handbook of research on teaching* (3rd ed., pp. 376–391). New York: Macmillan.

BIBLIOGRAPHY

Rosenthal, T. L., & Bandura, A. (1978). Psychological modeling: Theory and practice. In S. L. Garfield & A. E. Bergin (Eds.), *Handbook of psychotherapy and behavior change: An empirical analysis* (2nd ed., pp. 621–658). New York: Wiley.

Rosenthal, T. L., Moore, W. B., Dorfman, H., & Nelson, B. (1971). Vicarious acquisition of a simple concept with experimenter as model. *Behavior Research and Therapy, 9,* 217–227.

Rosenthal, T. L., & Zimmerman, B. J. (1978). *Social learning and cognition.* New York: Academic Press.

Ross, S. M., McCormick, D., Krisak, N., & Anand, P. (1985). Personalizing context in teaching mathematical concepts: Teacher-managed and computer-assisted models. *Educational Communication and Technology Journal, 33,* 169–178.

Rosswork, S. G. (1977). Goal setting: The effects on an academic task with varying magnitudes of incentive. *Journal of Educational Psychology, 69,* 710–715.

Rotter, J. B. (1954). *Social learning and clinical psychology.* New York: Prentice-Hall.

Rotter, J. B. (1966). Generalized expectancies for internal versus external control of reinforcement. *Psychological Monographs, 80*(1, Whole No. 609).

Rotter, J. B. (1982). *The development and application of social learning theory: Selected papers.* New York: Praeger.

Rotter, J. B., Chance, J. E., & Phares, E. J. (1972). *Applications of a social learning theory of personality.* New York: Holt, Rinehart & Winston.

Ruble, D. N. (1983). The development of social-comparison processes and their role in achievement-related self-socialization. In E. T. Higgins, D. N. Ruble, & W. Hartup (Eds.), *Social cognition and social development* (pp. 134–157). New York: Cambridge University Press.

Ruble, D. N., Boggiano, A. K., Feldman, N. S., & Loebl, J. H. (1980). Developmental analysis of the role of social comparison in self-evaluation. *Developmental Psychology, 16,* 105–115.

Ruble, D. N., Feldman, N. S., & Boggiano, A. K. (1976). Social comparison between young children in achievement situations. *Developmental Psychology, 12,* 191–197.

Rumelhart, D. E. (1975). Notes on a schema for stories. In D. G. Bobrow & A. M. Collins (Eds.), *Representation and understanding: Studies in cognitive science* (pp. 211–236). New York: Academic Press.

Rumelhart, D. E. (1977). Understanding and summarizing brief stories. In D. Laberge & S. J. Samuels (Eds.), *Basic processes in reading* (pp. 265–303). Hillsdale, NJ: Erlbaum.

Rumelhart, D. E., & Ortony, A. (1977). The representation of knowledge in memory. In R. C. Anderson, R. J. Spiro, & W. E. Montague (Eds.), *Schooling and the acquisition of knowledge* (pp. 99–135). Hillsdale, NJ: Erlbaum.

Rundus, D. (1971). Analysis of rehearsal processes in free recall. *Journal of Experimental Psychology, 89,* 63–77.

Rundus, D., & Atkinson, R. C. (1970). Rehearsal processes in free recall: A procedure for direct observation. *Journal of Verbal Learning and Verbal Behavior, 9,* 99–105.

Ryan, B. A. (1974). *Keller's Personalized System of Instruction: An appraisal.* Washington, DC: American Psychological Association.

BIBLIOGRAPHY

Sagotsky, G., Patterson, C. J., & Lepper, M. R. (1978). Training children's self-control: A field experiment in self-monitoring and goal-setting in the classroom. *Journal of Experimental Child Psychology, 25,* 242–253.

Sakitt, B. (1976). Iconic memory. *Psychological Review, 83,* 257–276.

Sakitt, B., & Long, G. M. (1979). Spare the rod and spoil the icon. *Journal of Experimental Psychology: Human Perception and Performance, 5,* 19–30.

Salatas, H., & Flavell, J. H. (1976). Retrieval of recently learned information: Development of strategies and control skills. *Child Development, 47,* 941–948.

Salomon, G. (1984). Television is "easy" and print is "tough": The differential investment of mental effort in learning as a function of perceptions and attributions. *Journal of Educational Psychology, 76,* 647–658.

Scardamalia, M., & Bereiter, C. (1983). The development of evaluative, diagnostic, and remedial capabilities in children's composing. In M. Martlew (Ed.), *The psychology of written language: A developmental approach* (pp. 67–95). London: Wiley.

Scardamalia, M., & Bereiter, C. (1986). Research on written composition. In M. C. Wittrock (Ed.), *Handbook of research on teaching* (3rd ed., pp. 778–803). New York: Macmillan.

Schaffer, L. C., & Hannafin, M. J. (1986). The effects of progressive interactivity on learning from interactive video. *Educational Communication and Technology Journal, 34,* 89–96.

Schunk, D. H. (1981). Modeling and attributional effects on children's achievement: A self-efficacy analysis. *Journal of Educational Psychology, 73,* 93–105.

Schunk, D. H. (1982a). Effects of effort attributional feedback on children's perceived self-efficacy and achievement. *Journal of Educational Psychology, 74,* 548–556.

Schunk, D. H. (1982b). Verbal self-regulation as a facilitator of children's achievement and self-efficacy. *Human Learning, 1,* 265–277.

Schunk, D. H. (1983a). Ability versus effort attributional feedback: Differential effects on self-efficacy and achievement. *Journal of Educational Psychology, 75,* 848–856.

Schunk, D. H. (1983b). Developing children's self-efficacy and skills: The roles of social comparative information and goal setting. *Contemporary Educational Psychology, 8,* 76–86.

Schunk, D. H. (1983c). Progress self-monitoring: Effects on children's self-efficacy and achievement. *Journal of Experimental Education, 51,* 89–93.

Schunk, D. H. (1983d). Reward contingencies and the development of children's skills and self-efficacy. *Journal of Educational Psychology, 75,* 511–518.

Schunk, D. H. (1984). Sequential attributional feedback and children's achievement behaviors. *Journal of Educational Psychology, 76,* 1159–1169.

Schunk, D. H. (1985). Participation in goal setting: Effects on self-efficacy and skills of learning disabled children. *Journal of Special Education, 19,* 307–317.

Schunk, D. H. (1986). Verbalization and children's self-regulated learning. *Contemporary Educational Psychology, 11,* 347–369.

Schunk, D. H. (1987). Peer models and children's behavioral change. *Review of Educational Research, 57,* 149–174.

BIBLIOGRAPHY

Schunk, D. H. (1989). Self-efficacy and cognitive skill learning. In C. Ames & R. Ames (Eds.), *Research on motivation in education. Vol. 3: Goals and cognitions* (pp. 13–44). San Diego: Academic Press.

Schunk, D. H., & Cox, P. D. (1986). Strategy training and attributional feedback with learning disabled students. *Journal of Educational Psychology, 78,* 201–209.

Schunk, D. H., & Gunn, T. P. (1986). Self-efficacy and skill development: Influence of task strategies and attributions. *Journal of Educational Research, 79,* 238–244.

Schunk, D. H., & Hanson, A. R. (1985). Peer models: Influence on children's self-efficacy and achievement. *Journal of Educational Psychology, 77,* 313–322.

Schunk, D. H., Hanson, A. R., & Cox, P. D. (1987). Peer-model attributes and children's achievement behaviors. *Journal of Educational Psychology, 79,* 54–61.

Schunk, D. H., & Rice, J. M. (1986). Extended attributional feedback: Sequence effects during remedial reading instruction. *Journal of Early Adolescence, 6,* 55–66.

Schunk, D. H., & Rice, J. M. (1987). Enhancing comprehension skill and self-efficacy with strategy value information. *Journal of Reading Behavior, 19,* 285–302.

Searle, J. R. (1969). *Speech acts.* Cambridge, England: Cambridge University Press.

Segal, E. (1977). Toward a coherent psychology of language. In W. K. Honig & J. E. R. Staddon (Eds.), *Handbook of operant behavior* (pp. 628–653). Englewood Cliffs, NJ: Prentice-Hall.

Seidel, R. J., Anderson, R. E., & Hunter, B. (1982). *Computer literacy: Issues and directions for 1985.* New York: Academic Press.

Self, J. (1988). *Artificial intelligence and human learning: Intelligent computer-aided instruction.* London: Chapman and Hall.

Seligman, M. E. P. (1975). *Helplessness: On depression, development, and death.* San Francisco: Freeman.

Shallis, M. (1984). *The silicon idol: The micro revolution and its social implications.* New York: Schocken Books.

Shapiro, E. S. (1987). *Behavioral assessment in school psychology.* Hillsdale, NJ: Erlbaum.

Shepard, R. N. (1978). The mental image. *American Psychologist, 33,* 125–137.

Shepard, R. N., & Cooper, L. A. (1983). *Mental images and their transformations.* Cambridge, MA: MIT Press.

Shipman, S., & Shipman, V. C. (1985). Cognitive styles: Some conceptual, methodological, and applied issues. In E. W. Gordon (Ed.), *Review of research in education* (Vol. 12, pp. 229–291). Washington, DC: American Educational Research Association.

Shuell, T. J. (1986). Cognitive conceptions of learning. *Review of Educational Research, 56,* 411–436.

Sigel, I. E., & Brodzinsky, D. M. (1977). Individual differences: A perspective for understanding intellectual development. In H. Hom & P. Robinson (Eds.), *Psychological processes in early education* (pp. 295–329). New York: Academic Press.

Silberman, H. F., Melaragno, R. J., Coulson, J. E., & Estavan, D. (1961). Fixed sequence versus branching autoinstructional methods. *Journal of Educational Psychology, 52,* 166–172.

Silver, E. A. (1981). Recall of mathematical problem information: Solving related problems. *Journal for Research in Mathematics Education, 12,* 54–64.

Simon, H. A. (1974). How big is a chunk? *Science, 183,* 482–488.

Simon, H. A. (1979). Information processing models of cognition. *Annual Review of Psychology, 30,* 363–396.

Skinner, B. F. (1938). *The behavior of organisms.* New York: Appleton-Century-Crofts.

Skinner, B. F. (1948). *Walden two.* New York: Macmillan. (Paperback version published in 1976)

Skinner, B. F. (1953). *Science and human behavior.* New York: Free Press.

Skinner, B. F. (1954). The science of learning and the art of teaching. *Harvard Educational Review, 24,* 86–97.

Skinner, B. F. (1956). A case history in scientific method. *American Psychologist, 11,* 221–233.

Skinner, B. F. (1957). *Verbal behavior.* New York: Appleton-Century-Crofts.

Skinner, B. F. (1958). Teaching machines. *Science, 128,* 969–977.

Skinner, B. F. (1961). Why we need teaching machines. *Harvard Educational Review, 31,* 377–398.

Skinner, B. F. (1966). Freedom and the control of men. In R. Ulrich, T. Stachnik, & J. Mabry (Eds.), *Control of human behavior* (pp. 11–20). Glenview, IL: Scott, Foresman & Company.

Skinner, B. F. (1968). *The technology of teaching.* New York: Appleton-Century-Crofts.

Skinner, B. F. (1970). B. F. Skinner . . . An Autobiography. In P. B. Dews (Ed.), *Festschrift for B. F. Skinner* (pp. 1–21). New York: Appleton-Century-Crofts.

Skinner, B. F. (1971). *Beyond freedom and dignity.* New York: Knopf.

Skinner, B. F. (1974). *About behaviorism.* New York: Knopf.

Skinner, B. F. (1978). *Reflections on behaviorism and society.* Englewood Cliffs, NJ: Prentice-Hall.

Skinner, B. F. (1984). The shame of American education. *American Psychologist, 39,* 947–954.

Skinner, B. F. (1986). What is wrong with daily life in the Western world? *American Psychologist, 41,* 568–574.

Skinner, B. F. (1987). Whatever happened to psychology as the science of behavior? *American Psychologist, 42,* 780–786.

Slavin, R. E. (1983). *Cooperative learning.* New York: Longman.

Snowman, J. (1986). Learning tactics and strategies. In G. D. Phye & T. Andre (Eds.), *Cognitive classroom learning: Understanding, thinking, and problem solving* (pp. 243–275). Orlando: Academic Press.

Sommers, N. (1980). Revision strategies of student writers and experienced adult writers. *College Composition and Communication, 31,* 378–388.

Spence, J. T. (1984). Gender identity and its implications for the concepts of masculinity and femininity. In T. B. Sonderegger (Ed.), *Nebraska Symposium on Motivation, 1984* (Vol. 32, pp. 59–95). Lincoln, NE: University of Nebraska Press.

Spence, K. W. (1936). The nature of discrimination learning in animals. *Psychological Review, 43,* 427–449.

Spence, K. W. (1937). The differential response in animals to stimuli varying within a single dimension. *Psychological Review, 44,* 430–444.

Spence, K. W. (1960). *Behavior theory and learning: Selected papers.* Englewood Cliffs, NJ: Prentice-Hall.

Sperling, G. (1960). The information available in brief visual presentations. *Psychological Monographs, 74* (Whole No. 498).

Spilich, G. J., Vesonder, G. T., Chiesi, H. L., & Voss, J. F. (1979). Text-processing of domain-related information for individuals with high and low domain knowledge. *Journal of Verbal Learning and Verbal Behavior, 18,* 275–290.

Staddon, J. E. R., & Simmelhag, V. L. (1971). The "superstition" experiment: A reexamination of its implications for the principles of adaptive behavior. *Psychological Review, 78,* 3–43.

Stallard, C. K. (1974). An analysis of the writing behavior of good student writers. *Research in the Teaching of English, 8,* 206–218.

Stein, B. S., Littlefield, J., Bransford, J. D., & Persampieri, M. (1984). Elaboration and knowledge acquisition. *Memory and Cognition, 12,* 522–529.

Stein, N. L., & Glenn, C. G. (1979). An analysis of story comprehension in elementary school children. In R. O. Freedle (Ed.), *New directions in discourse processing* (pp. 53–120). Norwood, NJ: Ablex.

Stein, N. L., & Trabasso, T. (1982). What's in a story: An approach to comprehension and instruction. In R. Glaser (Ed.), *Advances in instructional psychology* (Vol. 2, pp. 213–267). Hillsdale, NJ: Erlbaum.

Sternberg, S. (1969). Memory-scanning: Mental processes revealed by reaction-time experiments. *American Scientist, 57,* 421–457.

Strain, P. S., Kerr, M. M., & Ragland, E. U. (1981). The use of peer social initiations in the treatment of social withdrawal. In P. S. Strain (Ed.), *The utilization of classroom peers as behavior change agents* (pp. 101–128). New York: Plenum.

Sunshine, P. M., & DiVesta, F. J. (1976). Effects of density and format on letter discrimination by beginning readers with different learning styles. *Journal of Educational Psychology, 68,* 15–19.

Suppes, P. (1974). The place of theory in educational research. *Educational Researcher, 3*(6), 3–10.

Tait, K., Hartley, J. R., & Anderson, R. C. (1973). Feedback procedures in computer-assisted arithmetic instruction. *British Journal of Educational Psychology, 13,* 161–171.

Tarde, G. (1903). *The laws of imitation* (2nd ed.). New York: Holt.

Taylor, A. M., Josberger, M., & Whitely, S. E. (1973). Elaboration instruction and verbalization as factors facilitating retarded children's recall. *Journal of Educational Psychology, 64,* 341–346.

Taylor, R. P. (1980). *The computer in the school: Tutor, tool, tutee.* New York: Teachers College Press.

Tennyson, R. D. (1980). Instructional control strategies and content structure as design variables in concept acquisition using computer-based instruction. *Journal of Educational Psychology, 72,* 525–532.

Tennyson, R. D. (1981). Use of adaptive information for advisement in learning concepts and rules using computer-assisted instruction. *American Educational Research Journal, 18,* 425–438.

BIBLIOGRAPHY

Tennyson, R. D., & Park, O. (1980). The teaching of concepts: A review of instructional design research literature. *Review of Educational Research, 50,* 55–70.

Tennyson, R. D., Steve, M. W., & Boutwell, R. C. (1975). Instance sequence and analysis of instance attribute representation in concept acquisition. *Journal of Educational Psychology, 67,* 821–827.

Terrace, H. S. (1963). Discrimination learning with and without "errors." *Journal of the Experimental Analysis of Behavior, 6,* 1–27.

Thelen, M. H., Fry, R. A., Fehrenbach, P. A., & Frautschi, N. M. (1979). Therapeutic videotape and film modeling: A review. *Psychological Bulletin, 86,* 701–720.

Thomson, D. M., & Tulving, E. (1970). Associative encoding and retrieval: Weak and strong cues. *Journal of Experimental Psychology, 86,* 255–262.

Thorndike, E. L. (1906). *The principles of teaching: Based on psychology.* New York: A. G. Seiler.

Thorndike, E. L. (1911). *Animal intelligence: Experimental studies.* New York: Macmillan.

Thorndike, E. L. (1912). *Education: A first book.* New York: Macmillan.

Thorndike, E. L. (1913a). *Educational psychology: Vol. 1. The original nature of man.* New York: Teachers College Press.

Thorndike, E. L. (1913b). *Educational psychology: Vol. 2. The psychology of learning.* New York: Teachers College Press.

Thorndike, E. L. (1914). *Educational psychology: Vol. 3. Mental work and fatigue and individual differences and their causes.* New York: Teachers College Press.

Thorndike, E. L. (1924). Mental discipline in high school studies. *Journal of Educational Psychology, 15,* 1–22, 83–98.

Thorndike, E. L. (1927). The law of effect. *American Journal of Psychology, 39,* 212–222.

Thorndike, E. L. (1932). *The fundamentals of learning.* New York: Teachers College Press.

Thorndike, E. L., & Gates, A. I. (1929). *Elementary principles of education.* New York: Macmillan.

Thorndike, E. L., & Woodworth, R. S. (1901). The influence of improvement in one mental function upon the efficiency of other functions. *Psychological Review, 8,* 247–261, 384–395, 553–564.

Thorndyke, P. W., & Hayes-Roth, B. (1979). The use of schemata in the acquisition and transfer of knowledge. *Cognitive Psychology, 11,* 82–106.

Titchener, E. B. (1909). *Lectures on the experimental psychology of the thought processes.* New York: Macmillan.

Tolman, E. C. (1932). *Purposive behavior in animals and men.* New York: Appleton-Century-Crofts. (Reprinted 1949, 1951, University of California Press, Berkeley, CA)

Tolman, E. C. (1942). *Drives toward war.* New York: Appleton-Century-Crofts.

Tolman, E. C. (1949). There is more than one kind of learning. *Psychological Review, 56,* 144–155.

Tolman, E. C. (1951). *Collected papers in psychology.* Berkeley, CA: University of California Press.

Tolman, E. C. (1959). Principles of purposive behavior. In S. Koch (Ed.), *Psychology: A study of a science* (Vol. 2, pp. 92–157). New York: McGraw-Hill.

BIBLIOGRAPHY

Tolman, E. C., & Honzik, C. H. (1930). Introduction and removal of reward, and maze performance in rats. *University of California Publications in Psychology, 4,* 257–275.

Tolman, E. C., Ritchie, B. F., & Kalish, D. (1946a). Studies in spatial learning. I. Orientation and the short-cut. *Journal of Experimental Psychology, 36,* 13–24.

Tolman, E. C., Ritchie, B. F., & Kalish, D. (1946b). Studies in spatial learning. II. Place learning versus response learning. *Journal of Experimental Psychology, 36,* 221–229.

Trappl, R. (1985). Artificial intelligence: A one-hour course. In R. Trappl (Ed.), *Impacts of artificial intelligence: Scientific, technological, military, economic, societal, cultural, and political* (pp. 5–30). Amsterdam: Elsevier Science Publishers.

Treisman, A. M. (1960). Contextual cues in selective listening. *Quarterly Journal of Experimental Psychology, 12,* 242–248.

Treisman, A. M. (1964). Verbal cues, language, and meaning in selective attention. *American Journal of Psychology, 77,* 206–219.

Tulving, E. (1972). Episodic and semantic memory. In E. Tulving & W. Donaldson (Eds.), *Organization of memory* (pp. 381–403). New York: Academic Press.

Tulving, E. (1974). Cue-dependent forgetting. *American Scientist, 62,* 74–82.

Tulving, E. (1983). *Elements of episodic memory.* Oxford, England: Clarendon Press.

Ullmann, L. P., & Krasner, L. (1965). *Case studies in behavior modification.* New York: Holt, Rinehart & Winston.

Ulrich, R., Stachnik, T., & Mabry, J. (1966). *Control of human behavior.* Glenview, IL: Scott, Foresman & Company.

Underwood, B. J. (1957). Interference and forgetting. *Psychological Review, 64,* 49–60.

Underwood, B. J. (1961). Ten years of massed practice on distributed practice. *Psychological Review, 68,* 229–247.

Underwood, B. J. (1983). *Attributes of memory.* Glenview, IL: Scott, Foresman & Company.

Valentine, C. W. (1930a). The innate base of fear. *Journal of Genetic Psychology, 37,* 394–419.

Valentine, C. W. (1930b). The psychology of imitation with special reference to early childhood. *British Journal of Psychology, 21,* 105–132.

Veroff, J. (1969). Social comparison and the development of achievement motivation. In C. P. Smith (Ed.), *Achievement-related motives in children* (pp. 46–101). New York: Russell Sage Foundation.

Voss, J. F., Vesonder, G. T., & Spilich, G. J. (1980). Text generation and recall by high-knowledge and low-knowledge individuals. *Journal of Verbal Learning and Verbal Behavior, 19,* 651–657.

Vygotsky, L. (1962). *Thought and language.* Cambridge, MA: MIT Press.

Vygotsky, L. (1978). *Mind in society: The development of higher psychological processes.* Cambridge, MA: Harvard University Press.

Wallas, G. (1921). *The art of thought.* New York: Harcourt, Brace, & World.

Wang, M. C. (1980). Adaptive instruction: Building on diversity. *Theory into Practice, 19,* 122–128.

Wang, M. C. (1983). Development and consequences of students' sense of personal control. In J. M. Levine & M. C. Wang (Eds.), *Teacher and student perceptions: Implications for learning* (pp. 213–247). Hillsdale, NJ: Erlbaum.

Wason, P. C. (1960). On the failure to eliminate hypotheses in a conceptual task. *Quarterly Journal of Experimental Psychology, 12,* 129–140.

Watson, J. B. (1914). *Behavior: An introduction to comparative psychology.* New York: Henry Holt.

Watson, J. B. (1916). The place of the conditioned-reflex in psychology. *Psychological Review, 23,* 89–116.

Watson, J. B. (1919). *Psychology from the standpoint of a behaviorist.* Philadelphia: Lippincott.

Watson, J. B. (1924). *Behaviorism.* New York: Norton.

Watson, J. B. (1926a). Experimental studies on the growth of the emotions. In C. Murchison (Ed.), *Psychologies of 1925* (pp. 37–57). Worcester, MA: Clark University Press.

Watson, J. B. (1926b). What the nursery has to say about instincts. In C. Murchison (Ed.), *Psychologies of 1925* (pp. 1–35). Worcester, MA: Clark University Press.

Watson, J. B., & MacDougall, W. (1929). *The battle of behaviorism.* New York: Norton.

Watson, J. B., & Rayner, R. (1920). Conditioned emotional reactions. *Journal of Experimental Psychology, 3,* 1–14.

Weiner, B. (1974). An attributional interpretation of expectancy-value theory. In B. Weiner (Ed.), *Cognitive views of human motivation* (pp. 51–69). New York: Academic Press.

Weiner, B. (1979). A theory of motivation for some classroom experiences. *Journal of Educational Psychology, 71,* 3–25.

Weiner, B. (1985a). An attributional theory of achievement motivation and emotion. *Psychological Review, 92,* 548–573.

Weiner, B. (1985b). *Human motivation.* New York: Springer-Verlag.

Weiner, B., Frieze, I. H., Kukla, A., Reed, L., Rest, S., & Rosenbaum, R. M. (1971). *Perceiving the causes of success and failure.* Morristown, NJ: General Learning Press.

Weiner, B., Graham, S., Taylor, S. E., & Meyer, W. (1983). Social cognition in the classroom. *Educational Psychologist, 18,* 109–124.

Weiner, B., & Kukla, A. (1970). An attributional analysis of achievement motivation. *Journal of Personality and Social Psychology, 15,* 1–20.

Weinstein, C. E. (1978). Elaboration skills as a learning strategy. In H. F. O'Neil, Jr. (Ed.), *Learning strategies* (pp. 31–55). New York: Academic Press.

Weinstein, C. E., & Mayer, R. E. (1986). The teaching of learning strategies. In M. C. Wittrock (Ed.), *Handbook of research on teaching* (3rd ed., pp. 315–327). New York: Macmillan.

Wellman, H. M. (1977). Tip of the tongue and feeling of knowing experiences: A developmental study of memory monitoring. *Child Development, 48,* 13–21.

Wertheimer, M. (1945). *Productive thinking.* New York: Harper & Row.

Wertsch, J. V. (1979). From social interaction to higher psychological processes: A clarification and application of Vygotsky's theory. *Human Development, 22,* 1–22.

BIBLIOGRAPHY

White, R. T., & Tisher, R. P. (1986). Research on natural sciences. In M. C. Wittrock (Ed.), *Handbook of research on teaching* (3rd ed., pp. 874–905). New York: Macmillan.

White, R. W. (1959). Motivation reconsidered: The concept of competence. *Psychological Review, 66,* 297–333.

Whitely, S. E., & Taylor, A. M. (1973). Overt verbalization and the continued production of effective elaborations by EMR children. *American Journal of Mental Deficiency, 78,* 193–198.

Williams, D. R., & Williams, H. (1969). Auto-maintenance in the pigeon: Sustained pecking despite contingent non-reinforcement. *Journal of the Experimental Analysis of Behavior, 12,* 511–520.

Winett, R. A., & Winkler, R. C. (1972). Current behavior modification in the classroom: Be still, be quiet, be docile. *Journal of Applied Behavior Analysis, 5,* 499–504.

Winne, P. H. (1985). Cognitive processing in the classroom. In T. Husen & T. N. Postlethwaite (Eds.), *The international encyclopedia of education* (Vol. 2, pp. 795–808). Oxford, England: Pergamon.

Witkin, H. A. (1969). Social influences in the development of cognitive style. In D. A. Goslin (Ed.), *Handbook of socialization theory and research* (pp. 687–706). Chicago: Rand McNally.

Witkin, H. A., Moore, C. A., Goodenough, D. R., & Cox, P. W. (1977). Field-dependent and field-independent cognitive styles and their educational implications. *Review of Educational Research, 47,* 1–64.

Wittrock, M. C. (1978). The cognitive movement in instruction. *Educational Psychologist, 13,* 15–29.

Wittrock, M. C. (1986). *Handbook of research on teaching* (3rd ed.). New York: Macmillan.

Wolpe, J. (1958). *Psychotherapy by reciprocal inhibition.* Stanford CA: Stanford University Press.

Wood, G., & Underwood, B. J. (1967). Implicit responses and conceptual similarity. *Journal of Verbal Learning and Verbal Behavior, 6,* 1–10.

Woodward, J., Carnine, D., & Gersten, R. (1988). Teaching problem solving through computer simulations. *American Educational Research Journal, 25,* 72–86.

Woodworth, R. S. (1918). *Dynamic psychology.* New York: Columbia University Press.

Woodworth, R. S., & Schlosberg, H. (1954). *Experimental psychology* (Rev. ed.). New York: Holt, Rinehart & Winston.

Wylie, R. C. (1979). *The self-concept* (Vol. 2). Lincoln, NE: University of Nebraska Press.

Yerkes, R. M., & Dodson, J. D. (1908). The relation of strength of stimulus to rapidity of habit-formation. *Journal of Comparative Neurology and Psychology, 18,* 459–482.

Zeiler, M. (1977). Schedules of reinforcement: The controlling variables. In W. K. Honig & J. E. R. Staddon (Eds.), *Handbook of operant behavior* (pp. 201–232). Englewood Cliffs, NJ: Prentice-Hall.

Zimmerman, B. J. (1977). Modeling. In H. Hom & P. Robinson (Eds.), *Psychological processes in children's early education* (pp. 37–70). New York: Academic Press.

Zimmerman, B. J. (1985). The development of "intrinsic" motivation: A social learning analysis. *Annals of Child Development, 2,* 117–160.

Zimmerman, B. J. (1986). Becoming a self-regulated learner: Which are the key subprocesses? *Contemporary Educational Psychology, 11,* 307–313.

Zimmerman, B. J. (1989). Models of self-regulated learning and academic achievement. In B. J. Zimmerman & D. H. Schunk (Eds.), *Self-regulated learning and academic achievement: Theory, research, and practice* (pp. 1–25). New York: Springer-Verlag.

Zimmerman, B. J., & Koussa, R. (1975). Sex factors in children's observational learning of value judgments of toys. *Sex Roles, 1,* 121–132.

Zimmerman, B. J., & Ringle, J. (1981). Effects of model persistence and statements of confidence on children's self-efficacy and problem solving. *Journal of Educational Psychology, 73,* 485–493.

Zimmerman, B. J., & Rosenthal, T. L. (1974). Observational learning of rule-governed behavior by children. *Psychological Bulletin, 81,* 29–42.

Zuckerman, M., & Wheeler, L. (1975). To dispel fantasies about the fantasy-based measure of fear of success. *Psychological Bulletin, 82,* 932–946.

Author Index

AUTHOR INDEX

AUTHOR INDEX

AUTHOR INDEX

Subject Index

SUBJECT INDEX

SUBJECT INDEX